Ghost-Hunting

WITHDRAWN
PRINT

D1294317

for
dummies®
A Wiley Brand

Ghost-Hunting

by Zak Bagans

Host and executive producer of Travel Channel's
Ghost Adventures,
Founder/Curator of The Haunted Museum

A Wiley Brand

Ghost-Hunting For Dummies®

Published by: **John Wiley & Sons, Inc.,** 111 River Street, Hoboken, NJ 07030-5774, www.wiley.com

Copyright © 2020 Zak Bagans

Published simultaneously in Canada

For general information on our other products and services, please contact our Customer Care Department within the U.S. at 877-762-2974, outside the U.S. at 317-572-3993, or fax 317-572-4002. For technical support, please visit https://hub.wiley.com/community/support/dummies.

Wiley publishes in a variety of print and electronic formats and by print-on-demand. Some material included with standard print versions of this book may not be included in e-books or in print-on-demand. If this book refers to media such as a CD or DVD that is not included in the version you purchased, you may download this material at http://booksupport.wiley.com. For more information about Wiley products, visit www.wiley.com.

Library of Congress Control Number: 2019952067

ISBN 978-1-119-58475-9 (pbk); ISBN 978-1-119-58476-6 (ePDF); ISBN 978-1-119-58480-3 (epub)

Manufactured in the United States of America

C10015248_103119

Contents at a Glance

Table of Contents

Introduction

Thank you for picking up this book. I hope that it will be useful to you as a common sense guide to paranormal investigation. It wasn't written to say that I have all the answers when it comes to the paranormal. No one really does. We are all learning and discovering as we go, but I hope that you can learn something from the research that I have done over the years and make what it contains work for you.

About This Book

This book was written to provide a general reference for paranormal research and ghost-hunting. In a field that is always changing, it can be difficult to offer a specific guide. The field of paranormal research has been around for more than 170 years, and it's always changing. Many tried and true methods of investigation have been replaced by scientific equipment and new ideas, but I have tried to combine these things to help you as you search for compelling evidence in your own research.

This book has a very simple goal: Provide the reader with the essential information needed to conduct research into ghosts and the paranormal. But this goal is deceptively simple because the outcome of such research is not simple at all. In fact, it can be so complex and confusing that many people walk away from the paranormal field every day, scratching their heads and wondering if all the work and effort is really worth it. Trust me, it is!

Just remember that this is a guide that was written for *you*, the ghost-hunter. Obviously, I won't have all the answers about ghosts until I am one myself, but I can pass along the knowledge, ideas, and theories that have been gained by my own past experiences with hauntings. My hope is that you, as the reader and the researcher, will be able to take away at least one small piece of what you find in this book for yourself and use it in your own investigations. You'll be able to see what I have done and, hopefully, learn from what I have discovered over the years. If you manage to gain some new ideas and discover some new methods from this book, then I can consider it a success.

I should also point out that the ideas in this book are my own, based on my own years of research. Paranormal investigators, no matter how experienced, do not uniformly agree on what makes a place become haunted or even about what ghosts actually are. Everyone has his or her own ideas on the subject, and mine are certainly not meant to be the final word on it. I'm not afraid to state my opinions, though, and am willing to run the risk that you may not agree with them. That's fine by me — you don't need to agree with what I have to say. I just hope that you'll form your own opinions and at least find some things here that you can put to work for yourself.

So, what can you expect in the pages ahead?

Foolish Assumptions

In this book, I make some assumptions that very well may be foolish, about you, your ghost-hunting experience, and your goals.

>> You are fascinated with ghosts, hauntings, and the unexplained and may even have some experience with paranormal investigation.

>> You have patience and a determination to learn more about the subject matter in hopes of increasing your knowledge about the best ways to investigate the unknown.

>> You are willing to approach the subject with an open mind.

>> You are willing to devote time and energy to gathering authentic evidence of the paranormal and doing everything you can to rule out natural explanations for anomalies before assuming they are paranormal.

Icons Used in This Book

Throughout the margin of this book are small images, known as *icons*. These icons mark important tidbits of information:

TIP

The Tip icon identifies places where I offer additional tips that will enhance your investigation, knowledge, or skills.

The Remember icon bookmarks important notes about information that you'll want to remember.

The Warning icon helps to protect you from making the common mistakes that should be avoided by all ghost-hunters.

This icon highlights my words of wisdom or personal experiences.

Beyond the Book

In addition to what you're reading right now, this product also comes with a free access-anywhere Cheat Sheet that covers well-known ghosts and haunted places. To get this Cheat Sheet, simply go to www.dummies.com and search for "Ghost-Hunting For Dummies Cheat Sheet" in the Search box.

Where to Go from Here

I wish you good luck on the strange journey that you are about to begin into the world of paranormal investigation. Remember that genuine and compelling evidence of the spirit world doesn't always come quickly. It often takes a long time to find the authentic cases that you are looking for, but this book helps you tell the difference between the natural and supernatural events you encounter.

1

The Basics of Ghost-Hunting

Chapter **1**

Searching for Spirits: Why Do We Do It?

I was once assured by an award-winning physicist that we have nothing to fear from ghosts because they simply do not exist. They cannot walk among us, he said, because their feet would have to apply pressure to the floor. If they were able to do this, they could not pass through walls because being able to do one without being able to do the other would violate the scientific laws of action and reaction.

Ghosts, quite simply, he explained, cannot be real.

Like so many other scientists throughout history, this physicist was basing his ideas about spirits on his own personal beliefs. Science demands that for something to truly be "real," it has to be capable of being duplicated over and over again under scientific conditions. As we know, the supernatural rarely conforms to the idea of repeatable experiments. We can measure, document, and record, but ghosts seldom perform in the way that mainstream science requires. Ghosts avoid the laboratory. If you drag them out of the shadows and expose them to the harsh glare of what science is convinced is reality, they tend to vanish.

But yet, those of you reading this book believe that ghosts are real. So do I. Like many of you, I have seen them, felt them, experienced them, and, in some cases, have had them uncomfortably attached to me in ways that I do not appreciate.

How can they be real, though, if science says they cannot exist? If millions of Americans did not believe in ghosts, this book would not exist. Neither would the hundreds of other books out there or the television shows that fascinate so many people. Nationwide polls tell us that 1 in 3 Americans believe that houses can be haunted. An even larger percentage of people believe communicating with the dead is possible. If ghosts don't exist, why do millions of people believe that they do?

This is a perplexing question to most scientists and skeptics, but not others. Those who research the paranormal know that reports of ghosts and spirits have been with us for centuries, dating back to the days of Ancient Rome. Ordinary people have been having encounters with the spirits of the dead longer than history has been recorded and, of course, are still having them today.

Such encounters serve to keep mainstream scientists and hardened skeptics lying awake at night, unable to sleep and paralyzed by fear. This is not because they are afraid of ghosts but because they are afraid that the grip they have on society, demanding that they not believe in such things, has started to slip again.

This is not the first time that such a thing has happened. In the 19th century, scientists were shaken to the core by the rise of the Spiritualist movement, which believed that the spirits of the dead could communicate with the living. Angered by the fact that new innovations in the scientific field had just started to break the hold that superstition and religion had on society, they immediately set about to debunk everything possible about Spiritualism. And although many hoaxes were exposed, there were just enough genuine mediums among the fakes to send many of the scientists back to their universities and laboratories in fear. Others, like Sir William Crookes, Sir Oliver Lodge, and others, became convinced of the reality of life after death.

Today, with new technology assailing us from every side, scientists have once again assured us not to worry — ghosts, hauntings, and haunted houses are not real. In this modern era, such things cannot exist. There is nothing out there in the dark.

This is what they tell us, but we know differently, don't we?

My Approach to Ghost-Hunting

Using my own experiences with ghost research, I'm offering a system for investigating hauntings that has worked for me. I also discuss working with witnesses, dealing with ghost sightings, conducting interviews, finding haunted places, working with spirit communication devices, using equipment and new techniques and experiments you can use during your investigations, and much more.

I also delve into the basics of ghost research, including the nature of ghosts themselves and real-life haunted houses. I should note here that the term "haunted house" can mean a lot of things from old decaying mansions to new tract homes but remember that just about any place can become haunted, including churches, theaters, libraries, office buildings, and even caves, tunnels, and graveyards. What we call "haunting" activity in such locations can be any sort of unexplained happenings, like apparitions, footsteps, noises, odors, and more. For a spot to be considered genuinely haunted, the reported phenomena must be directly related to the place itself. For example, we can refer to a family that lives in a haunted house and decides to move out. If the house is really haunted, the next family who lives there should experience the same things as the previous one.

However, there are many different kinds of hauntings. No two cases are ever exactly alike. When conducting your research, you're bound to discover various kinds of activity and sometimes, believe it or not, it will be at the same location.

In some places, ghosts are seen. Some reports claim that they are white, mist-like forms that only resemble a person. They are sometimes transparent, and you are able to see through them. In other cases, the ghosts are reported as appearing very life-like. In fact, witnesses sometimes mistake the ghosts for living persons, at least until they vanish into the wall or disappear through a solid door.

Ghosts don't always make an appearance. In the majority of cases, ghostly noises are heard instead. Witnesses report everything from footsteps to voices, mumbling, whispers, knocking sounds, and more. And in other houses, furniture, knick-knacks. and solid objects fly about by themselves. At other times, doors open or close, lights and appliances behave erratically, or phantom smells come and go without logical explanation. In other words, you never know what you will find in a haunted location and hopefully, this book will help prepare you for that.

In addition to the wide variety of things that you might encounter at a haunted place, there are also a lot of things that you probably won't. There exist a great many misconceptions about ghosts and hauntings. Ghosts don't appear with sheets draped over their heads, rattling chains, and ghosts are usually not out to kill anyone or avenge their deaths. The instances of harmful ghosts are so rare that the few cases that have been documented have caused a huge sensation. That's not to say that people don't get hurt during hauntings or encounter negative or demonic entities. We deal with that in the book, as well.

There are also many misconceptions about haunted houses. For example, many believe that only old, ramshackle buildings can become haunted. This is not true, as many relatively new homes have been known to attract ghosts. Theories about ghosts, hauntings and more will be discussed throughout the book.

Even so, there seem to be few clear-cut answers when it comes to ghosts. For decades, ghost researchers have wondered what force or intelligence lies behind a haunting.

One view is that a location becomes haunted when some tragedy, like a death or a murder, takes place there. This is apparently true in some cases, but not in all. But are ghosts really the spirits of the dead, come back to haunt us? Are they somehow attached to the places where they lived and died? Or could ghosts be "memory pictures" of the past or "energy discharges" that replay over and over again? Could some ghosts be only the memory of something that is so real that sometimes we can see it? Could some ghosts be only in our minds? For example, perhaps a friend died, and soon after, we are walking down the street, look into a window and, just for a moment, see our friend's face looking back. The next day, perhaps we see him getting on a bus or driving a car in the opposite direction on a street. Is he really there? Is he a ghost? Or is this just a memory that is so vivid to us that we have made it real in our minds?

Ghosts can be any of these things and perhaps all of them. And I explore all these ideas in this book.

The Search for Life After Death

If you ask 100 different paranormal investigators why they hunt for ghosts, you are likely to get 100 different variations of the same answer. Many started simply, collecting strange tales and ghost stories, and then decided to see if there was anything behind the stories other than folklore and urban legends. Others started because they wanted to look beyond the horizon and beyond what is generally accepted as "reality." Many say that they want to help people. They want to ease the fears of people who are experiencing a haunting and either help them understand that nothing in their home will hurt them or assist them in getting rid of the spirit that is causing the problem in the first place.

Other researchers may say that they are seeking answers for scientific reasons, to prove that the theory about energy is correct — that it does not die but merely changes form. Some confess that they search for spirits in spooky places for the thrill of it. They like to be scared.

No matter the reason for their fascination with the spirit world, it really boils down to a search for the same thing — proof of life after death. Polls show that the vast majority of people believe in an afterlife. Three out of four Americans believe in the existence of heaven or hell. Paranormal researchers are trying to find the evidence that affirms the belief that so many of us already have. We are seeking the elusive answer as to whether our spirits have somewhere to go when our bodies cease to function. Pure faith is not necessarily enough for the researcher. We want to know that what we believe in is real and by capturing evidence of it, we can do so.

Although ghosts are more widely accepted than they were even a few years ago, paranormal researchers still have a long way to go to validate the things they believe to be genuine. To do that, we use equipment, investigative techniques, and advanced technology to hunt for evidence of ghosts. This validation is essential to the cause, for what good are beliefs if no evidence exists to back them up? If we choose not to seek that validation, we can be happy and contented in our belief that ghosts are real but in the end, we have achieved nothing.

Chasing Ghosts

As the reader often hears throughout this book, the best kind of tool available to you as a paranormal investigator is yourself. It is your research, your knowledge, and how you put them to use that guarantees your success as researcher. This book has the simple goal of providing the reader with the essential information needed to collect evidence of ghosts and the existence of the paranormal. This goal is not as simple as it sounds, though. Paranormal research can be challenging, complex, unnerving, and confusing. I can assure you that it is worth it, but like anything else you may do, it is only as rewarding as the effort that you put into it. Hopefully, this book can show you how to make that effort worthwhile and show you that paranormal investigation is not only enlightening but thrilling, too.

I hope that the information that you find here encourages you to pick up this book again and again and I hope that the ideas, theories, and accounts within spark your interest and inspire you to develop your own theories about ghosts and paranormal research. I have passed along my own knowledge, ideas, and experiences so that you can take what I have learned and adapt that to further your own search for knowledge.

Always remember that it is okay to say, "I don't know." Paranormal researchers do not uniformly agree on what makes a place become haunted, how spirits behave, or even about what ghosts actually are. There seem to be very few clear-cut answers but that should never stop us from searching for them. Ghosts may be the spirits of the dead, returned to haunt us, attached to the place where they lived and died. They may be residual memories, energy that repeats itself over and over again. Ghosts may be any of these things and perhaps all of them.

And that brings us back around to mainstream science.

We are in a field with no absolute answers and this makes it difficult to prove that ghosts exist but, I believe, not impossible. By definition, a ghost is a disembodied personality, and mainstream science states that no physical evidence of the human personality even exists. Science will not admit that such a thing is present inside of the body while it is still functioning, let alone outside of the body when we are dead.

But, of course, the human personality is real. It exists. It cannot be determined by scientific experiments, much like ghosts cannot. But we know it to be the truth. Hundreds of years ago, mainstream science believed that the earth was flat. A Greek named Pythagoras was the first to introduce the idea that the world was round, but it would not be for another 300 years before another Greek, Eratosthenes, would create a mathematical theory to back up the idea. Even then, it was dismissed by most as ridiculous. It would not be until Magellan finally sailed around the world in 1522 that proof of the world being round was finally accepted. His "experiment" finally proved that the earth really was round.

Someday, I believe that our own "experiments" will finally start to convince the skeptics that the paranormal is real. It will no longer be a matter of belief or faith but hard evidence that the dead do live on and that they can interact with the living.

Is All the Work Really Worth it?

At this point, you may have realized how much work it takes to be a reputable researcher, and you may be wondering whether it is worth it. I can assure you that it is. Tens of thousands of people around the country are involved in ongoing paranormal research, and I am fairly certain they all would agree with me.

We all may have different reasons for pursuing the paranormal, but it all boils down to doing the work. There are many things that a good paranormal investigator must be armed with. He or she needs equipment, cameras, and tools of the trade. He or she must know what to look for, how to operate the equipment, know what questions to ask, know how to properly investigate, know how to follow up, and more.

The common factor with all these things, though, is the investigator. As mentioned, he or she becomes the most important tool in any investigation. This person must use his or her mind, judgment, and powers of observation in every case. No equipment, recorders, or books are going to help in an investigation if the investigator is unwilling to pursue the paranormal to the best of his or her ability.

An investigator must always remember that the goal of this pursuit has many layers. Not only are we seeking evidence of spirits, but we are also there to help the client who called us in to investigate in the first place. It may be a distressed person or a frightened family and one of the investigator's main responsibilities is to assist them. At that time and place, you will seem like the best friend they have.

If you are just starting out, don't be surprised if it takes some time to track down a genuine case and some hard evidence. You will get involved in a lot of investigations and meet some very scared people who believe their house is haunted. You will likely find a lot of creaking floorboards, banging pipes, faulty outlets, and drafty windows before you ever find what you believe is a ghost.

Do not give up, though! Being a paranormal investigator can be a long, strange, frustrating trip but when you do find that first genuine case, you will be happy you decided to stick with it.

Chapter **2**

The Phenomenon of Ghost-Hunting

A belief in the supernatural has existed in every time period and in every part of the world. Ghosts have been one of the most enduring of man's preoccupations. Ghosts, phantoms, specters, wraiths, apparitions, and poltergeists — all manifestations of the supernatural — have always fascinated believers and skeptics alike. Evidence of this claim is not hard to find. We find them in books, in magazines, in films, and on television. It is rare to find a family that cannot dig up a ghost story or two that was told by some old relative and is still remembered today with a mix of both amusement and unease. Ghosts are a subject that touches everyone. If you haven't seen or encountered one, then you likely know someone who has.

In this chapter, I take a look at how the belief in ghosts and spirits began in the ancient world, became a phenomenon in the 19th century, and continues to haunt people today.

Ghosts in Antiquity

The idea of the dead returning to the material world dates back as far as Stone Age man, who buried his dead with ceremonies that were intended to ensure that the deceased's soul rested in peace. We can only guess to what extent these ancient men were bothered by spirits, but some of the earliest written records of mankind present many legends of apparitions that had already been around for centuries. Based on these writings, belief in disembodied spirits can be established among the people of Babylonia. They had adopted the beliefs of the Sumerians who lived in the valleys of the Euphrates, among whom it was a common belief that the dead visited the earth in spirit form.

Early man felt that these spirits fell into three distinct categories:

>> The soul of the dead

>> A phantom or demon whose mission it was to harass the living

>> The peculiar part-human, part-ghost spirit, which was the offspring between human beings and residents of the spirit world

The Assyrians were among the earliest people to define different spirits and give them names. There was the *utukku*, a ghost that lay in wait for unsuspecting travelers in deserted locations and graveyards. They could cause serious illness for those who merely saw them. The *alu* was a terrifying specter that sometimes appeared without a mouth, ears, or limbs and sprang on the unwary and "enveloped them as in a garment," to quote one record. The *alu* sometimes pursued a man to his home but the spirit most closely associated with haunting houses was the *ekimmu*, the spirit of an unburied body. Its appearance was said to predict a death in the family. This restless spirit was sometimes heard to moan and cry, and it served as the origin of the banshee and other visitants who became known for bringing news of death and disaster. The Assyrians believed that all these spirits were the direct result of failing to offer the proper rituals for the dead or leaving a corpse unburied.

There are not a lot of specific descriptions of ghosts in ancient texts, but the Babylonians have left behind the dramatic story of the *Epic of Gilgamesh*, which, over 4,000 years old, may be the oldest of all ghost stories. It tells the tale of a Babylonian hero, Gilgamesh, who appeals to the god Negral to restore his friend and is rewarded by an apparition that rises up like wind in the form of a transparent human shape.

Egyptians

The Egyptians had the most extensive array of spirits of demons in the ancient world, the majority of whom prowled the land seeking to harm humanity unless they were appeased by special offerings. The peculiar ideas that the Egyptians had about the human body influenced their belief in ghosts. They felt that man consisted of a physical body, a spiritual body, a shadow, a soul, a heart, a spirit called *khu*, a power, and a name. The *khu*, unlike the other ephemeral aspects of the person, became a wandering and unhappy spirit after death. It could not only cause illness in the living but could possess animals, driving them into a frenzy. The *khu* of suicides, executed criminals, those drowned at sea, and the unburied dead were believed to be the most malevolent of ghosts.

Apart from appeasing the ghosts by ritual offerings, the Egyptians believed they could communicate with the spirits of the departed. Sometimes in an effort to placate a particularly bothersome spirit, a scroll appealing to the dead man would be placed on his tomb. In the scroll, the haunted person would state that he had done nothing to deserve the torment and that when both met in the spirit world, he would be judged as a wronged individual. The spirit, fearing a threat of not qualifying for the delights of the afterworld, would hopefully cease the haunting.

Arabs

The Arabs, who also believed in many kinds of ghosts, were convinced that if a man were murdered, his ghost would rise from the ground where his blood had been spilled unless it could be restrained by driving a nail into the ground where the murder happened. This tradition, known as *nailing down the ghost*, foreshadows the idea of rendering a vampire harmless by staking it through the heart.

Exploring the histories of various nations during this early period, one finds how similar ghost traditions were — in particular the still relevant idea that ruined buildings are invariably haunted. Such a belief began from the idea that while ghosts would obviously prefer occupied buildings, these were often protected against intrusion by amulets and charms and therefore, they had to seek refuge where no such obstructions existed. In Assyrian texts, familiar adages like "hair standing on end" from fright can be found, along with "goosebumps" that would appear unless prayers were uttered immediately. In all the early stories, too, accounts of ghosts describe them as being of human shape and appearance. Not much has changed since the beginning of recorded time!

Greeks and Romans

The Greeks and Romans introduced the first really detailed descriptions of ghosts and their mythology. Both believed that the souls of the dead wandered about the earth to haunt the wicked, terrify the good, and interfere in the affairs of the living. The spirits of those who had lived good lives were distinguished by the name of *lares*. Wicked spirits were referred to as *larvae* or *lemures*. Sacrifices were often offered to them, and during festivals held in their honor, it was customary to burn black beans over their graves and to beat drums so that the noxious fumes of the beans and the noise of the drums would drive away ghosts in the vicinity.

Some of the best examples of Greek apparitions can be found within the pages of the *Odyssey*. During his travels, Ulysses has several encounters with ghosts. Spirits also appear in the *Aeneid,* and Virgil also informs readers that the Greeks believed that Charon was not permitted to ferry the ghosts of unburied persons over the Styx, so they wandered up and down the river banks for hundreds of years, after which they were finally permitted to cross. The satirist Lucian brought a little light relief to the subject by writing about a "ghost club" whose members met to discuss apparitions and other phenomena. Was this the first ghost-hunting organization in history — or at least the first time the idea was created?

Roman history is also filled with tales of ghosts and spirits, including a fascinating occurrence that was recorded by Pliny, the consul at Sura. There was a house at Athens haunted by a ghost who roamed through the building, dragging a heavy chain behind him. Athenodorous, the philosopher, rented the house and was determined to quiet the spirit. One night, the silence was broken by the rattling of chains, and the specter entered the room. At first, Athenodorous didn't pay any attention to it, but when the ghost rattled the chains again, he looked up and the ghost beckoned for him to follow. He was led out into the courtyard by the spectral guide, who pointed to a certain spot on the ground and then vanished. Puzzled, the philosopher marked the spot and the next day had the ground dug up. A skeleton of a man, wrapped in chains, was discovered beneath the earth. Athenodorous had it publicly burned, and after that, the ghost was never seen again.

The story of Caesar's violent end, foretold to his wife, Calpurnia, by a spirit became an important part of Roman lore, as did the legend of the emperor's spirit returning to haunt one of his assassins, Brutus. But this was not the only time the unfortunate Brutus was visited by a ghost. Another spirit, this time predicting his death, appeared to him when his army was waiting to do battle with the triumvirate in Greece. One night, according to the record of the incident, Brutus was in his tent working when he saw a ghost appear at his side. It was described as "horrifying in its gigantic proportions and pale, emaciated face." For a time, the specter was silent, and then Brutus asked it what it wanted. The spirit replied, "I am your evil spirit. You will see me again at Philippi." The ghost was right. Brutus encountered the ghost again on the night before his defeat and death.

Scandinavians

Scandinavia was also a region filled with stories of ghosts at this time in history. It was customary for the Nordic people to perform ceremonies at the tombs of the dead to appease the spirits and to make it easier for them to enter the halls of Valhalla.

Indians

In India, there were fearsome ghosts known variously as *virikas*, *paisachi*, or *bauta*, the latter being particularly horrific with small red bodies, the teeth of lions, and the habit of wandering around at night chattering in a nasal tone. It was customary in some parts of the country to build small shrines to them that were formed of a pile of stones on top of which was a sheltered spot where food and other small offerings could be left. There was also a class of men in the country called *cani* or *shaycana*, who were supposed to have the power to frighten away troublesome spirits. They charged a fee for their services and the price depending on the alleged powers of the ghost and its relationship to the family that hired them.

Chinese

The Chinese were another civilization with a dread of ghosts, particularly of those who had been murdered. According to legend, the Chinese spirit was first seen in shapeless form, the head forming first, then the feet, and finally, the body. The faces had no chins. Chinese tradition is filled with references to apparitions, seen in the clothing they wore on earth and surrounded by a green light. Chinese lore contains a list of 60 evil ghosts, each of which appeared for one day during a cycle of 60 days. To drive off these specters, the people hung talismans on their walls that were decorated with pictures of warriors and with money that was offered to convince the spirits to go away. They also took part in a curious ceremony called "Appeasing the Burning Mouths," which took place on the 17th day of the 7th moon, when plates of cakes were laid out with invitations on them that were addressed to the "Honorable Homeless Ghosts."

Japanese

A rich tradition of spirits also existed in Japan, where ghosts appeared in many forms. Among the most frequent were the apparitions of women with disheveled hair, clad in flowing white robs, and warriors carrying Samurai swords. Almost invariably, these phantoms were shown without legs and bearing scars that were appropriate to their earthly misdeeds. Japanese spirits are rarely friendly and are much more frightening than their western counterparts.

The Japanese had a tradition of what some have called *hungry ghosts.* They are said to be the souls of those who died from starvation while wandering the remote mountain trails of Japan, dying alone, and without a proper burial. The specters were cursed to roam the earth, seeking out others with whom to share their agony of eternal hunger. There were many tales of travelers navigating lonely mountain paths who suddenly found themselves overcome by an insatiable hunger, inexplicable fatigue, and numbness of the limbs. If not stopped, the attack by the spirit almost certainly led to death or insanity. According to lore, it was possible to avoid such a fate by having a small amount of food on hand, which would purportedly dispel the supernatural hunger.

Native Americans

The First Nation people of North America also had many beliefs in ghosts, and they revered the spirits of their ancestors. In 1890, spirit belief became a major religious movement among Indian nations. According to the teachings of the Northern Paiute spiritual leader Wovoka, proper practice of what was called the *Ghost Dance* would reunite the living with spirits of the dead, bring the spirits to fight on their behalf, make the white colonists leave, and bring peace, prosperity, and unity to Native American peoples throughout the region.

Belief in ghosts also featured quite extensively in the evolution of Christianity. There are many mentions of ghosts in the Gospels, such as when the Disciples saw Jesus walking on the water and "thought it had been a spirit." After his resurrection, they also assumed he was a ghost until he told them otherwise.

Perhaps the most famous ghost story in the Bible concerns King Saul, who, alarmed at the likely outcome of his battle with the Philistine army, visited a necromancer so that she could raise the spirit of Samuel for advice.

Classic Encounters with Ghosts

During the time between the fall of the Roman Empire and the discovery of America, there was a general consolidation of the belief in ghosts and the spirit world. Many of the superstitions and legends about phantoms, which had evolved in earlier times, were now given wider credence and this, combined with the interest in occult sciences in that era, gave rise to a widespread belief that the supernatural had a great influence on the affairs of man.

It was a grim time in history. The castles of the nobility were dank and forbidding. The homes of the peasants were wretched and rank. It is small wonder that each shadow took on a life of its own. Ghosts of the dead lurked inside every castle wall, phantom horsemen galloped through every village, and evil specters flitted through every home.

The Drummer of Tedworth

The story of the Drummer of Tedworth, probably the most famous ghostly tale of the 17th century, has been referred to as "one of the earliest well-attested poltergeist cases in England." The idea of a *poltergeist* was nothing new at that time. It was during the Dark Ages that the first reports of a noisy and troublesome ghost were recorded. The word poltergeist comes from German folklore and literally means "noisy ghost." Its activities — moving objects, flinging things into the air, creating noises like raps, bangs, scratching, and even occasionally human sounds like whistling, singing, and talking — no doubt gave rise to the classic phrase of "things that go bump in the night."

The case began in 1662 in a town that was then called Tedworth, in Wiltshire, in southwest England. It was a quiet and peaceful town, and local landowner and magistrate John Mompesson wanted to keep it that way. This was the reason he became very unhappy with a vagrant named William Drury, who came to town that spring. Drury was a former regimental drummer for Cromwell's army who had fallen on hard times and had a tendency to walk around at all hours drumming away and belting out battle hymns. It was an unwelcome noise to both the villagers and the magistrate.

Mompesson had Drury arrested and brought before the court. He was accused of using false papers and of swindling money from residents by demanding public assistance. Mompesson decided to let him off with a warning, but he confiscated Drury's drum and told him to leave the district. Drury begged and pleaded that his prized possession be returned to him, but the magistrate refused. Instead, it was taken to Mompesson's house until things could be sorted out. Drury himself seemed to vanish, and calm settled over the village — although not at the home of Mompesson and his family.

Soon after the Drury affair, Mompesson took a trip to London to take care of some business. When he returned a few days later, he was shocked when his wife informed him that strange things had been happening in their house. She told him that she had been kept awake by loud noises at night, and not long after, Mompesson heard them for himself. The house began to be plagued by the nocturnal banging of a drum, as well as by other less definable noises that sounded like scratching, thumping, and knocking.

On one such evening, he was awakened by a banging noise on the other side of his bedroom door, after which he grabbed a pistol and warily opened it to find nothing on the other side. Mompesson searched the house, pistol in hand, but no intruders were found. During the search, he was taunted by the knocking, banging, drum-like noises that seemingly came from nowhere.

Things began to escalate when the drumming became more urgent, coming from everywhere, even on the roof and under the floor. Objects were found moved about, and often in ominous ways, such as a Bible found atop the ashes of the fireplace and a knife situated upright in a bed.

The mysterious drumming sounds came nightly, and with increasing ferocity. Whatever was behind the supernatural drumming became ever more powerful, often moving heavy objects and flinging chairs across rooms. Such occurrences became commonplace and occurred in front of startled witnesses.

Spookily, a lot of the paranormal activity seemed to occur around the Mompesson children, with sounds often occurring in their rooms and their beds being banged by unseen forces. Scratching sounds seemed to follow them around, and, perhaps most unsettling, the children began to hear a disembodied voice that would chant "I am a witch, I am a witch" over and over again in raspy, inhuman voice that seemed to emanate from under their beds and from beneath the floorboards of the room.

The family recruited help from a clergyman named Reverend Cragg to try to contain the entity, which they had come to think of as demonic. This attempt only further irritated the mysterious force, which allegedly tossed furniture and shoes about in a rage, and struck Cragg in the leg with a heavy staff. It was immune from the minister's attempts to drive it off.

Before long, word of the haunting spread far and wide, and curiosity-seekers began showing up. Often, the visitors would see the phenomena for themselves. One of them, Sir Christopher Wren, heard the drumming at night and witnessed objects moving about. Another visitor was Reverend Joseph Glanvill, who also happened to be a member of the Royal Society and was a skeptic who arrived at the home with the intention of debunking the whole thing as nonsense.

By the time Glanvill arrived at the Mompesson home in January 1663, the occurrences had been taking place for over a year. After collecting eyewitness accounts from the family and the neighbors, he decided to stay at the house and try to determine what was going on. He suspected overactive imaginations or trickery, but his mind was soon changed. Glanvill witnessed the strange happenings for himself. He later wrote of hearing the eerie drumming, the scratching noises in the bedrooms of the children, knocking sounds, and even disembodied voices. By the time his investigation was finished, he was thoroughly convinced that the home had been invaded by a spirit or even a demon. It was Glanvill who first suspected that the disgraced drummer William Drury was somehow behind the whole thing.

When Drury was eventually located, it turned out that he had been arrested in Gloucester for theft and had been in jail the entire time. Seizing the moment, he openly admitted to using witchcraft as revenge against Mompesson for taking his beloved drum away from him. He was then put on trial for witchcraft with the events in Tedworth presented as the main evidence against him. He tried to make a deal with the magistrate, agreeing to lift the malicious curse in exchange for his freedom, but it was no use. He was whisked away to an English colony to be tried for other crimes. Drury's eventual fate remains unknown.

In the centuries since, the story of the Drummer of Tedworth has become widely regarded as a popular English legend and a curious haunting from another time. It's also attracted its share of criticism. Some believe the events were set in motion by Mompesson, hoping for fame and profit, or a hoax created by the household servants, who hoped to earn more pay while working under such terrifying conditions.

The Mompesson family, though, always stated that the story was completely true. They made no money from its telling and re-telling and gained nothing but notoriety. After all these years, it's impossible to know what really happened in Tedworth, but whatever it was, it became an integral part of the history of ghostlore and has endured for hundreds of years as an unsolved mystery of the paranormal.

Old Jeffrey

As a result of the tremendous advances in arts and sciences at the beginning of the 18th century, stories of ghosts and spirits began to fall into disfavor. A great many alleged hauntings were proved to be faked for personal motives, and many super-natural occurrences were dismissed as pranks. Yet, for all this skepticism, there were a number of inexplicable events during the century, which, in time, helped to encourage the scientific study of the nature and cause of ghosts.

John Wesley, the renowned minister, was one man who did not share the growing indifference toward the spirit world. He had strong personal reasons for his beliefs. His own family home at Epworth in Lincolnshire, where his father was a minister, had been visited in 1716 and 1717 by a spirit they had nicknamed "Old Jeffrey." The Epworth Poltergeist, as the ghost became widely known, was alleged to have disturbed Wesley's younger sister, Hetty, in her bed and to have caused noises and groaning sounds that could be heard throughout the house. Wesley himself was completely convinced of the existence of the ghost and wrote about it extensively, which gave it an enduring place in the history of the paranormal.

The Cock Lane Ghost

Just as famous as Wesley's spirit was the Cock Lane Ghost, which made its first appearance in 1762 and has since attracted the attention of countless writers and investigators. The story became a media sensation of the 18th century — a story of sex, mystery, a man accused of murder from beyond the grave, and a home turned upside down by a poltergeist. No matter what people believed about the outcome of the case, there was no denying the fact that it galvanized the city of London at the time and earned a permanent place in the annals of the paranormal.

Richard Parsons and his family lived in a house on Cock Lane, a working-class area of Smithfield, London. To his neighbors, Parsons was a respectable church clerk, but he was also a drinker and was not terribly responsible with his money. The fact that his best friend, James Franzen, ran a local pub, the Wheatsheaf, probably didn't help matters. Things seemed better for the family after Parsons met a couple in need of lodgings and soon, William Kent and his wife, Fanny, moved into rooms in the house on Cock Lane. Even better, William Kent was a money lender, and he readily loaned 12 Guineas to the down-on-his-luck Parsons, to be paid back at a rate of 1 Guinea each month.

The two families must have gotten along well at first because Kent soon confided in Parsons that he and Fanny were not married. Kent had actually been married a few years earlier to her sister, Elizabeth Lynes. They had kept an inn in Stoke Ferry in Norfolk, and after Elizabeth suffered a difficult pregnancy, Fanny moved in with them to help out. Elizabeth and the baby died, but Fanny stayed on as a housekeeper. Soon, the grieving husband was seeking solace from his supportive sister-in-law. As things became more serious, Kent traveled to London seeking advice on the prospect of marrying Frances, but the law at the time would not allow it.

In an attempt to remove himself from temptation, Kent moved to London, but Fanny wrote a series of passionate letters to him, and they were soon living together again, posing as man and wife, which was an offense at the time. Richard Parsons was now privy to some sensational information about the couple living under his roof.

The haunting began in 1759, while William Kent was out of town. Fanny was pregnant and wanted company with her lover away, so Parson's 12-year-old daughter, Elizabeth, stayed with her, sleeping in the same bed. One night, both of them heard strange knocking and scratching noises coming from inside the walls. Initially, Mrs. Parsons dismissed the sounds as the cobbler at work next door, but when the noises continued on Sunday, when the shop was closed, they began to wonder if more sinister agencies might be at work.

Things took a dramatic turn when James Franzen came to the house one day to visit the Parsons family. He was the reluctant witness to a spectral glowing figure in white on the staircase. Now, the family was convinced the Cock Lane house was haunted.

But why? Richard Parsons began to look for reasons why a ghost might be pestering his family. He was a Methodist, and if there was a ghost about, then surely it had a message to pass on to the living. The theory was soon proposed that the ghost was Kent's first wife, Elizabeth, returned from the grave to accuse her unfaithful husband of murder.

No one knows where such a wild idea came from, but it might be worth mentioning that Parsons had, by now, defaulted on his debt to Kent. Their friendship had cooled further when Kent instructed his solicitor to sue Parsons for the recovery of that debt. Soon after, Parsons happened to mention that the supposedly respectable couple who rented rooms from him was actually living in sin.

The Kents moved out, but their troubles were not over. The pregnant Fanny died from smallpox on February 2, 1760, and even though they were not married, her will left substantial funds for William Kent, much to the unhappiness of her family.

In January 1762, at about the same time that Kent's solicitor successfully recovered the debt owed by Parsons, Cock Lane was again the scene of supernatural happenings. Lodgers who had followed the Kents had been chased off by nocturnal knockings and scratching, and the young Elizabeth Parsons was reportedly experiencing unexplained fits and trances.

Parsons called in John Moore, a local Methodist rector who was sympathetic to the idea of spirits. He soon announced that the spirit now haunting Cock Lane was that of Fanny Kent herself — a second wife accusing William Kent of murder. Through a series of seances, it was established that Kent had poisoned her with arsenic and this, not smallpox, had killed her. There were plenty of people willing to believe this allegation, including Fanny's sister, Anne. Still upset about the terms of Fanny's will, Anne claimed that Kent had tightly screwed down the lid of her sister's coffin so that no one could check and see whether she had really died from the disease.

News of the shocking story — a tale of ghosts, sex scandal, and alleged murder — quickly spread, and Parsons was quick to cash in on it, holding nightly gatherings at his home for those who wanted to try to contact the ghost. Cock Lane became a destination for the curious and thanks to newspaper promotion, poor Fanny Kent went down in history as "Scratching Fanny."

William Kent found out about the events only through sensational newspaper reports. Horrified, he and his supporters attended some of the Cock Lane seances in order to deny the allegations against him. At one such séance, Elizabeth Parsons, who seemed to be the focus of the haunting, was publicly undressed and put to bed in front of a group of onlookers, while another relative, Mary Franzen, ran about the room calling for Fanny to appear. When this failed to entice the spirit, the room was cleared, and John Moore was able to persuade the reluctant spirit to manifest before allowing the onlookers back in. During the communications that followed, Kent felt compelled to defend his innocence against the ghost's accusations.

But his protestations didn't impress the ghosts or the public. The media sensation caused by the Cock Lane haunting was quickly changing from something other than just a spooky outing to something dangerous. People were becoming angry with William Kent.

With believers and skeptics skirmishing in the press and an angry mob calling for Kent to be hanged for murder, London's mayor, Sir Samuel Fludyer, was forced to take action. The veracity of the ghost would be tested by a special committee led by Reverend Stephen Aldrich and assisted by Dr. Samuel Johnson, the famous poet, playwright, essayist, moralist, literary critic, biographer, editor, and dictionary creator. Johnson wrote about a séance in the house where he and others present heard the alleged communications from the spirit but came to the belief that the haunting was the work of young Elizabeth Parsons and that there was "no agency of any higher cause."

More seances followed, and they produced the same knockings and scratching but when measures were taken to ensure that Elizabeth's hands and feet were in full view, the supernatural phenomena ceased. She was also observed, on one occasion, hiding a small piece of wood in her dress. Had she been faking it all along? Some believed that she had, but others insisted that she was desperate to continue the haunting because she was warned that her father would be sent to prison if the ghost was proven not to exist.

The newspapers were quick to pronounce the Cock Lane Ghost a hoax, but the story was not quite over.

Vindicated by the commission, William Kent now sought legal revenge. After all, the episode had publicly damaged his reputation, and ultimately, if the ghost had been deemed genuine, it could have cost him his life. Five people, including Richard Parsons and John Moore, were charged with conspiracy. Moore and another of the accused paid Kent a considerable sum in compensation and avoided jail. Parsons was not so lucky, and even though he was kindly treated by the public, who raised money for his defense, he still served two years in prison.

Centuries later, most believe that one of the most famous hauntings in British history was nothing more than a clever hoax, but perhaps we should consider one more piece to the puzzle. In the 19th century, an artist named J.W. Archer, visited the tomb where "Scratching Fanny" had been laid to rest 100 years before. Upon opening the casket, he found the well-preserved body of a handsome woman, with no visible marks of smallpox. She had been remarkably preserved — in just the way that arsenic did when used to embalm the bodies of the dead until it was discovered to be highly dangerous. Perhaps the Cock Lane Ghost had something worthwhile to say after all.

The Bell Witch of Tennessee

One of the most famous ghost stories in American history is that of the infamous Bell Witch of Tennessee (see Figure 2-1). This story has always appealed so much to me personally because the cave associated with this case is a location that I was able to investigate with *Ghost Adventures*. It was a case that occurred during a period when Americans had stopped believing in witchcraft but had not yet discovered Spiritualism. This may be, despite the amount of documentation that later appeared, one of the reasons that this case remains so mysterious. It may also be because it is one of the only accounts of ghosts in human history in which a spirit actually took credit for killing one of the principles in the case.

FIGURE 2-1:
The Bell Witch of Tennessee.

©*Travel Channel.*

The Bell Witch haunting began in 1817 in Robertson County, Tennessee. It occurred at the home of a prosperous farmer named John Bell, who lived with his wife, Lucy, and their children outside the small settlement of Adams Station. The family was well-liked, and John Bell had the respect of other men in the community.

Lucy was a beloved figure in the area, and her home was always open for travelers and for social gatherings. One of the children was a daughter, Elizabeth, who was commonly known as Betsy. She was a pretty young woman with several suitors, including a local farmer named Joshua Gardner.

The haunting on the farm began with a series of knocks on the front door of the house. When the knocks were answered, there was never anyone there. The knocks were soon followed by hideous scratching sounds. It sounded as though the wood was being peeled from the outside walls, although no cause could be discovered for the noises. Before long, the frightening sounds moved inside. They began as gnawing, scratching and scraping sounds that seemed to emanate from the bedroom belonging to the Bell sons. They would jump out of bed and light a candle, trying to find the source of the noise, but it would then stop. As soon as the candle was put out, they would start again. Soon, the sound of the rat-like scratching was joined by what sounded like a large dog, pawing at the wooden floor. Other noises were described as sounding like two large animals dragging chains through the house.

The crashing and scratching sounds were frightening, but not as terrifying as the noises that followed. It was not uncommon for the Bells to be awakened in the darkness by a noise like the smacking of lips, gulping sounds, and eerie gurgling and choking. They seemed to come from a human throat, and yet no living person was present. The nerves of the Bell family began to unravel as the sounds became a nightly occurrence.

The inhuman sounds were followed by unseen hands that began to plague the household. Objects were broken, and blankets were yanked from the beds. The presence seemed to bother Betsy Bell more than anyone else. Her hair was pulled, and she was pinched and poked, making her cry out in pain. She was once slapped so hard that her cheeks remained bright red for hours. She often ran screaming from the room in terror as the unseen hands grabbed and pulled at her. It was later noticed that the force became even crueler after she entertained her young suitor, Joshua Gardner. For some reason, the spirit seemed to want to punish her whenever Joshua would call.

John Bell felt helpless, unable to explain the mysterious occurrences. To make matters worse, he had also begun to develop a nervous condition that affected his tongue and jaw muscles. This affliction caused him great difficulty when trying to eat and chew. When his doctor's cures failed to help him, he started to believe that the illness was caused by the force that had invaded his home. Desperately seeking answers, he realized that he needed to appeal to someone outside the household for assistance. At this point, Bell decided to enlist help from his friend and neighbor, James Johnson.

At Bell's request, Johnson and his wife came to spend the night at the Bell farm. He was determined to get to the bottom of the strange events. That night, as everyone prepared to go to bed, Johnson read a chapter from the Bible and prayed fervently for the family to be delivered from the frightful disturbances, or at least for their origins to be revealed. As soon as the candles were extinguished, the violent events began. The gnawing, knocking, and scratching sounds were heard, and the disturbances continued to escalate as chairs overturned, blankets flew from the beds, and objects flew from one side of the room to the other.

James Johnson listened attentively to all the sounds and closely observed the other incidents that were taking place. He realized, from the sounds of teeth grinding and the smacking of lips, that an intelligent force seemed to be at work. He convinced John Bell to form an investigative committee of their friends so that they could solve the mystery.

Regardless of the diligence of the committee, the household remained in chaos. Word began to spread of the strange events and friends, and even strangers came to the farm to see what was happening. Dozens of people heard the banging and rapping sounds, saw objects move about, and had things thrown at them. Exorcists and witch-finders, all claiming they could expel the evil force from the Bell home, came from all over Tennessee and Kentucky. The disturbances soon sent them running from the house in terror.

The committee continued to search for answers. They set up experiments, trying to communicate with the force, and they arranged watches that lasted throughout the night. But nothing helped. If anything, the attacks increased in violence. Betsy was treated brutally and began to have fainting spells and sensations of the breath being sucked out of her body. She was scratched, and her flesh would bleed as though she was being pierced with invisible pins and needles.

They tried to communicate with the "witch," as the members of the committee had started to refer to the presence, asking it to speak and tell them what it wanted. They asked questions that required either "yes" or "no" answers or that could be answered with numbers. The replies would come in knocks or raps as if an invisible fist were tapping on the wall. This went on for some time, but the committee members continued to harass the presence with questions, daring it to speak. First, it whispered, as if it could not catch its breath, and then faint words began to be formed but they could not be understood, at least at first.

But the voice of the witch began to be clearly heard, and soon, the disembodied voice was coming from right out of thin air. When the questioners demanded to know who the witch was, the voice stated that it was a spirit whose rest had been disturbed, an ancient ghost, a murdered traveler, and much more. It lied, laughed, and made eerie predictions of future events.

Excitement in the community grew as word spread of the witch's communications. People came from everywhere to hear the unexplained voice. It attracted believers in the supernatural, along with skeptics, who were convinced the haunting was an elaborate hoax. Those who came to expose the charade left puzzled, unable to explain what was happening. The Bell family made no money from the crowds of people who came to the farm, camped on their property, ate their food, or wandered about the house. John Bell refused to take their money. He did not consider the witch a wonder, or an object of delight. To him, the creature was an "affliction" and her presence in his home a "calamity."

Visitors came and went, but the violence in the house continued. Objects still moved about, the family was still kept awake most of the night by banging sounds and the voice of the spirit and, most disturbing, the attacks on Betsy and John Bell continued. Strangely, the spirit would sometimes treat Betsy with tenderness, only to attack her with terrible force later that same day.

The attacks were serious but were nothing compared to the agony suffered by John Bell. His tongue and throat often became so swollen that he was unable to eat for days at a time. He had difficulty swallowing and drinking water. As the haunting progressed, he began to come down with other unexplainable symptoms, like a bizarre facial paralysis that made it impossible for him to speak. They lasted for days and even weeks at a time.

The attacks on John Bell remain a mystery. There is no explanation as to why the witch hated him so much. From the beginning, the spirit made it clear that it intended to get "Old Jack Bell" and torment him until the end of his life. In addition to his illness, Bell was also physically abused by the witch, just as Betsy was. Whenever his name was mentioned in the presence of the spirit, it would scream and called John every vile and offensive name imaginable. His doctor was helpless and unable to find a cure for his sickness. The witch laughed at his efforts and declared that no medicine could cure him. It was determined to kill him but refused to say why its hatred for the man was so strong.

After nearly four years of the haunting, John Bell's physical condition had grown much worse. The jerking and twitched that paralyzed his face continued, as did the swelling of his throat and tongue, and violent seizures that caused him to lose consciousness. He collapsed in October 1820 and was forced to remain in bed for eight days. During this time, the spirit stayed by his side. It raved and cursed and prevented him from sleeping, wishing loudly that he would die and leave the world a better place.

Bell recovered, but after another attack by the witch a short time later, he was back in his sick bed. This time, though, he never left it. After suffering from several violent seizures, Lucy Bell asked her oldest son, John, Jr. to fetch his father's medicine from the cabinet. He discovered that all of the medicines that his father had been prescribed were gone and had been replaced by a small, "smoky-looking vial," half-filled with dark liquid. It turned out that John Bell had been given a large dose of it during the night, even though all the family members denied having ever seen the bottle. It was suggested that the mysterious liquid be tested so John, Jr. dipped a piece of straw into the vial and gave a few drops to a family cat. The animal was dead in less than a minute.

John Bell never regained consciousness and died on the morning of December 20, 1820. His final moments were met by great joy from the witch. The spirit laughed heartily and expressed the hope that Bell would burn in hell. With those chilling words, she departed and was not heard from again until after the funeral.

The burial was held a few days later, and it has been said that the funeral was the largest ever held in Robertson County, before or since. Bell was laid to rest in a small cemetery, a short distance from the Bell house. After the grave was filled, the mourners began to walk away. As they left the scene, the voice of the witch returned, singing loudly in the cold morning air and celebrating the death of John Bell.

After the death of John Bell, the witch seemed to lose interest in everyone in the family, except for Betsy Bell. After her father's death, Betsy believed that the witch would finally leave her alone and allow her to be courted by Joshua Gardner. This was not the case, however. The spirit never made it clear why it objected to Gardner. It simply hated him and never explained why. The disembodied voice pleaded with Betsy to end her relationship with the young man and made it clear that it would continue to punish her until she did. When Betsy realized that the haunting would never end until she followed the witch's orders, she broke things off with Joshua. He soon left Robertson County, and they never saw each other again.

The witch remained with the family until 1821. One evening while they were sitting at supper, there was a tremendous noise in the chimney. The witch's voice rang out and told the Bells that she was leaving — but would come back in seven years. With that, the haunting came to an end.

In 1828, only Lucy Bell and two of her sons remained in the homestead, although John, Jr. lived nearby and experienced most of the witch's new manifestations. Things started again as they originally had, with scratching, items moved around, and covers pulled from the bed. However, since Betsy had long since moved away and John Bell was dead, the witch seemed to have no one to torment. Lucy and her sons ignored the new happenings, and within two weeks, the manifestations stopped. John, Jr. claimed that the witch visited him several times in his home, allegedly making prophecies of future events, from the Civil War to the end of the world. She also promised to return in 107 years and plague one of his descendants. But 1935 came and went without any appearance of the Bell Witch.

To this day, the story of the Bell Witch remains a classic American haunting. It has never truly been explained, which is what made it such an incredible experience for me to be able to investigate such a legendary place. As part of the investigation, we were able to interview an ancestor of one of John Bell's friends, who had experienced the spirit first-hand at his own home. One night, the spirit had manifested in his cabin, and he managed to somehow capture the presence, wrapping it up into a blanket. He attempted to throw it into the fire, but it escaped. Family lore passed along his story from one generation to the next, with one line in particular standing out in the account. As his ancestor told it to me, "I almost killed that bitch."

When we brought this man's ancestor into the investigation, we started picking up voices inside of the Bell Witch Cave. We also obtained evidence of what seemed to be a portal in the large room of the cave, documented using night vision equipment, as well as some sensors from Bill Chappell. When the ancestor went into the cave alone, it sounded as though rocks were being thrown at him.

I believe that we even made contact with the Bell Witch at one point. We recorded some absolutely incredible audio recordings of what sounded like a pig grunting and recorded an animal-like manifestation with thermal imaging cameras within the cave. We were unable to debunk any evidence of the we obtained, further adding to the mysterious nature of a hauntings that has continued for more than two centuries.

Spiritualism and the Beginning of Paranormal Research

There is little doubt that the birth of the Spiritualist movement in the middle 19th century created the need for paranormal investigation. It was because of the claims of the Spiritualists, concerning their alleged contact with the dead, that the need for investigations of such claims came about. These investigations were not done so that the Spiritualists could be exposed as frauds, although this sometimes happened, but because the evidence that was being presented had to be questioned.

The investigations that followed, and which later began to focus less on mediums and Spiritualists and more on hauntings, set the standard for the ghost-hunters to come. They established the need to question the evidence of ghosts, ruling out all possible natural explanations for the activity before accepting that it might possibly be real.

Although the idea that man was able to communicate with spirits had existed already for centuries, modern belief in such a practice came about in March 1848 in Hydesville, New York. The movement, which would come to be known as *Spiritualism*, remained strong for nearly a century, enjoying its greatest revival after World War I. The practice was founded on the belief that life existed after death and that the spirit existed beyond the body. Most importantly, it was believed that these spirits could, and did, communicate with the living.

Spiritualism was born at the home of the Fox family in Hydesville after two young daughters in the family, Margaret and Kate, began claiming that they could communicate with a spirit that was haunting their home. Using an alphabet code that was created by knocking and rapping sounds, they alleged to carry on conversations with the spirit.

The two daughters were both purported to have mediumistic powers, and the news of the unearthly communications with the spirit quickly spread. By November 1849, they were both giving public performances of their skills, and the Spiritualist movement was born. The mania to communicate with the dead swept the country and filled the pages of newspapers and magazines.

From the very beginning, the Spiritualist movement has been marred by controversy and questioned by skeptics. But the public was not easily discouraged. In fact, they were fascinated with the reports of "spirited communications," and those who spoke with the dead became famous. They gave public demonstrations of their abilities and drew crowds that numbered into the thousands. Seemingly overnight, Spiritualism became a full-blown religious movement, complete with scores of followers, its own unique brand of phenomena, and codes of conduct for everything from spirit communication to séances.

The Spiritualists believed that the dead could communicate through what were called *mediums*. These were sensitive women and men who were in touch with the next world and, while in a trance, could pass along messages from the other side. Many of these practitioners also produced physical phenomena that were said to be the work of the spirits. These phenomena included lights, unearthly music, the levitation of objects, disembodied voices, and even full-blown apparitions.

All of this was produced during what were called *séances* (or sittings), which were regarded as the most exciting method of spirit communication. Any number of people could attend, and the rooms where the séances took place often contained a large table that the attendees could sit around, smaller tables that were suitable for lifting and tilting by the spirits, and a cabinet where the mediums could be sequestered while the spirits materialized and performed their tricks. The sessions reportedly boasted a variety of phenomena, including musical instruments that played by themselves and sometimes flew about the room, glowing images, ghostly hands, and, of course, messages from the dead.

While each séance was different, most had one thing in common in that they were always held in dark or dimly lighted rooms. Believers explained that the darkness provided less of a distraction to the audience and to the medium. They also added that since much of the spirit phenomenon was luminous, it was much easier seen in the darkness.

Those who were not so convinced of the validity of the movement offered another explanation. They believed the dark rooms concealed the practice of fraud. These early questioners would go on to become the first paranormal investigators of the era.

But while the Spiritualist movement brought the study of ghosts and spirits into the public eye, it also provided fame, and sometimes infamy, to many of those involved. Not only did the mediums gain notoriety, but so did many of the investigators, and in many cases, the movement led to their ruin when they were exposed as fakes. It was obvious that Spiritualism was riddled with cases of deliberate fraud. It seemed easy to fool the thousands of people who were looking for a miracle, and many of the mediums began lining their pockets with money that they had swindled from naive clients.

Of course, that's not to say that all Spiritualists were dishonest. Many of them, like the famous author Sir Arthur Conan Doyle, truly believed in the validity of the movement. Some of these good-hearted but gullible people were easily taken in by frauds. However, there were a few mediums of the era whose skills were never logically explained.

Spiritualism saw a huge increase in popularity after the Civil War. The rise in interest was credited to the number of deaths that occurred during the war. Families and individuals lost many loved ones, and now, thanks to Spiritualism, these lost loved ones were no longer lost at all. They could be communicated with and contacted as if they were still alive. Spiritualism managed to fill a huge void for the everyday person, who now had something to cling to and a belief that their friends and family members had gone on to a better place.

Interest in Spiritualism faded and by around 1900, had largely died out as a popular movement. It had never really been an organized field and, thanks to dissension in the ranks and internal politics among the leaders, it was nearly gone by the turn of the century. The exposure of many frauds also took their toll and with science not being forthcoming about legitimizing the proof of Spiritualistic tenets, the movement began to fall apart. Some of the diehard believers remained faithful but the general public had moved on to other things.

A little more than a decade later, though, World War I brought thousands of the bereaved back to séances when the movement went through its second heyday. Public interest later cooled, and by the 1930s, the era of the physical medium was gone. Most agree that this period was largely killed off by the continued attacks by magicians, investigators, and debunkers, who exposed fraud after fraud and gave even the legitimate practitioners a bad name. Soon, the mediums no longer wanted to expose themselves and abandoned the physical medium effects of flying trumpets and spirit materializations and turned to mental mediumship instead.

Today, psychic mediums are common in the world of paranormal research, just as they were more than a century and a half ago, when the field was just getting started.

Rapping with the Fox sisters

On December 11, 1847, two weeks before Christmas, John and Margaret Fox and two of their daughters moved into a small wooden-frame house in the village of Hydesville, New York. Legends say that the house was haunted before the Fox family came to live there. Those in the neighborhood often referred to it as "the spook house." Later tales claimed that the spirit that resided in the house was that of a peddler who had been murdered many years before.

But the Fox family had no interest in ghosts. John Fox and his wife, Margaret, were both past 50. The two girls, Margaretta (known as Maggie), 10, and Catherine (called Kate), 7, were both pretty girls with dark hair and eyes. Their stay at the cottage in Hydesville was meant to be a temporary one. John had purchased some land nearby, and while a home was being built, he rented the cottage in town where they could live. It became an unlikely place for the birth of an enormous national movement that would attract millions of people and dramatically change the way that Americans would come to view life and death. But it was in that small house, in that small town, where Spiritualism began on a cold March night in 1848.

The first three months that the Foxes lived in their rented home, life was fairly normal. It wasn't long, though, before friends and neighbors began sharing stories of the house's "spooky" reputation for "mysterious rapping noises." The family tried to ignore the tales because they were already experiencing the strange happenings for themselves. The noises became worse toward the end of the winter. The banging and rattling sounds pounded loudly each night, disturbing them all from their sleep.

At first, John Fox thought nothing of the sounds that his wife and children reported and were so frightened by. He assumed that they were merely the sounds of an unfamiliar dwelling, amplified by active imaginations. Soon, however, the reports took another turn. Kate woke up screaming one night, saying that a cold hand had touched her on the face. Maggie swore that rough, invisible hands had pulled the blankets from her bed. Even Mrs. Fox swore that she had heard disembodied footsteps walking through the house and then going down the wooden steps into the dank cellar.

John, not a superstitious man, was perplexed. He tried walking about the house, searching for squeaks and knocks in the floorboards and along the walls. He tested the windows and doors to see whether vibrations in the frames might account for the sounds. He could find no explanation for the weird noises, and Mrs. Fox admitted that she was upset by the inexplicable sounds and the mysterious footsteps. She concluded that some "unhappy restless spirit" was haunting the place.

On the evening of March 31, John began his almost nightly ritual of investigating the house for the source of the sounds. The tapping had begun with the setting of the sun, and although he thoroughly searched the cottage, he was no closer to finding the source of the sounds. Then, Kate began to realize that whenever her father knocked on a wall or doorframe, the same number of inexplicable knocks would come in reply. It was as if someone, or something, was trying to communicate with them.

Finding her nerve, Kate spoke up, addressing the unseen presence by the nickname that she and her sister had given it. "Here, Mr. Splitfoot," she called out. "Do as I do!"

She clapped her hands together two times, and seconds later, two knocks came in reply, seemingly from inside of the wall. She followed this display by rapping on the table, and the precise number of knocks came again from the presence. The activity caught the attention of the rest of the family, and they entered the room with Kate and her father. Margaret Fox tried asking aloud questions of fact, such as the ages of her daughters. To her surprise, each reply was eerily accurate.

Unsure of what to do, John summoned several neighbors to the house to observe the phenomenon. Soon, news of the spirit rappings attracted so much attention that a great many visitors began showing up at the Fox home, many of them demanding entry, numbering up to 500 people in a single day.

Celebrity status

The startling stories about the Fox house quickly spread throughout the surrounding area and beyond. The events attracted curiosity from both believers and skeptics. This was no mere ghost story. This was a situation in which it seemed that the Fox sisters and an alleged unseen entity had established a communication network that was unlike anything people had heard about before.

With the ability to receive a response from the spirit inhabiting their house, the young Fox sisters had tapped into the public's enthusiasm for the supernatural. Within a matter of months, what began in Hydesville spread to surrounding communities, and from there, via newspapers, to the large cities. There was no way to explain why this one particular event so vividly captured the imagination of the public. It was as if people suddenly found confirmation of the spirit world's ability to communicate with the physical world.

It wasn't long before an older sister, Leah, began putting the two girls on public display. She arranged a public lecture and demonstration at Corinthian Hall in Rochester, the city's largest auditorium, and the admission was the steep price of $1 per person.

Of those who attended the demonstration that night, many were certain they had witnessed genuine spirit communication, while others were just as sure they had witnessed a fraud. If the skeptics of the city expected to witness a public exposure of fraud in return for their dollar, they were sorely disappointed because no one could explain what caused the rappings. A committee of leading citizens reported itself completely unable to give a natural explanation for the rappings, which each of them had heard. Disappointed, the debunkers formed a second committee, which would announce a solution at a later date. When that date came, they also declared that they had been unable to detect any trickery.

More public demonstrations followed, and word began to spread beyond New York to cities all over the country. The girls became nationally known, which was unusual in an era when such celebrity was rare. A few months later, with their popularity still surging, they began traveling around the country, appearing in a variety of venues. The publicity around them was intense. Some newspapers and public venues hailed them as frauds and others as sensations. Regardless, people flocked to see them in massive numbers, all of them gladly paying for the privilege. They toured the country, becoming hugely popular, and their séances became more elaborate, with objects moving about, spirits appearing, and tables levitating. They also gave private demonstrations for those customers who could afford them.

Age of Spiritualism

The Age of Spiritualism had begun and was already generating money. Skeptics, to their dismay, were powerless to curb the enthusiasm of hundreds of thousands of people who sought contact with the spirit world. There was a sudden demand for mediums, and although the Fox sisters were there first, they soon had competition that would force them to fight for a place in an increasingly crowded market. Other mediums were soon breaking into the scene for their share of the limelight.

Since no one had been able to declare that the sisters were frauds, the public concluded that they must be genuine. The girls were embraced by such celebrities as James Fenimore Cooper, William Cullen Bryant, Harriet Beecher Stowe, and newspaper editor Horace Greeley, who provided quarters for the girls at his home. P.T. Barnum, that sensational showman, read and enjoyed news accounts of the Fox sisters' powers, and he featured them at his American Museum, where they became a huge attraction.

In 1853, the Fox sisters even held a séance in the White House for Jane Pierce, the grieving wife of President Franklin Pierce. Her son, Benjamin, had been killed in a railroad accident when the family was on its way to Washington, D.C. and she had never stopped mourning him. The two young mediums were invited to the White House, where they were expected to receive spirit raps from Benjamin in the next world. Exactly what occurred during this séance is unknown. The sisters never revealed any details about their White House experience, but rumors circulated that it was successful.

Even though most major American newspapers branded Spiritualism a fraud and a swindle, the criticism was largely ignored by people enthusiastically seeking out mediums to contact the spirit world. Skeptics continually ranted against Spiritualism, but a huge number of Americans weren't listening. What they preferred to hear was a message from parents, aunts, uncles, cousins, and children in the next world.

Notwithstanding the genuine problem of fraud and trickery in the Spiritualist movement — and there was plenty — people were anxious for a sign from a departed loved one or some message from beyond the veil. A significant change in the American attitude about death was taking place, for Spiritualism was encouraging a new outlook about the possibility of the afterlife.

A sad ending for the sisters

But life was not easy for the first celebrity mediums. Later in life, both fell on hard times. They suffered through years of séances, public appearances, tours, tests, and scrutiny, much of it antagonistic. Those who knew the sisters felt they had been physically and emotionally drained by their grueling schedule. They simply were not sophisticated enough to understand when they were young that they were being exploited by their older sister, their promoters, and their desperate audiences. Nor did they fully comprehend the depth and hostility of the religious and scientific controversy that surrounded Spiritualism. They were the first to venture professionally into the new movement, and each paid the price for it.

Maggie abandoned mediumship for love. In Philadelphia, she met and fell in love with famed Arctic explorer Elisha Kent Kane, the dashing son of an aristocratic family, who did not deem Maggie worthy of marrying into their line. They did exchange vows and rings in the company of friends but were never legally wed. Unfortunately, the affair ended in tragedy when Kane died in 1857. Maggie was left broken-hearted and almost penniless. She had abandoned being a medium but now had to take it up again. She began drinking, and her health and her mental state began to decline.

Kate, however, continued her career. She worked as a personal medium for wealthy New York banker Charles Livermore and then traveled to England to perform as a medium in 1871. She made herself available for testing with some of the eminent scientists of the day and performed with other well-known mediums. Her reputation as a medium earned Kate a visit to Russia, where she demonstrated her gifts for the czar. In 1872, she married a barrister named Henry Jencken, with whom she had two sons. After his death, she returned to America to find that her fame had faded, and her prospects were grim. Like her sister, she turned to drink.

By that time, Maggie was still a medium, albeit a reluctant one, forced to continue practicing because of her dire economic situation. She was living in poverty in 1888 when she was hired to give a lecture at the New York Academy of Music, during which she denounced Spiritualism as a complete and total sham. The years of alcohol abuse, loneliness, and grief had taken their toll on her, and she weighed the idea of committing suicide before finally choosing confession instead. She walked out on stage to announce that she and Kate had created the strange rappings heard in their Hydesville home by simply cracking their toes. She also stated that their sister, Leah, had forced them into performing as mediums for the public.

While the critics laughed, devoted Spiritualists denounced Maggie's confession as the ravings of a sad and tired drunk. The convoluted story soon became stranger. In early 1889, Maggie recanted her confession. She explained that the financial pressures she faced were responsible for her temporary disavowal of Spiritualism. She also implied that influence from certain groups who were hostile to the subject, likely churches, forced her into the erroneous confession.

The confession and the retraction did nothing for Maggie's career. The public was angry, indignant, and confused. But both Maggie and Kate were plagued by poverty, alcoholism, loneliness, and a variety of serious physical and emotional problems, so the turmoil that surrounded them probably didn't matter as much as it once might have.

In the end, the confession really didn't mean much either. It should have been a crippling blow to the credibility of Spiritualism, but it came too late to destroy a movement that had captivated the country for four decades. Spiritualism was not dead, much to the frustration of its enemies.

Both Kate and Maggie died tragic deaths. Kate drank herself to death in July 1892 at the age of only 56. Her body was discovered by one of her sons. Maggie died in March 1893, at age 59.

Their legacy

The Fox sisters, shown in Figure 2-2, went to their graves with the question of their authenticity still unsolved. But the significance of the Fox sisters' story goes far beyond whether or not the women were genuine mediums. The importance of their story is the fact that Spiritualism became a massive movement in American history and attracted millions of believers, from common homes to the White House. It happened because of those two young girls, who either communicated with a spirit or managed to scare their parents with rapping noises one cold night.

FIGURE 2-2:
The Fox sisters.

Courtesy Library of Congress.

It the end, the truth of that night may not matter. From a historical perspective, one has to be amazed that two young girls from a tiny farm community caused a stir that captured the attention of millions of Americans for more than half a century. Spiritualism became a significant force that spurred science, psychology, and theology to think in new ways. While it challenged long-held beliefs, it motivated millions to question the very nature of life and death. It also proved to be a very important solution to grief, especially after the Civil War. The movement that the sisters began grew to be much larger than just two women. Their confessions and recantations came too late to stop Spiritualism and the surge of interest that it created in the supernatural that continues to this day.

Levitating with Daniel Dunglas Home

For the most part, the 19th century did not offer the kind of celebrity status that we are so familiar with today. With only newspapers, periodicals, pamphlets, and word of mouth, news spread slower, and it was more difficult for actors, musicians, and even spirit mediums to attract a cult following. There was, however, one exception to this rule, and his name was Daniel Dunglas Home (pronounced "Hume"), and he became the most famous and enigmatic physical medium of the era. In his day, no one was better known or more successful, and Home used his purported paranormal powers to mingle with the rich, the royal, and the famous. Even to this day, he stands unique among the scores of Spiritualists that thrived in the 19th century because many of the feats that he allegedly performed have yet to be duplicated by anyone.

Home, shown in Figure 2-3, was born in Edinburgh, Scotland on March 20, 1833, but was adopted by his mother's sister and came to live with his aunt in America when he was nine. Legend has it that Home was sent away because of his psychic talents, inherited from his mother, which were already beginning to manifest when he was an infant. Family members reported that his cradle would rock by itself, as though moved by an unseen hand, and at age four, Home accurately foretold the death of a cousin. He was a sickly and strange child and believed by his family to have remarkable powers. Home went to live with his aunt in Connecticut. His health continued to decline, and he was diagnosed with tuberculosis. Unable to exert himself as most boys could, he spent most of his time walking in the woods and reading his Bible. He later became a very talented pianist, and he also came to believe that the spirits of the dead constantly surrounded him.

He had many paranormal experiences as a child, but when he was 15, the Fox sisters created a sensation and Spiritualism was first embraced by the public. Not long after, Home's own paranormal talents began to increase. He was living with his aunt at the time, and she grew to believe that the eerie events that took place around the boy were the work of the Devil. She went to the length of calling in three ministers of different denominations to pray over her nephew, but it did little good. Angry and frightened, Home's aunt threw him out of the house and left the imaginative and delicate young man to make his own way in the world.

For most of the rest of his life, Home had no place of his own to live. Staying in various households as a guest, he traveled about, holding séances for those who were interested. His séances, however, were different than most others because he always held them in brightly lit, rather than darkened, rooms. Home had attended many other séances in the past and regarded most mediums as frauds. He decided to do the opposite of what was being done elsewhere, showing the public that he had nothing to hide. Much has been made of the fact that Home never accepted direct payment for his mediumistic abilities. Most psychic investigators believed that any medium who accepted money for their services had a blatant motive for fraud. So, Spiritualists have long maintained that Home must have been genuine. However, there are other kinds of "payments." Throughout his life, Home was taken care of by "kind friends," who likely would have never heard of him had it not been for his abilities. He ate at the tables of the rich and entertained with the noble, the brilliant, and the powerful. In short, he did very well for a poor young man with no visible means of support.

Séances

During the séances that Home began to perform, he displayed a wide array of psychic abilities, including rappings, ghostly hands that ended at the wrist and which reportedly shook hands with audience members, moved tables, chairs and other objects, played spectral music, spelled out messages from the dead using lettered cards, and amazingly seemed to be able to shrink his body in size. While he was doing these things, he would ask the sitters to hold his hands and feet to prove that he was not somehow manipulating the objects with secret devices or wires. He claimed that friendly spirits, over which he had no control, made all his feats possible. Once he became known, by his own admission, he never again knew privacy or peace. He was constantly in demand by thousands for his psychic abilities.

Other physical mediums of the era attempted to create similar effects and materializations, but none of them could demonstrate such things with the skill of D.D. Home. A Home séance, at the very least, was marvelous, entertaining, and intriguing theater. If it gave evidence of the spirit world or some supernatural ability, that made it even more extraordinary.

Home was so confident of his abilities that he encouraged séance participants to stop him at any time to search for any concealed devices, the kind which were used by stage magicians. But no one ever discovered him engaged in trickery. Many were stumped when they were sure that they had determined how his psychic effects were created, only to be proven wrong.

The power to levitate

Tables lifted off the ground, spirit hands appeared and then vanished, and musical instruments played on their own. Yet, of the many Home demonstrations, the one that still provokes the most wonder — and the most debate — was his ability to fly (see Figure 2-3). Historically, levitations have been associated with the holiest of various faiths: Catholic saints, Hindu fakirs, and a few mystics. Otherwise, levitating was the domain of the theatrical magician, who created an illusion for the entertainment of his audience.

FIGURE 2-3:
The levitation of Douglas Home.

Getty Images, Hulton Archive

Home initially demonstrated his power to levitate in August 1852 at the home of a Connecticut industrialist named Ward Cheney. At the séance, music was heard playing, although no instruments were present. But that was not his most amazing feat of the evening. To put it bluntly, Home managed to fly.

Present that night at the séance was a reporter, F.L. Burr, whose assignment it was to find something incriminating against Spiritualism in general and especially about Home, who had debunkers in an uproar with his excellent reputation. However, instead of writing an expose of the evening, Burr instead wrote that Home levitated several feet off the ground. He was unable to determine how the feat had been accomplished.

Home claimed that he had no idea how he did it. He stated that an "unseen power" simply came over him and lifted him into the air. Home's supporters, of course, claimed his abilities were entirely supernatural and evidence of his psychic abilities. He could not only levitate himself, but he also sometimes caused séance participants to rise and float around the room. At one sitting, a woman felt her hand being inexplicably raised, and nothing that she did would bring her arm back down again. Suddenly, in front of stunned witnesses, she was lifted from her seat, dangled in the air for a few moments and then was mysteriously placed back in her chair.

European travels

In the spring of 1855, Home traveled to England. In a biography that was later written by his second wife, it was asserted that he needed a rest because of poor health brought on by his numerous séances and was advised to visit England for a change of climate. He arrived in April, looking pale and feeling physically ill and depressed, but he settled in London, where his reputation as a famed medium preceded him. He was soon back at work around the séance table.

Home did not stay in London for long. Over the course of the next few years, he traveled throughout Europe, performing seances for the rich and famous. He met authors, poets, and scholars, gave a demonstration for Napoleon III and Empress Eugenie, and visited Russia to display his powers for Czar Alexander II. While there, he married the daughter of a Russian nobleman, Alexandrina De Kroll, whom he had met in Rome. One of the witnesses at Home's wedding was noted author Alexandre Dumas.

Home was in France in 1862 when he predicted that Abraham Lincoln would be killed by an assassin. Later that same year, his wife, Alexandrina, died and he found himself in financial trouble. Her family contested his rights to any inheritance, and it would take another decade for the case to be resolved in his favor. In London, Home resumed his sittings for noted figures like William Makepeace Thackery and others.

The Ashley Place levitation

Between 1867 and 1869, Home became part of several séances that have intrigued psychical researchers, skeptics, and believers ever since. His frequent levitations expended a great deal of his energy, especially considering his frail health, and yet he continued them. One demonstration, in particular, has been studied, debated, and analyzed since it occurred in December 1868. The Ashley Place levitation has been called the "most famous case in the history of levitation" and still stands as one of the landmarks in the history of Spiritualism.

At Ashley Place, Home was in the company of two young men who were well-known to London society: Lord Lindsay and Lord Adare, the latter a close friend of Homes and the owner of Ashley Place. Also present was Adare's cousin, Captain Charles Wynne. These three irreproachable witnesses reportedly watched as Home went into a trance, floated out the window of the third floor, and came in through the window of another room.

How was this achieved? The longest-held belief is that they were accomplished by some supernatural power. Some scientists have experimented with levitation, describing their explorations into what is known as *electro-gravity* or *anti-gravity effects.* Parapsychologists have suggested levitation may be the result of psychokinetic or telekinetic energy. Yet another theory offered is that levitation can be induced by hypnotic suggestion. Eastern mystics who have demonstrated levitation for centuries have been credited with having a special breathing technique that makes it possible.

Just as there have been numerous theories to explain Home's seeming ability to levitate, there have been just as many efforts to demystify it, too. How he was able to apparently suspend himself in mid-air has been an ongoing source of debate and controversy. There are no less than 100 separate incidents of levitation attributed to Home, yet no single theory to explain how he was able to do this in front of large and small groups of bewildered witnesses.

Home's abilities attracted attention everywhere he went, and the press never failed to report about him. Some of the explanations offered for his strange abilities were nothing short of bizarre. For example, with the Ashley Place levitation, it was suggested he had done it by rigging up harnesses and pulleys outside of the house. However, it should be noted that it was the first time that Home had visited the house, so he had no opportunity to rig up elaborate machinery or engage the services of anyone to do it for him. There is no evidence to say that he ever resorted to such tricks. In addition, he was not exactly a robust character, thanks to his tubercular condition. It would have been impossible for him to go fumbling about on ropes and pulleys outside of the window of Lord Adare's mansion on a cold December night.

Wild speculation

After his death, dozens of explanations were given as to how Home accomplished this feat through trickery, but not even one of these theories was ever proven. In addition, the most prominent stage magicians in the world, including Harry Houdini, all claimed they could duplicate his stunts on stage, but, for some reason, they never did. During his career, Home was never caught cheating, but this didn't stop skeptics from wildly speculating about how he accomplished his strange feats.

Over a two-year period, Home reportedly held around 80 séances, and in 1869, the London Dialectical Society arranged for a committee to study Spiritualism. The group's members included several hard-nosed skeptics, one an outspoken atheist. When Home was tested at four separate séances, the results were less than what was expected. There was some evidence of spirit raps and some table tipping, but little else. It was said that Home's energy was at a low point, thanks to his continuing struggle with tuberculosis, and he was simply too weak to summon the power that he possessed. The committee's conclusion was that little had occurred, but the group acknowledged that Home had been open and willing to be studied through the entire process.

Retirement

In 1871, Home married again. His new wife, Julie de Gloumeline, like his first wife, was a wealthy, attractive, upper-class Russian woman. They'd met in St. Petersburg, Russia, where he was conducting séances.

By 1876, Home's health had become noticeably worse, forcing him into retirement. Thanks to his marriage, money was no longer a concern. His long struggle with tuberculosis had shortened his life, yet he made it clear that he had no fear of death. He lived quietly for another ten years, cared for by his wife, and died quietly in Paris on June 21, 1886, at the age of only 53.

Home's death did not end the curiosity and controversy that encompassed him in life. Although he was never publicly detected committing any fraud or deception, no one could say with certainty how he produced some of the amazing manifestations that have been credited to him. Years after his death, debunkers were convinced in hindsight that somehow Home had employed deception — and yet they could not point to any proof of it.

Home left many unanswered questions in his wake. Theories and speculation will always continue, boiling down to two possibilities: Daniel Dunglas Home was a unique and remarkable individual who truly possessed the powers that have been attributed to him, or he was one of the most clever and cunning frauds in history. It's likely that we will never discover which one is the truth.

Investigating the Eddy Brothers

The stories were everywhere in 1874. They were not only in the Spiritualist periodicals of the time; stories even appeared in the popular press. They all reported the same thing — some very strange happenings were taking place on a small farm outside Chittenden, Vermont. The farm belonged to two middle-aged, illiterate brothers, William and Horatio Eddy, and their sister, Mary. The Eddy clan lived in an unkempt, two-story house that was infested with supernatural beings in such numbers that nothing like it had been reported before, or since. People were coming from all over the country and from around the world to witness the manifestations for themselves. Spiritualists had started to call Chittenden the "Spirit Capital of the Universe."

Of course, not everyone believed the stories before they arrived. One of the most skeptical was Henry Olcott, who had read about the Eddys in a New York newspaper. Intrigued, he convinced the *New York Tribune* to send him to Vermont to investigate the wild tales. Olcott had no interest in the supernatural prior to this journey. Born in New Jersey in 1832, he attended college in New York City, studying agricultural science. While still in his early 20s, he received international recognition for his work on a model farm and for founding a school for agriculture students. During this same time, he published three scientific works. He went on to become the farm editor for the *Tribune*. When the Civil War broke out, Olcott enlisted in the Union Army. He was appointed as a special investigator to root out corruption and fraud in military arsenals and shipyards. He was soon promoted to the rank of Colonel and after the war, was part of a three-person panel that investigated the assassination of President Lincoln. After the war, Olcott studied law and became a wealthy and successful attorney.

Olcott could never explain what prompted him to read the article about the Eddy brothers or why he was interested enough to travel to Vermont to investigate the claims made about him. But whatever the reason, it changed his life.

Olcott traveled to Vermont with newspaper artist Albert Kappes. Together, they planned to investigate the strange events at the Eddy farm, and if the stories were a hoax, they would expose the Eddy brothers in the newspaper as charlatans. Olcott's first impression of the Eddys was not a favorable one. The two distant and unfriendly farmers were rough-hewn characters with dark hair and eyes and New England accents so thick the New York attorney and writer could scarcely understand them.

A sad past

The story was that the Eddys came from a long line of psychics, including a distant relative that was convicted of witchcraft at Salem in 1692. Their grandmother had been blessed with the gift of "second sight" and often went into trances, speaking to entities that no one else could see. Their mother, Julia, had been known for frightening her neighbors with predictions and visions. Her gifts were unwelcomed in the Eddy home. Her husband, Zepaniah, was a cruel and abusive man. He beat his wife, and later, when it was discovered that his sons also had strange powers, he beat and whipped them. As children, the Eddys were unable to attend school. When they did, books flew, desks levitated, and rulers, inkwell, and slates flew about the classroom.

Zepaniah continued to beat his sons, trying to make the disturbances stop. Instead, they grew worse. If they went into a trance, he would pinch and slap them, trying to wake them up. It didn't work. They were bruised until they were black and blue. Once, on the advice of a friend, he doused the boys with boiling water. When this didn't work, he also allowed this friend to drop a red-hot coal into William's hand. The boy didn't awaken from his trance, but he bore a scar on his palm for the rest of his life.

Unable to control the boys, Zepaniah sold them to a traveling showman who, for the next 14 years, took them all over America, Canada, and Europe. It was a brutal and degrading life. As part of their "performance," audience members were allowed to try and awaken the boys from their trances. The Eddys were locked into small wooden boxes to see whether they could escape, and hot wax was poured into their mouths to see whether they could produce "spirit voices" when they were unable to talk. The skeptics poked, prodded, and punched the sleeping brothers, leaving them scarred and damaged for the rest of their lives. On several occasions, they were even stoned and shot at by angry mobs.

The Eddys eventually returned home after the death of their father. Along with their sister, Mary, they turned the family farm into a modest inn called the Green Tavern. It was there that Olcott first met the brothers, and it was there that they began holding seances for Spiritualists who traveled to see them from across the country and overseas.

An outdoor séance

During Olcott's first night at the farm, he was witness to an outdoor séance. He was led through the woods with a few other participants to a natural cave in a deep ravine. Olcott later learned that it was called Honto's Cave, in honor of the Native American spirit who often appeared there. Olcott suspiciously investigated the cave but found it was little more than a few rocks on top of one another, forming a natural arch. There was only one way in or out. He determined there was no way that anyone could slip in or out of the cave without being seen.

Horatio Eddy acted as the medium for the séance. He sat on a camp stool under the arch and then was draped in a makeshift "spirit cabinet" formed by shawls and branches that had been cut from small saplings. As Horatio rested there, a gigantic man, dressed as a Native American, emerged from the darkness of the cave. A few moments later, more spirits appeared above the cave entrance and in the surrounding rocks. Olcott counted ten different spirits at the site. The last, the spirit of William White, the late editor of a Spiritualist newspaper, emerged from within Horatio's cabinet. He was dressed in a black suit and white shirt was supposedly recognizable to witnesses who had read the newspaper and recognized his picture from it. He vanished at the same time the others did. Moments later,

Horatio appeared from the cabinet and signaled that the séance was at an end. After the bizarre display was over, Olcott and Kappes carefully searched the cave and the surrounding area for footprints in the soft earth. They found no footprints — there was no trace that anyone had been there.

The séance room

Olcott was intrigued, but not convinced. The whole thing would have been too easy to stage, he believed. It would be different when he could see one of the séances inside of the house. The Eddys had built a séance room on the second floor of the inn. Olcott and Kappes thoroughly examined it. They drew charts and diagrams and took numerous measurements, sure that they would find false panels, secret doors, or hidden passages, but found nothing. Determined not to give up, Olcott hired carpenters and engineers to come and search the place, but the experts found nothing unusual. The walls and floors were as solid as they seemed. There was no trickery taking place with the structure of the house, which made what Olcott witnessed on the following nights even stranger.

Each séance was basically the same. On every night of the week — except for Sunday — guests and visitors would assemble on wooden benches in the séance room. A platform, which had been assembled there, was lit only by a kerosene lamp, recessed in a barrel. William Eddy, who acted as the primary medium, mounted the platform and entered a small cabinet. A few moments later, soft voices began to whisper in the distance. Often, it would be singing, accompanied by spectral music. Musical instruments came to life and soared above the heads of the audience members, disembodied hands appeared, waving and touching the spectators, and odd lights and unexplained noises appeared and filled the air.

Then, the first spirit form emerged from the cabinet. They came one at a time, or in groups, numbering as many as 20 or 30 in an evening. Some were completely visible and seemed solid. Others were transparent and ethereal. Regardless, they awed the frightened spectators. The spirits ranged in size from over six feet to very small. Most of the ghostly apparitions were elderly Yankees or Native Americans, but many other races and nationalities also appeared in traditional Russian, African, and Asian garb.

Olcott could not explain where they had come from. He had examined the spirit cabinet and platform and had found no trap doors, nor hidden passages. In fact, there was no room in the cabinet for anyone other than the medium himself. Olcott was familiar with the workings of stage magicians but could find none of their tricks present at the Eddy house.

The apparitions not only appeared, but they also performed, sang, and chatted with the sitters. They produced musical instruments, clothing, and scarves. In all, nearly every type of supernatural phenomena was reported at the Eddy farmhouse. These included rappings, moving physical objects, spirit paintings, automatic writing, prophecy, speaking in tongues, healings, unseen voices, levitation, remote visions, teleportation, and more. And, of course, there were the full-bodied manifestations of which Olcott observed more than 400 during the weeks he visited the house. He concluded that a show like that which he had seen would have required an entire company of actors and several trunks of costumes.

Yet, Olcott's inspection of the premises revealed no place to hide either actors or props. The idea of stage actors was further dispelled by the convincing manner of the spirits. One woman spoke in Russian to the alleged spirit of her deceased husband. Several other dialects were also heard. This seemed impossible because the Eddy's could barely read and write and were scarcely capable of speaking coherent English.

In addition, such an elaborate show would have cost a fortune to produce each night. They would have had to pay actors, invest in costumes, and hire someone to create the "marvels" of the spirits. This would also have been impossible given that the brothers were almost penniless. Most of the visitors who came to the farm did not pay, and the rest gave only $8 per week for room and board at the inn. No admission was ever charged for the séances. In Olcott's mind, fraud would have been physically and financially impossible. In fact, the whole thing was impossible, but he was convinced that it was real.

Life-changing results

Olcott spent ten weeks at the farm. He left the place disliking the house, the food, the weather, and the Eddy brothers themselves, but he also left convinced that the two men were making contact with the dead. He wrote this in the newspaper and then wrote a massive book about the Eddys called *People from Other Worlds*. It was filled with precise drawings of the apparitions, the farm, the house, and even detailed plans of its construction, proving that no hidden passages existed. He also recorded hundreds of different supernatural beings and collected hundreds of affidavits and scores of eyewitness testimony to the amazing events. He also reproduced dozens of statements from respected tradesmen and carpenters who had examined the house for trickery. A modern reader would have to look very hard to discover anything that Olcott did not investigate.

Eventually, the Eddys had a falling out and spent the rest of their lives apart. Horatio died in 1922. William lived to be 99 and died in 1932. He never participated in séances again. If either of the two men had any secrets about the weird events at their home, they took those secrets with them to the grave.

No one knows what really happened at the Eddy Farm in Vermont. To read this story today, we are first inclined to dismiss the events as fanciful tales from another time, but this might be a mistake. Colonel Olcott had impeccable credentials for investigating fraud, so the story can't be dismissed out of hand. His extensive documentation, along with his investigative skills, suggests that the events were not part of a hoax. Olcott remained skeptical and analytical throughout his stay at the farm, and yet he came away convinced that the Eddys had the power to contact, and communicate with, the dead.

Colonel Olcott came away from Chittenden a believer. The once skeptical military investigator was convinced that the dead could communicate with the living.

In fact, he was so convinced of the reality of the spirit world that he left his career and his wife and devoted the rest of his life to the study of the occult and the arcane. He cofounded the Theosophical Society and moved to India. Olcott spoke in temples and open squares in India and Sri Lanka, where he urged young people and their families not to relinquish their traditions and to argue against colonialist missionaries. He lobbied the English authorities to permit a national celebration of Buddha's birthday, during which worshippers rallied around an international Buddhist flag that Alcott helped design. He raised money for schools and educational programs and wrote a book about Buddhism that is still read in Sri Lankan classrooms today.

After his awakening at the Eddy farm, Olcott understood himself to be on the mission of a lifetime. It was a mission that touched Hindu and Buddhist cultures so deeply that Olcott may be the single most significant Western figure in the modern religious history of the East. Decades after his arrival there, the Buddhist nation of Ceylon enshrined his image on a postage stamp and marked his death with a national holiday.

And it started with a séance in Vermont. Whatever one decides to believe, it cannot be denied that something amazing and mysterious occurred on the farm of the Eddy brothers, although what this may have been, we may never know for sure.

The First Ghost-hunters

Between 1876 and 1900, the world saw scores of amazing discoveries and inventions — the telephone, electric lights, the science of fingerprinting, the Kodak "box camera," medical improvements, automobiles, motion pictures, wireless telegraphs, the discovery of radioactivity, airships, and more. By 1893, when Tesla's alternating current turned Chicago's World Columbian Exposition into a city of lights, most people who had grown up after the Civil War had started to think that the new technology of the approaching 20th century was more exciting than the Spiritualism that had come of age in the 1800s.

At the same time, however, thanks to many poets and writers, more Americans began to explore alternative thinking and mysticism as a path to a spiritual truth. Writers like Walt Whitman encouraged readers to contemplate Eastern beliefs, and America's sense of religious curiosity began to threaten the more conservative Christian denominations, which were already battling Charles Darwin's highly contentious and controversial theory of evolution. Even though every important scientist in the country had embraced his explanation for the origin of the species, it was a direct contradiction to Christianity's certitude in the literal world of the Bible that God had created the universe in six days.

Spiritualism remained popular in America and England, but it began to be looked at in a different way by the general public. People had grown tired of fraudulent mediums, plus people were living longer and had healthier lives, so there was less thought about imminent death. In the increasingly mechanized society of the era, many felt that psychic phenomena needed to be explained scientifically and rationally. It seemed obvious to many that strange things took place, and now such things needed to be explained.

What seemed to be needed was a serious, scientific investigation of Spiritualism and other psychical claims, carried out by an organization of objective researchers who were dedicated to seeking the truth — whatever that might be. The Spiritualist movement had always lacked a cohesiveness and a single authoritative voice to represent it. This was the reason why its ranks were so riddled with fraud and why its many claims had remained unproven for decades. But all that was about to change.

The Society for Psychical Research

In 1882, paranormal research took a giant leap forward from séance room to scientific setting when a group of insightful British men, most of them educated at Cambridge University, formed a new association for investigating the paranormal — the Society for Psychical Research, or SPR, as it came to be called. It made its purpose very clear from the start: "To examine without prejudice or prepossession and in a scientific spirit those faculties of man, real or supposed, which appear to be inexplicable on any generally recognized hypothesis."

Why what can only be called as a landmark moment in supernatural history occurred first in England and not in America remains a bit of a mystery. It's thought that perhaps since Britain was a much older and longer established society that it was "better organized" in the 19th century. It had its own thriving Spiritualist movement, with many mediums and dozens of publications. America was larger, much more diverse, spreading to the west, and the people had a streak of independence that the Europeans thought of as "unruly." Many British scientists and thinkers, whether opponents or supporters of Spiritualism, seemed less intimidated about delving into the field than their American counterparts.

Regardless of why it happened, the first investigation society formed itself in Great Britain. Events were set into motion one day toward the end of 1881, when a respected physicist from Dublin, Professor William Barrett, was invited to the London home of journalist and Spiritualist Edmond Dawson Rogers. The two men were engaged in a lively discussion about Spiritualism when Rogers suggested that a society be formed with the goal of encouraging the greatest scientists in England to investigate psychical phenomena. Barrett, who'd long had an interest in mesmerism and Spiritualism, embraced the idea. He knew there had been earlier attempts to create such organizations in England and America, but all were short-lived. Barrett was determined to make sure this one worked, which would require the right people to be involved.

Barrett took the idea to his friend Frederick W.H. Myers, and then to Edmund Gurney, but neither man was optimistic about the success of such a society. Myers was a professor at Cambridge with a curiosity about what evidence existed for a spirit world. Gurney was a scholar with an interest in telepathy and hypnotism. However, they agreed that if Professor Henry Sidgwick would serve as the group's president, they'd lend their support to the effort. Sidgwick, a well-respected philosopher at Cambridge with a reputation for being highly skeptical and critical, agreed to the job.

On February 20, 1882, the Society for Psychical Research was formed with Sidgwick at the helm. Including the president, a 19-member council was named: 13 of them were Spiritualists, 6, including Sidgwick, were not. One Spiritualist chosen was an author, Mrs. George Boole. Several months later, unhappy that she was the only woman who had been appointed to the council, she resigned. It would be nearly 20 more years before another woman — Sidgwick's wife — was appointed. This seems ironic considering the fact that women had long dominated the Spiritualist movement.

The group was successful from the start, perhaps because of the ages of the founding officers and members. Most were in their 20s and 30s at the time — the oldest was Sidgwick at 43. Despite its scientific goals, the SPR was not founded by only scholars and scientists. The group was composed of a variety of occupations, including a schoolteacher, accountant, businessman, lawyer, and hotel owner. All of them had been brought up in religious homes. They did their best to maintain high standards of scholarship in their journal, and the members took their investigations and research very seriously.

Sidgwick divided the SPR members into committees, each to investigate a particular phenomenon, including telepathy, hauntings, physical mediumship, spontaneous experiences, and mesmerism. Each committee was charged with issuing reports of their findings. Sidgwick also named those he considered best qualified to examine specific topics: Barrett researched dowsing; Gurney studied phantasms of the living; Mrs. Sidgwick was responsible for a study of apparitions; and Richard Hodgson, trained in law and with a fierce dedication to exposing frauds, investigated Theosophy. Other SPR members delved into deathbed visions, clairvoyance, and the statistical probabilities of chance.

The SPR investigators and their respective committees worked so hard that, within just a few years after the society's foundation, they were already producing more than 500 pages of research each year. During this time, the society earned a reputation for being notoriously tough in its investigations.

An investigation led by Richard Hodgson examined famed physical medium, William Eglinton. The society became interested in the medium after hearing the widely spread reports of the phenomena that occurred during his séances, including apports that "appear from nowhere," phantoms, and that he "levitated to the ceiling." Eglinton was best known for his slate writing skills, which he began demonstrating in 1884. He once gave a séance attended by British Prime Minister William Gladstone, who was so impressed that he joined the SPR. The well-known English naturalist Alfred Russell Wallace, who had helped Darwin devise his theory of evolution, was also convinced that Eglinton was genuine.

The SPR gathered many accounts from people who had attended Eglinton's séances, and, despite the number of awestruck accounts, the investigators knew that slate writing was open to trickery. It was Richard Hodgson who spoiled the medium's game. He watched Eglinton carefully and concluded there was fraud afoot. Eglinton, he said, employed "distraction," among other deceptions. On that basis, the SPR declared that Eglinton's manifestations were nothing more than "clever conjuring." Others were less skeptical and spoke on Eglinton's behalf. The SPR angered the Spiritualist community and Eglinton responded by publishing dozens of testimonials a Spiritualist newspaper. After thousands of sittings — and only a handful of accusations of fraud — Eglinton gave up mediumship and became a successful journalist.

Over the course of the next couple of decades, the society managed to weather both scandal and embarrassment, as mediums they endorsed were found to be fraudulent; Frederick Myers got involved in a sex scandal with a female psychic investigator who turned out to be a fraud; Edmund Gurney was found dead under strange circumstances; and in 1888, the founders of the Spiritualist movement, the Fox sisters themselves, publicly confessed to being fakes. Even though the credibility of this confession was in question, it was still used by other scientists to make the SPR members look like fools. By the early 1900s, the reputation of the society was rather tarnished, but nevertheless, still intact. The society's work continues today.

Harry Price

Other organizations followed in the wake of the SPR, testing mediums and attending séances, trying to discover whether the paranormal events that were allegedly occurring were real. As science lost interest in chasing spooks, magicians and amateur investigations took up the cause, intent more on debunking fraudulent mediums than with delving into the authenticity of incidents connected with the next world. In time, as the mediums changed their methods, even those investigations died out. Science had turned to investigating the mysteries of the human mind — ESP, telekinesis, and clairvoyance — and ghosts would have likely been relegated to the dusty back rooms of haunted history, if not for the men and women who began seeking spirits in the 1920s and 1930s. These new investigations didn't focus on mediums and Spiritualism — they were strictly looking for ghosts.

It wasn't until this new era that psychical research truly began to delve into hauntings and what caused them to occur. Almost all psychical research had initially questioned whether the effects that occurred during séances could be linked to the dead. The new research was different. It wasn't as concerned with the dead who were returning, but with the dead who were still on earth. In other words, are ghosts real? And do they haunt the places that were linked to them in life?

The first celebrity ghost-hunter

There were a number of researchers who became active during this era, but the most prominent was Harry Price (see Figure 2-4). His influence on the paranormal field of the early 20th century is beyond measure, and that influence continues today. Most present-day ghost-hunters emulate Harry Price with every investigation they conduct and, sadly, few of them have any idea they are doing it.

Harry Price, although disliked and distrusted by many, remains one of the most important figures in the formative years of ghost research. He had a highly charismatic personality, and his energy, enthusiasm, and passion for the paranormal made him the first "celebrity ghost-hunter." He was instrumental in making ghost research accessible to the general public, realizing that only by making the research entertaining could he attract the attention of the masses. And there is no question that Price loved attention. Mixed throughout his legitimate research were the bizarre attempts that he made to investigate a talking mongoose and a spell that would turn a goat into a man. With every step of the way, he had newspapers, radio newscasters, and reporters following his every move.

FIGURE 2-4:
Harry Price.

Getty Images, David Scherman

His flamboyant showmanship, his larger-than-life personality, and his refusal to go along with those who wanted to keep the paranormal confined to a laboratory made Price many enemies in the psychical research field. Much of that resentment came from the fact that Price had no real scientific training but was still so skillful at what he did. He was a deft magician and an expert at detecting fraud, so he was never taken in by the many phony mediums that plagued paranormal research when he was first starting out. His success became a point of contention for those who considered themselves established paranormal researchers.

His work was groundbreaking, no matter what other investigators and main-stream scientists thought of him. His investigation at the house known as Borley Rectory, shown in Figure 2-5, became the first documented attempts to track down evidence of a haunting at a single location. He created the ghost-hunter's "tool kit" and also developed the first how-to guide for investigating a haunted house.

An early ghostly encounter

Harry Price was born on January 17, 1881, in London, the son of a grocer and trav-eling salesman. He was educated in New Cross, first at Waller Road Infant's School and then at Haberdashers' Aske's Hatcham Boy's School. At 15, he founded the Carlton Dramatic Society and wrote a number of plays. One of the plays that he wrote was about an early experience that he had with a poltergeist. He was still a teenager, and he and a friend obtained permission to stay in what was regarded locally as a haunted house. The stories claimed that a ghost could be heard walking heavily down the main staircase each night, so Price and his friend set up a camera that could be fired remotely so that they could catch the spirit on film.

On that fateful night, both boys clearly heard footsteps pacing on the upper floor of the otherwise empty house. Moments later, the footsteps came down the stairs, and Price pushed the button that fired off the camera and flash powder. The boys were hiding in an adjoining room, and the light was so bright the darkened room was illuminated by the glare from under the door. At the same moment that the flash went off, the footsteps on the stairs faltered and stumbled, a sound that the boys could plainly hear. It was followed by what sounded like someone falling. After the young men got over their astonishment, they retrieved the camera and fled the house. After the plate was developed, they found that the photograph that they attempted to take of the ghost was nothing more than a washed-out, over-exposed negative, but Price would never forget the time that he and his friend frightened a ghost.

His passion of paranormal phenomena

After graduating from school, Price worked several jobs, including as a journalist and paper salesman. He developed a lifelong interest in magic and conjuring, and his expertise in sleight-of-hand and magic tricks helped him immensely in what would become his all-consuming passion: the investigation of paranormal phenomena. In 1908, Price met and married a wealthy heiress, Constance Mary Knight. With his fortunes secured, he began his pursuit of the unknown.

By the time that Price joined the Society for Psychical Research in 1920, he had already begun his career as Britain's most famous ghost investigator. He had spent many hours at alleged haunted houses and in the investigation of Spiritualist mediums. He was also an expert magician and soon made a name for himself within the SPR for using his magic skills to debunk fraudulent psychics, then in keeping with what was the main thrust of the current SPR investigations. Unlike most magicians of the era, though, Price endorsed some mediums that he believed were genuine.

Price's first major success in psychical research came in 1922 when he exposed the spirit photographer William Hope, who was making a fortune taking portraits of people that always seemed to include the sitter's dead relatives. Price investigated and soon published his findings. He claimed that Hope used pre-exposed plates in his camera, which he learned by secretly switching the plates the photographer was using with plates of his own.

He went on to conduct dozens of séances with a young woman named Stella Cranshaw, which produced many remarkable events. Price designed his own equipment to be used in the séance room so that the phenomena she produced could be studied scientifically. One of them was a special table with the inner portion of it being a wire cage where items that were to be manipulated could be placed. The first time that it was used, several musical instruments were placed inside, and a rattle was somehow thrown out of the closed cage. Another was the *telekinetoscope*, a clever device that used a telegraph key that when depressed would cause a red light to turn on. A glass dome then covered the key so that only psychic powers could operate it. During the séances, the red light often turned on, even though the switch could not be manipulated by hand. Price continued to test — and in many cases, expose — mediums, trying to measure aspects of each séance in a scientific manner. He managed to record strange temperature drops and other phenomena that finally convinced him of the reality of the paranormal. From this point on, he devoted more of his time to pursuing genuine phenomena rather than debunking mediums, which did not sit well with the SPR. Price had already been in a number of disputes with the SPR, and the relationship became so strained that Price decided to form the National Laboratory for Psychical Research in 1923. It would take another three years to get it up and running, but it so angered leaders at the SPR that they returned Price's donation of a massive book collection.

Price had little use for nonsense and made a formal offer to the University of London to equip and endow a Department of Psychical Research and to loan the equipment of the National Laboratory and its library. The University of London Board of Studies in Psychology responded positively to this proposal. In 1934, the

National Laboratory of Psychical Research, which held Price's collection, was reconstituted as the University of London Council for Psychical Investigation with C. E. M. Joad as chairman and with Price as Honorary Secretary and editor, although it was not an official body of the University. His collection of books, papers, and materials were donated to the University by his widow in 1976, and they remain on display there today.

The Ghost Club

Meanwhile, in 1927, Price joined the Ghost Club, a sort of rival organization of the SPR, and remained a member until it temporarily closed in 1936. It would be Price who re-established the Ghost Club in 1938, with himself as chairman, modernizing it, removing the connections to Spiritualism, and turning it into a group of mostly open-minded skeptics who gathered to discuss and investigate the paranormal. He was the first to admit women into the club.

While the various dramas were playing out on the organizational stage, Price was still investigating the cases that came along, from mediums to general strangeness. In 1926, he learned of a Romanian peasant girl named Eleonora Zugan, who was apparently experiencing violent poltergeist phenomena, including flying objects, slapping, biting, and pinching. He also investigated a famous medium named Rudi Schneider. Price then rocked the paranormal community with the announcement that Rudi was a fraud. As evidence, he produced a photograph that was taken during a séance and which showed Rudi reaching for a table.

One of Price's strangest cases was that of Gef, the Talking Mongoose of Cashen's Gap. The case began in 1931 with a disembodied voice plaguing the Irving family, who lived at Cashen's Gap, an isolated spot on the Isle of Man. The voice claimed that it belonged to a mongoose, a weasel-like creature. It told the Irvings that it ate rabbits, and it spoke in various languages, imitated other animals, and even recited nursery rhymes. Price never found any evidence to suggest the creature was real, but later studies do suggest that the Irving house may have been experiencing a poltergeist outbreak caused by a human agent.

Borley Rectory

The year 1929 marked a turning point in Price's career, although the case in which he first became involved with that summer would not be made public for several years in the future. The house that was at the heart of the case, a deteriorating old place in Essex called Borley Rectory, would take over Price's life and, more than anything else that he did, make him both famous and infamous.

Price's interactions with Borley Rectory brought him a windfall of new publicity in newspapers and on the radio. He also wrote two books about the house. Despite what his critics said about him, there was no question that Price was the most famous ghost-hunter in England — and perhaps in the world after LIFE magazine ran a piece about Borley Rectory in the 1940s. Publicity aside, though, his books about the house set the standard for psychical investigations and marked the first time that the general public was exposed to detailed accounts of paranormal research. Even today, Price's books about Borley Rectory make for compelling reading, and it's easy to understand why they turned into the bestsellers of the day.

The tiny parish of Borley is located in a quiet, sparsely populated county near the eastern coast of England, not far from Essex's border with Suffolk. Harry Price began the chronicle of the lonely place in 1362 when Edward III bestowed the Manor of Borley upon the Benedictine monks. But that early history of the future rectory was so shrouded in mystery that all that was known for certain is that the manor was in the possession of the powerful Waldegrave family for at least 300 years. Between 1862 and 1892, the Reverend H.D.E. Bull, a Waldegrave descendant, was the rector of Borley. A year after his appointment, he built Borley Rectory. Despite local warnings, he had built the house on a site believed by locals to be haunted. His son, the Reverend H.F. Bull, succeeded him as rector and remained in the position until his death in 1927. The rectory was then vacant for over a year, until October 1928, when the Rev. Guy Eric Smith was appointed to the role. However, he quit the rectory just one year after moving in, plagued by both the ghosts and the house's deteriorating state.

There had been strange happenings reported in and around the rectory for many years before the residency of the Reverend Smith. The Bull family often discussed the ghosts and often reported seeing a ghostly nun walking the grounds. Prior to 1939, there had been 14 legitimate sightings of the nun, and 3 of those people had also seen a spectral coach, and horses "with glittering harness," sweep across the grounds. Two others had claimed to see an apparition of a headless man on the property.

In June 1929, a story about ghostly occurrences at Borley appeared in a newspaper. The next day, Harry Price received a telephone call from a London editor and was asked to investigate. He was told about various types of phenomena that had been reported there and given a lengthy list of weird happenings — phantom footsteps, whispers, the headless man, a girl in white, the spectral coach, the ghost of Henry Bull, and, of course, the phantom nun.

Price was told that local legend claimed that a monastery had once been located on the site and that a 13th-century monk and a beautiful young nun were killed while trying to elope from the place. The monk was hanged, and his would-be bride was bricked up alive within the walls of her convent. Price scoffed at the idea of such a romantic tale but was intrigued by the many stories associated with the house.

Price was accompanied on his first visit to Borley by V.C. Wall, a well-known journalist, and Miss Lucie Kaye, his long-time secretary. Together, they listened to the experiences of Reverend Smith and even observed some minor examples of poltergeist phenomenon for themselves. Price also conducted a long interview with Miss Mary Pearson, the rectory's maid, who had seen the ghostly coach and horses twice and was firmly convinced the house was genuinely haunted.

Later that night, the group held a séance in the Blue Room of the house, where many of the manifestations had allegedly occurred. They were startled when a piece of soap jumped up off the floor with no assistance. The following day, Price conducted more interviews and spoke with the Coopers, a couple who had lived in a cottage on the rectory grounds. They had moved out in 1920, blaming uncomfortable feelings caused by the ghosts.

The events that occurred, and the witness interviews that were documented, were enough to convince Price that something supernatural was going on at the house. That early summer afternoon kicked off Price's more than decade-and-a-half long obsession with Borley Rectory. He became fascinated with the house, and it came to represent the most exciting and baffling puzzle of his career.

Price's second visit to Borley came two weeks after the first. In addition to witnessing a religious medal that appeared without explanation, there were several times when bells — once used to summon servants — rang throughout the house, although the bell wires had been cut many years before. The constant ringing was a source of great annoyance for Reverend Smith and his wife, and this, along with other unnerving manifestations, convinced the couple to abandon the house on July 14, 1929.

Over the course of the next 14 months, the rectory remained empty, and yet the happenings reportedly continued. According to local accounts, a window on the house was opened from the inside, even though the rectory was deserted, and the doors were securely locked. The main staircase was found covered with lumps of stone, and small pieces of glass were said to have been scattered about. Locals who lived nearby reported seeing "lights" in the house and hearing what were described as "horrible sounds" around the time of the full moon.

Even though Rev. Smith and his wife moved out of the house because of the ghosts, things had really been rather peaceful up until that point. All of that would change, though, in October 1930, when the Reverend Lionel Foyster and his wife, Marianne, replaced Smith. The Foysters' time in the house would see a marked increase in paranormal activity. People were locked out of rooms, household items vanished, windows were broken, furniture was moved, odd sounds were heard, and much more. However, the worst of the incidents seemed to involve Mrs. Foyster, who was thrown from her bed at night, slapped by invisible hands, forced to dodge heavy objects that flew at her, and was once almost suffocated with a mattress.

The activity during this period was more varied and far more violent than before. There is no question that Reverend Foyster, Marianne, their adopted daughter, and later, a young boy who stayed with them as a guest, went through some strange and sometimes terrifying experiences. The manifestations reached their peak when a series of scrawled messages began appearing on the walls inside the house, written by an unknown hand. They seemed to be pleading with Mrs. Foyster, using phrases like "Marianne, please help get" and "Marianne, light mass prayers."

Things got so bad by May 1931 that the Foysters left the rectory so that they could get a few days of peace and quiet. In June, Dom Richard Whitehouse, a friend of the Foysters, began an investigation. He found things inexplicably scattered all over the unoccupied house, but never saw any of the activity occur. When the family returned, the violent manifestations began again, usually directed toward Marianne. One night, she was hurled from her bed three times. By October 1935, the Foysters had reached the limits of their endurance. They decided to leave the house, and the church decided to sell the place, as they now believed that it was unfit for any parson to live in it.

The church offered the house to Harry Price — for about one-sixth of its value — but after some hesitation, he decided not to buy the place. Instead, he signed a lease to rent it for a year. Price planned to conduct an extended, around the clock investigation of the house, using scores of volunteer investigators to track and document anything out of the ordinary that occurred there. As it turned out, the investigation was never that organized. Even so, in spite of often poor record-keeping and periods when the house was unoccupied, the year-long investigation remains a landmark in the annals of the paranormal.

A landmark investigation

Price's first step was to run an advertisement in the personal column of the *Times* on May 25, 1937, looking for open-minded researchers to camp out at the rectory. They were to record any phenomena that took place in their presence. The advertisement read:

HAUNTED HOUSE: Responsible persons of leisure and intelligence, intrepid, critical, and unbiased, are invited to join rota of observers in a year's night and day investigation of alleged haunted house in Home counties. Printed Instructions supplied. Scientific training or ability to operate simple instruments an advantage. House situated in lonely hamlet, so own car is essential. Write Box H.989, The Times, E.C.4

Price was deluged with potential applicants. After choosing more than 40 people, he then printed the first-ever handbook on how to conduct a paranormal investigation. It became known as the *Blue Book.* A copy was given to each investigator, and it explained what to do when investigating the house, along with what equipment they would need. As part of the investigation, he coined the idea of a *ghost-hunter's kit,* which included tape measurers to check the thickness of walls and to search for hidden chambers, still cameras for indoor and outdoor photography, a remote-control motion picture camera, finger-printing kit, various powders to use for checking for footprints, and even portable telephones for contact between investigators.

During the investigations, the researchers were allowed to search for facts any way that they wanted. Some of them employed their own equipment, others kept precise journals, and others turned to séances. The observers that Price recruited came from all different professions, outlooks, and interests, but all of them contributed to the pile of data that began to accumulate. Many of them spent nights in the empty rectory, where one room had been set up to serve as a base and where various instruments had been installed. Some of them came alone, and others came in groups, skeptics, believers, and debunkers alike. A good many of them neither saw nor heard anything, but quite a few of them had strange experiences. These experiences were wildly varied, from footsteps to moving objects, to strange sounds, or eerie lights. Many of them witnessed full apparitions — rarely seen by just one person at a time — and the majority of those sightings were of the phantom nun.

The end of the rectory but not the story

After Price's investigation came to an end, it was purchased by Captain W.H. Gregson, who planned to live there. Unfortunately, his occupancy was a short one. On February 27, 1939, Gregson was unpacking books in the library when an oil lamp overturned and started a fire. The blaze quickly spread, and the rectory was gutted. The building itself was finally demolished in 1944, but the story was far from over.

The publication of Price's first book on Borley, The Most Haunted House in England, brought Price a deluge of letters. The wall-writings, the planchette messages, and the various reports from the observers led to arguments, new theories, and new facts. Price was able to point out the parallels and similarities in a dozen other hauntings.

The rectory was in ruins, but this did not keep the curious away. Throughout the years of World War II, visitors often explored the rubble and occasionally spent the night in the eerie remains of the building. In 1941, H.F. Russell, a businessman, paid a visit to the Borley grounds with two of his Royal Air Force officer sons. While there, he claimed that he was seized by an invisible presence and dashed to the ground. Two years later, some Polish officers spent the night in the ruins and claimed to see and hear several chilling sounds and sights, including the infamous nun.

Other visitors included a commission from Cambridge University, which was formed by A.J.B. Robertson of St. Johns College. Robertson and his colleagues were interested in the inexplicable "cold patches" in the house. They investigated the house from 1939 until the demolition of the rectory in 1944.

Weird events continued to at the site where Borley Rectory once stood. They were frequent enough that Price made plans for a third book about the place, although it was never completed. As his research progressed, Price lined up 50 new witnesses to more recent phenomena, including Rev. Henning, officials from the BBC, local residents, and strangers.

But Harry would never write that third volume on the history of Borley Rectory. He died from a heart attack in his home in Pulborough on March 29, 1948. After his death, his critics began to claim that he had faked the phenomena at Borley Rectory, even though none of those critics took part in the investigations at the house or had even been there. Many came to Price's defense, but the number and variety of disturbances recorded by the many different investigators who took part in the year-long study speaks volumes about the authenticity of the events. Price did not witness the majority of the observations, accounts, and reports. He was not even present most of the time. Instead, the reports came from independent observers who often had no idea that others were experiencing the same events at other times.

There is still debate today about the validity of "England's Most Haunted House." And perhaps that's the reason that the story of Borley Rectory has never really died — and Harry Price remains such a fascinating and controversial figure. No matter what disparaging things have been written about him, there is no question that he earned his place in the history of the paranormal. He was a pioneer and a new brand of ghost-hunter, much different from the scientists, debunkers, and Spiritualists who thrived in the past. He was the first modern ghost-hunter and would set the stage for those who followed in his wake.

Hans Holzer

The 1950s brought the age of rocket ships and space flight, and while some Americans were less interested in psychical worlds than in those that lay beyond the stars, there was no question that interest in ghosts was again on the rise. During the 1930s and through World War II, interest in the paranormal had cooled somewhat. Americans were more focused on the hard times of the Depression and the war than they were on anything that might be conjured up in a séance room.

As the 1950s dawned, though, ghosts became popular again. New books were published, and magazines began appearing on newsstands with articles not only about hauntings but Spiritualism, too.

It was during this period that a man who would become one of the most famous names in modern ghost-hunting came to prominence. His name was Hans Holzer (see Figure 2-6), and his books, television appearances, and investigations would earn him a generation of fans. A frequent guest on late night talk shows, he was also a consultant to Leonard Nimoy's *In Search Of*, and appeared on the ground-breaking show several times. Among Holzer's fans were Elvis Presley and Dan Akroyd, who has admitted, "I became obsessed by Hans Holzer, the greatest ghost-hunter ever. That's when the idea of my film *Ghost Busters* was born." Holzer was the first paranormal researcher to become widely known in America and had a tremendous impact on paranormal culture during the 20th century.

FIGURE 2-6:
Hans Holzer.

Wikimedia Commons

Holzer was born in 1920 in Vienna, Austria. His interest in the supernatural was sparked at a young age by ghost stories that were told to him by his uncle. At the University of Vienna, he studied ancient history and archaeology, but with World War II imminent, his family fled to the United States in 1938. Holzer settled in New York City, where he remained for the rest of his life. He enrolled at Columbia University, where he studied Japanese and at the London College of Applied Science, he earned a master's degree in comparative religion, followed by a Ph.D. with a specialty in parapsychology. His career was varied enough to include a teaching position at the New York Institute of Technology, an annual lecture schedule, television and feature film production, numerous appearances on radio and television, and the publication of 138 books during his lifetime.

His first book, *Ghost-hunter*, was published in 1963 and became a bestseller. Calling himself a "scientific investigator of the paranormal," Holzer believed that ghosts did not know they were dead. "A ghost is only a fellow human being in trouble," he said. He considered intelligent spirits to be "stay behinds," lingering after death and remnants of a still-active intelligence. He was convinced that ghosts relived their final moments of life over and over again like a needle stuck in the grooves of a vinyl record. Holzer was determined to help these unfortunates realize that they were indeed dead, allowing them to depart their captivity on earth. He believed that many hauntings were simply imprints or recordings left behind, and not the presence of stuck souls.

These were groundbreaking ideas at the time and helped to make Holzer the go-to expert for television and radio shows. Unlike many paranormal investigators, Holzer did not shy away from mediums and sensitives. He never had much use for equipment — carrying only a camera and a reel-to-reel tape recorder during his investigations — and preferred to check out alleged haunts with well-known trance mediums like Ethel Johnson-Meyers, Sybil Leek, and Marisa Anderson. He traveled all over the country, and throughout the world, searching for evidence of ghosts.

Holzer's most infamous investigation became the so-called Amityville Horror case. In January 1977, Holzer, with Ethel Johnson-Meyers in tow, visited the house at 112 Ocean Avenue in Amityville, New York. The owners claimed that the house was haunted and were driven from the house in terror by demonic happenings. A year before they had moved in, a young man named Ronald DeFeo, Jr. had murdered his entire family in the house. The story of the haunting that allegedly occurred in the house remains controversial after all these years. Many maintain that the entire story was a hoax.

Holzer married once and had two daughters. He divorced after the birth of his second daughter and passed away in 2009. The prolific author left an indelible mark on the paranormal field. There is no question that he was one of the most authentic personalities and well-intentioned ghost-hunters to emerge from the early days of the modern era. His legacy should be remembered today as one of the researchers who moved the paranormal away from the shadows of the séance room and into the bright lights of the public arena.

Ed and Lorraine Warren

Hans Holzer was not the only prominent ghost-hunter to emerge on the public scene in the 1950s. In 1952, a Connecticut couple named Ed and Lorraine Warren (see Figure 2-7) founded the New England Society for Psychic Research, which would become one of the first actual ghost-hunting groups in modern history. It wasn't long before they came to be regarded as recognized authorities when it came to ghosts, demons, exorcisms, and haunted houses.

FIGURE 2-7:
Ed and Lorraine
Warren.

Ed and Lorraine Warren were both born in Bridgeport, Connecticut — Ed in 1926 and Lorraine a year later — but did not meet until they were teenagers. Ed's father was a state trooper and devout Catholic and enrolled Ed in parochial school. The Warren family lived in a large, older home that was rented out by an elderly woman with a mean disposition. Ed was five years old when she passed away, and he always told the story of seeing his first apparition when she showed up in his bedroom closet a few days after she died. His father always told Ed that there must be some logical explanation for the paranormal experiences he had, but his father never came up with one. Ed was often so terrified by the ghost in his closet that he refused to stay home alone.

And she was not the only ghost he saw, Ed claimed. Another spirit that frequently visited was his late aunt, who had been a nun. During her visitations, she allegedly told Ed that he would someday consult with priests, but would not become one, which Ed used as his reasoning for his life as a self-proclaimed demonologist. The Warrens moved out of the old house when Ed was 12. By then, he had gotten used to the strange happenings in the place and, in fact, used his exposure to the super-natural as fuel for his future research into the paranormal.

Just three blocks from the Warren home lived Lorraine Rita Moran, daughter of an affluent Irish family. Lorraine attended Laurelton Hall, a Catholic girl's school in nearby Milford, and it was while at school that she learned her gift for clairvoy-ance at age 12. On Arbor Day that year, the nuns organized a tree-planting for the students, and as soon as her sapling was placed in the ground, Lorraine began staring at the sky, seeing the tree as it would look when it was full-grown. The nuns considered her psychic ability to be sinful and sent her off for a weekend retreat of prayer.

When Ed was 16, he was working at the Colonial Theater in Bridgeport and met Lorraine. The following year, on September 7, 1943, his 17th birthday, he enlisted in the U.S. Navy. He spent the war as an armed guard aboard a Merchant Marine ship. He and Lorraine married on May 22, 1945. They were both 18. Their only child, Judy, was born just six months before Ed left the Navy. After the war, Ed attended Perry Art School, which was affiliated with Yale, but left to travel around New England, painting and looking for haunted houses.

Ed's favorite pastime was to hear stories about local haunted houses and then make a little money by painting the house and selling the painting to the house's owners. Even more, he loved to be invited inside and allowed to look around. Eventually, his experiences with ghosts led the Warrens away from a career as itinerant artists to full-time work as paranormal consultants. Frightened homeowners confided in the Warrens about their experiences, and the Warrens soon found themselves giving advice to not only the owners of the homes but to interested strangers, as well. Finding that the negative energy associated with teenagers and young adults attracted spirit activity, the Warrens began giving lectures at colleges to encourage their listeners against unwittingly inviting trouble into their lives.

The Warrens amassed a large archive of detailed interviews and reports from haunted families, as well as from other investigators, along with photographs, audio and video recordings of paranormal activity, and even founded an occult museum of haunted objects, dolls, and other items.

The Warrens investigated all over America and overseas. After being invited to a place, they arranged a visit as soon as possible. Once at the site, they usually split up, with Ed conducting interviews of the witnesses and Lorraine walking through the house to see whether she could discern any spirit activity. Lorraine could usually detect a presence almost immediately and would be able to tell whether they were earthbound, human spirits, or demonic. Earthbound spirits, she maintained, usually remained at a place because of a sudden, violent, or tragic death and often didn't realize that they needed to move on to the other side.

But a demonic presence was an entirely different matter. These inhuman spirits attempted to overpower their victims through physical, mental, and emotional abuse. The Warrens always stressed that God did not let evil visit humans, but that humans must in some way invite malevolence into their lives by using a Ouija board or by experimenting with witchcraft and the occult. Once allowed inside, demons took control in three stages: infestation, oppression, and possession. In severe circumstances, the final outcome could be death.

During the infestation stage, the Warrens claimed that the demon's goal was to create chaos and fear through strange happenings — footsteps, whispers, inexplicable sounds, moving objects, and so on — and would inspire fear by knocking on doors three or six times, mocking the Holy Trinity. Too often, they said, the work of a demon could be dismissed as pranks or overactive imaginations, but make no mistake, the diabolical was at work.

Once fear has taken hold, the oppression stage begins when the demon dominates the victim's will. According to the Warrens, this meant an increase in demonic manifestations in the house, like screams, heavy breathing, footsteps, hellish moans, inhuman voices coming from the television, smells of sulfur and rotting flesh, movement of large objects, and the materialization of a dark form that the Warrens believed personified evil. The victim would start to believe that he or she was insane and would have dramatic personality changes and mood swings.

Finally, if there had been no intervention for the victim, then they would be possessed by an inhuman evil. This usually meant that the demon would speak through the victim, foul odors and fluids would emanate from the body, and they would no longer resemble themselves. But if the afflicted could get help, then hope existed that the demonic presence could be expelled through exorcism. The Warrens stated that the expulsion of the demon had to be a religious process and had to be performed by a priest who had been named as an exorcist by the church. As a demonologist, Ed could identify the problem and offer prayer and support, he said, but could not perform the actual exorcism.

Over the course of their careers, the Warrens estimated that they investigated over 8,000 cases, including the famous Conjuring case that has been adapted for film, the Snedeker haunting in Connecticut, the Smurl Case in Pennsylvania, the Amityville Horror, and many others. Besides their demon rescue work, lectures, and tours to promote the ten books that were written based on their experiences, the Warrens also created the occult museum and the paranormal research group.

In March 2001, Ed Warren collapsed from heart problems after a trip to Japan. He was hospitalized for a year and was in a coma for several months. He spent the next four years being cared for by Lorraine, who was by his side when he passed away on August 23, 2006. Lorraine passed in April 2019 while this book was being written.

There is no question that the Warrens enjoyed a long and well-publicized career. For no other reason, they deserve credit as two of the best-known ghost-hunters of the modern era. Like Hans Holzer, they were dealing with hauntings long before many modern ghost-hunters were even born. And that, if nothing else, makes their legacy as one of the most famous couples in the paranormal live on.

Chapter 3

Believing in Ghosts and Spirits

E ach year, as fall turns to winter and Halloween grows near, we are reminded about the realm of the dead. Our ancestors contemplated death at the same time we do, celebrating the beginning of the dark half of the year when, it was widely believed, the barrier between the living and the dead grew thin and ghosts could be commonly encountered.

This chapter explores the American belief in the supernatural and talks about after-death communication.

Incorporating Ghosts into the Christian World

In the seventh century, hoping to convert the people of northern Europe to Christianity, Pope Gregory I directed missionaries not to stop the pagan celebrations of the people in the region. He wanted them to absorb them into the Church. Accordingly, over time, the festival that celebrated the dead became All Saint's Day, when speaking with the dead was considered religiously appropriate. The night before, when the veil between worlds was the thinnest, between All Hallows Evening, or Halloween.

Not only did pagan beliefs about the spirits of the dead continue, but they became a part of many of the early Church's practices. Pope Gregory himself suggested that people who saw ghosts should say a mass for them. The dead, as far as he was concerned, might need help from the living to make it to Heaven.

During the Middle Ages, a belief that the souls of the dead could be trapped in Purgatory led to the Church's practice of selling *indulgences,* which were payments to the Church to reduce the penalties for sins. The widespread belief in ghosts made the sale of indulgences very profitable for the Church.

These beliefs contributed to the Reformation, the division of Christianity into Protestantism and Catholicism, led by Martin Luther. In fact, Luther's "95 Theses," nailed to the door of All Saints Church in 1517, was largely a protest over selling indulgences. Subsequently, ghosts became identified with "Catholic superstitions" in most Protestant countries.

A dismissal of ghosts as a superstition by some people didn't end the debate about their existence, however. Over time, many turned to science to deal with the issue. By the 19th century, *spiritualism,* the movement that claimed the dead could converse with the living, became mainstream and featured popular techniques like séances, talking boards, spirit photography, and more. Although spiritualism faded in cultural importance after World War I, many of its approaches are still used by ghost-hunters today, who often use scientific techniques to try to prove the existence of spirits.

Ghost Stories

A belief in ghosts is not just part of the Christian world. Most, if not all, societies have ghosts in their culture. For example, in Taiwan, about 90 percent of people report having seen a ghost. Along with many Asian countries like Japan, Korea, China, and Vietnam, Taiwan celebrates a Ghost Month, which includes a Ghost Festival in honor of the dead. This is a time when spirits are believed to freely roam among the living. As in many traditions, Taiwanese ghosts are seen as either friendly or unfriendly. The friendly ghosts are commonly ancestral or familial ghosts that are welcomed into homes during festivals that celebrate them. Unfriendly ghosts are those who are angry and haunt the living.

Ghost stories — no matter where they take place in the world — have central themes. Ghosts generally seem to haunt for good reasons. These range from unsolved murders, lack of proper burials, suicides, preventable tragedies, and other ethical failures. Ghosts, when we look at them in this light, are often seeking justice from beyond the grave. They often make demands from individuals, or from society as a whole. Ghost sightings are often a reminder that wrongful deeds done in life can carry a heavy spiritual burden.

And yet, ghost stories are also hopeful. Their existence promotes the idea of life after death, and in this way, they offer a chance to be in contact with those that have passed on. They give us a chance for redemption and a way to atone for past wrongs. A belief in ghosts can be part of a healing process, for both our minds and our souls.

Exploring American Belief in the Supernatural

If you believe in ghosts, you're not alone. In a recent poll, it was suggested that 45 percent of all Americans believe that ghosts or the spirits of the dead can return to haunt certain places and situations. Some 32 percent of them also said that ghosts and spirits can hurt living people, while 43 percent said that ghosts — if they are real — are harmless. In fact, a survey conducted by a realtor group suggested that 30 percent of Americans are open to living in a haunted house. Still, 42 percent of people said they would never consider it.

Widening the scope, 65 percent of Americans stated that they believe in some aspect of the supernatural — reincarnation, spiritual energy, yoga as a spiritual practice, astrology, connecting with the dead, consulting a psychic, or having a ghostly encounter. There were also 49 percent who said they'd had a "religious or mystical experience."

Another recent study, carried out by Chapman University, discovered that believers are willing to accept a wide range of paranormal phenomena, from ghosts and aliens to ancient civilizations and Bigfoot. The study, which looked into the fears of average Americans, found that 52 percent of the participants agreed that places can be haunted by ghosts and spirits.

After-Death Communications

It should come as no surprise to learn that so many Americans believe they have encountered a ghost — or that they may encounter one in their lifetime. Ghosts and spirits go hand-in-hand with grief and loss, and there is no one among us who has not been touched by the grief associated with losing a family member or loved one. That grief can be so unsettling that many who mourn express concern that they are losing their minds. Those in mourning are bombarded with unusual thoughts, experiences, and emotions. Many believe that such grief can make us open to experiences that go beyond what is typical for the mourning process. These events are referred to as *after-death communications* and are defined as a spiritual experience that occurs when someone is contacted directly and spontaneous by a family member or friend who has died.

Those who have exhaustively studied the phenomenon have listed the main categories of experiences.

>> **Sensing a presence:** This is the most common type of after-death communication and most describe it as a physical sensation that a deceased loved one is nearby.

>> **Hearing a voice:** A person in mourning hears the voice of the deceased as though he or she was in the room.

>> **Feeling a touch:** Individuals report the deceased touching them, patting their arm, touching their hand, or embracing them.

>> **Smelling a fragrance:** The mourner becomes aware of a smell that was associated with the deceased, like flowers, a certain perfume, or even cigar or pipe tobacco.

>> **Visual experiences:** Sightings of the deceased can range from spotting hazy apparitions to more lifelike, full-body forms. The most common place for these occurrences is at night, at the foot of the bed. Many refer to these as *twilight experiences,* meaning that they occur during altered states of consciousness such as when falling asleep, awakening from sleep, or while praying.

>> **Dream communications:** These types of experiences occur while the mourner is asleep, and yet they are not regular dreams. They are reported to be more real and intense than a normal dream.

>> **Physical phenomena:** These may include lights turning on and off, objects moving about, or doors opening and closing. However, most mourners who experience such things state that they are temporary and most commonly are referred to as simply a sign from the deceased to let the living know they are well in their new existence.

>> **Symbolism:** Mourners may see signs that their loved one is still with them. They can take make forms, including feathers, butterflies, flowers, and much more. For example, after a woman experienced the death of her son, she began to find coins everywhere she went. The dates on the coins were always significant dates in her son's life — birth, surgery, and death. She believed they were signs that he was still with her, and the positive impact on her grief was immeasurable.

After-death communications occur with people of all nationalities, ethnicities, religious affiliations, income, and levels of education. Those who report such experiences are typically free of mental illness. Widows and widowers most commonly report these communications, with women being more likely than men.

But as common as these experiences are, people are still reluctant to talk about them for fear that others will believe they are suffering from mental issues. In truth, questioning your sanity is typical of the sane person who has one of these experiences. It can often take years for someone to be brave enough to open up to others about such an experience. Mourners are aware these events are out of the ordinary and that some people will dismiss them as hallucinations caused by a grieving mind. Those who dismiss or trivialize the experience often do not realize how important the events are for the bereaved. For some, they provide hope and are viewed as spiritual signs. The experience is a link with their loved one, which can sustain them through their darkest times.

After-death communication provides an ongoing connection to the deceased and suggests to the living that death is not the end. They serve as a source of comfort, consolation, strength, and take away at least some of the pain of grief.

Arthur Conan Doyle

Many after-death communications are not merely sensations or dream-like experiences. Some can be blatant messages from the dead. In the past, such messages came to the living from Spiritualist mediums, who eased the pain of thousands of people after the American Civil War and World War I. These were times of great resurgence in the belief that the dead could communicate with the living and those who lost loved ones flocked to séance tables.

Such experiences could literally change a person's life. For example, famous author Sir Arthur Conan Doyle, creator of Sherlock Holmes, become one of the world's greatest proponents of spiritualism after a message he received through a medium after World War I. His best friend and brother-in-law, Malcolm Leckie, had been killed during the war. A short time after his death, the Doyle family had a guest in their home named Lily Lauder-Symonds, a gifted medium. While she was there, she conducted a séance for the family and delivered a message from Malcolm. Years before, he and Doyle had shared a private joke about a guinea coin that Leckie had given to Doyle as his first fee when he became an Army doctor. Doyle had cherished the small token and wore it on his watch chain. The message that Doyle was given by Lauder-Symonds concerned the guinea, an item that most people, including the medium, knew nothing about. After that incident, Doyle became convinced of life after death.

Harry Houdini

Although he became known as a debunker of fraudulent spiritualism mediums in the 1920s, magician Harry Houdini was a lifelong believer in the possibility of the supernatural. After the death of his mother, he tried to contact her spirit for many years. Failure after failure followed, and when the clever illusionist saw through the tricks being performed by frauds, he began exposing their secrets, earning him the dislike of most of the spiritualist community.

Houdini, though, was not a true skeptic. He publicly stated, "I am willing to be convinced. My mind is open, but the proof must be such as to leave no vestige of doubt that what is claimed to be done is accomplished only through or by supernatural power."

To prove that he did have an open mind, the magician made a pact with several of his friends that if he should die, he would make contact, if at all possible, from the other side. He devised a secret code with the one person that he trusted most, his wife Bess, so that if a message should arrive from the beyond, that she would be able to determine that it was really from Houdini.

Early in Houdini's career, he and Bess had performed an act in which they used a code that contained both alphabetical and numerical symbols. Before his death, Houdini used that code to create a secret message with Bess that he promised to communicate with her after his death if spirit communication was possible. After all, Houdini was a master of impossible escapes — if anyone could escape death, it would be Houdini.

Not long after Houdini died, the famous Houdini Séances began. While Bess planned to honor her husband's requests about attempting contact with him after death, this may not have been what prompted her to seek the secret code that he promised to try and send her from beyond the grave. Bess wasn't trying to simply honor Harry's wishes; she was lost without him. She desperately needed to hear from him because she had no idea what to do with her life without Harry's guidance. With her beloved husband gone, Bess was drifting, depressed, and empty.

She tried to move on with her life but spent a lot of her time attempting to contact her late husband. Every Sunday at the hour of his death, she would shut herself in a room with his photograph and wait for a sign. She spread the word that she was waiting for a secret message from Harry, and word spread far and wide that Bess had offered $10,000 to any medium who could deliver a true message from Houdini.

Almost weekly, a new medium came forward, claiming to have broken the code. The public was still fascinated by the idea of spirit communication. Ouija boards were still selling as a novelty, and there were still a few mediums to be found.

Those who wrote or contacted Bess with what seemed to be nothing more than guesses about the Houdini code were turned away, until 1928, when Bess heard an announcement by a medium named Arthur Ford that consisted of a single word that came, not from Houdini, but from his mother, Cecilia Weiss. The word was "forgive."

Bess soon made a startling announcement of her own — Ford's message was the first that she had received which "had any appearance of the truth."

"Forgive" was the one word that Houdini had always hoped to hear from his mother in the séance room. It had to do with an incident that happened many years before. When his brother Nat's wife, Sadie, had abandoned him to marry another brother, Leopold, Houdini had been shocked and angry. The once close-knit harmony of the family had been destroyed. Harry could not bring himself to forgive his brother unless his mother told him to. She died before he could discuss the family crisis with her. This was the one reason that he had searched so tirelessly for a genuine medium and was so infuriated when he found nothing but frauds.

Arthur Ford, the founder of the First Spiritualist Church of New York, had a good reputation as a medium. He was at the start of his career at the time of the Houdini message. Professionally, he rarely socialized with other psychics and openly denounced fraud. He was accused of trickery himself, and while he always denied it, after his death, his private papers revealed that he cheated from time to time by researching the backgrounds of famous people who came to his sittings. He had an almost photographic memory and kept voluminous files of newspaper clippings and notes, which provided material for his readings.

In 1928, his one-word message to Bess Houdini managed to get Ford plastered across the front pages of newspapers across America. Bess was cautiously optimistic that the message was genuine, or so the newspapers claimed. In November, another message came to Ford, this time, he said, from Houdini himself. In a trance, the medium relayed an entire coded message: "Rosabelle, answer, tell, pray, answer, look, tell, answer, answer, tell."

After this information was relayed to Bess, she invited Ford to her home, and he asked her if the words were correct. She said they were, and Ford asked her to remove her wedding ring and tell everyone present what "Rosabelle" meant. This was the word that made the message authentic, a secret known only to Bess and Harry themselves. It was the title of a song that had been popular at Coney Island when they first met. The rest of the message was a series of code words that spelled out the word "believe." The code was one that the Houdinis had used during a mind-reading act they perfected in their early days of performing.

For all intents and purposes, this made the message genuine. This was the final clue that Houdini had promised to relay from the next world. He had become the first medium to pass on a message from Houdini from the other side. A splashy story appeared in the newspaper, touting Arthur Ford as the man who broke the Houdini code — but, almost as soon as it appeared, the controversy began.

Accusations of fraud began to be leveled against Ford. Bess had apparently deemed the message authentic at first, but friends quickly urged her to retract her support. The charge against Ford was led by Houdini's friend, Joseph Dunninger, who stated that he was quite willing to believe that Ford delivered the correct code and message to Bess — because it was in common use by sideshow performers and had even appeared in a biography written about Houdini two years before he died. Ford was skewered by the press, skeptics, and Houdini's fellow magicians. On their advice, Bess withdrew the offer of $10,000.

And they may have been right. Although it would not be discovered until after he died, more than four decades after the alleged Houdini message, Arthur Ford collected extensive files on many of the people that he did readings for, offering them seemingly random information about their lives to make his séances seem authentic. He could have easily found the information about the mind-reading act code and used it to try and pull one over on Bess.

But, here's the weird thing: Dunninger and various skeptics were able to claim that Ford tricked Bess with the code, but they never explained how he had managed to come up with his original message — the one he said was from Harry's mother and the one that got Bess's attention in the first place. There was nothing in a Houdini biography about the word "forgive" — the word that Houdini had been hoping to hear from Cecilia when he first began trying to make contact with her spirit. The family disagreement between Houdini and his brothers was not publicly known. It was a private side to his life that he had not shared. Arthur Ford went to his grave claiming that he had received a genuine message from Houdini, and perhaps he did. Strangely, this would not be the last mystery concerning after death communications from the famous magician.

Bess Houdini continued to hold séances in hopes of communicating with her late husband, but as the years went by, she began to lose hope that she would ever hear from him. The last official Houdini séance was held on Halloween night of 1936, ten years after Houdini had died. A group of friends, fellow magicians, occultists, scientists, and Bess Houdini herself gathered in Hollywood, on the roof of the Knickerbocker Hotel. Eddy Saint, a former carnival and vaudeville showman who had also worked as a magician, had arranged the gathering.

Coverage for the Final Houdini Séance was provided by radio, and it was broadcast all over the world. Eddy Saint took charge of the proceedings and started things off with the playing of "Pomp and Circumstance," a tune that had been used by Houdini to start his act in later years. He noted for radio audiences, "Every facility has been provided tonight that might aid in opening the pathway to the spirit world. Here in the inner circle reposes a medium's trumpet, a pair of slates with chalk, a writing tablet and pencil, a small bell, and in the center, reposes a huge pair of silver handcuffs on a silk cushion."

Saint and the rest of Bess's inner circle attempted to contact Houdini for over an hour before finally giving up. Bess reluctantly admitted that she no longer believed that her husband could communicate with her. She had tried for years and her hope was gone. She ended her statement with a final farewell, "Good night, Harry!"

The séance came to an end, but at the moment it did, a tremendously violent thunderstorm broke out, drenching the séance participants and terrifying them with a terrific display of lightning and thunder. They would later learn that this mysterious storm did not occur anywhere else in Hollywood — only above the Knickerbocker Hotel. Some speculated that perhaps Houdini did come through after all, as the flamboyant performer just might have made his presence known by the spectacular effects of the thunderstorm.

A personal experience

Not all after-death communications are as spectacular as Harry Houdini's (see preceding section). Most are deeply personal, which is what happened in my life. My father passed away in December 2018, while I was filming *Ghost Adventures* at the Binion Hotel. It happened during our last day of filming, which made for a very tough day for me. I had never dealt with that kind of grief before. I had never lost a parent, so not only was it sad, but it really felt like a part of me died with him.

It is no surprise that I could feel my father's energy around me in the weeks that followed. But then he began to visit me in my dreams — five times on five consecutive nights. These were not ordinary dreams. They were so lucid and so real that I knew he was visiting me. In the dreams, he was telling me things, and I remember grabbing my phone so that I could record him in my dreams. When I awoke, I reached for me phone, convinced that I had audio and video evidence that my father had been there. That's how real the dreams were.

In the last dream, I was driving in a car with him, and we were going to his home in Michigan. To get to the little island that he lived on, we had to cross two bridges. One of them was manned by a toll operator. In the dream, my father told me that he did not want to go to the toll bridge because the attendant would just see a car driving by itself with me in the passenger seat. He said that I was the only one who could see him, and we laughed together about this.

He had one last message for me: to call my stepmother, his widow, and to tell her to look in his toolbox. When I woke up, I sent a text to my stepmother and told her to check his toolbox. I had no idea why. A few minutes later, I heard back from her. She was stunned! She had been looking everywhere for the spare key to their house and had been unable to find it until I told her to look into the toolbox. It was there! I have no doubt that this was a real-life visitation from my father.

My father did not return to my dreams, but I had one last encounter with his spirit. I went hiking one afternoon, and at a point on a mountainous trail, I saw him standing there, clear and solid in every way. I believe it was at that moment that he was ready to move on. I don't think he could do it until he relayed the messages that he needed to send. Since that time, I have never dreamed about my father and I've never seen him again, but I know that he stayed with me for a short time, until his business here on earth had been completed.

Chapter **4**

What's Science Got to Do with It?

There is no question that without the events of the past, there would be no hauntings for us to seek out, research, or examine. Ghosts simply cannot exist without history, and neither can the field of paranormal investigation. Without the investigators of the past, there would be no modern-day ghost-hunters. Television shows like mine, *Ghost Adventures,* would not exist without the first investigators who began trying to see whether what they were seeing, hearing, reading about, and photographing at haunted places and in séance rooms was truly real. They needed to know whether the impossible was possible after all. In this chapter, we look at how history and science intertwine.

The Relationship Between Science and the Supernatural

The first paranormal investigators were scientists, and their initial investigations concerned the events that were being reported by the spiritualists in the early years of the movement. Scientists were in a fragile place when spiritualism was born. By the 1850s, science had managed to challenge the hold that religion maintained in American society and had started to offer a new version of truth for people to examine. The days of miracles were over, they stated, and the world should be examined under the harsh light of reality.

And then spiritualism came along. It offered proof of life after death, of spirits, and of communication with loved ones who had passed away. The public was fascinated by it and science began to be ignored, so the scientist establishment fought back. Resentful over the fact that it had managed to loosen the hold that religion had on society, only to lose its footing to spiritualism, the debunking of mediums began to be encouraged. Editorials and printed articles professed a blatant disregard for anything that hinted at the supernatural. If it could not be explained, it did not exist.

After all of these years, unfortunately, not much has changed. The relationship between science and the supernatural remains as tenuous now as it was in the 19th century. Those courageous and open-minded individuals who dared go beyond the acceptable limits of debunking, to examine or test psychical claims, often paid a heavy price when colleagues scorned them and called their reputations into question.

From practically the first reports of spirit rappings in New York in 1848, the people who openly doubted the Fox sisters' claims of communication from the spirit world included those who had a skeptical, or so-called rational, view about the supernatural. Most men of science were hopeful that anything to do with the supernatural had been banished to the darkest corner of human experience to be forever forgotten.

But those who assumed that ghost stories would go away could not have been more wrong. Once millions of Americans became fascinated by spiritualism, it was folly to think that they were not thinking about what awaited them after death. In addition, ordinary people did not really care about what scientists thought, or what they did not believe in. Scientists would often claim they were acting on the public's behalf, protecting them from the dishonesty of spirit mediums. Grief-stricken people, though, were more concerned about hearing from a departed loved one than they were about the psychological or scientific explanation about how what they believed in could not be true. Many of them insisted that such questions were not the responsibility of scientists anyway. They should be relegated to the domain of religious beliefs and faith, not to science, an "orderly branch of knowledge involving systemized observations and experimentation."

Testing for spirits

Psychic happenings were elusive, and the question of testing for an invisible spirit world seemed to be impossible to most people.

Scientists were unsure how to even deal with what was being reported during séances. They didn't know what to call it, so it made it difficult to determine how to test its existence. At the time, there was no generally accepted definition of the inexplicable field that came to be known as *paranormal.*

The spirit world rarely cooperated with those investigating it. It did not conform to any established scientific protocols. When many mediums were exposed as frauds and charlatans, it became a convenient excuse for skeptics and establishment scientists to discredit all of them. However, there were many cases in which no trickery was detected. Those were usually ignored. Too often, doubting scientists found the easiest way was to conclude that all psychic events were fraudulent. It was a lazy and insincere approach. The press was also quick to jump on any allegation of fraud but was rarely moved to say that a medium, which had never been shown to be fraudulent, might be genuine.

In fairness, scientists, doctors, and psychologists of the 19th century have very little knowledge, equipment, or experience with which to test the paranormal, even if they had wanted to do so.

The role of spiritualism

The irony was that spiritualism played an important, although an unwitting, role in the development of American psychology. Prior to the concepts of Sigmund Freud, spiritualism was already paving the way for theories about the conscious and subconscious mind.

But neurology, psychiatry, chemistry, physics, and other disciplines that would later factor into the study of the paranormal by scientific means were not well understood in that era. For example, theories to explain mediumship ranged from claiming it was blatant fraud, to involuntary muscle action, to physical disease, to insanity. Some believed that mediums experienced hallucinations or delusions that were due to "excessive excitement of the nervous system." In this way, hysteria could be used as an explanation for psychical experiences.

Spiritualists often contended that contact with the spirit world was something electromagnetic. Electricity was the wonder of the 19th century because it was clearly present, could be proven, and had been tested. In addition, the electric telegraph connected the United States from New York to California, so the analogy that defined mediumship as the *spiritual telegraph* was quickly adopted.

When finally, in the 1850s, the movement officially became known as spiritualism, few scientists showed any interest at first. The cynical ones dismissed it as humbug, and it would take a few years before any of them would take the time to attend séances and begin to examine the reports of strange happenings.

Applying the laws of science

During those early years of the movement, scientists who wanted to investigate the claims of mediums often functioned independently. There was little coordination among those interested in paranormal research and there would not be a permanent American organization dedicated to psychical research until 1885, and that was three years after the British created the Society for Psychical Research (SPR). The British were first, ahead of the Americans, in their examination of mediumship and other paranormal phenomena, including survival after death, crisis apparitions, hauntings, clairvoyance, telepathy, premonitions, and telekinetic events.

In the middle 19th century, interest in spiritualism by traditional American science was erratic and haphazard. Perhaps most scientists did not consider the subject worthy of serious attention. In those relatively rare cases when a scientist came forward to examine a paranormal claim, he was expected to debunk and dismiss it. William B. Carpenter, a noted British physiologist of the period, was disgusted by the fascination with spiritualism in America and Britain. He called it an "epidemic delusion," similar to the witchcraft hysteria that had ravaged both continents in past centuries. Some early physicians believed mediumship and a propensity toward psychic experiences was an illness that required treatment and needed to be treated.

Science and spiritualism meet up

At the same time that spiritualism was starting to grow in the middle 19th century, new advances were also being made in the fields of science and technology. To some, it seemed that science and spiritualism could not be further apart, each functioning in an entirely separate world. But this was not really the case. They had to meet at some point.

In that period, there was no force in nature that was more intriguing to the general public than electricity. The marvel of electricity, truly coming into its own with the successful introduction of the telegraph in 1844, just four years before the events in Hydesville, joined science and spiritualism in the minds of those who believed that spirit contact was of an electric nature.

Many considered spiritualism to be a "scientific religion," and the comparison to electricity was obvious in the popular term of "spiritual telegraph," a reference to how mediums got in touch with the other side. In addition, both spirit contact and electricity were invisible forms of energy.

There were many theories that circulated that linked spirits and electricity. One theory was that souls vibrated with a mysterious electrical charge that could be detected by mediums. Others believed the opposite was true — that mediums acted as a signal to spirits, which is why they chose to make contact with them. Of course, there were many who feared that electricity might run wildly amok. This meant that the mediums might be taken over or inhabited by negative spirits that they could not control. No one truly understood how electricity worked. It might be just as dangerous as it was beneficial.

In 1853, Michael Faraday, one of England's most respected scientists, turned his attention to spiritualism. Faraday was both a physicist and chemist who became widely known for his experiments with electromagnetism and for inventing the first electric generator in 1831. He was deeply religious and had no personal desire to become a spiritualist. His interest in the movement was generated by annoyance that psychical researchers were not testing spiritualist claims with what he considered was the correct scientific approach. So, Faraday began his own series of experiments. In the early 1850s, that meant looking into spirit raps and table tipping, the most popular scientific manifestations of the time.

After Faraday observed many demonstrations of table tipping, he drew his conclusion about what was causing the events to occur. His theory was that the unconscious expectations of the sitters were creating a muscle pressure that was causing the tables to move. Faraday designed an apparatus to measure even the tiniest movement of the séance table. He found that those motions were sufficient to make a small, lightweight table seem to move on its own. Skeptics often point to the same theory to explain why the planchette on a talking board moves from letter to letter. Of course, most spiritualists disagreed with Faraday's theory, maintaining that people's hands attracted "spirit energy" and the messages came from discarnate beings.

Faraday's conclusion may be an explanation for a limited number of psychical occurrences, especially telekinetic activity. But it left many unanswered questions about spiritualism, including how mediums were able to give accurate messages, and did not explain other phenomena, like spirit materializations, clairvoyance, telepathy, and hauntings. And perhaps he knew it. When Faraday had the opportunity to test D.D. Home, the noted scientist refused, so he never got Home into his laboratory. There's a very good chance that Faraday knew that Home might exhibit powers that he would not able to so easily explain.

Despite the interest shown in spiritualism by some members of mainstream science, true scientific investigation of the paranormal remained a scattered effort in America until late in the 19th century. It was as if researchers were waiting to see if the movement hung around long enough to be worthy of study. They found out that it was just as baffling as it was when it first arrived on the scene and debate continued whether everything from spirit raps to physical phenomena — flying trumpets, ectoplasm, materializing spirits — were even possible.

There also remained a valid concern about exactly what instruments could investigate something as unstructured as spirit phenomena. What could be built? And what would it measure? There were legitimate questions asked about the possibility of clairvoyance, premonitions, and telepathy. Were they psychical or supernatural in nature? Were they caused by an energy that was not yet discovered? Or did they originate from discarnate entities? Such questions only annoyed the spiritualists, for it called into question their strong belief that all psychic experiences were attributed to the spirit world.

The issue of testing was critical. Scientists were adamant about the fact that, in order for psychical energy to be proven, it had to be measured under strict conditions. In an era that was fascinated by electricity, modern machinery, and theories about invisible energy, a form of measurement was essential. It was no surprise that legitimate scientists wanted to measure the abilities of spiritualists in a way that guaranteed a non-biased result. And it wasn't as if professional mediums objected to being tested. In fact, many in the movement actually urged scientists to examine psychical phenomena. However, the nineteenth and early twentieth centuries were a time when there were few organized academic studies of the paranormal, and the handful of university-backed investigations always came to the same conclusion: there was no scientific evidence of psychical phenomena. And even though there was no conclusive scientific evidence that paranormal events were not real, the prevailing rationalist opinion was that you had to prove it to be so, before it could be accepted as so.

Many cynics suggested that professors had made up their minds to oppose the paranormal before they examined it, regardless of what was presented. This certainly seemed to be the case. It seemed the answers were already in before the questions were ever asked. Didn't this make the resulting tests to be completely biased? Whatever the explanation, the paranormal was rarely welcome in the hallowed halls of American academia.

Sir William Crookes and the Paranormal

Some academics pushed for investigating the spirit world. Among them was the famed British physicist Sir William Crookes, who was one of the first scientists in England or American to advocate the scientific investigation of psychical phenomena. Although his investigations would take him dangerously close to scandal, his research began with the best of intentions.

His interest in spiritualism was spurred by the death of his younger brother in 1867. After he consulted with several mediums, Crookes decided that he would personally investigate spiritualism. His decision was greeted with wide approval.

The popular press felt sure that Crookes would soon show that spiritualist claims were nothing more than ridiculous humbug. Crookes appeared to share that view. When he announced that he was going to begin his investigations, he stated that he had no preconceived notions on the subject and then added, "The increased employment of scientific methods will produce a race of observers who will drive the worthless residuum of spiritualism hence into the unknown limbo of magic and necromancy." This statement was taken as a disclaimer of belief in spiritualism, but if Crookes' private beliefs had been better known, his words would have been more clearly interpreted to mean that he intended only to disprove the "worthless residuum" who were frauds. In diary entries that were written just months before his investigations began, he noted that he was already a firm believer in the possibility of an "unknown power."

Crookes was born in London in 1832 and was largely self-taught, with no regular schooling, until he enrolled in the Royal College of Chemistry at age 16. He graduated in 1854 and took a position as the superintendent of the meteorological department at Radcliffe Observatory, Oxford. A year later, he took a teaching position as a professor of chemistry at Chester Training College but resigned after one year because he was not given a laboratory in which he could do research. Although he tried to find another teaching position, he was never successful and most of his later work was done in a laboratory at his home. In 1856, Crookes married Ellen Humphrey, with whom he had eight children, and from his home, he began writing and editing for scientific journals. In 1861, Crookes achieved the first of his scientific discoveries: the element thallium and the correct measurement of its atomic weight. This got him elected a Fellow of the Royal Society at age 31.

Then, in 1867, came a turning point in Crookes's life with the death of his youngest brother, Phillip. The two men had been very close, and Crookes was distraught over his brother's death. Like others of the time who suffered a great loss, he turned to spiritualism for answers. At the urging of his friend and fellow scientist, Cromwell Varney, Crookes and his wife attended several séances to attempt contact with Phillip. Although the details of these sessions are unknown, Crookes believed they were successful. One of his first séances was with the famous medium D.D. Home, where Crookes was amazed to see phenomena that he never dreamed possible before. The scientist was not content to simply observe Home's manifestations, he also attempted to re-create them in the laboratory and, according to his records, this was successful.

Crookes invited members of the Royal Society to take part in his testing, but they declined. However, he brought four others with him to act as witnesses during his examination of Home. Crookes conducted many tests using the best instruments available in the 19th century. In a long series of experiments using weights, balances, and other devices to register changes in the weight of objects under the medium's hand, Crookes became convinced that he was in the presence of a real physical force that was previously unknown but just as real and measurable as electricity or gravity. To determine whether Home could somehow manipulate electromagnetic energy, Crookes wrapped an accordion in copper wire and then placed it in a metal cage. He ran an electrical current through the wire, which he believed would block any magnetic energy coming from Home. The medium was still able to make the accordion play, leading Crookes to believe that he possessed an independent psychic force. He published a report that stated this, and it stirred up tremendous controversy and led to horrific criticism of the esteemed scientist. His previous work in the scientific field was all but forgotten and his colleagues railed against him as an eccentric fool.

Crookes' conclusions were criticized on many fronts. Few dared to accuse the great man of fraud, but several felt there was fraud in the construction of his testing apparatus. Even the critics admitted, though, that Crookes had been more than willing to make changes in the equipment to increase its sensitivity and make it harder for Home to interfere with it. This seemed to dismiss the problems with the equipment. A second wave of opinion fell back on the standard "It must have been a hallucination," accusing not only Crookes of being hypnotized by the medium, then recording false data, but also claimed that Home somehow caused the equipment to hallucinate, as well. Finally, there is the always popular solution that none of Crookes' experiments mattered anyway. Critics continue to claim that Crookes violated one of the scientific world's most inflexible requirements. To be valid, an experiment must be repeatable — when the conditions are the same, they must produce identical results.

Instead, Crookes said, "The experiments have been very numerous, but owing to our imperfect knowledge of the conditions which favor or oppose the manifestations of this force, to the apparently capricious manner in which it is exerted, and to the fact that Mr. Home himself is subject to unaccountable ebbs and flows of the force, it has but seldom happened that a result obtained on one occasion could be subsequently confirmed and tested with apparatus specially contrived for the purpose." This meant simply that Home was able to dictate the experimental conditions, such as the degree of lighting used and the relative positions of where the experimenters stood during the sessions. Whenever the setup was not to his liking, Home could conceivably declare that the spirits were absent or weak. Of course, he never did this, but the debunkers declared that he could have, which, in their opinion, nullified the results.

Whether or not most of Crookes's scientific colleagues were intrigued by his experiments, many former skeptics were convinced of the reality of Home's phenomena. The report may have damaged Crookes's credibility with other scientists, but it was tremendously influential to the public and started the scientist on a second career that was only a little less important than his previous work and certainly much more colorful than his role as an establishment scientist.

Although the scientific community frequently criticized him, Crookes continued his investigations into the spirit world, testing mediums and publishing material on the science of the afterlife.

Unfortunately, Crookes's most famous investigations were not those with Daniel Home, but with the controversial medium Florence Cook. During the 1870s, she was one of the spiritualist movement's most famous mediums. She was known for her ability to produce full-form spirit manifestations in a well-lighted room. Her best-known materialization was that of her spirit guide, Katie King (see Figure 4-1). She would appear from behind the curtains of Florence's spirit cabinet and walk among the sitters at her séances. Katie was not a mysterious and ethereal figure. Her body was almost indistinguishable from that of a living girl. She was a beautiful young lady in fact — and unfortunately — very closely resembled Florence Cook.

FIGURE 4-1:
Katie King.

Everett Collection Inc./Alamy Stock Photo

All, of course, noticed the difference in attire from Florence's long, dark, full dress with sizable sleeves, to that of Katie, who emerged from the spirit cabinet in which Florence was bound, out of sight of the sitters. She looked quite a lot like Florence, except that Katie had a quantity of white cloth draped over her head. She was young, pretty, dressed in a white gown, barefoot, and in short sleeves, a rather revealing costume for the Victorian era, and not at all the way that Florence dressed.

Florence always entered her spirit cabinet when she wanted to go into a trance. As long as 30 minutes might pass before the curtains parted and Katie emerged, leaving Florence unconscious in the cabinet. Occasionally, when Katie was present, Florence could be heard sobbing and moaning inside the cabinet, as if the manifestation were draining her energy. At first, Katie simply smiled and nodded to the audience, but later, she began to walk among them, offering her (strangely solid) hand and talking to them. She was fond of touching the sitters and allowing them to carefully touch her, as well. After Katie returned to the cabinet, Florence would be found, still tied up and seemingly exhausted.

Spiritualists considered Katie's materializations a marvelous phenomenon. Skeptics were sure the manifestations were just a thinly disguised Florence Cook. But many wondered how Florence, who was tied up in the cabinet, could release herself from her bindings to become Katie and then tie herself up again as she had been before. One observer, a British minister, after witnessing one of Florence's séances, remarked, "Spiritual or material, it was clever." In other words, even if you did not believe that Katie was a spirit taking physical form, it made for an entertaining evening. Florence and Katie were soon famous on both sides of the Atlantic.

Around this same time, Daniel Home was undergoing testing by Sir William Crookes. Florence quickly got in touch with Crookes and offered to add her own contribution to psychical research. Crookes was delighted to investigate the now-famous partnership between Florence and Katie and happily agreed to a series of private séances.

Once the investigations started, Crookes invited Florence, and occasionally her mother and sister, to stay with him at his home on Mornington Road in northwest London. Crookes knew that most spiritualists had a distrust of scientists and he hoped to rectify this by inviting the young woman into his home and befriending her. Mrs. Crookes was in the house, but was not much in evidence, as she was expecting a child at the time and was usually confined to her room.

In March 1874, Crookes obtained what he felt was "absolute proof" that Florence and Katie were two separate entities. During a séance, Katie had walked among the sitters for a time and then retreated behind the curtain where Florence had been bound to a chair. In a minute, she reappeared and asked Crookes to accompany her behind the curtain. According to his account, he found the unconscious form of Florence Cook, still bound with sealed tape. Katie had vanished, leaving Florence behind. But he still had not seen both of the women at the same time. That opportunity came on March 29, he said, when Katie invited him into the cabinet after he had turned out the gaslight in the room. He carried with him a phosphorus light, which cast only a very dim glow. However, Crookes claimed to be able to see adequately. He saw two women there but never saw their faces. Regardless, Crookes was convinced that Florence and Katie were not the same person.

Crookes may have been convinced, but many séance attendees were not. Many of them insisted on extreme measures to prevent Florence from practicing trickery. Customarily, before the séance would begin, Florence would be bound with a cord or sealed with tape. Each time, the bindings were found to still be intact at the end of the evening. Once, Florence's hair was nailed to the floor. Believe it or not, Katie still appeared.

After Crookes began regularly testing Florence, he produced several dozen photographs of Katie King and was allowed to test her appearances with Florence in plain sight. During the test, Florence reclined on a sofa behind a curtain and wrapped a shawl about her face. Soon, Katie appeared in front of the curtain. Crookes checked to be sure that Florence was still lying on the sofa, and he saw that she was — although incredibly, he never moved the shawl to be sure that it was really her.

In all, Crookes created 55 photographs of Florence and Katie, but only a handful of them remain today. The rest were destroyed, along with the negatives, shortly before his death in 1919. Crookes used five cameras, two of them stereoscopic, operating simultaneously during the sessions. Many of the photos were both poorly shot and questionable in authenticity, and while many of them purported to show both Katie and Florence at the same time, they offered little proof that they were two separate beings. In one, Katie is seen standing in the background while Florence is slumped over a chair, apparently in a trance. Unfortunately, though, an "ectoplasmic shroud" hides Katie's face.

One of Crookes's assistants was a man named Edward Cox. He was one of Britain's best-known psychical researchers at the time, as well as a practicing attorney. He had helped with the testing of Daniel Home and was supportive after he had witnessed his levitations and other psychical abilities. Cox had a sharp eye for details and was well-acquainted with the trickery that some mediums engaged in. In addition, he was skeptical about the existence of spirit phenomena even though he believed in the possibility that some inexplicable "forces" existed — forces that had "both power and intelligence, but imperceptible to our senses."

Cox's opinion of Florence Cook was largely negative, and his notes implied that he felt she was a fraud. To prove it, he devised a very simple test that would conclusively prove if Florence and Katie were the same person, or if they were two separate beings — one human, and one a ghost. Cox suggested that a dab of indelible India ink be placed on Florence's forehead. Then if the alleged spirit, Katie, emerged from the cabinet with ink on her forehead, then she was obviously Florence, pretending to be the ghost. But strangely, Crookes never followed Cox's suggestion, and the simple ink test was never done.

Crookes didn't seem to need proof of Florence's integrity. He often defended her to critics. He stated that Florence agreed to every test that he put her though, without hesitation, and that he had never seen the slightest inclination that she was trying to deceive him.

Still, many were not convinced. Critics stated that Katie looked so much like Florence because that's who she was. It was not simply good enough to cite Crookes's integrity and his stature as a scientist to convince someone of the authenticity of the séances. Edward Cox knew that both Florence and Katie were "solid flesh." Both breathed and even showed beads of perspiration. He thought it was highly improbable that a spirit entity would manifest such clearly human functions.

Was it possible that Florence employed a double to pretend to be Katie King? Many historians — and every skeptic, of course — have reached that conclusion. It's not as outrageous as it might sound. During the investigations, a young medium named Mary Showers stayed at the Crookes's residence while Florence was there. She performed a sort-of double act with Florence. The two of them went into trances together and would create two manifestations — one of Katie and one of Florence Maple, a ghost who bore more than a passing resemblance to Mary. Would it not have been possible for Mary, or even Florence's sister, to have stepped into the spirit cabinet and pretended to be an unconscious Florence, slumped over with her face covered, while Florence walked around as Katie? Or couldn't Mary, who was only in her teens in the middle 1870s, have posed as Katie, which might explain why some thought Katie appeared to be younger than Florence?

If it had been a hoax, then we have to wonder how Sir William Crookes, an eminent scientist, inventor of the radiometer, and discoverer of the element thallium, could be so easily duped by a fraud. If he knew it was a hoax, it seems unlikely that he would have risked his well-earned reputation to go along with it.

Many years later, a British researcher came up with an explanation. He believed that Crookes and Florence were having an affair, right under the nose of the scientist's wife. That would explain Crooke's willingness to either believe in the existence of Katie King or colluded with her to manufacture fraudulent results in the tests. At the time the two of them met, Crookes was in his early 40s and married with a large family; Florence was 18. His infatuation with the pretty young woman, it was said, clouded his judgment and objectivity. By stating that Florence was genuine assured him easy access to her affections. Having a scientist of Crookes's reputation declare her legitimate served Florence well, even if it meant a sexual relationship with him. In short, the two of them may have been using each other. Of course, there is no hard evidence of this, but it would be naïve not to at least consider the possibility of it.

There is one other possibility to explain the manifestations — that they were real. Florence may have been a genuine medium, Katie King may have been an actual spirit, and Crookes's investigations were not as flawed as they appeared to be. Although Crookes behaved strangely for a man with a scientist's regard for detail — such as omitting names and addresses of witnesses from his record — this may have been for privacy reasons.

We will never know what really happened. What is sure, however, is that Katie King "departed" in May 1874, and Florence never manifested her again. With Katie now gone, there was no point in Florence staying on for further investigations. In fact, she told Crookes for the first time, she had been married about two months before to Edward Corner.

Crookes soon returned to his work as a physicist. He was supportive of future psychical investigations, but he was never directly involved with them again. Some believe that Crookes's abandonment of the field was because he was aware of Florence's hoax or was heartbroken when she left him. But, of course, those suppositions are based on the idea that they had an affair, of which no real evidence exists.

After Katie departed, Florence went into retirement for six years, but then returned to the spiritualist scene manifesting a new spirit, this one named Marie. This new spirit partner managed to provide even more entertainment than Katie had, singing and dancing for the sitters at her séances, and providing contact with the spirit world. Her popularity eventually faded, and she retired in 1899. She passed away in 1904 at the age of only 48.

In 1875, Crookes earned the Royal Medal for his work and one year later invented the *radiometer*, a device which demonstrated the effects of radiation on objects in a vacuum, and a special device called the Crookes Tube that went along with it. This invention would lead to the discovery of cathode rays, X-rays, and the electron.

Crookes went on to serve on scientific committees, earned prestigious awards for his discoveries, and invented an instrument that would be used to study subatomic particles, and yet he never wavered in his belief in spiritualism. In 1916, after the death of his wife, Crookes attempted to communicate with her but was unsuccessful. He died in April 1919, never questioning that fact that the spirit world was genuine and that there were things his beloved science would never truly be able to explain.

He left behind the final word on the reality of the paranormal. "I never said it was possible," Crookes once wrote. "I only said that it was true."

William James and "One White Crow"

In 1885, three years after the founding of the Society for Psychical Research in England, William Barrett encouraged the founding of a similar society across the Atlantic and the American Society for Psychical Research (ASPR) was founded in Boston by several scientifically minded researchers. The society soon gained the support and interest of famed philosopher and psychologist William James. His investigation of the medium Leonora Piper — and his conclusions — make up one of the most important incidents in America's paranormal history.

James, one of the most respected scientists in 19th-century America, was a man of intellect and integrity and was unafraid to wade into the turbulent waters of psychical research. He had already earned a reputation as one of the most influential thinkers in the country, a seminal figure in philosophy, and a pioneer in the psychology field when he began making a name for himself in the study of the paranormal.

Born in New York City in 1843, James came from an unusual family that encouraged intellectual curiosity. One of his four siblings, Henry, became a popular novelist. By the time that William was 3, he had already traveled to Europe and eventually learned to speak several languages. He was a brilliant young man, accomplished in both philosophy and psychology, and also earned a degree from Harvard Medical School. He joined the faculty there before he turned 30 and taught there for many years.

Once his interest in psychical research began, he became one of its outstanding voices. One of his goals was to reunite science and religion by extending science so that it embraced the relationship between "mind, body, and spirit." This concept, abandoned as medicine became increasingly specialized in the 20th century, returned as the holistic health movement of recent decades. James also regarded traditional, Bible-based religious beliefs to be "absurd," but recognized the useful role that they played in people's lives. He believed that the core of genuine spirituality was an inner, mystical experience, one of the basic tenets of the more recent New Age movement. James's philosophy about religious dogma being not necessarily the same as spirituality is an outlook embraced today by millions of Americans, proving that William James was a man ahead of his time.

James's search for a personal spiritual perspective began his interest in psychic phenomena, but it would be his careful investigation of trance medium Leonora Piper that would convince him once and for all that paranormal abilities were real.

Leonora Simonds Piper was born in Nashua, New Hampshire, in June 1859, and the first inkling of what awaited her in the future occurred when she was only 8 and was playing in the garden one day. She felt a sharp pain in her right ear and then a whispered voice that said, "Aunt Sara, not dead, but with you still." Terrified, she ran into the house and told her mother. It later turned out that Aunt Sara had died at that very moment.

In 1881, Leonora married a shop assistant named William Piper of Boston, with whom she had two daughters, Alta and Minerva. Her mediumship began in earnest in 1884 after Piper's father-in-law took her for a medical consultation with J.R. Cook, a blind clairvoyant who had a reputation for psychic cures. Piper lost consciousness at Cook's touch and entered a trance of her own. Later, she attended a home circle sitting with him and again entered a trance. This time, she produced a message for one of the other sitters, a well-known local judge who stated that the contact she made with his dead son included the most accurate message he had received in almost 30 years of his interest in spiritualism. This incident made her popular throughout the city, and many clamored for readings with her. Leonora was both disarmed and disturbed by the unexpected attention, but she reluctantly began agreeing to a limited number of sittings in her home. This was how she came to the attention of William James.

One of the sittings was for James's mother-in-law, who had heard about Leonora through friends. She made an appointment with her out of curiosity. After her sitting, she returned to the James's home very excited and told the James that, while in a trace, Leonora had told her facts about relatives, living and dead, that she could not have possibly have known about in any normal way. James laughed at her credulity and called her a victim of a medium's trickery. He gave her an explanation as to how mediums accomplished their fraud, but his mother-in-law refused to consider this and returned for another séance the following week. This time, she convinced her daughter to accompany her. Both women were now impressed with the medium and returned to Cambridge to tell James all about her. Again, the professor tried to discourage them, but they would have nothing to do with it. Instead, they insisted that James visit the medium himself and, irritated that they would not accept his logical explanations for the alleged spirit messages, he agreed.

When James arrived at the Pipers' home, he was surprised to note the complete absence of spiritualist props — no cabinet, no red lights, circles of chairs, trumpets, or bells. The sitters, of which there were two or three others present, merely sat wherever they liked in Leonora's modest but comfortable parlor. Leonora herself also surprised the professor. She was quiet and shy, and there was nothing flamboyant about her, as he had observed with so many other mediums. She politely warned her guests that there would be nothing sensational about the séance and that she did not manifest spirits or cause things to fly about. She would simply go into a trance and one of her spirit controls would then take over. She had no control over whether messages would be given.

James was greatly surprised and impressed by her abilities. Leonora summoned up the names of his wife's father and even that of a child that he and his wife had lost the previous year. He gave her no information to work with and, in fact, was purposely quiet throughout the séance so that she would have nothing with which to guess facts from.

James arranged more sittings and asked whether she would be amenable to stringent testing. At that time, he was forming the ASPR and was searching for worthwhile subjects to study. She agreed and James undertook a lengthy investigation of Leonora's séances that lasted 18 months, during which time he supervised nearly every aspect of her readings — his purpose being to eliminate any possibility of collusion or fraud on her part. His observations convinced him that Leonora had no advance knowledge of her subjects for whom the readings were highly accurate, and her only help seemed to come from her spirit guides. James's tests were also able to rule out mind reading on Leonora's part. She was psychically strongest on the first names of subjects, personalities, and health problems of both sitters and the dead. While she did not engage in theatrical displays during her sittings, on rare occasions, she inexplicably produced the sweet smell of flowers. Aside from that, she was strictly a mental medium who produced eerily accurate messages from the spirits to their friends and families.

James was certain that Leonora Piper possessed genuine psychic ability, and although he could not determine the source, he remained doubtful about the spirits as an explanation. He questioned whether some other form of psychic phenomenon was responsible. He was firmly convinced that she had abilities that were beyond the ordinary, however, and as he famously wrote, "To upset the conclusion that all crows are black, there is no need to seek demonstration that no crows are black; it is sufficient to produce one white crow; a single one is sufficient. My white crow is Mrs. Piper."

William James's study of Leonora Piper came to an end because of work obligations, but he did not believe that the study of her should be at an end. He contacted SPR members in England about her, and Richard Hodgson came to the United States, took up residence in Boston, and continued the testing of Mrs. Piper. The SPR arranged for Leonora to be paid an annual stipend so that her tests would give the SPR unprecedented and exclusive access to her as a medium.

Like James, Hodgson began his work with Leonora assuming her to be a fraud. His research in England had unmasked several fraudulent mediums and had given him a working knowledge of conjuring. He knew what to look for in a hoax and expected to find the similar qualities in Leonora Piper. He made appointments for 50 sitters with her, keeping their identities secret from the medium, and kept detailed records of the séances. He even hired private detectives to follow her about and to make sure that she was not compiling information about possible sitters. Although she never behaved in any suspicious manner, Leonora continued to produce eerily accurate information about people she had never met and about whom she knew nothing.

After a sufficient number of tests had been conducted, James wrote up Hodgson's conclusions, and neither man believed Leonora had resorted to fraud or trickery, especially considering the "close observations as to most of the conditions of her life." James noted in 1898 that he would be willing to wager money that Mrs. Piper was honest.

Even after the report was published, Hodgson was not yet finished with Leonora. He had an idea that would impose even stricter controls on her: He would take her to England. Once there, she would be in an unfamiliar country and among people she did not know. Mrs. Piper agreed and traveled to England in November 1889. She resided at the home of F.W.H. Myers in Cambridge, and it was more than just hospitality that prompted the invitation — as his guest, Myers could observe all of Leonora's comings and goings. He chose sitters for her séances at random, and their identities were unknown to her. She was in England from November 1889 to February 1890 and gave 88 sittings. She was carefully supervised the entire time. She was watched everywhere she went, as was anyone she spoke to, and anything she read was cautiously censored. While most would have felt confined by such scrutiny, Leonora remained remarkably patient and cooperative. She even consented to have her mail opened and read by SPR investigators.

The records of the SPR show that some of the séances were nothing short of remarkable. Just about anyone who studied Leonora came away with the same conclusion: She had some kind of supernormal power or ability, but, of course, there was a lot of disagreement about what exactly it was. The so-called spirit theory was disagreeable to the scientific men, who opted instead for the possibility of telepathy, clairvoyance, hallucinations, some unknown energy — anything but ghosts. Hodgson was firmly in agreement with these men of science. He did not believe that the dead could communicate with the living — until something extraordinary happened that changed his mind.

Hodgson, a very private man, rarely spoke of his personal life with Leonora Piper, despite the fact that he had spent countless hours with her observing her sittings, and they had developed a cordial relationship. One day when he was the subject of a reading, Leonora told Hodgson that the spirit of a young woman was communicating a message she wanted him to know. The spirit identified herself to Leonora and then told the medium that she had recently passed away. Hodgson was stunned because he immediately knew who Leonora was talking about.

Years earlier, when he had been a young man in Australia, Hodgson fell in love with a girl that he very much wanted to marry. However, her parents refused to allow it because of the differences in the couple's religions. Hodgson was heartbroken, moved to England, but never married. He never saw or spoke again to the young woman that he'd lost. But she reached out to him after her death and communicated with him through Leonora Piper. Hodgson was both shaken and moved by the message, but he had no way to confirm or deny it — he did not know what had happened to her when he left Australia. But one thing that he did know was that Leonora's communication was not based on telepathy, and further, Leonora could not have known about this personal and painful part of his life long ago.

Hodgson soon sent word to Australia and contacted old friends who would know of his beloved's fate. It was exactly as Leonora said: The woman had died just a short time before. Apparently, she had never stopped thinking of him and after death, had contacted him the only way that she could. Hodgson was saddened by this turn of events, but he couldn't help but marvel at Leonora's gift.

This incident had a profound effect on Hodgson, who had always rejected the spirit hypothesis to explain mediumship. In 1897, he wrote in the *SPR Journal* that he now had no doubt that he had experienced genuine spirit communication. This was quite a statement from the no-nonsense investigator who had spent most of his career exposing one fraud after another. After 15 years of investigating Leonora Piper, he finally — reluctantly — accepted that the dead had communicated through her. He issued a second statement on the matter and planned a third report but died suddenly of heart failure at the age of 50 in 1905. At the time, Hodgson was the secretary for the ASPR and an important part of the organization. His death left a daunting vacancy to be filled.

Interestingly, there is a little more to the Hodgson story. After his untimely death, his spirit allegedly communicated messages to several people, including an SPR colleague, James Hyslop, and a British medium named Mrs. Holland.

Hodgson left an indelible mark on the paranormal field. His many years of study and testing of Leonora Piper were of great value to the scientific research of the paranormal, and he also trained Columbia University philosophy professor James Hyslop to become one of the best psychical researchers in American history. Even before his death, Hodgson had tasked Hyslop with continuing the investigation of Leonora's ability. Like his friend, Hyslop was quite skeptical of mediumship before he met Leonora in 1888. He employed every caution possible when testing her and required at least a dozen sittings with Leonora to become convinced that he was witnessing genuine mediumship. Her sessions with him changed his mind after he received messages from his late father, brother, and several uncles.

Meanwhile, Leonora Piper was still very involved with ASPR investigations. By 1906, several of the original members of the SPR had died, including Hodgson, Edmund Gurney, and Frederick W.H. Myers. There were a number of cross correspondence experiments conducted to determine whether these three men could — or would — communicate from the after-life. The results seemed to indicate that several of the mediums who participated in the tests, including Leonora, each received part of a spirit message from them that had to be deciphered and pieced together to form a complete communication. Although the conclusion seemed to suggest the accuracy of the communications went beyond mere chance, the study never achieved the kind of acclaim that it should have.

Leonora Piper continued to be tested by investigators until her retirement in 1927. By then, she was in her late 60s. She died on July 3, 1950, and has since come to be regarded as a medium of the first rank. She gave much of her life in the service of science, and, as a result, many who had previously doubted the possibility of survival after death became convinced of its reality. There is no question that her contributions to psychical research were enormous. A large number of documented eyewitness accounts, evidence from the many tests Leonora had undergone, and published reports by researchers and scientists provided an unequaled amount of material about the history of mediumship.

There seems to be little doubt that she was, in the words of William James, the "white crow" that proved that not all crows are black.

Thomas Edison and Communicating with the Dead

One of the most compelling examples of mixing science with the spirit world is the story of the alleged Telephone to the Dead that was invented by American genius, Thomas Edison (see Figure 4-2). The inventor of the light bulb — along with countless other amazing advances in technology — at one time expressed an interest in creating an electronic method of communicating with the dead. Unfortunately, though, it appears that the device was never created, and no plans for one were ever discovered among the voluminous piles of paperwork that Edison left behind when he died.

A self-taught genius, Edison began experimenting with scientific theories as a child. His vision and incredible curiosity led to inventions like the light bulb, the phonograph, storage batteries, the film projector, and much more. He worked tirelessly — Edison was a notorious insomniac —to create ways to make the world work better, communicate better, and to be better entertained. Throughout his life, he maintained that it was possible to build anything if the right components were available. This idea would later be applied to a machine that he believed might be able to communicate with the spirit world.

FIGURE 4-2:
Thomas Edison.

Courtesy Wellcome Collection

Despite his theories about the possibility of such a machine, Edison was not a believer in the supernatural, nor was he a proponent of the popular spiritualist movement. He had always been an agnostic, and although he did not dispute the philosophies of religion, he didn't necessarily believe in their validity. He believed that when a person died, the body decayed but the intelligence lived on. He thought that the so-called spirit world was simply a limbo for disembodied intelligence.

He took these theories a step further by announcing that it might be possible to devise a machine that could communicate with the inhabitants of this limbo. An article in the October 1920 issue of *American* magazine was entitled "Edison Working to Communicate with the Next World." The news of the invention made headlines around the world. In an essay that Edison wrote in 1920, he stated:

Now what I propose to do is furnish psychic investigators with an apparatus which will give a scientific aspect to their work. This apparatus, let me explain, is in the nature of a valve, so to speak. That is to say, the slightest conceivable effort is made to exert many times its initial power for indicative purposes. It is similar to a modern power house, where man, with his relatively puny one-eighth horse power, turns a valve which starts a 50,000 horse-power steam turbine. My apparatus is along those lines, in that the slightest effort will be magnified many times so as to give us whatever form of record we desire for the purpose of investigation.

Beyond that, I don't care to say anything further regarding its nature. I have been working out the details for some time; indeed a collaborator in this work died only the other day. In that he knew exactly what I am after in this work, I believe he ought to be the first to use it if he is able to do so. Of course, don't forget that I am making no claims for the survival of the personality; I am not promising communication with those who have passed out of this life. I merely state that I am giving psychic investigators an apparatus which may help them in their work, just as optical experts have given the microscope to the medical world. And if this apparatus fails to reveal anything of exceptional interest, I am afraid that I shall have lost all faith in the survival of the personality as we know it in this existence.

According to journals and newspapers, Edison began working on the apparatus, but if he did, no plans or prototypes were ever found. Regardless, he continued to talk about its possibilities. He mentioned the machine again a short time later: "I have been at work for some time building an apparatus to see if it is possible for personalities which have left this earth to communicate with us and I hope to be able to finish it before very many months pass."

Apparently, though, he never completed it. Even though this mysterious instrument has since been dubbed the Telephone to the Dead, Edison's version of it has never been found.

However, Edison may have built something. In an essay, he mentioned working on an item that he likened to a valve that would amplify the ability for the spirits to manipulate the object so that "It does not matter how slight is the effort, it will be sufficient to record whatever there is to be recorded."

In a 1933 issue of *Modern Mechanix* magazine, an article claimed that a secret meeting took place in Edison's lab in 1920 where he tried to communicate with the dead. Complete with illustrations, the article describes how Edison set up a beam projector and photoelectric receiver with delicate instruments that would register anything that crossed the beam's path. A group of scientists sat in the room for hours, but nothing happened.

If the story is true, then Edison did maintain an interest in the spirit world up until the time of his death, but he almost certainly gave up on plans for any kind of telephone. The article about this experiment was published about in 1933, which was two years after Edison's death and 13 years after the experiment, but it never addressed what happened to this device. Like the plans for the Telephone to the Dead, no plans for this device was discovered either. The Edison estate has stated that he was never involved in work with a device to communicate with the dead because no plans, or instruments, have ever been found.

In the years following his death, curators at both of the Edison museums in Florida and New Jersey searched extensively for the components or the prototype for the machine to communicate with the dead. No trace of it was discovered, but the accounts of the mysterious machine did not end with the inventor's death. Joseph Dunninger, a famous magician and a personal friend of Edison, claimed that he was once shown a prototype of the machine. If this was true, then he was perhaps the only one who saw it.

In 1941, two of Edison's associates allegedly made contact with him during a séance that took place in New York. During the sitting, Edison's spirit allegedly claimed that plans and schematics for his apparatus were in the care of three of his assistants. Edison said that his valve machine had been completed but had never worked correctly. Then, in a second alleged séance, Edison made some suggestions about altering the apparatus so that it might work. Inventor J. Gilbert Wright was present at this séance and claimed that he made the changes that Edison told him about. Wright reportedly worked on the apparatus until his death in 1959, but that was the last that anyone ever heard of it.

Since that time, the machine to communicate with the dead has never resurfaced, making the device the greatest mystery of Edison's complex and intriguing life.

Examining Mysteries with J.B. Rhine

By the late 1920s, spiritualism was in decline. As it withered away, organized scientific interest in the paranormal also slowed, until very little research was being conducted. Frustration and disappointment discouraged many scientists from further testing. Following the deaths of most of the original SPR and ASPR founders who had dedicated themselves to psychical research, the next generation of their members was hampered by the extensive revelations of fraud that had plagued the spiritualist movement for years.

There were several reasons for the "death" of spiritualism. It was forced from America's center stage in the first quarter of the 20th century by the development of new measurements of the unseen worlds in the realms of psychology and physics, soft science, and hard science. By the late 1920s, the world of the unseen — inhabited by spirits and invisible beings — had become the subject of real scientific scrutiny. We could see neither the atom nor the subconscious, but both medical and physical science had shown them to exist. They had been discovered and proven by science in a way that the paranormal had never been.

Physical mediums and séances gave way to low-key, less flamboyant practitioners, the best of whom used their gifts to communicate with the deceased and bring messages of hope and comfort to the living.

It was the abilities of the psychics and mediums who weathered the near demise of the spiritualist movement who captured the attention of the last remaining scientists with an interest in the unknown. One of them was Joseph Banks Rhine, a young psychology instructor who joined the faculty of Duke University in Durham, North Carolina, in 1927. He would not oversee the destruction of paranormal studies. In fact, he elevated it by finally placing it in the kind of scientifically controlled and academic setting that so many before him had longed to see. Through his long and distinguished career, J.B. Rhine moved psychical research in the twentieth century to a place where both defenders and detractors agreed that he became of the most important figures in American parapsychology.

Rhine was born in the small western Pennsylvania town of Waterloo in 1895. By 1925, he had graduated from college and earned a Ph.D. in biology. Five years later, he married his childhood sweetheart, Louise Weckesser, who shared his life and work, becoming a highly regarded parapsychologist herself. Early in their careers, the Rhines agreed that they had little interest in teaching biology. Instead, they dedicated themselves to researching psychical phenomena.

Rhine's initial interest in the paranormal had come about in 1922, when he attended a lecture about spiritualism by author Sir Arthur Conan Doyle. He was further intrigued when he participated in psychical research experiments conducted at Harvard University by Dr. Walter Franklin Prince, who had been president of the ASPR. While in Boston, the Rhines attended a séance with the well-known medium Mina Crandon (a.k.a. Margery) but left dissatisfied, convinced she was a fraud. Rhine was unhappy with the ASPR for supporting her as a genuine medium. He concluded that experimental science was the best way for psychical research to advance, and he named the new field of study *parapsychology.*

In 1926, an opportunity arose for the Rhines to study under Dr. William McDougall, who would become the chairman of the psychology department at Duke University. They jumped at the chance, resigned their teaching positions, sold all their furniture, and moved to Boston, where McDougall was then teaching. At first, Rhine attempted to study mediumship but soon found it as frustrating as other scientists before him. What he wanted was proof — verifiable, scientific, replicable proof. He was finding that hard to achieve. But passionate about his research, Rhone was determined to drag psychic phenomena out of the séance room and into the scientific laboratory.

In 1927, Rhine's mentor, Dr. McDougall, moved to Duke University and the Rhines soon followed. Rhine taught psychology as an instructor, but the bulk of he and Louise's time in the first few months was devoted to analyzing the records of a man named John Thomas, who had compiled 750 pages of notes on conversations he had with his late wife through spirit mediums. Rhine was convinced that the mediums referred to information about Thomas and his wife that they could not have known by conventional means. But, he noted, this did not mean that the information was actually coming from the dead woman — it could easily have been coming from Thomas's mind.

To Rhine, this seemed to be a much more plausible area of research — the ability of the human mind to obtain information outside of the limiting principles of time, space, and physics. He was convinced that such abilities existed, and he termed them "extra-sensory perception."

Rhine abandoned the search for proof of survival after death and instead began to focus on ESP. His first tests for telepathy were informal. He used a numbered card or a normal playing card to see whether his subjects — ordinary people, usually students, and not mediums or people who had a reputation for being psychic — could guess a card without seeing it. What he found, however, was that people tended to have favorite cards and would suggest those rather than try to really guess what card was being displayed. Rhine wanted an entirely new set of cards, with images that had no previous associations in the minds of his subjects. For this, he turned to a colleague in the psychology department, Dr. Karl Zener.

Zener, whose usual work specialized in conditional responses, selected five simple symbols for the deck he created for Rhine — star, square, circle, cross, and three wavy lines — because people didn't seem to have specific feelings for or against any of them. The deck came with five sets of five symbols, meaning that the chances of guessing the first card correctly were one in five, but the chances of making ten or more correct guesses in a run of 25 cards were at least one in 20. Figure 4-3 shows the deck of cards.

FIGURE 4-3:
Zener's psychic cards.

Shutterstock.com

The tests were fun and popular with Duke students, so the Rhines had no shortage of subjects. In 1931 alone, they conducted 10,000 ESP tests with 63 students, many of them scored better than chance. Some scored so well above chance that they were statistically significant, like Duke divinity graduate student Hubert Pearce, who once made 25 consecutive correct identifications, a full run of the Zener deck.

In 1934, Rhine published *Extra-Sensory Perception*, considered by many psychic researchers to be a milestone work in the history of the paranormal. While most parapsychologists reacted positively and realized Rhine's work was significant, skeptics, of course, criticized Rhine's test conditions because there was likely no amount of evidence that would change the minds of those with a single purpose of debunking the paranormal. They criticized his methods of compiling statistics, or just flatly stated that his work had no value. There were also those who questioned whether subjects might have been able to read through the backs of the cards, and thus see the shapes on them. This was one of the most ridiculous of the accusations since Rhine had taken every possible precaution to prevent such sensory clues. Rhine was a trained scientist and was conducting studies under controlled conditions. He ignored the detractors and continued the experiments.

The popular reaction to Rhine's work was largely uncritical and approving. By the mid-1930s, even as the country remained in the grips of the Great Depression, the media took note of Rhine's tests, and soon there were stories in some of America's most popular magazines. In 1935, Rhine's work saw a massive boost when a wealthy patron gave him and his lab $10,000 a year for two years, with the possibility of extending that to $10,000 a year for five years if all went well. With the money, Rhine set up his own lab, still under the Duke auspices, but separate from the psychology department. Thanks to the donor, the lab was the most well-funded at the university.

Meanwhile, the general public's appetite for ESP research was seemingly limitless. By 1937, you could buy Zener cards from the local newsstand for ten cents a pack. Rhine's books reached a wide audience, ESP experiments became the subject of radio shows, and everyone wanted to talk about telepathy. Rhine's reputation as the country's preeminent parapsychologist meant that people who'd had weird, inexplicable experiences or felt that they had abilities that others did not, thought of him as their champion — a scientist who actually believed in what others called the impossible.

But there was a downside. As Rhine became better known and accepted by the public, criticism of him and his wife increased. Some of it was particularly hostile, and most of that came from fellow psychologists. The public's embrace of parapsychology did not make it acceptable to most other scientists. Despite the initial promise of the lab, and the hundreds of thousands of trials that the Rhines believed established the validity of ESP, parapsychology still had the taint of the occult.

McDougall, Rhine's champion and mentor, and William Preston Few, the Duke president who agreed to Rhine's lab, had both died. Rhine had few defenders, and overall, most psychologists of the era remained antagonistic toward Rhine and the paranormal in general.

The reason wasn't very complicated: Most of them were concerned with stubbornly protecting their own theories and careers. If Rhine was correct about ESP and could prove it genuine, traditional assumptions about the limits and capabilities of the human mind would have to be reconsidered. It was easier to dismiss Rhine than to face the new threat of paranormal theories.

Regardless, the Rhines continued their work through the 1930s and resumed it after World War II with more students at the Duke Parapsychology Laboratory. As time passed, though, the connection between the lab and the university began to fall apart. Even though the Parapsychology Lab was funded from outside sources (including the Office of Naval Research, the Army, and the Rockefeller Foundation), its lack of support within the university put it in jeopardy. In 1948, the Lab became a nonteaching independent unit within the university, losing its access to graduate students and further distancing itself from the school.

When Rhine retired in 1965, the lab closed. He founded a nonprofit research center, the Foundation for Research on the Nature of Man, to continue the research and continued to be involved in ESP research until his death in 1980. The Rhine Research Center still exists today, but perhaps its greatest legacy was the other organizations that formed in its wake, including the Parapsychological Foundation in New York in 1951, and the Parapsychological Association in 1957. The Psychical Research Foundation was founded in 1960, in Durham, North Carolina, and began specializing in poltergeist cases and out-of-body experiences. As interest in the paranormal grew, it branched out into past lives research, dream telepathy, psychic healing, near-death experiences, remote viewing, and more.

What remains clear after all these years is that J.B. Rhine was a pioneer in psychical research. He was truly the first to find the middle ground between science and the paranormal, where real research could take place.

Ghosts Don't Always Perform on Command

Today, it seems remarkable that scientists of the past, like J.B. Rhine and others, were able to establish paranormal research centers or to have their work taken seriously. To say that paranormal research is still on the fringes of the established scientific community is a massive understatement. The National Science Foundation, in its surveys on the public perception of science, refers to ESP and the study of psychic abilities as pseudoscience. The official case for the existence of "real" ESP is considered tenuous because attempts to replicate studies that seem to prove such abilities exist have not been consistently successful — largely because no academics are willing to put in the kind of time that J.B. Rhine and others did. They dismiss it all as junk science and not worthy of bothering with.

When it comes to ghosts, the perception by mainstream scientists is even worse. No matter what kind of evidence seems to be gathered, nothing changes the mind of scientists. They still maintain that ghosts don't exist. They cannot walk among us, scientists say, because their feet would have to apply pressure to the floor. If they were able to do this, they could not pass through walls because being able to do one without being able to do the other violates the scientific laws of action and reaction. Ghosts, quite simply, cannot be real.

Mainstream science demands that for something to be real, it must be able to be duplicated over and over again in a scientific setting. Unfortunately, the supernatural does not conform to the idea of repeatable experiments. We can measure, document and record, but ghosts do not perform on command in a structured setting, which is what scientists demand. Ghosts cannot be trapped in the laboratory. If you drag them out of the shadows and expose them to the harsh glare of scientific reality, they tend to vanish. Thanks to this, science tells us, ghosts cannot exist.

But do most people feel this way? No, they don't. We have looked at the nationwide polls and millions of people believe in ghosts, hauntings, and communication with the dead. If they cannot exist, then who do so many people believe they can?

This is a perplexing question for mainstream scientists, but it isn't to ghost-hunters and psychical researchers. First-hand accounts of ghosts have been with us for centuries, dating back to the beginning of recorded history. People have been having encounters with the spirit world since that time and are still having them today. Scientists may say that ghosts don't exist but those who delve into the paranormal know differently.

By definition, a *spirit* is a disembodied personality or a consciousness. At this time, science says we have absolutely no physical evidence that a personality or consciousness exists. This means that they must maintain that it cannot exist outside of the body either. But we know it exists. We also know that since it exists inside of the body, then there is no reason why it cannot exist outside of it, too. Our consciousness is a form of energy and as one of the greatest scientists in history,

Albert Einstein, once said, "Energy cannot be created or destroyed, it can only be changed from one form to another."

It's baffling why this concept is so easy to understand for a paranormal investigator but not for a mainstream scientist. They refuse to believe it, much in the same way that they refuse to accept the idea of paranormal research as legitimate science. They cannot understand it, and worse yet, most of them simply don't want to. It has never been until scientists have been shown the error of their ways that they will grudgingly admit they could have been wrong. For many years, the world's greatest scientists insisted that the earth was flat. They largely ignored those who tried to prove otherwise until Magellan sailed around it in 1522. Other scientists claimed that the earth was hollow and that the sun revolved around it or, more recently, that Pluto was the ninth planet in our solar system. In each case, infallible science turned out to be wrong.

Perhaps someday, they will admit that paranormal research also has its place in the scientific field. Until that time, we can simply continue to do what we have been doing, keeping an open mind and working hard to gather the most authentic and credible evidence that we can.

Adapting the Scientific Method

Perhaps the best way to put an end to the misguided stereotype that paranormal investigation is a pseudoscience, practiced by gullible investigators is to apply the methods used by scientists to your investigations.

Many believe that this can only be done by using electronic devices, but this is not the case. Ghost-hunting devices — scientific equipment adapted to be used in the paranormal field — have only been used in the field since the 1970s. Before that, researchers had little or no electronic equipment that could be used to monitor locations or to search for anomalous activity that might be present in a place they were investigating. Theories were developed that suggested that spirit activity created an energy that caused a disruption in the magnetic field of a location and that energy might be detectable using measuring devices. In those days, researchers used Geiger counters to check for changes in the radioactivity levels of locations.

By the 1990s, new theories were developed suggesting that many haunted locations had high levels of electromagnetic energy. Other theories stated that the spirits themselves were electromagnetic in origin or that perhaps the ghosts used the energy present to manifest. Either way, activity connected to spirits could be monitored using electronic devices that measured levels of electromagnetic energy, leading to wide usage of such devices.

These devices are widely used today, and if used correctly, are an integral part of a scientific investigation. The devices are pieces of equipment that have been adapted to be used for ghost research. Their use is based on the theory that they can pick up distortions and disturbances in energy fields caused by ghosts. This remains a theory, not a fact. For this reason, devices are always best used to provide corresponding evidence. They should be used in conjunction with first-hand experiences, when monitoring locations, and with other investigative techniques. No single piece of evidence can stand on its own. In other words, anomalous readings on an EMF detector can only be seen as hard evidence of a ghost if the readings can be backed up by something else, like a cold spot, a personal experience, or even readings on other equipment at the same time.

We can give even more credence to readings collected with electronic devices when we employ the scientific method during every investigation. An investigator must remain both open-minded and skeptical. We cannot always assume that something that occurs is a ghost. Phenomena must be questioned, and we must be willing to admit that national explanations might exist.

To get the root cause, a scientific investigator must ask questions based on the scientific method:

» Why is the event occurring?

» Is there a natural explanation for the event?

» Is this incident connected to any other reported events?

» Is there other research that has found connections between the events that you have observed?

» Have other researchers drawn the same conclusions?

» What is your theory as to the cause of the event?

» Does it agree with fellow investigators, or is it new?

» Can this theory be tested under controlled conditions?

» What predictions can be made based on this theory?

» Were tests based on this theory significant, and did they help to draw further conclusions?

By using these steps, a paranormal investigator can follow the same line of questioning that a mainstream scientist uses in their own work. Of course, there are variables that occur with the paranormal that doesn't occur in a laboratory, but you'll be on the right track. By using this method, other investigators can use the same experimental protocols and can attempt to reproduce your results. If done successfully, there is theoretically no limit as to what can be achieved with your investigations.

Using History as Science

There is, of course, no guarantee that science will accept the findings of paranormal researchers, even if every investigation is conducted using the most careful scientific methods. Mainstream science has very little interest in "things that go bump in the night." However, there is a way to gather additional evidence of a haunting that cannot be dismissed as pseudoscience and that is with historical research. It is possible to actually prove that a location is haunted using history.

Here is an example of what is meant by this: A family moves into a house and begins experiencing strange things. Doors open and close, lights turn on and off, and objects vanish, turning up in odd places a few days later. They are also startled when they see the apparition of a man at the top of the staircase. He vanishes when they approach him. Bewildered by the weird events, they contact the previous owners of the property and learn that they also experienced the odd happenings and saw the ghostly man. In fact, they describe him exactly as he was seen by the current occupants of the house. Checking back even further, they discover that other previous owners of the property also shared these same experiences. Before this, none of them were aware that others had experienced these things, and they had not discussed the happenings with anyone outside of their immediate family.

The house was haunted, and they had solid historical evidence of it. This was not a science experiment that was conducted in a laboratory, but it was a case that would have held up in court if haunting a house was against the law.

The incident described is based on a true story. The witnesses to the haunting had never compared notes about the situation and, the various families combined, had lived in the house for a period of more than 50 years. During each occupancy, the homeowners independently saw and experienced the ghostly activity without ever realizing that someone else had experienced it, too. In addition, all the witnesses identified a photograph of the home's original owner as the ghost that they had seen. They did this without hesitation, not knowing that the former residents had also picked out this same photo.

Skeptics who insist that ghosts are not real convince themselves that anyone who experiences the paranormal is either drunk, mentally ill, or is lying. In a situation like the one described, every single witness would have had to have been mentally ill and, to make it worse, would have had to have experienced some sort of shared hallucination that spanned five decades. Anyone thinking logically must admit that this extremely unlikely, even impossible.

They could not have been lying about their experience because they would have no idea what to lie about. They were unaware that others had shared their experience and yet it had been repeating itself for many years.

REMEMBER

During investigations, it is imperative to collect historical evidence by gathering witness testimony and details about the events that are occurring. If possible, we can also compare the current witness testimony with the accounts of those who lived in the house before. By stepping backward in time, we can compile a full personal history of the location. This is all a little simplified in this example but having different witnesses, from different time periods of the location, with matching experiences makes for compelling and convincing evidence of a haunting.

Anyone can learn to do good historical research and in turn, become an even better ghost-hunter. This is your chance to hone your ghost-hunting skills with detective work and use another kind of science to give your investigations the credibility they deserve.

Chapter **5**

Seeing the Spirit World as Entertainment

G hosts have been a part of popular culture entertainment since the beginning of reported time. When our ancestors gathered around the fire on a cold winter's night, spooky tales of ghosts and spirits were inevitably part of the evening's entertainment. Accounts of hauntings appear among the remains of the world's oldest cultures, and the Greeks and Romans enthralled each other with stories of the afterlife.

When printed books came along, the public continued to seek out tales of horror and ghosts. Horace Walpole's *The Castle of Otranto* is widely believed to be the first Gothic novel, establishing a blueprint for a dark literary genre that was obsessed with terror, death, and the supernatural. The Victorian traditions of ghost stories during the Christmas season created a genre of its own, which is best represented by *A Christmas Carol* by Charles Dickens.

In the pages of the 19th century's "penny dreadful" books to the pulp magazines of the 1920s and 1930s, ghost stories have always been a part of our popular culture. In those days — just like today — many of the most popular stories, plays, and presentations were based on real life.

Truth is, as they say, always stranger than fiction.

Having Fun with the Spirit World

When news spread of the knockings in Hydesville, New York, the Fox sisters became almost instant celebrities. (For details on the Fox sisters and their story, see Chapter 3.) The newspapers and the public couldn't get enough of them. The Spiritualist movement swept across the country, even in those days before radio, television, and mass communication. People became obsessed with the idea that the living could communicate with the dead — and receive a reply — and almost everyone wanted to be involved with it. By the early 1850s, an estimated two mission Spiritualists were in the United States, and the movement showed no signs of slowing down. It was easy to find people, from the lowliest tenement homes to the very steps of the White House, who believed in contact with the spirits.

It was a time of prominence for some of America's greatest literary celebrities, all of whom also had a great effect on the popular culture of the country. Almost all of them expressed curiosity for the growing Spiritualist craze.

Writing about the spirits

Ralph Waldo Emerson was a transcendentalist, who believed in the afterlife. This movement taught that divinity can be found in all nature and humanity. Henry Wadsworth Longfellow shared his views. Henry David Thoreau, also a transcendentalist, expressed interest in reincarnation. William Cullen Bryant took part in séances, and so did Nathaniel Hawthorne, who then rejected Spiritualism, but created a Spiritualist character for his 1852 novel *The Blithedale Romance*. Throughout his life, he acknowledged that he had witnessed apparitions. In one incident, Hawthorne, who often went to the Boston Athenaeum, a research library in the city, always noticed an elderly minister there reading. One evening, as usual, Hawthorne saw the same gentleman in his usual chair. He was stunned to learn that the man had already died before he saw him. Hawthorne concluded that he had seen the man's ghost, which continued to appear for several more weeks.

Herman Melville, author of the 1851 book *Moby Dick*, was a believer in the afterlife. Walt Whitman understood *phrenology* (an occult science based on the measurements of the skull) well enough to allude to it in his poetry. Later in the century, Henry James included Spiritualists in his books, and the creator of Sherlock Holmes, Sir Arthur Conan Doyle, became one of the greatest proponents of Spiritualism in history.

The popular English poet Elizabeth Barrett Browning, drawn to Spiritualism, joined in séances conducted by the famed medium Daniel Dunglas Home. However, her husband, Robert Browning, despised Home and publicly mocked Spiritualism as a fraud, hoping in some small way to injure the reputation of the medium.

Novelist William Thackeray, whose works included *Vanity Fair*, attended séances given by the Fox sisters and D.D. Home, but admitted his reaction to Spiritualism was "mixed" at best.

In 1852, the best-selling author Harriet Beecher Stowe published one of the most influential books of all time, *Uncle Tom's Cabin*. It was responsible for changing public opinion in the northern states against slavery. Stowe was seriously interested in the new Spiritualist movement and attended séances, as did noted abolitionist and newspaper publisher William Lloyd Garrison, whose interests also included mesmerism and phrenology.

Poet Emily Dickinson mentioned the spirit world in her writings, and author Louisa May Alcott discovered that supernatural events did not occur only at séances. Alcott, who later wrote the classic novel *Little Women*, was only 25 in 1858 and lived at her family's home in Concord, Massachusetts. Despite the great interest in Spiritualism, she remained uninvolved. But she found out that one did not need to be a Spiritualist to have an experience with ghosts. When her sister, Beth, died from scarlet fever, Louisa was present at her side, along with her mother. Louisa later wrote that both of them saw a light mist rise up from Beth's body at the moment of her death and vanish in the air.

Participating in mediums, séances, and spirit circles

The Fox sisters were not the only mediums of note. (See Chapter 3 for more on the Fox sisters.) People were hungry for more. Mediums, séances, and spirit circles could be found in most communities, large and small, throughout the country. New York City reported hundreds of known mediums and no less than 40,000 serious believers in spirit rapping. (For more on spirit rapping, see Chapter 2.) Across the country, especially in the Northeast and New England, the number of mediums exploded. Philadelphia claimed 50 to 60 private spirit circles and scores of mediums. In Ohio, more than 200 spirit circles were reported. In 1854, Illinois Senator James Shields presented the U.S. Congress with a petition containing 15,000 signatures, calling on the federal government "to investigate communications from the dead." U.S. Senator N.P. Tallmadge and Ohio Congressman Joshua Giddings were among the politicians who practiced Spiritualism.

Whether the spirit communications of the Fox sister had been fake or genuine didn't seem to matter. They had made an impact that had changed the country. By 1855, the New England Spiritualist Association estimated some two million believers across America.

Creating magic shows

As the popularity of the movement continued to spread, many publications, both supportive of and opposed to Spiritualism, were being printed across the country. By 1851, New Yorkers had a new daily newspaper to read called *The New York Times*. It immediately took a strong anti-Spiritualism stance, but if Spiritualism caught your fancy, dozens of publications devoted to the movement were readily available in towns and cities across the country.

But séances and publications about them still weren't enough. The public wanted more. They didn't want to take a chance that they might see one in a séance room — they wanted a sure thing. It was a professor named John Henry Pepper who decided to start offering that in 1863.

Pepper was an analytical chemist, who in 1852 became director of London's Royal Polytechnic Institution, an establishment that worked to disseminate scientific knowledge to the public. Pepper believed that this could be done by making science entertaining, and he especially liked explaining complex concepts and devices by using optical illusions and programs that produced grand dioramas and dissolving views. It was in this way that he came to devise the "Ghost Show," which enchanted audiences in Britain, Canada, America, and Australia.

The Ghost Show allowed an audience the illusion of interacting with the phantoms on stage and its primary effect relied on the same principle that lets a person see successive reflections of themselves in an automobile window while riding in a lighted vehicle at night. The ghost was an actor positioned in front of the stage, but below it, concealed from the view of the audience. Hidden beneath the stage, a projectionist illuminated the actor, whose image reflected in a mirror and from there onto a large, mostly invisible, glass pane. A variety of startling apparitional special effects were possible, making the spirit seem to menace either the actors onstage or the audience itself.

Despite efforts to patent his performances, Professor Pepper's show was soon being copied all over Europe. The illusions drew huge crowds, who came to see terrifying specters rising from graveyards, ghosts menacing actors on stage, and more.

In addition to these artificial manifestations, real ghosts were still entertaining sitters at Spiritualist séances, much to the chagrin of scientists and skeptics who wanted nothing more than to expose fraudulent medium for the tricksters they were. Some of the most adept at re-creating the allegedly miraculous phenomena of physical mediums were stage magicians. They began putting on shows that duplicated, and then exposed, the ghostly effects. The methods practiced by the mediums were simple, these men claimed, and were merely stage illusions just like the ones being created before audiences in vaudeville theaters across the country. "If I can only get your attention intently," one magician claimed, "an elephant could pass behind me and you would not see it."

Shows that "exposed the spirits" became increasingly popular as the fascination with Spiritualism began to wane in the early 20th century. Performers like Houdini, Harry Kellar, Howard Thurston, and scores of others drew massive audiences as they performed mock séances on stage, after which they turned on the lights and showed the audiences how the tricks were accomplished. It broke all the rules of magic, but they felt that it was for a good cause.

Transforming into spook shows

As Spiritualism was taking its last shuddering breath in the late 1920s, a new form of spirit entertainment came along to take its place. The pioneers of what became known as the *spook show,* which included magicians like Howard Thurston, began developing the format of the midnight ghost and magic shows in the early 1930s. The spook shows of those days mainly appealed to young people in their late teens and 20s. This audience, in the days of the Great Depression, was looking for a way to escape from the toil of poverty and the despair of everyday life. Theater owners loved the idea, too. They had huge movie palaces they were struggling to fill and needed the extra cash flow. The shows were cheap to produce, but offered audiences a lot of fun for very little money.

Even though the shows were never really advertised as such, the spook shows were essentially magic performances. They were an offshoot of the séance re-creations that magicians used to explain how tricks were accomplished by mediums. In the spook shows, though, séances occurred but were never explained, letting audiences wonder if what they had seen was real or trickery. The advertising always emphasized the presence of ghosts and, as many shows were held in the grand old vaudeville houses of the early century that had been converted for movies and sound, the atmosphere certainly invited these conclusions.

Each show usually began with a brief lecture on ghosts, followed by a 45-minute demonstration of telepathy, clairvoyance, cold readings, and conjuring tricks that emphasized the mysterious. They featured floating objects, mysterious music, séance cabinets, and more. The highlight of the show, however, was the grand finale, often called the *dark séance.* All the lights in the theater would be extinguished, and soon ghosts and other fearsome creatures would suddenly appear on stage and would fly about over the heads of the audience. After several minutes of wild screams and laughter, the lights would come back on, as the spirits would have vanished. Moments later, the magician would bid the audience good night, and the flickering images of a B horror film would illuminate the theater's screen.

This final part of the evening was probably the most important reason for the success of the spook shows. By performing after hours, the spook show operators had no problem convincing theater managers to open their houses for them. In fact, exhibitors were more than eager to book midnight ghost shows, as it filled their theaters at a time when they would have been otherwise empty. These novel attractions were able to do a week's worth of business in a single night, and a well-planned show could earn the operator several thousand dollars a week, which put many bank accounts back in the black during the Depression years.

Viewing Ghosts at the Movies

Ghosts have been part of movie history since the very beginning. In 1896, groundbreaking French filmmaker George Melies made a short film called *The Haunted Castle*, which excited audiences on Christmas Eve. Films in those days had no storyline and were simply an excuse to thrill a crowd with a new form of entertainment. After the audience saw people, ghosts, a bat, a skeleton, and props appear and disappear on screen, they were convinced that had witnessed the supernatural at work.

In 1900, the inventor of the motion picture camera himself, Thomas Edison, made a film about ghosts called *Uncle Josh in a Spooky Hotel*. It featured a mischievous ghost that appeared and disappeared behind two men.

For the most part, ghosts remained offscreen until the 1930s. When the protagonists of a film visited a haunted house, like in *The Cat and the Canary*, the supernatural was usually explained away as trickery. When the film *Dracula*, directed by Tod Browning, appeared in 1931, audiences were shocked when they discovered that the titular character was an actual vampire — a supernatural being. This film opened the floodgates for the American horror films that followed, many of which were about ghosts and haunted houses.

While not an inclusive list, these are some of the best ghost films that have been made:

>> *The Uninvited* (1944)

>> *The Innocents* (1961)

>> *Carnival of Souls* (1962)

>> *The Haunting* (1963)

>> *The Legend of Hell House* (1973)

>> *The Changeling* (1980)

» *The Shining* (1980)

» *Ghost Story* (1981)

» *Poltergeist* (1982)

» *Lady in White* (1988)

» *Ghost* (1990)

» *The Frighteners* (1996)

» *Stir of Echoes* (1999)

» *The Sixth Sense* (1999)

» *What Lies Beneath* (2000)

» *The Devil's Backbone* (2001)

» *Session 9* (2001)

» *The Others* (2001)

» *Ju-On: The Grudge* (2002)

» *The Ring* (2002)

» *1408* (2007)

» *The Orphanage* (2007)

» *Insidious* (2010)

» *The Awakening* (2011)

» *Woman in Black* (2012)

» *Crimson Peak* (2015)

Some of cinema's most popular ghost films were those based on true stories. One of the first to earn national attention was the adaptation of the bestselling book, *The Amityville Horror.* The book and film told the story of the Lutz family, who moved into a house on Long Island where murders had occurred just one year before. They soon discovered that the house was haunted, fleeing for their lives after only 28 days. While the "truth" behind the Amityville story has become controversial in recent years, the story was wildly popular when the film was released in 1979.

Another film that was based on a true story was *The Conjuring*, which hit theaters in 2013. The film chronicles the story of the Perron family, who moved into a haunted house in the 1970s. The real-life story involved the famed ghost-hunters Ed and Lorraine Warren, who were portrayed on screen by Patrick Wilson and Vera Farmiga. The film was so popular that it has since spawned a number of sequels and spin-offs.

In 1984, audiences made *Ghostbusters* one of the biggest films of the year. The supernatural comedy seems to be an unlikely true story, but it is. In 1972, Harold Ramis was a student at Washington University in St. Louis, Missouri. There was a notoriously haunted location on campus called Whittemore House, and staff members called in a local paranormal investigation team to take a look. Ramis was so impressed with the idea of a group of ghost-hunters that he later turned the idea into a film.

Changing Ghost-Hunting with the Internet

Popular culture in America has always had a great effect on people's interest in the paranormal. Much of that has been because of the technology available at different times in our history. Spiritualism and the print media came into their own during the same era. Public séances were highlighted by the growth of popular culture in the late 19th century. Radio broadcasts, such as *War of the Worlds,* a show that aired on October 30, 1938, spread fear of the unknown.. Hosted by Orson Welles, the reality format of the broadcast caused panic among those who thought it was covering an actual alien invasion. The Internet would change things in ways that no one could imagine.

Much like it was in the early 20th century, the paranormal had fallen under the purview of scientists by the late 1980s. Aside from a few scattered groups and individuals, amateur researchers weren't doing much by that time,. By the early 1990s, though, academic support for the paranormal had waned. The Duke Parapsychology Lab was reshuffled. John F. Kennedy University had stopped offering parapsychology degrees in 1987. But the decline in academic interest came at a time of increased developments in personal technology. In other words, average people could now afford technology that had once been only in the hands of colleges and government offices. Audio, video, and emerging digital photography made documenting all aspects of life — including the parts with spirits, haunted houses, and disembodied voices — easier.

Everything was changed by a household item that increased in popularity during the 1990s — the computer. Before the mid-1990s, only a small percentage of American homes had a computer. Aside from doing paperwork or writing term papers, computers had little use for the majority of people — and then the Internet came along. That previously unknown entity, used only by academics and the military, opened a whole new world for average people.

When the Internet began gaining in popularity, it suddenly made it easy to discover information, share photos and theories with others who were interested in ghosts, and form groups of people who could go out and look for haunted places. As Harry Price had done decades before by opening up the world of ghosts to the average person, the Internet had made it possible for amateurs to get involved in paranormal investigation. (For more on Harry Price, see Chapter 3.)

Compared to today, the Internet seemed impossibly small back then. In the middle 1990s, only a few dozen websites about ghosts were on the World Wide Web. Of course, that quickly changed, and even though most websites were pretty basic in those days, they began to draw a lot of interest. The Internet offered a refuge for ghost enthusiasts who were looking for those who shared their interests. Before the Internet, finding people who shared an enthusiasm for ghosts was much harder. Most people were limited by the size of their community or by finding stories in newspapers and books about great places to investigate. Comparing notes with people on the opposite side of the country was now possible.

A huge surge of interest not only about ghosts and the paranormal, but in cameras, equipment, investigation techniques, and more occurred. For the first time, everyone with an interest in the paranormal had a forum at their disposal where they could talk about anything and might actually have an audience for what they had to say. Technology, this time through the Internet, had transformed the definition of the paranormal community.

Watching How Television Changed It Again

Chronologically speaking, television shows about the paranormal came before the Internet. In 1987, the first version of *Unsolved Mysteries*, hosted by Robert Stack, began sending cold chills up the spines of viewers across America. While technically more about unsolved crimes than the paranormal, it did feature many stories about hauntings and psychic experiences.

In the 19702, *In Search Of . . .* was television's first program to deal with true stories of the paranormal. From 1992 to 1997, the syndicated series *Sightings*, a paranormal documentary-style show, became the first program since *In Search Of. . . .* to deal strictly with the unexplained, ghosts, hauntings, and more. While other similar shows would follow, *Sightings* was really the first to change the way that Americans looked at the paranormal on television.

But what really sparked the resurgence in paranormal interest at the time was a Fox program called *The X-Files*. It wasn't because the show focused on ghosts — that was a rare thing in the series — but because it tapped into the paranormal psyche of America. It also highlighted an interest in aliens, conspiracies, and rising distrust in large government. *The X-Files* created a ready-made audience for paranormal reality TV. When the show ended in 2002, reality TV as its own genre was about to redefine television.

In 1989, the show *COPS* — which follows the men and women of law enforcement, as the opening voiceover went — premiered on Fox. It was the first actual reality show and remains the longest-running show of that type in history. *COPS* was a direct result of the 1988 Writer's Guild of America strike, which lasted for 22 weeks. Networks scrambled to come up with alternative programming that didn't need writers. The economic benefits and convenience of reality-type TV were first considered during this prolonged strike, although it was almost a decade before the genre was fully in place. The strike, as well as advances with home computers and video editing systems, made reality TV possible. Handheld cameras further solidified the possibility, and by the late 1990s, the public was familiar with grainy and jerky footage from camcorders since just about every home in America had one.

Paranormal reality shows came along about a decade after the premiere of *COPS*, and by 2000, the resurgence in interest in the paranormal that the Internet and the production of shows like *Sightings, Strange Universe, Haunted History*, and others spawned finally brought about the first wave of paranormal reality shows. The very first show in America came from an unlikely source — MTV.

In 1992, MTV introduced a groundbreaking endeavor in reality television called *The Real World*, a show about "seven strangers, picked to live in a house, to find out what happens when people stop being polite and start getting real." The concept provided a first-hand look at people's lives, albeit, from the safe distance on the other side of the TV screen, and, most important, it claimed to be real. These same elements make paranormal shows so appealing. Other reality-type shows in the past, going back as far as the classic *Candid Camera*, had existed, but *The Real World* started the kind of reality television that we know today — with a story, plot, and characters.

Eight years later, MTV, seeing the popularity of the paranormal in the country, decided to launch a reality show of a different kind on the network called *Fear*. It was a game show of sorts, and while it only lasted two years, paranormal reality TV would not be what it is today without it. The initial concept of the show was different than what made it on air, and the show eventually changed to be less about hunting ghosts and more about scaring people.

The idea behind *Fear* was to send a series of contestants into reputedly haunted locations alone. The contestant who managed to make it through the night won the game. Each contestant was given a series of tasks that initially involved ghost-hunting, but eventually turned into just scary challenges to make people cry. However, *Fear* did introduce significant innovations for the genre. For the first time, contestants filmed themselves and, perhaps most importantly, did so using night vision cameras with their grainy, green look as a video technique. Before long, the murky greenish-gray image would be a staple for reality TV. The show started a trend in reality TV, but it was canceled after two seasons. It was popular but very expensive to produce.

Other shows followed, all tapping into the paranormal, but not quite bringing the audience into the mix the way that reality shows would soon do. Fox Network began offering *Scariest Places on Earth* and *Real Scary Stories* for kids. Each was a scripted show, hosted by Linda Blair from *The Exorcist* with voiceovers from *Poltergeist* actress Zelda Rubinstein that sometimes dabbled in investigations.

In England, in 2002, a new show was launched called *Most Haunted*. It was popular in Britain, as well as in America after it started airing on the Travel Channel. The show featured a group of paranormal enthusiasts, such as actresses, psychics, and university-trained parapsychologists, as they traveled around the country in search of ghosts. Ridiculed by many for its unbelievable theatrics and lack of any solid evidence, *Most Haunted* was still something new in the world of reality television. It got the attention of American production companies, who started looking for a way to develop paranormal programming in the United States. A scramble began to find paranormal investigators to participate in televised ghost-hunts.

In 2004, the SyFy Channel began airing episodes of a new show called *Ghost-hunters,* featuring two average guys, Jason Hawes and Grant Wilson, who searched for evidence of ghosts. Unlike *Most Haunted*, the investigators on *Ghost-hunters* carried out actual investigations, without the theatrics of the other show. In many cases, especially in the early seasons of the show, they were apt to explain to property owners why their location was not haunted. Ghosts weren't everywhere, not on this show at least. The show ran for 11 seasons, finally coming to an end in 2016. During the height of its popularity, Grant Wilson left and came back, featured a number of established investigators as guests, and spun off several other short-lived series, like *Ghost-hunters International* and *Ghost-hunter's Academy*.

GHOST ADVENTURES

In early 2004, before the first episode of *Ghost Hunters* aired, I began filming the original documentary of *Ghost Adventures.* My desire to start investigating the paranormal began several years earlier when I saw my first full-bodied apparition in Michigan. I turned my attentions to film production and made an independent film that documented my investigation of alleged paranormal activity in and around Virginia City, Tonopah, and Goldfield, Nevada. The film aired on SyFy in 2007 and enjoyed tremendous ratings. Knowing that I was on to something original, I pitched the idea of a *Ghost Adventures* series to a production company and made a deal right off the bat to bring the show to the Travel Channel. A year later, the series began (see figure).

©Travel Channel.

The show was an immediate success. The idea of the lockdown investigation was some-thing unique to paranormal reality television. In each episode, we were literally locked into a building, with no escape, saturated in the spiritual energy of the location, for bet-ter or worse. In addition, we never failed to let the cameras see our natural reactions and personalities, no matter how frightened we became. This raw emotion touched a nerve with audiences, who wanted to see paranormal investigators on television as gen-uine people, not actors who had to pretend to be scared. Viewers loved the show, and they still do. All these years later, we have never taken a break, never been off the air, and still film for months at a time. The appeal of the show has never worn off, thanks to our amazing fans and loyal viewers, our ratings have remained strong. We recently celebrated our highest, record-breaking season so far.

One of the really great things about doing the show has been the fans. We meet people all the time who say they have been watching since the beginning or have made the night a new show airs into a family watch party. Those same fans have watched us grow and evolve over the years. They saw us start out as novice investigators and have watched how our experiences have changed us. They have seen the disturbing and demonic investigations and watched as things turned out bad for us. Those are the moments that have sculpted us into who we are today as investigators. As people, though, we're still the same as we always were. I think our audiences know that, and they know we are just as passionate about what we do as when we started.

I love what I do. I feel that it's fate that I'm doing this show. I feel that the spirits that have been around me since I was young have put me on this path. It's not a coincidence. Other television shows out there have been on as long as we have, but you can often see that they're losing their passion and enthusiasm for what they are doing. *Ghost Adventures* is the reverse of that. We are only getting more enthusiastic. We've been overexposed to the spirits at all the locations we have visited. They have created such a sensitive attuning in us that we are now so hypersensitive to the spirits — and the spirits know that. So, not only are we a television show, but we're also a massive experiment for paranormal research, seeing what happens when you take the same few guys and expose them to more than 1,000 investigations at some of the most intensely haunted locations on the planet. This is what we've become and who we've become.

There is no end in sight for *Ghost Adventures,* so our grand experiment will continue for many years to come.

Chapter **6**

Preparing to Look for Ghosts

Whether you're a true believer in the paranormal or a skeptic looking for proof, ghost-hunting can be an amazing experience that blends the spiritual with the scientific. If you've ever wanted to have a first-hand encounter with the supernatural or have ever wondered if the spirit continues on after death, then you're on the right track by reading this book.

But before you being ghost-hunting, it's important that you not only have the right mindset, but that you're aware of a few important factors before you begin.

Getting in the Right Frame of Mind

It has often been said that the most important tool in a paranormal investigation is the ghost-hunter himself or herself. It's imperative that we use our mind, our judgment, common sense, and powers of observation to the utmost of our ability. No cameras or fancy gadgets can replace a good investigator.

The subject of ghosts and paranormal phenomena has fascinated people since the dawn of history, and interest continues to grow at a rapid pace. Perhaps this growth is because ghost-hunting is one of the few subjects left where an amateur can make a real and valuable contribution to a subject that may have a tremendous long-term impact.

Ghost-hunting can be exciting, and it can also be physically exhausting and mentally challenging. Most of the time, the main requirement to be a ghost-hunter is having a lot of patience, because nothing is happening. But when things do, it can be extremely rewarding — and may not be for the faint of heart.

REMEMBER

Today's ghost-hunters have a lot of different resources (like this book) that offer the tricks of the trade, including what to do and how to stay safe. Just as important, they have the information they need to ensure a professional investigation. Investigation of the paranormal should always be taken seriously, with respect and an abundance of caution.

Ghost-hunting with an Open Mind

To become an effective ghost-hunter, you need a few important qualities, such as objectivity, patience, strength of character, and honesty. Perhaps the two most important qualities are an open mind and a healthy skepticism.

Skepticism doesn't mean that you don't believe in the possibility of the paranormal, however. The actual definition of a skeptic is a person who keeps an open mind to all possibilities. Unfortunately, the true definition of the word has been corrupted over the years to mean someone who is close-minded to everything, or a debunker.

Healthy skepticism plays an important part in science and stimulates research and critical thinking. By contrast, debunkers are committed to the belief that paranormal events are impossible, or at least so improbable that they should merit no serious attention.

Maintaining a healthy balance

The important thing is to maintain a healthy balance. Balance is often described as being "optimistically skeptical." You can believe in ghosts but not believe that every ghost story has something to do with ghosts. You can believe that houses become haunted but still want to rule out every natural cause for a haunting before deciding that a ghost is causing the activity. There is no shame in believing through evidence. Evidence of ghosts and spirits is what paranormal researchers should be looking for. Regardless of how differently each of us may go about the search, we all want the same thing. We all want to obtain the most authentic evidence of the spirit world that it is possible to find.

Critics and debunkers don't believe that most ghost-hunters are credible. They label us as fantasy-prone personalities, a designation used to describe an otherwise normal person's propensity to make things up. They claim that we use scientific equipment incorrectly to bolster our claims of paranormal activity. Even though most paranormal investigators work hard to be professional and reliable, honor our commitments to client confidentiality, and use the scientific methods for our investigations, it's never enough for the critics.

Fitting into the scientific framework — or not

For generations, science has been used as a framework to understand the world and the things that take place in it. One of the main theories in science is that events can be tested by anyone at any time. In other words, if a scientist makes a claim that he can improve the taste of your food by adding certain chemicals to it, you do not have to take his word for it. You are more than welcome to do your own research on the subject, try the food with and without the chemicals and even get another scientist to do tests that either prove or disprove the claims.

Can hauntings and paranormal phenomena fit perfectly into the scientific framework? Not exactly. Paranormal activity is described as *anomalous* because it completely contradicts all the standard and existing scientific theories. For this reason, mainstream science tends to ignore any observations, ideas, or events that even hint at the supernatural. This viewpoint is something that the debunkers use to try and negate any paranormal research that emerges.

This narrow viewpoint of mainstream science has become so ingrained in our society that most people automatically doubt anything unusual they might hear. For example, when someone sees a ghost, most people will quickly question their observations and perhaps even their sanity. It doesn't help matters that ghost sightings infrequently happen and, because they are so unexpected, are hardly ever captured on film or experienced by a large number of people. This is the reason that dismissing such reports is so easy.

Hauntings are scoffed at by the critics, but they're unable to explain the fact that there exists a consistent record of ghost sightings and related events that date back for centuries. Ordinary people have reported the presence of ghosts from early times up to the modern day. Could they have all been mistaken, lying, or insane? That hardly seems likely, and if you have no other reason to maintain an open mind when it comes to ghosts and hauntings, that alone should suffice.

Achieving a balance

A balance must be struck by the ghost-hunter between the hard-edged world of science and the outright acceptance of the true believer. In many cases, a natural explanation can be found for the strange happenings that are reported, but once again, can all those who encounter ghosts be mistaken? Science will say yes, but we can't afford to accept the trappings of mainstream science as total and absolute fact. The theories of the past are constantly changing and being adapted and updated to fit new information. There is no way to know what science may accept as fact in the future.

Just because critics and debunkers choose to treat the paranormal with scorn is no reason why it should not be studied. In fact, science's lack of interest in the subject is just the reason why fascinated amateurs need to fill the gap. If even a single paranormal anomaly is proven to exist, then the scientific theories in use now will no longer fit. They will have to be changed completely because they would cause what scientists called a paradigm shift.

If such breakthroughs ever come, it will be because of balance, common-sense investigations. In far too many cases, ghost-hunters go into their investigations as true believers, convinced that a location is haunted just because a witness claims that it is. They accept that the events reported are genuine and attempt to prove that this view is correct. Common sense tells us that this approach is not the right one. In truth, it is just as wrong as the approach taken by debunkers at the other end of the scale.

Debunkers always see reports of strange phenomena as a misinterpretation of naturally occurring events. They're not looking for any kind of evidence except that which shows the paranormal can't exist. They often express themselves by saying that "extraordinary claims demand extraordinary proof," and while most of us don't disagree with this statement, such investigators are determined to ignore any evidence that they may find that is contrary to their personal beliefs.

These methods are completely at odds with one another but are also strikingly similar. Both methods presuppose something about the nature of the phenomenon they're trying to explain. Real science doesn't work this way, nor is it the way to conduct a proper investigation into anything, including (as a detective could tell you) a criminal act or, in our case, an allegedly haunted house.

Throughout the rest of this book, we urge you to keep an open mind. If we can ever hope to explain paranormal events, we must research them without prejudice going in. A good investigator must follow the facts where they lead, find out what phenomena are present to study, and then study it with the best methods available to him. Obviously, we can assume as we enter an investigation that the events reported may not be paranormal, but we can't assume that they must not be. We must eliminate the mundane first, before reaching any conclusions about whether the events are paranormal or not. Only after the normal explanations have been eliminated should we proceed along supernatural lines.

Things to Know Before You Begin

Before deciding to enter the field of paranormal research, you have many things you should think about, including the skills you need to document and prove your efforts.

The following sections walk you through some things you may not have through of when you first became interested in ghosts.

Gathering information

The first stage of any investigation is to gather all the facts. You should interview witnesses, examine the site, and exhaust all the possibilities. This is the first, and perhaps most important, step, and unfortunately, this step has led to the often disappointing conclusion of what seemed to be a promising case. Incidents that first seemed to be linked to a haunting are often explained away by a presentation of possible solutions. Only if the case survives this first step is it worth pursuing any further. If it does and the haunting involves what may be recurrent phenomena, then it's time to monitor the area and possibly have a chance to observe the happenings for yourself. (For more on monitoring the area, see Chapter 13.)

TIP

Being a ghost-hunter can be a lot like being a detective. As an investigator, you must learn to use your observational skills. Even if you've mastered the skills of field work and equipment, you still have to develop the skills you need to observe your surroundings with a critical eye. To do so, you must access the location objectively and let go of any preconceived notions you have about the site or situation. Always consider the facts and then make your own observations and judgments.

Keeping accurate records

You always need to take good notes to keep track of the events during your investigations, even if someone else is simultaneously filming the investigation. Notes can be a valuable way or recording important information because a camera can't catch every angle at once, nor can it show what you may have experienced personally, like a touch, cold spot, or impression.

Follow these pointers when recording your experience:

>> Make note of anything you think is significant and record any possible ordinary explanations.

>> Later, eliminate all events and discrepancies that seem to be suspect and the ones for which natural explanations exist (see the next section).

>> List the remaining items separately, in order of significance, so that your list makes logical sense.

>> Don't discard the less significant items. Instead, move them to the bottom of the lost and make note of them as the investigation proceeds. It's possible that they may move up the list if they're repeated.

For an example of what accurate records look like, see Chapter 15.

Analyzing your evidence

Seek meaningful probabilities from the facts that you have gathered so that you can eliminate the guesswork from your conclusions. Dispassionately reviewing the evidence from your personal experiences allows you to add them to your audio recordings, equipment readings, and video recordings to make a balanced assessment. For details, see Chapter 15.

Affording the research

Most ghost-hunters do not go into the field without thinking about how much it will cost them financially. Ghost-hunting is not usually a job that you can make a living at. Although paranormal investigating can be rewarding on a personal level, it is not a particularly lucrative field. Most people who go into it do so primarily for the unselfish reason of helping other people. While most investigators never charge for their services, many teach classes, write books, work as media consultants, and make money from peripheral aspects of the paranormal. Others accept donations or asked to be reimbursed by their clients for hotel costs and travel expenses.

Opinions differ widely, and there is frequent debate about the ethics of charging for investigations or allowing clients to reimburse for expenses. Some won't charge a client under any circumstances, while others accept payment only from organizations and never from individuals.

The other costly aspect of paranormal investigation is the equipment involved. If you want to build your own ghost-hunting toolbox, acquire equipment as your budget allows. Many different kinds of equipment, in many different price ranges, are available for use in the field. Spending a small fortune on equipment that you may not even use is far too easy, so be sure to keep your investment to a minimum until you're sure that your interest in the paranormal will continue. (For more on the equipment you need, see Chapter 9.)

Even then, owning the most expensive equipment that is available isn't essential to a reliable investigation. Investigators have shown significant results using very inexpensive gear, so be sure not to let the cost of equipment discourage you. It can't be stressed enough that the most important tool in an investigation is yourself.

2

Investigating Ghosts and Hauntings

Chapter **7**

Researching the Spirit World

What causes a place to become haunted? No one really knows. In fact, there are so many types of hauntings from human ghosts to animal ghosts and even ghost ships that no one has ever been able to come up with a general theory that can explain all of them. Any single theory would have to cover an immense variety of phenomena, and it just can't be done. Such a theory would have to explain why apparitions are seen in one location, but not in others. It would have to provide a solution for phantom footsteps, cold spots, strange smells, and much more. Developing such a theory is no easy matter, especially as few researchers can really agree about what underlying force causes a haunting in the first place.

But, of course, the lack of a single, all-encompassing theory is no reason to give up on a search for answers. No one has all the answers, but everyone seems to have an opinion. There are many reasons for hauntings and many kinds of paranormal activity that have been linked to ghosts. Are they all the work of spirits? Your own investigations will have to answer that question to your satisfaction. In this chapter, I present the many different theories and evidence, and you can use the information in conjunction with your own research.

What Are Hauntings?

According to the definition, a *haunting* is the repeated manifestation of strange and inexplicable sensory phenomena at a certain location. This does not mean that a haunting is always associated with a ghost but, for now, assume that hauntings are connected to paranormal activity.

There are no general patterns to hauntings, which is what makes them so hard to define. Some phenomena may manifest on occasion, or even continually, for periods that last from several days to centuries. Other manifestations may only occur on certain anniversaries, in accordance with distinctive weather conditions or for reasons that make no sense whatsoever.

The public assumes that hauntings always involve apparitions, or the ghosts of the dead, but *apparitions* (a visual manifestation of a haunting) are connected to a minority of cases. Most hauntings involve noises like phantom footsteps, unexplained sounds, tapping, knocking, and even voices and whispers. They can also include strange smells, sensations like the prickling of skin, cold spots and breezes, and being touched by unseen hands. Other hauntings can involve poltergeist activity, such as furniture and objects being moved about, broken glass, doors that open and close by themselves, and the manipulation of lights and electrical devices, circuits, and outlets (see Figure 7-1).

FIGURE 7-1: Poltergeist activity.

Mary Evans Collection, Diomedia.com

Visitors to haunted places often report a variety of emotions, including anger and fear when negative forces are at work. Other sites seem to involve friendly, or at least benign, emotions.

While attempts have been made categorize certain types of hauntings, many locations manage to defy this labeling and manifest a variety or a combination of different types. It has also been shown that some locations seem to act as a catalyst for activity, sometimes causing visitors to manifest their own unconscious phenomena. This can often give rise to accounts that don't fit into any category at all.

Traditional Hauntings

The *traditional, or intelligent, haunting* is perhaps the most widely accepted kind of ghostly activity, although it is not as common as many might think. In this kind of case, the spirit or entity involved is an intelligent or interactive presence in a haunted location. It is there because of a connection to the site or to the people at the location.

This ghost is most simply described as the personality, or consciousness, of a person who once lived and has stayed behind in our world instead of passing on at the time of death. This may happen in the case of murder, a traumatic event, a suicide, or even because of some unfinished business in the person's life. At the time of death, the spirit refused to move on because of these events. The spirits may also linger because of emotions that tie them to the Earth, from anger to love. In other cases, there is the chance that the spirit didn't even realize they had died. This may occur when a death is sudden or unexpected, like with an accident or a murder.

These spirits now consist of the energy that once made up the personality of a living person. Now that the human body is gone, that energy is all that remains. These interactive spirits can be benign or very negative. This might be explained by the fact that they are the personalities of people who were angry or bitter in life. This often explains the types of activity (or behavior) being exhibited at the haunted location. The spirits are simply human personalities and seem to retain the same traits they had when alive. If a person was kind and caring in life, the spirit will be a benevolent one. On the other hand, if that person was angry or cruel, those qualities are likely to manifest.

These negative spirits can be frightening and, in rare cases, can actually harm the living. This is generally not the case, though, and most injuries related to haunted houses occur because of physical objects that are moved or when someone injures himself in an accident because of their fear of the phenomena.

In the case of the intelligent entity, the variety of phenomena can include knocking and tapping sounds, noises with no logical cause, disturbance of stationary objects, doors slamming, lights turning on and off, and much more. The ghost tends to manifest itself in physical ways, including cold chills and smells. It usually seems to want to bring attention to itself, and such cases can literally drag on for years at a time.

As an investigator, you can deal with this kind of haunting in several ways. Because some of these spirits have remained behind because of some sort of incomplete business, it is a hard obstacle to overcome. The spirits may have remained in this world because they have relatives or loved ones that have been left behind. Or they may have left unfinished tasks that they feel cannot be completed by anyone else. They may not rest because of some injustice that was done to them or perhaps because of something as simple as wanting to be around to see their children grow up.

It is worth noting is that the annoyance factor in a case like this will be high. It is likely that the spirit will attempt to get the attention of the living occupants of the location. These spirits can be known for hiding objects, moving things about, turning things on and off, and other nuisances that can be compared to a child seeking attention. It is possible that the spirit may by looking for assistance to cross over or to accomplish a certain task. It has also been documented that the spirit may just be seeking the company of the residents or even the investigators in the case.

For the most part, the idea of these spirits remaining behind in this world is rather sad, if not tragic. In all our excitement over finding a ghost, we also must keep in mind that many spirits are confused over what has happened to them and may not even realize they are dead. Many of them may have died suddenly. Others may try to cling to life, afraid of letting go of the tangible, material world. Because of this, they are drawn back to places where they experienced joy, peace, and happiness in life. Many of these spirits may just feel too alive to want to pass on to the other side.

These ghosts sometimes need help to be convinced that they do not belong here anymore. They can be shown the right way and introduced to the idea that there is more for them in the next world than there remains for them in this one. There are many ways to approach this and, surprisingly, a number of people who are skilled in such matters. They accomplish their tasks in different ways, ranging from simple explanations to perhaps a prayer offered by a clergyman of the spirit's faith.

SIGNS OF A TRADITIONAL HAUNTING

Most intelligent spirits will manifest in physical ways to try to interact with those at the location:

- Slamming doors

- Windows that open and close

- Cold chills and a strong presence

On rare occasions, the spirit will be seen, and when it is, it will most likely look as it did when alive.

While this sounds a lot like spiritualism, it isn't. In such cases, we can historically verify the existence of the ghosts by connecting their current manifestations, and the rare instances when they are actually seen, to the time when they were among the living. We can take the witness accounts of the ghost and compare them to contemporary photographs or descriptions of the person the ghost is alleged to be. This is where history can literally make the case for us and connect a haunting to a person from the past.

Residual Hauntings

The *residual haunting* is likely the most common type of haunting. Such hauntings are more prevalent than most realize, and a large percentage of paranormal activity falls into this category. When investigating haunted places, be careful not to confuse this type of activity with an intelligent haunting (see preceding section). It is possible that residual hauntings have little to do with what we think of as ghosts.

The simplest way to explain this kind of activity is to compare it to an old film loop or a recording. It can be a scene or image that plays over and over through the years. Many of the locations where these hauntings take place experience an event (or a series of events) that imprints itself on the atmosphere of the place. This event can suddenly discharge and play itself at various times, just as a recording would. The events are not always visual either. They are often replayed as smells, sounds, and noises that have no apparent explanation. The famed phantom footsteps that are reported at many haunted locations are a perfect example of this.

Often, the mysterious sounds or images that are recorded relate to traumatic events that have taken place and that have caused some sort of disturbance (or impression) to occur there. This is the reason why so many battlefields, crime scenes, and areas related to violence have become famous for their hauntings.

A residual haunting may not be caused by trauma or violence, though. Sometimes, the image or sound might be created by an event that has been repeated over and over again. These frequent and repetitive releases of energy also seem to be capable of leaving a lasting impression. A good example of this can be realized from the large number of haunted staircases that have been reported over the years in homes and public buildings. It's possible that because of the number of times that people go up and down these sets of stairs the energy expended leaves a mark on the site.

These locations act like giant storage batteries, saving up impressions of sights and sounds from the past. Then, as the years go by, these impressions appear again as if a film projector has started to run. No one seems to know how this might work, but there are many theories.

Some theories have connected atmospheric conditions to residual hauntings. It has been suggested that perhaps barometric pressure, or even temperature, may have something to do with hauntings becoming repeatedly active. Some have noticed an increase in paranormal activity in the winter months, when more static electricity is in the air. It might also have something to do with the phases of the moon. Since the full moon has been known to affect the ocean tides, it is possible that it affects hauntings, too.

For years, investigators have referred to the *stone tape theory* as a possible cause for residual hauntings. This idea suggested that the building materials of various structures could absorb the energy and then replay it again later. Researchers noted that most buildings where residual hauntings occurred were older structures. Of course, this could also be explained by the age of the building. The number of people that passed through an old structure over time, and the tapestry of history played out in it, seemed a more convincing reason for the haunting to occur.

One of the most promising theories behind residual hauntings involves water. Thousands of haunted places are associated with water. Many of them are on rivers or lakes or have an underground water source nearby. Since water is a great conductor of electricity, perhaps it can be a conductor of paranormal energy as well.

This brings us back to the stone tape theory. The main problem with it is that no one has ever found a satisfactory explanation as to how the haunting that is "recorded" on a location occurs, or how the solid fabric of the location was able to retain the energy of the events that took place. A possible answer to this question was discovered by science many years ago and has only recently been introduced into the paranormal field.

For well over two centuries, people have been using homeopathic remedies and medicines to a great degree of success. With these medicines, a natural therapeutic agent is given to a person with an illness, but this agent is often so toxic that in order for the person not to be harmed by it, it has to be diluted with water. In fact, the original substance is often diluted to the point that all traces of the agent are effectively removed. The person is given nothing more than ordinary water. It seems impossible that anyone could be cured of an illness using nothing but water, but it happens. The sick become well using homeopathic remedies, which is why they have been used for so long. Scientists ignored this for years, but people continued to use the remedies, not caring how or why they work.

Homeopathic medicines remained a mystery until the 1980s, when a respected French scientist named Jacques Benveniste, an expert in the field of allergies, made a strange discovery. In his research, he was studying a type of blood cell involved in allergic reactions called the basophile. When basophiles encounter something that a person is sensitive to, they activate, causing symptoms like red blotches and itching. Benveniste developed a test that could tell whether a person was allergic to something. He added a kind of dye that turned only inactive basophiles blue. In this way, by counting the blue cells, he could determine whether an allergic reaction had taken place. But then something very strange occurred with his experiments.

A technician reported that something had apparently gone wrong. A solution had been diluted so strongly that it was at the level of a homeopathic medicine. In other words, it was now just ordinary water. Even so, a reaction had been observed in the basophiles. They reacted exactly as they would have if placed in the presence of the allergen. Suspecting that an error had been made, the experiment was repeated, but once again, the basophiles reacted.

Baffled by what seemed to be impossible results, the team carried out hundreds of experiments, but the results remained the same. The water, diluted to the point that all trace of the original substance was removed, continued to react as if the substance was still present. Dr. Benveniste could come to only one conclusion: The water had a memory.

The experiment was repeated over and over again and since that time has been carried out by scientists all over the world. Although it remains controversial, most scientists will admit that water molecules do seem to retain a memory of substances that they have been in contact with. This seems to lend credibility to homeopathic remedies and, by extension, to residual hauntings.

Water is a component of almost everything. You wouldn't know it, but an average brick wall, as one example, is made up of nearly 15 percent water. The human body is, of course, largely made up of water, as is the ground under our feet. It's not hard to imagine that the water that exists within everyday objects could have a memory of events placed into its molecules.

It would work in the same way that we have always theorized that events imprint themselves on locations and become residual hauntings. In the case of a homeopathic remedy, it's necessary for the water to be strongly agitated during the dilution stage, the same stage where the memories are imprinted. When the water is stirred vigorously, a large amount of kinetic energy is being released into the water. The water also develops a slight electromagnetic charge by this motion, and it could be this charge that implants the memory.

To take it one step further, we can look at the experiments performed by Dr. Masaru Emoto in the 1990s, during which he observed the physical effect of prayers, music, and environment on the crystalline structure of water. He hired photographers to take pictures of water after being exposed to different emotions. When he screamed or yelled angrily at the water, it froze into harsh, jagged crystals. But when he spoke loving to it, played music, or read peaceful poetry, the water formed beautiful, tranquil crystals.

Compare the event of agitating the water with a violent, traumatic, or even repetitive event that occurs and serves to agitate the physical location. It's possible that this event could leave a memory imprint on the water at this location, just as the chemical compounds and the stirring motions leave an imprint on the water of the homeopathic medicine.

We can even take this idea one step further by examining other ghostly activity that has been associated with residual hauntings. Many investigators have discovered through their own research that residual hauntings often seen to fade away over the years, as if the battery that charges them just seems to wear out. If these hauntings are caused due to some sort of water memory, then perhaps the shelf life of the haunting expires as the water begins to evaporate. As the original molecules dry up, the copy of the memory that they hold becomes weaker and weaker. The original molecules may have passed their imprinted memory to neighboring molecules, but with each successive copy, the memory becomes less distinct. This would be similar to making photocopies of a document; each generation of the copy becoming less clear and more damaged that the one that proceeded it. In time, it's possible that the memory would just disappear altogether.

It's also been noted that residual hauntings often seem to become more active following disturbances caused by renovations or remodeling. Again, a water recording may offer an explanation for this. Inside of some structures, water may be locked in and prevented from evaporating, like inside a wall or in the foundation. Disturbing that may cause the water that has been stored for decades to be released and in this way, allow its memory to be played. This stored water could hold a higher quality copy of the original event, and this new ghost (which, in truth, would be an old one) might make it seem that the location is active again. Once this water also evaporates, the haunting then fades away once more.

This certainly seems to give a lot of credence to the idea of residual hauntings and may open an entirely new series of experiments to bolster the credibility of paranormal phenomena. Many of these experiments can be carried out with relatively simple research on the part of the field investigator, making serious observations and measurements of the amount of water present within haunted locations. A basic hygrometer can keep an eye on humidity levels, and meters can be used to measure the amounts of water within the structure of a building. Over time, we may be able to build a database of water and humidity levels at haunted locations and compare them with levels measured at nonhaunted sites. Doing this, we should be able to establish real evidence of residual hauntings.

The question remains, though: When we have ghostly figures, strange sounds and smells, how can we tell the difference between a traditional and a residual haunting? In some cases, the two very different types of activity can manifest in similar ways. However, the most important signs will be different.

SIGNS OF A RESIDUAL HAUNTING

The following signs indicate a residual haunting:

- Apparitions reported will be like moving pictures and will typically be seen in the same spots, walking down the same hallway, appearing in the same window, doing the same motion over and over. They will be unaware of the living people around them. Such cases do not have any interaction between the ghost and the witnesses.

- Strange sounds, such as footsteps, voices, knocking, and rappings, are common.

- There may be high levels of humidity at the location, as this seems to be a possible sign that a residual haunting is taking place. It's been suggested that water embedded in the location may hold a sort of recording of the haunting that is taking place.

Remember: Residual hauntings will not involve missing or vanished items, as there is no consciousness present. While windows or doors may be opened and closed, it is because of energy expending itself, not because it is physically being manipulated by spirits.

It boils down to the interaction between the haunting and the witnesses. Apparitions that are seen during a residual haunting, which are mere images, will not interact with the witnesses at the location. The apparition will be little more than a moving picture, or it may appear to be completely solid, but will vanish when approached or confronted. It is possible that the images and activity may be atmospheric in nature. The haunting may be influenced by storms, temperature, artificial energy sources, or even the proximity of living persons. These factors may determine when activity occurs, and it is important that a log of activity is kept. In this way, a pattern can be developed as to when activity occurs, and the researcher has a much better chance of experiencing it.

Poltergeist-Like Activity

In years past, poltergeists (a German word for "noisy ghosts") were commonly blamed for violent and destructive activity during a haunting. Researchers believed this activity was caused by the spirits or an outside force, but today, most investigators don't think this is the case. While intelligent and interactive spirits may be involved in some cases, many hauntings have a force behind them that, while paranormal, has nothing to do with ghosts.

During a poltergeist outbreak, a variety of phenomena can occur. There are reports of knocking and tapping noises, sounds with no visible cause, disturbance of stationary objects like household items and furniture, doors slamming, lights turning on and off, fires breaking out, and much, much more. They can leave a family plagued by such activity frightened and confused, and most initially call the police for help before they ever consider the services of a paranormal investigator.

SIGNS OF A PK HAUNTING (HUMAN AGENT POLTERGEIST)

In a PK haunting, the movement of physical objects can be sudden and violent and occur more frequently than in cases involving actual, interactive spirits. Reports will often escalate as time goes by but will peak early and then fade away.

Keep an eye out for a young female or an adolescent to be present in the house. Usually the activity will be centered around this person in particular. This person can be isolated or removed from the house to rule out connected activity.

Always try to rule out human involvement (including fraud) before assuming that the phenomenon has anything to do with ghosts.

The most common theory behind this poltergeist-like activity is that it is caused by a person in the household, classified as the *human agent.* The agent is usually an adolescent girl and normally one that is troubled emotionally. It is believed that she unconsciously manipulates physical objects in the house by *psychokinesis* (PK), the power to move things by energy generated in the brain. This kinetic type of energy remains unexplained, but even some mainstream scientists are starting to explore the idea that it does exist.

It is unknown why this energy seems to appear in females around the age of puberty, but documentation of its existence is starting to appear as more and more case studies have become public. It seems that when the activity begins to manifest, the girl is usually in the midst of some emotional or sexual turmoil. The presence of the energy is almost always an unconscious one, and it is rare when any of the agents realize that they are the source of the destruction around them. Unaware they are the source, most believe that a ghost or some other supernatural entity is to blame. The bursts of energy come and go, and most poltergeist-like cases will peak early and then slowly fade away.

It should be noted that while most cases like this manifest around young women, it is possible for puberty-age boys (and even older adults) to show this same unknowing ability. As with the young women, the vast majority will have no idea that they are causing the activity and will be surprised to find there is even a possibility that strange things are happening because of them.

Cases like this offer an excellent chance for the researcher to document strange activity. Unfortunately, though, the case will have nothing to do with ghosts, and there is really no way to help the home owners. The family is usually more in need of a good counselor or mental health provider than a paranormal investigator. Luckily for the home owners, poltergeist cases of this nature usually come and go very quickly.

Portal Hauntings

Portals — or, as some call them, thin spots" — are the most controversial types of hauntings in the paranormal field. It is the least understood and least traditional type of hauntings, and few investigators can agree about what they are and why they exist.

The idea of a portal, possibly to another dimension, is not a new one. It has been suggested that there exist places all over the world that serve as doorways from our world to another. These doorways may provide access for entities to come into our world. They may be the spirits of people who have lived before, or they may be something else altogether. Some researchers even believe that they could be otherworldly beings from some dimension that we cannot even comprehend.

As bizarre as this sounds, it may not be as strange as it seems. The entities that have been sighted, reported, and even photographed around what many believe to be portals could be much stranger than ghosts. If locations like this do exist, and they are some sort of doorway, it's possible that these spots may have been labeled as being haunted over the years by people who saw something near them that they couldn't explain.

There are many locations across the world where strange events occur over and over again, without explanation. Some have suggested that these locations may be active because of natural, magnetic lines that run beneath the Earth. These lines are believed to cross the entire Earth, moving both north and south and from east to west. Spots where these lines cross one another are thought to be especially active.

The idea of such lines was suggested by a man named Alfred Watkins in 1925. The idea came to him when he was examining a map of Herefordshire, England, and he noticed an alignment of ancient sites. He gave such alignments the name of *ley*, a Saxon word that meant "a clearing in the woodland." The lines are believed to be alignments of powerful Earth energy that connect sacred sites, such as churches, temples, stone circles, megaliths, burial sites, and other locations of spiritual importance. The true age and purpose of such lines remain a mystery. Watkins suggested that all holy sites and places of antiquity were connected by ley lines and using an old Ordnance Survey, he claimed that the leys were the "old straight tracks" that crossed the landscape of prehistoric Britain and represented sites that were built from the very dawn of human settlement there.

After Watkins's theory was published, fascination with ley lines spread across the world and the idea of such lines remains a subject of speculation and debate to this day. Many contend that the ley lines mark paths of Earth energy, which can often be detected by dowsing and which may have been sensed by early humans. For this reason, they chose to locate their sacred sites along the pathways and especially at points where the lines cross one another. Points where the ley line paths intersect are believed to be prone to anomalies, such as Earth lights, hauntings, and even UFO sightings. It is believed that the energy here is at its greatest, and some might even describe such sites as portals.

These glitch areas may be found anywhere — cemeteries, churches, even under a home or building. In fact, these doorways, and the unknown entities that pass through them, might be the explanation for some of the most frightening encounters reported by witnesses at haunted places. These are cases of very negative spirits and violent entities, terrifying visions, and even strange beings that may have never been human at all.

It is possible that these sites were considered haunted long before anything modern was located there. Some believe that our ancestors, and perhaps the Native Americans who came before them, felt the psychic draw associated draw associated with ley lines and other Earth energies there and decided to protect it in some way by building there. Perhaps they felt there was something sacred or spiritual about the place and, without realizing why, placed a monument or building at the location, making it a protected spot.

Or perhaps the settlers deduced that somewhere was not quite right about the site and believed that their strange feelings about it were evil or demonic. There has been a long tradition in this country about haunted or mysterious places being dubbed with "devil names" as a way of warning people away from something the discoverers did not understand. It's possible that superstitious settlers also felt that many of these portal locations were evil in some way. In some cases, they placed a holy or religious site upon it. This might explain the myriad of haunted churches that exist in this country and might also explain why some people believe that cemeteries are haunted, as well.

But I don't think that portals exist simply because they are located along ley lines. I believe that some of them can be opened up by dark rituals, connected to black magic or something equally as sinister. By performing such a ceremony, I believe they are invited inhuman entities — demons — and negative energies into a location. If the portals do not get closed down properly, they stay open, perhaps for years. Even if the physical structure at the site is torn down and replaced with something else, the haunting will continue.

It can be difficult, but not impossible, to sense a portal at a location that you are investigating. For myself, when I feel a spirit, it feels like it passes through me, like it is transient, but I can document it with whatever equipment that I am using at the time. For example, when I did the "Demon House" investigation with Dr. Barry Taff and, in the basement, we used a Tri-Field meter to try to detect whether there was any kind of anomalous electromagnetic energy — or even a portal — in the house (see Figure 7-2). The police had referred to this as a gateway to Hell where multiple demons had come through. I believe this portal was opened on purpose by someone performing a ritual there, based on the strange objects we found buried beneath the basement floor at that spot. Dr. Taff repeatedly said that he detected a moving energy in the basement that kept moving about the room. This was consistent with the reports from police officers and family members about the entities that moved so quickly about that they could feel them moving in and out of them. I feel that our equipment scientifically backed up the witness accounts.

FIGURE 7-2:
The Demon
House.

Courtesy of Zak Bagans.

I also believe that you can sense portals without equipment, too. As an investigator and an empath, I can go to a location and feel any portal that exists there. It is a strong energy that knocks your equilibrium off. In my experience, encountering a portal has felt like a strong static shock, and I have also felt a strange sensation on the top of my head, like being electrocuted while someone is grabbing my skull. I've felt pure fear and pure panic, based on what sort of entity that was using the doorway, whether positive or negative. I felt the presence of a portal at the ancient site of Stonehenge and at the Hoia Baciu Forest in Romania, where there is a perfect circle in the woods where nothing grows. I believe that was also a portal.

TIP

Sometimes, the way you feel is more accurate than your equipment. Some investigators may see a high reading, or spike, on their detection device and mistakenly assume that it is picking up wiring in the wall. But if there is nothing artificial that could be creating the spike, it could be a portal. The more that you investigate, the more you will begin to train your body and really develop an accurate sense for what you are feeling and experiencing. For me, feeling a spirit and sensing a portal are two very different sensations.

A portal can be activated, and reactivated, sort of like by a combination lock in the environment, when the temperature, humidity, moon phase, and other factors synchronizes in just the right way. In a way, they can be similar to a traditional haunting, in which strong emotions, deaths, and violence can cause paranormal events to occur. In this case, though, they can open a portal and allow entities to come through that have nothing to do with the history of the house. These entities might trap, or hold onto, the spirits connected to the house for some reason and cause the haunting to continue.

SIGNS OF A PORTAL HAUNTING

Many events that seem to fit into the category of a portal haunting occur in locations that a researcher might not first suspect, like a church, cemetery, or outdoor site. Be aware of stories that involve glowing balls of light that are seen with the naked eye, odd creatures, strange shapes, or unexplained images.

With a home or building, these doorways can be harder to ascertain. In this type of haunting, though, the spirits that are present may be more numerous than in a traditional haunting and are unconnected to the history of the building. The site is nothing more than a crossover point, which can be confusing to those doing research, but may offer tremendous possibilities for research.

Research into hauntings and the possibility of nonhuman entities is a subject of great controversy. For centuries, there have been tales of nature spirits and elementals who spring from the Earth. They have never been human but choose to interact and to communicate with us. In more modern times, researchers have theorized that such spirits may be beings that pass between dimensions. They use the portals and doorways to pass back and forth, and such spirits have a reputation for being kind and benign, as well as dangerous and violent.

Theories about portals are still being formulated today and while there is a lot of speculation about what they are and how they work, it is important to keep an open mind about the idea. A lot more study and research needs to be done into this unexplained facet of paranormal research.

Demonic Hauntings

Another controversial type of haunting is one that also involves something more dangerous, and more frightening, than ghosts. *Demons* are widely believed to be supernatural and malevolent entities that exist in many religions around the world, under different names. Some consider them fallen angels, sent to Earth with Lucifer, whose sole purpose became to revolt against God and his followers. In the New Testament, Jesus was said to have driven out many demons.

Others believe that demons are malevolent spirits, non-human creatures that have been present on Earth for as long as man, or even longer. These entities are neither religious nor supernatural, but something connected to history that we do not yet understand. They are dangerous, though, as the numerous accounts of them have made clear.

The annals of the paranormal are filled with stories of demons possessing individuals, but there are also many claims of them infesting homes, just as spirits do during a traditional haunting. No one knows for sure why demons prey on certain families or individuals. It is suggested that their innate hatred of mankind causes them to pick people and places at random. However, certain behaviors do seem to attract them.

Some of the reasons cited for demonic hauntings include dealing with the occult or practicing black magic, devil worship, using a Ouija board, or even purposely summoning a demon. It's also suggested that overwhelming stress, anger, and violence can catch the attention of a demon and perhaps allow it into a person's life. Each of these have one thing in common: They are all things that attract negative energy to a person or place. They serve as an engraved invitation to any harmful entities that are out there, looking to wreak havoc. No matter where a person believes that demons come from, any of these things can be asking for trouble.

Common symptoms

Several common symptoms suggest a demon infestation in a home. The initial goal of these entities it to create chaos and fear through strange happenings. Too often, the work of a demon can be dismissed as pranks or overactive imaginations, but make no mistake, the diabolical just may be at work.

Unexplained noises

Real-life accounts of demonic hauntings claim that the sound of a demon is a harsh growling sound that is unlike that of an animal. It may occur in a specific place, like a basement or closet. It sometimes sounds like a threatening voice, speaking a family member's name. Other sounds might also occur, including banging, stomping, or scratching from inside the walls. One sign of a demonic haunting is the repeated sound of three knocks, which has been interpreted as a mockery of the Holy Trinity.

Frightened animals

It is widely believed that animals, including pets, can see things that people cannot. They seem to be especially tuned in to demonic activity. Stories cite instances of dogs barking at empty air, becoming terrified by something that is unseen by human eyes.

Terrifying dreams

Many victims of demonic hauntings have reported strange and terrible dreams that accompany unexplained activity in their home. The dreams often include entities that hover above the bed, attack the occupants, and appear as glowing red eyes. They are said to be much more disturbing than any ordinary nightmare and always include an inordinate amount of violence.

Manipulation of religious objects

There have been many reports of holy objects being broken, damaged, or disturbed during demonic hauntings. Bibles, rosaries, crucifixes, and other religious objects are regarded by the entities as a threat to their presence at the location.

Offensive odors

One of the most common events to occur during a demonic haunting is an unexplained stench that may fill the house. The terrible putrid smell has been described as both sulphur-like (rotten eggs) or the smell of a decomposing corpse.

Physical and psychological disturbances

Negative entities can act like parasites, latching onto people and draining them of their energy. They can cause all kinds of unexplained symptoms, including emotional swings, accidents, and even scratches or cuts on a person's body. Subjects have also reported feelings of unease, nausea, and mysterious illnesses. It is thought that the goal of this is to wear a person down and make them more susceptible to demonic possession. Many begin to experience health problems, financial issues, and more.

Oppression

This stage of the haunting begins with an increase in demonic manifestations in the house, like screams, heavy breathing, footsteps, hellish moans, inhuman voices, bad smells, and movement of large objects. The victim could start to believe that he or she is insane and have dramatic personality changes and mood swings. People in the oppression stage of the haunting often turn to alcohol, drugs, or other kinds of destructive behavior. This stage can often be mistaken for depression or some form of mental illness. However, the "illness" is coming from the entity in the house. Those affected will often withdraw from family and social situations and may start to entertain thoughts of suicide.

Possession

The presence of a diabolical entity in a home may very well be the precursor to the possession of a person. That may, in fact, be the entire purpose of the haunting. Inhuman spirits have long been believed to try to overpower their victims through physical, mental, and emotional abuse. Everything that had already happen during the haunting was a way to weaken and break down the victim and get inside of their mind.

My approach to demonic hauntings

I have had a lot of experience with demonic hauntings in my career. In fact, some of the most important cases that I have dealt with would definitely be described as demonic. I tend to approach such cases in a unique way, almost as a doctor would examine someone with a suspected terminal illness. I begin by looking for the symptoms, so to speak. Like a doctor, I know these people need help in ridding themselves of this mysterious "disease," which is afflicting them and destroying their lives. Unfortunately, in most cases, they don't have a "specialist" to help them and give them a straight answer.

I deal with this kind of situation in a straightforward way. Before I go in and start giving them information that can alter their lives and finances by telling them to move out of their house, I start comparing what is happening with them to other cases of demonic hauntings. One thing that I have found about these cases is that the entities involved are very secretive. They do not want to be figured out. They do not like the power of religion forced upon them. It seems that as soon as you start trying to decipher their motives and talk about them with the people whose lives they are affecting, they will lash out against you, the investigator, or they will escalate the events of the haunting.

To give an accurate diagnosis of a demonic infestation, oppression, or possession is to link up the symptoms of the case. Malevolence had somehow gotten into these person's lives, and once inside, the demon will wreak havoc. In severe circumstances, the final outcome could be death.

In so many cases, I have seen families literally torn apart by these kinds of hauntings. They desperately need help, and it is always a relief to have someone come in who can accurately diagnose and explain what they are dealing with. Just having someone who can see the signs of what they are dealing with gives them hope that they are not crazy and that they are not imagining the strange things that are occurring to their family. I have had experience with all this. I have had an exorcism performed on me and have battled demonic attachments. By being able to share that with people in the same situation, it helps them realize that they can be free from it, too.

EXORCISMS

In some extreme situations, exorcisms have been necessary with demonic hauntings. An *exorcism* is the religious or spiritual practice of evicting demons or other spiritual entities from a person or an area that is believed to be possessed. An exorcism is not usually the work of an investigator. It is recommended that you contact someone experienced in these matters to help the client or family you're assisting.

It is imperative to go into such a case with knowledge and a game plan. There is always a solution, which can often mean calling in an exorcist that I work with to start battling the demonic entity.

Haunted Objects

There are many accounts from paranormal sources of what some researchers have called *possessed possessions,* items to which ghosts and negative spirits become attached. Older, antique items seem to be especially prone to attachments like this and can include anything from books to mirrors, jewelry, decorative items, clothing, and much more. I became so fascinated with these kinds of items that I opened the Haunted Museum in Las Vegas, where visitors can view and experience hundreds of haunted objects.

In the following sections, I list some of the most famous haunted objects in history, including four that I have had personal experience with. Two of them, the Dybbuk Box and Devil Chair, are on display at the museum.

The Dybbuk Box

According to Jewish folklore, a *dybbuk* is a dark spirit that takes over the bodies of living people and uses them for evil. Legend has it that a dybbuk can be trapped inside of a box and prevented from causing mischief — unless the box is opened, that is.

Several years ago, the Dybbuk Box, shown in Figure 7-3, came up for sale on eBay. The seller listed a vintage wine cabinet that came from the estate of a woman who survived a World War II concentration camp. The seller, an antique dealer named Kevin Mannis, claimed that the first owner's granddaughter was terrified of the box, warning him that her grandmother said it held a dybbuk. After buying the cabinet, he was plagued by a series of unfortunate events and recurring nightmares of an old hag that would brutally attack him, causing him to wake up with bruises on his body. He also experienced an overpowering stench of cat urine in his home. Tragically, his mother suffered a stroke while opening the box. Not surprisingly, he decided to get rid of it.

The box eventually ended up in the hands of Missouri medical museum director Jason Haxton, who was skeptical about the powers attributed to the box. He soon changed his mind. After acquiring the box, he began to experience a series of medical maladies, including bleeding eyes and strange rashes. He also began to dream of being attacked by an old hag and would also awake with bruises on his body. Kevin Mannis told me that while the box was in Haxton's basement, a man died there, and his body was found lying next to the box. He eventually became so unnerved by the box that he reached out to scientists and rabbis, who instructed him to build a wooden ark, lined with 24-carat gold, place the box inside, and bury it in the ground.

FIGURE 7-3:
Dybbuk Box.

©Courtesy of Zak Bagans, The Haunted Museum.

The box was opened during the time that it was owned by Jason Haxton. He retrieved it from its burial site for a special appearance on my television show, *Deadly Possessions*. I arranged to have the box placed in a containment room so that Kevin Mannis, the previous owner, could confront his fears about the box. When he opened it, he found the contents were intact. There was a dried rose, two coins from the 1920s, a small gold kiddish wine goblet, two locks of hair, an octopus-legged candlestick holder called a *shabbat*, and an engraving of the word "shalom," which means "peace" in Hebrew.

When Kevin opened the box, the lights in the building started to flash, strange sounds were heard, and strangest of all, Kevin turned to face a wall, and he got a very weird expression on his face. His voice changed, and he started to recite a story about a shadow man. He then started speaking in tongues and making bizarre whistling sounds. He was sweating profusely and began to cough uncontrollably.

I purchased the Dybbuk Box from Jason Haxton and placed it on display at the Haunted Museum. Because of the sinister nature of the box, only visitors over the age of 18 who have signed a waiver are allowed to see it. During the time that it has been on display, there have been people who have fainted, become dizzy, and even sick. Visitors have also witnessed a shadowy cloaked figure that has been seen passing directly through the closed doors of the room where it is on display. One of my tour guides has had her face shoved into the case that holds the box by an unseen force.

In 2018, my friend, singer-songwriter Post Malone, visited the Haunted Museum. During his visit, we were together in the Dybbuk Box room, and both heard the unmistakable sound of a little girl's voice. Moments later, something began to affect us. This sensation prompted me to remove the protective case from the box. Something was telling me to open the box. After a very tense moment between Post and myself, I touched the box. I began to panic and to scream, cry, and hyper-ventilate. Concerned, Post reached out and touched my shoulder. When he did, I felt something pass through my body. When we left the Museum, Post saw the dark shadow figure that so many people had encountered follow us out. The next day, he sent me a photo of a mysterious bruise that appeared on his arm. After his visit, he was involved in an emergency landing in his private jet, his car was involved in an accident, and armed robbers targeted a home in San Francisco that they believed to be his. I believe that a curse from the box affected him in a series of three events.

On Halloween 2018, *Ghost Adventures* aired a live special from The Haunted Museum, when I planned to open the Dybbuk Box myself. During the time that I had owned the box, I had been too cautious to open it because of events that had transpired with it in the past. I had planned to open the box on live television, but in the end, I did not. I am a very empathic person. After the many cases that I have been involved with, my body has become sort of a tuned instrument when it comes to the paranormal. I believe that the Dybbuk Box was aware that we were on live television that night. It had no interest in performing. It does things on its sched-ule, in its own time, not according to our clock. I felt as though the energy in that room started peaking. It was overwhelming. I could feel that something very bad would have happened if I had opened that box.

It was affecting many people in the room that night, and people watching it on television couldn't understand the seriousness of what was happening. I did not want to sacrifice our safety and health just for the sake of entertainment. It was mostly influencing myself, Aaron, electronic engineer Gary Galka, and renowned psychic medium Chris Fleming. In addition, other things were happening with the production itself that I felt were trying to prevent the box from being opened. This became apparent when Gary Galka and Chris Fleming began receiving some very disturbing messages using different pieces of communication equipment. I believe the Dybbuk Box disturbed and disrupted everything that we were trying to do. And it worked. I made a very abrupt decision to end things with the box unopened.

A lot of people questioned my decision, but I know that I did the right thing. I know what the Dybbuk Box had done to me, I know what it has done to others, and I know what it has done to my friends. The coincidences of what they have gone through and the curse of it are too coincidental to ignore.

The box remains on display at The Haunted Museum, where it is regularly seen by the thousands of visitors who come to experience it every month. Approach it at your own risk.

I say that from experience. I have a bizarre connection to the Dybbuk Box. It will pull me into that room, and sometimes I talk to it in whispers and words that I don't understand. Sometimes, I cannot even open the door to the room. At other times, I feel that I can control it. It is a very strange relationship that I have with the Dybbuk Box and at some point, perhaps I will be able to truly understand it.

The Devil's Rocking Chair

In 2019, I purchased another macabre object for The Haunted Museum. Dubbed the Devil's Rocking Chair, it is of unknown origin but was passed on to the Glatzel family in the early 1950s. It was simply a piece of household furniture until the summer of 1980 when it became the center of a tragedy that struck the family. The sinister relic became a part of one of America's most notorious exorcisms, which involved two demonic possessions and an eventual murder. It is believed that the chair, quite literally, was cursed by the Devil.

The horror began in July 1980 when David Glatzel, 11, became possessed by a demon. One night, he woke up screaming, claiming that he had been visited by a "man with big black eyes, a thin face with animal features, jagged teeth, pointed ears, horns, and hooves." David was, everyone agreed, not the kind of kid who liked scary movies or who was likely to make things up, and he was visibly shaken by this experience. He became withdrawn and quiet. His older sister, Debbie, asked her fiancée, Arne Johnson, if he would stay with her family for a while and see whether it would help David get out of his depression.

Arne, of course, agreed, but things didn't get better. David reported more nightmares about the terrifying man, who promised to take his soul. Odd scratches and bruises began to appear on the boy, and all the injuries seemed to happen while he was asleep. Odd sounds, which Arne couldn't explain, were heard in the attic. Worst of all, David began to claim that he was now seeing the Beast while he was awake. He was always seen sitting in the family's rocking chair, which the Beast now claimed as his own. David (and later, Lorraine Warren) was the only one who saw the Beast in the chair, but family members often saw it rocking back and forth, seemingly under its own power.

The family first brought over a priest to bless the house. This didn't help. In fact, it made things worse. The sounds in the attic got louder, David's visions increased, and he began to hiss at his family and speak with multiple voices. He started to quote from *Paradise Lost*, a book that most 11-year-olds aren't exactly familiar with. During the night, someone had to stay up and watch David, who woke every 30 minutes, sometimes having seizures.

Desperate for help, the Glatzels called Ed and Lorraine Warren, who began making regular visits to their home, bringing more priests with them, and performing exorcisms. Many of those exorcisms took place while David was seated in the rocking chair. The chair itself moved about the house on its own, mysterious disappearing and reappearing in different places. Most incredibly, it levitated on numerous occasions in full view of witnesses, including the Warrens, clergy members, and shocked family members. It happened once while David was sitting in it during an exorcism.

After a final exorcism, the demon left David. He soon began to show signs of improvement. However, his sister's fiancée, Arne Johnson, was not so lucky. Apparently, the demon left David and entered him. He started making the same kind of growls and hisses that David had made, as well as slipping into trances for a period of months before killing his landlord, Alan Bono, with a five-inch pocket knife, stabbing the man over and over as Debbie watched. Bono died a few hours later in the hospital, and Johnson was picked up by the police two miles from the murder scene. Eight months later, Johnson appeared in court with a plan to enter a plea of not guilty, due to demonic possession.

For the first time in American legal history, demonic possession was used as a reason for murder. It didn't work. Judge Robert Callahan refused to accept the plea since there was no evidence to show that Johnson was possessed. Johnson eventually went to prison for his crime. He was found guilty of first-degree manslaughter and received a 10- to 20-year sentence, although he only served 5. Arne and Debbie married after he was released.

For many years after the horrifying events of 1980, the rocking chair remained in storage. When the Glatzel family later moved, it went with them. However, over time, it became apparent that there was something very wrong with the chair. Whoever sat in the chair, whether innocently or because they knew its strange history, were suddenly stricken with incapacitating sciatica or abnormal back problems. Some were so bad that they required surgery. Once close family member was unable to walk upright more than ten years after testing the legend of the chair.

Today, the Devil's Rocking Chair is at The Haunted Museum. There are stains on the original cushion from holy water and blessed oils that were part of the exorcisms conducted by Catholic priests and Ed Warren. An evil presence surrounds it, and even before it was on display, it was already causing problems in the building. Soon after it arrived, the door containing the chair opened by itself with no one touching the switch, a power cord used to light the chair was yanked out of the wall by an unseen force, and on the first day of the chair being unveiled to the public several tour guides began to cry uncontrollably as well as a woman fainting above the chair which resulted in this exhibit being shut-down. I also heard from the shipper who picked up the rocking chair from the Glatzel house, and he told me that he was plagued by terrible nightmares after coming into contact with it.

Like the other cursed items at The Haunted Museum, the Devil's Rocking Chair will be safely displayed so that creates the least amount of havoc in the building. Even so, there remains the chance that the menacing aura that surrounds it will have an effect on those who are brave enough to visit it.

"The Hands Resist Him"

No one could have known that a photograph that was taken of Bill Stoneham when he was 5 would go on to become one of the most famous cursed paintings in history.

At the time, Stoneham's father was in advertising and did a lot of traveling. His family was staying at his grandmother's apartment in Chicago to save money. The place was so small that Bill had to sleep on a mat in a closet filled with coats and dresses. He regularly played with a little girl from the neighborhood, and one day, his parents had both kids pose in front of a glass door for a photo. They couldn't have known that, two decades later, Stoneham would turn the ordinary photograph into a terrifying painting that has become the stuff of Internet legend.

In 1972, Bill's first wife, Rhoann, wrote a poem called "Hands Resist Him." It was about Bill's experience of being adopted and never knowing his biological siblings. At the time, the couple lived in California, and Bill was under contract with art gallery owner Charles Feingarten to produce two paintings each month, for a fee of $200 each. With his next deadline approaching, he used his wife's poem and the old photo of himself with the neighbor girl as inspiration.

Stoneham called the painting "The Hands Resist Him," and he turned it over to Charles Feingarten for a large gallery show in 1974. At the show, the painting was purchased by actor John Marley, most famous for his role as the movie producer in *The Godfather* who wakes up with a severed horse's head in his bed. The gallery show also led to the painting's first press mention when it was reviewed by noted art critic Henry Seldis.

And then things got strange. Between 1978 and 1984, three of the men closest to the painting died: Seldis in 1978, Feingarten in 1981, and Marley in 1984.

The painting disappeared from public view after Marley's death and it would be another 26 years before Bill Stoneham heard about his painting again. He would later find out that it had been abandoned behind a California brewery that was turned into an art space. In 2000, the painting resurfaced in a listing on eBay. The family selling it had a chilling story to tell.

Their kids claimed that the boy and the doll in the painting were fighting and coming into their room at night, so Dad set up a camera to show them they were just imagining things. There was nothing to be afraid of. Instead, he saw the boy crawl from the painting. He quickly put the painting up on eBay with a disclaimer.

These details proved to be a huge draw for buyers. The eBay listing was viewed more than 30,000 times. Some of these viewers even complained to the seller about experiencing supernatural occurrences after merely visiting the listing. They claimed to hear voices on in their homes. Others said that they became ill after viewing the painting. Another claimed to have blacked out.

By the time the painting was sold to gallery owner Kim Smith for $1,025, its legend had spread across the Internet. Today, the painting is in storage at Smith's gallery in Grand Rapids, Michigan. He has been asked to see the painting only a handful of times over the years but still receives messages each week from people who are terrified by it.

I tried to purchase this painting for The Haunted Museum but was unable to make a deal with the current owner. However, I was unable to stop thinking about it, so I started doing some research and got in touch with the artist, Bill Stoneham. Oddly, when we spoke, Bill told me that he sensed a strange connection to me and that it was fate that I had called him. He eventually ended up painting for me the prequel to "The Hands Resist Him," which he called "The Hands Invent Him." Figure 7-4 shows this prequel painting. It portrays the inside of the window from the original painting.

This was a surreal experience for me, and it ended up becoming even eerier. Bill did not want me to see the painting until it was completed and shipped to me. While the painting was in transit, several staff members of The Haunted Museum and I began hearing the sound of a child's tricycle traveling the halls of the building. The sound was often accompanied by the ringing sound of a bicycle bell. Around this same time, a light bulb mysteriously exploded in the Oddities Room. It was located above an old coin-op machine that was on display. This particular machine had a long hose coming out of it with a hand on the end.

Stoneham Studios

Once the painting arrived, I realized that it depicted a long hose with a hand on the end of it, ringing the bell on a tricycle. I was in absolute shock over this. I had no logical way to explain the connection between the painting and the events that occurred at The Haunted Museum except to say that Bill Stoneham is a very mystical person. He creates tarot cards and is very much in touch with the other side. Somehow, our connection created a link between me and two different versions of the "Hands" paintings.

Robert the Doll

The life-sized straw doll had been a birthday present for Robert Eugene Otto — or Gene, as his family called — and the young boy loved it. It was given to him by his grandfather, who bought it while on a trip to Germany in 1904. Dressed in one of Gene's sailor suits, the doll, shown in Figure 7-5, became his favorite toy. He took it everywhere and began calling it Robert after himself. Soon, things became a little strange.

The stories say that the Ottos and their servants would often hear Gene in his bedroom, having conversations with himself in two different voices. On many occasions, the family was awakened in the middle of the night by Gene's screams, only to find the frightened boy in bed, surrounded by overturned furniture and scattered toys. Gene claimed that it was Robert who had messed up the room.

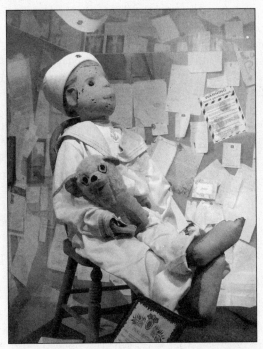

FIGURE 7-5:
Robert the Doll.

Wikimedia Commons/Key West Art & Historical Society and David Sloan

When things moved about the house and when toys were broken or lost, Gene always stated that "Robert did it!" And while his parents didn't quite believe the boy, they were unnerved by the strange events and bothered by stories told by the servants of hearing small footsteps and laughter in the house when it should have been empty. People who passed by the Otto house at 534 Eaton Street in Key West, Florida, even claimed to see the doll staring out the window at them. When Gene left home to study art, Robert was moved to the attic, where he remained for many years.

In 1930, Gene married Annette Parker in Paris, and after his parents passed away, he moved back to the Otto home in Key West. He retrieved Robert from the attic and returned him to his old turret room on the second floor, which he turned into his studio.

There are many tales in Key West about Annette's disdain for the doll. Conflicting rumors are still told, some alleging that she died from insanity after locking Robert back in the attic, while others claimed that Gene died with Robert at his side. What we do know is that Gene passed away in 1974 and his wife died two years later.

Robert stayed with the house when it was sold to Myrtle Reuter, who owned it for the next two decades. Those who passed by the house always saw Robert looking out of the second-floor turret room window. Today, Gene's former residence operates as a bed and breakfast called the Artist House, and visitors can even stay in the old turret room.

Robert the Doll isn't there anymore, however. He now lives at the Fort East Martello Museum, safely locked away in a glass box that has been outfitted with alarms. Those who come to see him are warned to be careful. It is said that curses will befall those who take photographs of Robert without asking his permission first. While this seems hard to believe, the walls near his glass case are covered with letters from scores of visitors and nonbelievers, writing to beg for Robert's forgiveness and asking him to remove the bad luck that he placed on him because of their carelessness.

Annabelle

The history of Annabelle remains a bit of a mystery, but we do know that it has long been one of the most famous items locked away in the occult museum of haunted and cursed objects that was owned by investigators Ed and Lorraine Warren.

According to the Warrens, the Raggedy Ann doll, shown in Figure 7-6, was given to a nursing student named Donna by her mother in 1970. Within days, Donna and her roommate noticed that the doll appeared to change positions when no one was looking. When it began to show up in different rooms of the house, seemingly under its own power, they decided to get help. A psychic told them that the doll was possessed by the spirit of Annabelle Higgins, a little girl who had died under mysterious circumstances. The spirit apparently claimed that she only wanted to be loved. Feeling sorry for her, Donna and her roommate gave Annabelle permission to remain with the doll.

A short time later, though, the doll — or the spirit inside of it — attacked a friend of Donna's, and they contacted a priest. The priest contacted the Warrens, who declared that Annabelle Higgins was not a spirit but a demonic entity posing as the little girl. The doll ended up with them, and it was locked away in their museum for safekeeping. Since then, she has been blamed for a number of fatal and near-fatal accidents involving those who doubt the spirit's power.

FIGURE 7-6:
The Annabelle
doll.

Wikimedia Commons/Warren Occult Museum/Altor

Not long after opening the Haunted Museum, I invited Tony Spera, Annabelle's current owner, to bring the doll to Las Vegas for a special episode of *Ghost Adventures.* I knew the stories. I was aware that Annabelle was said to be so evil that she was kept locked in a case and handled only with gloves and holy water for less than a minute at a time. It was said she was even responsible for harming people and even killing one visitor to the Warrens' museum in Connecticut.

When Tony Spera agreed to let Annabelle out of her case and brought in the doll, we were all warned not to touch her. But as she was placed in the middle of the room, something drew me to her. I touched Annabelle. All the people watching the show saw me do it, as did Tony, who got angry and put her back in the case, warning me that I was in danger.

All that I can say to the people who criticized me for touching Annabelle is that while they may think they know what it's like to be in these kinds of situations, they don't. I absorb and sense energies around me at a very high level. Whether it's from living people, residual energy, objects, or from spirits. I've been like this my entire life. I am not a psychic medium. I am a sensitive. It's a rush, it's draining, it's exhilarating, and it's terrifying all-in-one, depending on who or what I'm in contact with.

There are layers and layers of negative energy around Annabelle, and I was completely affected by everything that was happening. I became very sad for no reason at all. I truly believe that Annabelle was manipulating me, sending me into a trance. I didn't want to touch her, but I felt compelled to do so. I simply did not have direct control of myself at that moment.

But, yes, I wish that I had not done it. Touching her led to many strange events, and it was a dangerous thing to do. If you ever decide to tempt fate and fool around with a cursed or haunted object, think again. The legends that surround many of them may seem far-fetched but, as many unlucky people can tell you, they got started for a reason.

Chapter **8**

Where the Ghosts Are

N o matter what skeptics and debunkers would like to tell you, haunted places are more common than a lot of people think. If you are willing to do the work, you are going to find them. Always remember, however, to never go searching for a haunting where you are not wanted. Some people do not want to be told they have a resident ghost. Some simply do not want to talk about it and some do not want the attention or the publicity. An ethical paranormal investigator is a lot like any other kind of profession. The ones who bother and pursue witnesses and owners of haunted places are just like the worst harassing salesperson. This is never a good thing for your reputation. Never be pushy or demanding about an investigation. You have to accept the fact that some people just do not want the curtain pulled open to expose their ghosts to the light of day.

Homes and other private locations are not the only places to find ghosts. An allegedly haunted place that is open to the public can provide hours of research for any ghost-hunter. The history of such spots may provide good leads when it comes to finding the resident ghost. Many times, the folklore and legends of the place are a great place to start. These stories may have a root in genuine phenomena. The lesson here is to not ignore the stories that sound too good to be true because there may be more to them than meets the eye.

The problem is that you have to know how to separate the ghostlore from the ghosts. *Ghostlore* is the practice that society has of trying to explain strange events by attaching a legend to them. In many cases, stories of a "lady in white" or a "headless railroad brakeman" have been invented to try and add understanding to sightings of ghostly white shapes and mysterious glowing lights. Without these chilling stories, the weird locations may never be explained. To put it simply, people just have a need to try and explain things. They crave a reason for everything, supernatural or not.

In many cases, these locations are truly haunted. Unfortunately, though, the true facts behind the haunting may not have anything to do with the legend that is associated with it. There may be another reason entirely for the strange phenomena reported but, many years before, witnesses felt the need to attach an explanation to events they could not understand. A witness may have glimpsed some sort of pale apparition that looked like a flowing dress, and thus, the legend of a "lady in white" was born.

In other cases, a story may have gotten started at some point in the past and then was embellished and enhanced to the point that it soon bears little resemblance to real events. In some cases, the owners or caretakers of the property may even know the truth but don't bother with it, feeling that the fanciful story is better than the real thing.

Regardless, you should always pay close attention to the legends and folklore of a location. Strange, hard to believe, and possibly too good to be true, they may have been started for a reason.

Finding Ghosts

The following is a list of some of the places where paranormal researchers have had good luck in finding ghosts and hauntings throughout the years. After each category, I noted a couple of locations that we investigated on *Ghost Adventures* that I felt really illustrated the reason why each of these types of locations made the list.

Homes

Many private residences, and not just old ones, have a tainted past that may include murder, suicide, or some other tragic event. Many times, these events cause a place to become haunted when the spirits connected to the event choose not to leave. These spirits can be positive or negative and haunted houses boast all kinds of different phenomena. Residual hauntings are also common, especially in older structures.

In some cases, the history of the house itself may not reveal the reason the location is haunted. It might be the land, which is why many new homes also become the scene of hauntings and unexplained events. Finding a source for the haunting may require researching the history of the land. It may have once been occupied by another house, a building, a farm, or perhaps even an old cemetery.

Lemp Mansion

In 2014, we investigated the Lemp Mansion and Brewery, along with the Cherokee Cave system that once stored the Lemp's lager. After years of tragedy and several Lemp family suicides, the house has become known as one of the most haunted places in the country. (See Figure 8-1.)

FIGURE 8-1:
Ghost Adventures at Lemp Mansion.

Lizzie Borden House

In Fall River, Massachusetts, we were locked inside of the Lizzie Borden house in 2011. This was the scene of one of the most infamous murders in American history.

Cemeteries

In most cases, ordinary cemeteries are not haunted. They are simply repositories of earthly remains. However, many burial grounds do become haunted. When a house becomes haunted, it is usually because of events that occurred prior to someone's death, or because of it. A haunted cemetery is the opposite. Hauntings occur because of events that happen after death, including tragic events, desecration of graves, vandalism, and rituals that can open portals within the confines of the cemetery. A tremendous amount of research into cemetery hauntings has been done over the years and, although controversial, these sites remain worthy of further investigation.

One thing to be careful of, though, is to check into your state and local laws about entering cemeteries after dark. Some areas expressly forbid it whereas others allow it as long as the cemetery is not posted against trespassing. Be very careful to make sure that you are not breaking the law.

Bachelor's Grove Cemetery

In 2012, we took part in an incredibly active investigation at what's been called one of the most haunted burial grounds in America. It is a haunting caused by grave desecration, grave robbery, and devil-worshipping rituals. (See Figure 8-2.)

FIGURE 8-2:
Ghost Adventures at Bachelor's Grove Cemetery.

Wikimedia Commons/Mark Bergner

Concordia Cemetery

We traveled to El Paso, Texas, in 2017 to investigate this haunted cemetery where countless ritual jars are left on graves and where "Night Stalker" serial killer Richard Ramirez was introduced to the occult rituals and devil worship.

Theaters

The entire range of the human emotion is expressed inside of a theater and this seems to attract spirits who use this energy to manifest. A theater also inspires a lot of devotion from the people who work and perform in them, causing many of them to remain behind after their deaths. The saying goes that "every good theater has a ghost" and many theaters are prime locations for all kinds of spirits.

You can normally expect two very different types of hauntings in these locations, both traditional haunts, and residual ones. Thanks to the massive expressing of energy that goes on inside of the buildings, you can expect to hear reports of ghostly footsteps, phantom applause, voices, laughter, and more. All these phenomena normally signal that residual energy is present. You should also take note of the hundreds of stories about haunted theaters where the ghosts of former actors and staff members linger, which makes them a favorite spot for many ghost-hunters.

Yost Theatre

We did a lockdown at the Yost Theatre in Santa Ana, California, in 2013. This venue that dates back to the early 1900s now plays host to some of the world's best electronic DJs and also, a number of spirits.

Silent Movie Theatre

In Los Angeles, in 2017, we took part in a lockdown at the infamous Silent Movie Theatre on Fairfax Avenue. During the investigation, information emerged about the double-murder of the theater's owner and a candy counter girl, about the strange death of a silent film preservationist who lived at the theater, and we made contact with deceased actor Douglas Fairbanks, Jr.

Ghost towns

You don't have to believe in spirits to enjoy a visit to one of the ghost towns that can still be found across the western landscape of the United States, but you may become a believer if you do. The abandoned mining towns and once-thriving settlements of the region were once filled with people, along with their hopes and dreams. But fires, disasters, deaths, and mines that eventually stopped producing forced the residents to move on to better places. Today, these towns exist as collections of buildings and other structures telling the story of years gone by.

The chaos, violence, and desperation of long ago have left an impression on these places and hauntings from the past, as well as former residents themselves, often linger behind.

Bannack Ghost Town

In 2014, *Ghost Adventures* traveled to Montana and the ghost town of Bannack, which is now a state park. We investigated Hotel Meade, the former site of the county courthouse of Beaverhead County. During the lockdown, we included more buildings, including the "crying baby house," which was believed to be used as a quarantine hospital to isolate children with scarlet fever, the old Methodist church, the saloon, the schoolhouse, and also the pond where a teenage girl drowned in 1916.

Virginia City, Nevada

In the original documentary film, *Ghost Adventures*, we traveled to Virginia City to investigation the most haunted locations in the ghost town — the Silver Queen Hotel, the Old Washoe Club, the Virginia City Cemetery, and a cabin near the Yellow Jacket Mine. That visit turned out to be so compelling that we returned in 2011 and were locked down at the St. Mary's Art Center, the Silver Queen Hotel, and the Miner's Cabin at the Yellow Jacket Mine. We returned to the Washoe Club once more in 2018 for a chilling exchange with the spirits. Our visits to ghost towns have produced some of our most compelling evidence.

Schools and colleges

Many schools have had tragic events that had led to hauntings. Some may be caused by deaths on campus, either those of students or staff members, whereas others may be caused by the energy that lingers from having so many young people clustered together. The best way to pursue ghost stories and sightings at a college is to pass the word to a student or two that you are interested in hearing their stories or by talking to someone on the security or maintenance staff. Teachers and custodians are the best contacts for other schools.

Keep in mind that ghostlore plays a big role in the alleged hauntings on every campus. Nearly every school has a local legend or rumor about a murdered co-ed, a vanished student, or a death that never actually occurred. They make great stories for late night parties but don't have much resemblance to reality. Do not dismiss such stories entirely, though. They may still have some element of the truth to them as explanations for a genuine haunting that is taking place.

Lewis Flats School

In 2018, we investigated the mysterious Lewis Flats School in Deming, New Mexico, which was located on land that is haunted by the spirits of the Apache, who waged a violent struggle against settlers in the region in the 19th century.

Albion Normal School

One of the most sinister schools that we have investigated was the Albion State Normal School in Idaho, where we did a lockdown in 2017. The school was believed to contain dark energy, caused by occult graffiti, which was affecting the staff. During an interview, both investigator Jay Wasley and the witness were marked by strange symbols that appeared behind their ears.

Hotels

Thousands of people pass through the hotels and motels in every city and small town each year. With all those people coming and going, it is not hard to imagine that there may be a ghost or two around. A little investigation into the history of an older hotel may find that a suicide or murder has taken place there. Even newer hotels often have events that occur, including murders, rapes, assaults, and mysterious deaths. Each of these emotional events can certainly leave a haunting behind. Many investigators believe that residual hauntings are like "leaving a little piece of yourself behind" and hotels are the perfect place for this to occur.

Keep in mind that unless your location is a historical bed and breakfast, an abandoned motel, or an old hotel that advertises its ghosts, asking at the front desk may not do an investigator much good when trying to secure a haunted room for the night. The best way to find out about stories that are not so well known — and which room may have an otherworldly occupant — is to ask one of the maintenance staff or the housekeeping workers. You just might discover they have a good story to tell.

Be prepared to spend some money, though. You can't investigate a haunted hotel without spending the night there.

Stanley Hotel

Most people know the Stanley Hotel in Estes Park, Colorado, as the inspiration for Stephen King's book, *The Shining*, but the hotel is truly haunted. In 2010, we investigated the hotel and found that its reputation as a haunted place is well deserved. (See Figure 8-3.)

FIGURE 8-3:
Ghost Adventures at the Stanley Hotel.

Crescent Hotel

This historic hotel in Eureka Springs, Arkansas, is considered one of the most haunted places in the country. For years it was a resort hotel, but later it became a cancer hospital operated by a phony doctor named Norman Baker. Hundreds died there and left many restless ghosts behind. We investigated the hotel in 2019, captured a curtain moving on its own, and made contact with an active and very notorious spirit. (See Figure 8-4.)

FIGURE 8-4:
Ghost Adventures at the Crescent Hotel.

Battlefields and crime scenes

These two types of locations go hand-in-hand. They are linked because of the tragedy that occurs at both kinds of sites. These locations deal with a sudden loss of life and this can sometimes cause a spirit to linger behind in confusion. There have been many cases over the years of spirits who reportedly did not realize they were dead or whose life ended so abruptly they did not cross over.

The tragedy and the trauma involved can also create residual hauntings as the terrible events reply themselves over and over again. Many witnesses report seeing lines of troops on battlefields, still marching to battle, or hearing the sounds of guns, screams, and cries from long ago.

Perryville Battlefield

Although not as famous as other American battlefields, we found that this battlefield in Kentucky is just as haunted. Perryville was the scene of the most destructive Civil War battle in the state, ending with more than seven thousand men wounded, killed, or missing. The battle marked the South's last serious attempt to gain possession of Kentucky and today, is one of the most unaltered Civil War sites in the country.

Freakshow Murder House

Few places are as sinister as a murder site, which we discovered in 2017. We investigated the scene of a 1996 double murder in Los Angeles's Chatsworth neighborhood. During the lockdown, we tried to help the current owners of the house, who sell and store oddity antiques in the house, by gathering evidence of paranormal activity.

Hospitals and asylums

Working hospitals frequently have tales of ghosts and hauntings they are no doubt the hardest places for any researcher to get into for an investigation. In many cases, even getting permission to hear the anecdotes from people who work there among the spirits is difficult. Hundreds of hospitals have resident ghosts — from phantom nuns to spectral patients — but getting anyone to talk about them is nearly impossible.

Most investigations at locations that fit into this category must be done after the hospital has closed down. Spirits are said to linger behind at scores of abandoned hospitals and mental institutions. It seems that the former residents have left an impression behind, especially in cases of mental disturbance or extreme tragedy, when both residual impressions and conscious entities can leave an indelible mark.

Waverly Hills Sanitorium

This former tuberculosis hospital in Louisville, Kentucky, has definitely earned its reputation for being extremely haunted. In 2010, we did a lockdown at the hospital for search for evidence of the spirits that remained behind from the thousands of patients who died there. We were not disappointed. (See Figure 8-5.)

©Travel Channel.

FIGURE 8-5:
Ghost Adventures
at Waverly Hills
Sanitorium.

Rolling Hills Asylum

Also, in 2010, *Ghost Adventures* went to Bethany, New York, for a lockdown at this haunted former asylum. During its years in operation, the homeless, alcoholics, orphans, tuberculosis patients, and the criminally insane all took refuge at Rolling Hills. This led the building to become a mixing pot of tragic cases and dark personalities, which has led to the haunting of today.

Jails and prisons

When compiling any sort of list of the most haunted places in America, prisons and jails fall high on the chart. The amount of trauma, pain, and terror experienced by men who are incarcerated often leaves a lasting impression behind. The horrible events carried out by such men, which led to them being locked away from society — along with the horrible events that occur behind prison walls — often cause the spirits of the men who lived and died behind bars to linger behind.

America's prisons, jails, and reformatories can be terrifying places for those in this world and the next.

Alcatraz

This "escape proof" location is one of the most famous prisons in American history, but it is also one of the most haunted. Dubbed the "Evil Island" by Native Americans in the region, "The Rock" served as a federal prison from 1933 until 1963, housing some of the most infamous criminals in American history, like Al Capone, George "Machine Gun" Kelly, and the "Birdman of Alcatraz," Robert Franklin Stroud. It has been plagued by tales of inmates tortured by unseen entities, as well as dozens of ghosts. We had many strange experiences while on Alcatraz in 2013, especially in the solitary confinement Cell 13, where an entity with glowing red eyes may have been responsible for the death of an inmate. (See Figure 8-6.)

FIGURE 8-6:
Ghost Adventures in Alcatraz.

Library of Congress/Jet Lowe

Yuma Territorial Prison

In 2016, we investigated what has been called the "Hell Hole Prison." The Yuma Territorial Prison earned the nickname thanks to the intense heat of the location and the inhumane punishments that the inmates faced for even the smallest infractions. Our lockdown that night included contact with former inmates who perished under such inhumane conditions.

Chapter **9**

The Ghost-Hunter's Toolkit

There is a lot more to paranormal investigation than ghost detective devices. This may seem like a funny way to start a chapter about using tools to detect the presence of ghosts, but it is true. The most important tool in a paranormal investigation is the ghost investigator himself or herself. It is imperative that you use your mind, your judgment, and your powers of observation to the utmost of your ability. No cameras or fancy gadgets can take the place of a good investigator.

In the early days of paranormal investigation, technology usually consisted of a camera, some string, a jar of flour, and any homemade device the ghost-hunter could create. Of course, we would never want to go back to those days. If a ground-breaking investigator like Harry Price had possessed a thermal imaging camera in his day, he would undoubtedly have been using one instead of a black string and some flour. Even in those primitive times, investigators still managed to get some amazing and compelling evidence of hauntings. They were forced to rely on their abilities and common sense.

We do not want to forget about common sense, even in these modern times of gadgets, high-tech cameras, EMF detectors, and spirit boxes. Paranormal investigations consist of interviewing witnesses, examining the location, collecting evidence, and waiting around for something to happen. These things are essential, not things of the past. People are always in a hurry today and impatience seems to prevail in every walk of life, including in paranormal research. Some investigators fail to take the time to learn to use their equipment correctly. They do not understand how cameras work, and worse.

There is a lot to know when you begin your paranormal investigations, and you should always be learning and having an open mind about exploring new things and new ideas. Keep that in mind as you read the chapter ahead and discover the basic, the essential, and the high-tech items that can be used for paranormal investigating.

Exploring the Basic Items for Investigations

In the 1930s, during his investigation of England's Borley Rectory, ghost-hunter Harry Price became the first investigator to compile a list of items that he believed everyone should carry in their ghost-hunter's kit. (See Figure 9-1.) They included

>> A pair of soft felt overshoes (for creeping about in silence)

>> A steel measuring tape

>> Screw eyes, lead seals, a sealing tool, white tape, a tool pad and nails and small, electric bells (for the construction of motion detecting devices)

>> Dry batteries and switches (for secret electrical contacts)

>> A camera, film, and flash-bulbs

>> A notebook; red, blue, and black marking pens; sketching pad; and drawing instruments (for maps and diagrams)

>> A ball of string and a stick of chalk (to mark movement of objects)

>> Bandages, iodine, surgical tape and a flask of brandy (for injuries)

>> Electric torch, matches, and candles

>> A bowl of mercury to detect tremors in a room or passage

>> Cinematograph camera with electrical release

Although the tool kits of early paranormal investigators undoubtedly sound very quaint to modern readers, the essential list of basic items today is not all that different from what was used decades ago. In fact, whereas some of the items are updated versions of the tools from Price's original kit, some of them have not changed at all.

FIGURE 9-1:
Harry Price's
ghost-hunting kit.

Wikimedia Commons

Most of the basic and essential items in the tool kit can be purchased and used by anyone but even basic items require knowledge and practice in order to be used correctly. It goes without saying that any electronic equipment that you buy should be carefully used and practiced before you use it in an investigation. You want to know what it was originally designed for, what it can do, and what the readings actually mean. It can never be stressed enough that you should never carry out an investigation if you do not know how to properly use your equipment. Nothing destroys your credibility faster than compiling what amounts to false data from a location that may not be haunted at all.

New paranormal investigators are urged not to ignore the basic items on this list in an attempt to impress people with how many expensive gadgets they have. Researchers operated for many years, obtaining great results, using nothing more than basic items, good instincts, and a camera. We are lucky today to have so many new items at our disposal but never forget that intelligence, logic, and good detective work are essential to your research, no matter what kind of technology you have.

This is a list of items that no investigator should be without while conducting paranormal investigations. You never know when they may be needed, and many of them complement other items in the chapter ahead. It is also recommended that you purchase tool bags or padded cases in which to carry your equipment.

Here is the list of basic items:

>> Notebook and pen (recording notes, witness statements, and making diagrams)

>> Sketch pad and drawing pencils (for maps of location)

>> Measuring tape (checking distance and witness accounts)

>> Extra batteries (you never know when they may fail)

>> Flashlight (this requires no explanation)

>> Recording device (for witness accounts and for electronic voice phenomenon or EVP)

>> Small tool kit (some electronic devices require screwdrivers)

>> Camera (for documenting the location and anomalous photographs)

>> Video camera (for documenting the location and investigation, plus interviews)

>> Portable motion detectors (great for securing locations)

>> Two-way radios (allow the group to stay in contact and they avoid the electromagnetic interference caused by cellular phones)

In addition to these basic items, others may be useful, although not essential, for an investigation. Eminent ghost researcher Peter Underwood suggested several items for a tool kit, including reels of black thread, adhesive tape, twine, and wire, all of which could be used to seal off a room or windows. He also added an assortment of small screws, nails, tacks, screw-eyes, a small hammer, pliers, luminous paint, a pen-knife, several magnifying glasses, a scale (for measuring the weight of any item that is apparently moved by paranormal forces) and a string gauge, which could measure the force necessary to close or open a door or cabinet.

Ghost-Hunting Experiments

Paranormal investigations can sometimes lead to trial by error for the researcher, so several items are worth bringing with you to a location to test out theories about ghosts and about the workings of the human mind.

Working with trigger objects

The idea of working with trigger objects began in England in the early 1900s and eventually, it caught on in the United States, too. Psychic trigger objects are items that are used to try and elicit a response from a spirit at a location. The idea is that the ghost spots the object and moves it. Meanwhile, the investigator records the interaction between the spirit and the psychic trigger. Such experiments are easy to set up, record, and replicate.

No set rules exist as to what these objects should be, but common sense should be applied. For example, don't use anything dangerous, like knives or firearms, in hopes that a ghost may react to it. If it does, the consequences may not be what you were looking for.

Trigger objects should be relevant to the culture of the alleged spirit being investigated. For example, using a religious relic or crucifix may be helpful when investigating a church or using period items when investigating ghosts related to the Civil War. As a side note, it is also worth trying this experiment with sound recordings as a sort of "lure" for ghostly activity. Many investigators use music from the era believed to be connected to the ghost to try and stir up activity.

One thing to always remember is that trigger objects need to be portable and easy to carry around with you. The idea is that they can be moved about by the ghosts, so the smaller they are, the better the chance that they can be manipulated by any spirits present. Here is a basic method for using psychic triggers during your investigations:

1. **Carefully select your trigger objects and consider the idea of using objects that may be familiar to the alleged spirits.**

   If you are investigating an old house, perhaps an old key, some period money, or household item may be appealing.

2. **Conduct your baseline tests, as you would for any investigation. Check humidity and temperature readings from the area.**

   You need to have a base atmospheric level for the area where the trigger objects tests are carried out so that you know when anything out of the ordinary occurs.

3. **Make sure that the objects are placed on a level surface. Take a piece of paper and arrange the object, or objects, on it. Then, take a small ruler and place it next to the items and photograph the scene.**

   In this way, you can show how far the object actually moves, if it does manage to move at all. This gives you an accurate scale when you are filming and photographing the objects.

4. **Using a pencil, carefully trace around the objects so that an outline remains on the paper when they are removed.**

5. **Next, take a photograph of the arrangement from directly above it. This is your reference point so that you can assess any movement that takes place. Make sure that you have all the objects and the ruler in the photograph.**

You can also take photographs from other angles if this is relevant. For example, if you are using a slightly large toy in order to enhance contact with a child's spirit, and you initially position it to so that it faces in one direction, you need to take a photograph of it in that position in case it moves when you leave the area. Using just an overhead photograph for reference may not help you to know whether anything unusual has happened.

6. **Consider setting up motion detectors around the spot where the objects have been placed. This serves the dual purpose of letting you know when objects move and making sure that they have not been tampered with.**

7. **After the set-up has been arranged, place a video camera on a tripod and place it so that it is directed at the trigger objects. If possible, consider using several cameras to monitor the scene from different directions.**

8. **After this has been completed, leave the area where you have placed the trigger objects and go to another part of the location. If they have been placed in a room, close and lock the door to this room and then seal it with motion detectors, or even standard tape.**

If the motion sensors inside of the room signal movement, you have two options: you can either return to the objects to see why the alarms have gone off and reset them, or you can leave the area alone and let the sensors reset themselves. The latter option is preferable because the cameras will still be recording the room and the trigger objects.

9. **Leave the objects alone for at least one hour or longer if possible.**

Because we have no idea of the mechanics necessary for a spirit to move a solid object, we can have no idea how long this may take to occur.

10. **When you do return to the psychic trigger objects, take photographs, just as you did in step 5. Make notes on whether the objects have moved, but do not touch them until the experiment is completely at an end.**

Testing for psychic abilities

Another kind of experiment that may be worthwhile for an investigator is a test that can be carried out to check for psychic abilities — both those of the home-owners and the investigation team. It is believed that everyone possesses at least a small amount of psychic ability. It has been theorized that at some point in our distant past, humans possessed a more developed "sixth sense" than most of us have today. Some people, however, have been able to retain these abilities and have even been able to put them to use. These psychics, sensitives, and empaths are able to make contact with spirits, catch glimpses of the future, and even occasionally move objects with just the power of the mind.

This type of psychokinesis is more a part of paranormal research than many of us realize. Many ghost-hunters find themselves embroiled in cases where no evidence of ghosts exist, but they are faced with reports of items that move about by themselves, doors that slam open and closed, and more. Many of these cases may come down to genuine instances of human agent "poltergeist" hauntings when a person in the household is unknowingly responsible for the activity being generated.

Testing those involved in the case you are investigating can be done in a few different ways. You can use the standard Zener cards that were developed by J.B. Rhine at Duke University. These cards, which come in five designs (square, circle, star, cross, and wavy lines), have been used for decades when testing students and possible subjects with extra sensory perception. They are simple to use, and researchers simply keep track of how many accurate guesses the test subject makes as to what card is held by the investigator out of their eyesight.

You can also make a simple device that may be useful in testing subjects for PK abilities. Ideally you should start your experiments with a light object as a psychic trigger. Untrained abilities of this nature probably have never been used consciously before, so you shouldn't ask subjects to move, say, your television with the power of their minds. Instead, ask them to move this simple device. Just follow these steps:

1. **Construct a paper cylinder.**

   You can either make one with a little Scotch tape or use the cardboard core from a roll of toilet paper instead.

2. **Make a strip of thin metal that is about a quarter of an inch thick and just slightly wider than the top of your paper or cardboard cylinder.**

   With a pair of strong scissors, cut the metal from an aluminum soda can or, with metal snips, a coffee can. The type of metal does not really matter, but it must be flat and even. After the strip is cut correctly, use a metal punch or even a nail and hammer to make a dent in the metal as close to the center as you can — not a break or a hole, merely a depression in the metal.

3. **With a small blade, cut a slot on either side of the paper cylinder about a half inch from the end. It should be small enough that your metal strip can be slipped in on one side and come out the other.**

As mentioned, the strip should be a little wider than the cylinder so that a small amount sticks out of both sides of it. It should also be adjusted so that the indention that you put in the metal is near the center of the cylinder, with the dented-in side facing down into the cylinder.

4. **Get a block of wood about an inch thick and about four-inches square. In the center of the wood, drill a very small hole large enough to accommodate the tip of a steel knitting needle. The hole should be tight enough so that the needle will stand straight upward and not fall over.**

In place of the needle, you can also use a small metal rod, but it must be perfectly straight, not light enough to bend, and have a good tip on it.

5. **When you are sure that the needle is secure in the wood, carefully lower the paper cylinder down over it until the needle's free point meets the depression in your metal strip. Adjust the strip until the cylinder hangs evenly and balances on the end of the needle.**

You may want to add a few drops of adhesive to make sure that the metal strip remains in the same place in the cylinder. This is optional, though, and if you plan to take the device apart after using it, there is really no point to gluing it into position.

Your PK tester is now complete, but it must be covered so that natural air currents can't reach it. You can cover it with a large mouth jar or a glass dome, which you can usually find at a hobby or craft store. The entire apparatus, now covered, should then be placed at about eye level on a shelf or table that is free from vibration.

For the experiment — and you should try this yourself or with members of your team before using it with a witness —move a few feet away from the device and begin thinking about the paper cylinder revolving on the end of the needle. Concentrate on making the cylinder turn, but do it only for about ten minutes at a time. You may be surprised at what happens — or you may not.

Not everyone can make this work. With some people it takes patience and with others, it never works at all. Don't be disappointed if you can't make the cylinder turn and also, don't be disappointed if your suspected "human agent" can't make it rotate either. It's possible that this person may still be responsible for some of the activity but is totally unable to control it. This is not an exact science, but perhaps a device like this one can get you a little closer to some solid answers in your investigation.

And if nothing else, it's an interesting way to test your own abilities — or lack of them — and by experimenting in such a way, you may learn more about yourself and the other investigators that you are working with.

Ghost-detection Devices: The Basics

Electronic devices serve a variety of purposes during an investigation. They are used to document your location and can serve as both an alert that a spirit may be present and also for showing what is *not* a ghost. The devices in our tool kits are pieces of equipment that have been adapted for ghost research. Use of such devices is based on theories that have been developed over the last few decades that point to the idea that the devices can pick up distortions in energy fields that may be caused by ghosts.

These devices are not foolproof. Most were originally designed to check for electromagnetic surges caused by household wiring and industrial equipment so adapting them for the paranormal requires a lot of knowledge about exactly how they work and what the readings mean. For this reason, these devices are best used in conjunction with eyewitness accounts, when monitoring locations, and with other investigative techniques. No single piece of evidence can stand on its own, which is why investigators are always looking for corresponding evidence during their research. In this case, anomalous readings on an EMF meter become more intriguing when they are backed up by something else, like a cold spot, witness account, or with other equipment at the same time.

Electronic equipment can be expensive, which is a sobering thought for investigators on a tight budget. However, other items that are low in cost and have been around for centuries can also be used to check for magnetic energy.

The compass

For those who may not be able to afford an electronic device, a compass can be purchased in just about any sporting goods store in your area. There is no way to guarantee the validity of the results that you may obtain, but ghost-hunters have been using compasses for many years, often with successful results. The reaction that you get from a compass is basically the same reaction that you get from a simple EMF detection device.

The best way to use the compass is to carry it into an allegedly haunted location, leaving the compass open and flat out on the palm of your hand. Your arm should be bent at the elbow and level, extended at an angle from your body so that the compass is directly in front of you. The needle on the compass moves each time you change direction, and, according to reports, it begins to spin when it encounters a ghost or some sort of anomalous energy field.

Even though the compass is a very basic item, the reported behavior of the device in a situation involving paranormal energy is actually quite consistent with much higher-tech devices. The theory is that the device reacts to abrupt changes or fluctuations in the energy field of the location. A spinning compass needle would certainly show that something unusual is going on.

Dowsing rods

The art of dowsing has been around for centuries, perhaps even thousands of years. It is the oldest form of divination known to man and has been used for a variety of different reasons, including searches for underground water, discovering the location of unmarked graves, determining the sex of unborn children, and even locating ghosts.

How dowsing actually works remains a mystery, but it has proven to be uncannily accurate over the years. Even the American Society of Dowsers admits that "the reason the procedures work is entirely unknown."

The standard practice of dowsing is to search for underground water sources. Many cities, counties, and corporations keep a dowser on the payroll. In most cases, a dowser searches an area with either a Y-shaped rod or two L-shaped rods in his hands. He concentrates on what he is looking for, which is usually a water source, and when he finds the right spot, the rods either bend downwards or cross over one another. No one knows how this works, it simply does.

To use dowsing rods to find ghosts, most dowsers recommend using two L-shaped rods that have been made from brass or some lightweight metal. Some dowsers even use metal coat hangers, so no standard material exists. The rods should be about two-foot long and bent into an L-shape, which fits into your hand. Then, hold the short end of the rod so that the longer piece points outward, away from your body. The rods should be held loosely so that they have room to swing easily back and forth.

After that, begin searching the building or location. It has been suggested that it's possible that by searching, and by concentrating on what you are looking for, you can find ghosts, anomalous energy, and some say even dimensional portals, using dowsing rods.

Walk about the location and follow where the rods lead you. They are supposed to point in the direction of any energy they detect. After you have discovered the energy source, the rods cross, signaling that the area in question has been found.

Ghost-detection Devices: The Advanced

Paranormal researchers of the past had little or no electronic equipment that could be used to monitor locations or to search for anomalous activity that may be present in a place they were investigating. In recent times, new theories have been developed which seem to suggest that many haunted locations have high levels of electromagnetic energy present in them.

Some scientists have pointed to these energy fields, which have been discovered to cause headaches, dizziness, and even hallucinations, as an artificial explanation for all ghost sightings. Paranormal researchers have developed their own theories suggesting that ghost themselves may be electromagnetic in origin or perhaps that the ghosts use this energy to manifest. The magnetic energy may also explain how residual hauntings occur, causing events and images to impress on the atmosphere of the location.

Although we still do not know exactly what electromagnetic fields and paranormal events have in common, researchers first began adapting electronic devices as a way to detect paranormal energy as early as the 1970s. This began the development of theories about spirits causing disruptions in the magnetic field of locations, making them detectable with measuring devices.

Today, Electromagnetic Field (EMF) detection meters are the most commonly used devices in the field. They are used to search for evidence of spirit activity and also for ruling out artificial sources of energy that may interfere with an investigation. Electromagnetic fields are present around any object that possesses an electrical charge, whether it be artificial or natural. They were never designed to detect ghosts. They were supposed to be used in the building and scientific trades to detect energy leaks and problem areas. They can certainly — and were designed to — be influenced by things that are not paranormal.

Electronic devices are always useful in an investigation, complimenting the other tools that we use and the other research that we do. The researcher should use the devices to both rule out artificial changes in the electronic field and to search for corresponding evidence to go along with the investigation is gathering. That evidence can be gleaned from witness accounts, photographs, temperature changes, or whatever else may occur. In this way, we can truly use this information to document a haunting.

Using an EMF meter

The majority of EMF detectors have been designed to read in the 30 to 500 Hz range. They are calibrated at 60 Hz, which is the standard setting for most household fields. What most meters are designed to gauge are the currents induced inside of the location by artificial fields. Most common fields are around 60 Hz. It remains unknown whether paranormal energy is above or below this standard setting, which can make things difficult. The three basic theories are: ghosts are made up of electromagnetic energy; they disrupt the energy in the location; or they use the energy to manifest. Any or all of these scenarios may be correct, which makes it possible for EMF meters to track energy that is beyond normal.

The following section deals with different EMF meters, such as the one shown in Figure 9-2, that are used in investigations. We include usage directions, as well as some extra information and some things to watch out for so that they can be used correctly.

FIGURE 9-2:
A meter.

Basic EMF meters

Quite a few basic EMF meters that feature both analog and digital scales are on the market. Most basic meters range in price from about $30 to $100. The devices are easy to use if you follow some common sense directions.

An EMF meter should be carried in your hand, with your fingers wrapping around the bottom of the meter and your fingertips holding the side. Do not place your hand over the end of the meter, because your body will interfere with the readings. It should be noted that most basic meters do not have sensors on the sides of the meter, only in the front. This means that the energy fields must be approached from this direction only in order for them to be picked up. The best way to do that is to bend your elbow so that the meter is held out in front of you at a distance from your elbow to hand. Your arm can be extended for further reach, but do not bring the meter closer to your body.

When conducting a study of a location, gently move the meter from side-to-side as you walk. Moving it up and down too quickly can cause false readings and spikes to occur. As you walk, be on the lookout for sudden and extreme bursts of energy to be registered on the meter. If such an event does happen, try to pinpoint the source of the field. Usually, strong readings and surges of energy are signs that you are picking up an artificial energy source like an appliance, an electrical outlet, or even a hidden line in the wall or the floor. Always try to find a natural source for the energy readings before you begin thinking that you have found a ghost. These basic devices easily pick up artificial fields and should be used with caution.

Meters like this are beginning models and are very simple in design. Anyone who is searching for a more sophisticated device should try one of the more advanced models available. However, don't discount a basic meter completely. Although, admittedly, they are not as sensitive as other meters, and can be hard to use in indoor investigations, they work quite well for those who investigate cemeteries, historic sites, and outdoor locations. Because little in the way of interference exists at these sites, just about anything you pick up with the meter will demand an explanation. With no artificial fields in evidence, a basic meter is one of the best detectors to use in such circumstances.

TriField EMF meter model TF2

TriField meters, manufactured by AlphaLab Inc. in Utah, are some of the finest EMF meters on the market. Although their lowest-tier model still falls into the realm of a standard meter, it is far more sensitive than any other basic meters that are available. This newer model has replaced the older TriField 100XE model. It is an AC gaussmeter, AC electric field tester, and a radio power density meter in a single unit, which combines all the features needed for fast, accurate measurements of electromagnetic fields.

Most interesting for paranormal investigators, though, is the special frequency weighted mode that properly scales the magnetic and electric measurements to indicate the full magnitude of currents produced by each type of field inside the human body. It has a large LCD bar for accurate readings and an adjustable back-light for use in dark locations.

For the best use of this meter, it should be held with the right or left hand curled underneath the device so that the fingertips wrap around the opposite edge. You should never hold the meter so that your hand blocks the top of it. This can block the detection of all electrical fields. Even though you cannot block magnetic fields this way, you should err on the side of caution and hold it with your hand around the center.

Hold the meter extended in front of your body, again using the distance from your hand to your elbow as a guide. Move the meter back and forth and watch for abrupt and sudden surges of energy. You should notice that you are detecting a background radiation of the location that falls between 2–3 milligauss on the ana-log scale. This is normal. Watch for sudden changes and fluctuations that drive the needle much higher on the scale. When you find one, you should again try to rule out any artificial interference before you accept the readings as evidence of any-thing paranormal.

TriField Natural EM meter

This is perhaps the best and most sensitive meter on the market for paranormal investigations. What makes this meter so beneficial to paranormal research is the fact that it registers only DC or "natural" electrical and magnetic fields. This is the type of field that is given off by humans and animals and possibly, by paranormal energy, as well. It makes a great addition to any investigator's arsenal, but it can also be tricky to use, so it may not be best for beginners.

The Natural EM meter was originally designed to detect changes in extremely weak DC fields. It is equipped with both an analog scale and an audible signal that moves whenever a field changes from its previous level. The meter was also designed to ignore artificial (AC) fields that are generated by man-made power sources, which is why it became so popular with researchers.

Originally, the meter was used to do field experiments on the energy levels of geo-magnetic storms, including unusual solar activity in the earth's ionosphere and the electrical activity of ordinary thunderstorms. The meter is very sensitive to changes of as little as 0.5 percent of the strength of the earth's magnetic fields. When set on "magnetic," the meter can detect the movement of any magnetic sources at the location. A tone sounds when the field increases or decreases. After the meter detects a change and then the field becomes stable for more than five seconds, the tone ends, and the meter returns to a base reading. The meter then remains at rest until the field changes again. The user can determine the amount of change that signals the audible tone by using a "squelch" knob on the side of the meter. Any changes in the strength of the magnetic field will register.

When the dial is set to "electric," the meter becomes sensitive to electric fields as weak as 3 volts per meter. As an example of how sensitive the meter is, this is the equivalent of taking a ten-foot-square room and filling it with enough energy to lift a single grain of salt. Typical electric fields will fluctuate at about 1–2 volts per meter. Because of this, the minimum sensitivity on this model has been set to 3 V/m and has been designed to disregard "background noise." Regardless, the meter remains so powerful that it can pick up the electrical field of humans and animals, sometimes through a wall. You can actually see the changes for yourself by holding the meter in one hand and moving your other hand across the top of it. For this reason, the meter can even function as a motion sensor. However, it isn't foolproof because some people have such a charge to their bodies that they cannot use this meter without causing constant interference.

This particular meter also features a "sum" setting, which combines the readings from the electric and magnetic fields of the location. The meter does not differentiate between the two and the scale and signal don't change whenever either field changes.

It can be complicated to use, and this is why the meter is best-suited for those who have been working in the field for some time. It can be learned by just about anyone, though, so long as they have the time and the patience to experiment with it.

Although this meter can be used as a handheld device, it's very delicate and just about any change in motion can cause it to react. For this reason, it's probably best used as a stationary device to pick up transient fields. The meter is capable of detecting activity in an entire room and the device can be easily monitored by either a video feed or even by a researcher, as long as they remain quiet and relatively still during the investigation. This enables the ghost-hunter to detect any unseen changes or fields in the location and it is very effective. To make the meter especially sensitive in the "electric" and "sum" settings, place it on a metal stand or surface.

Using Other Detection Devices

Making a list of every electronic device that has been — or will ever be — adapted for use in paranormal investigations would be an endless task. If you have technical skills, you can consider building some of your own equipment, but for those who want to purchase the many different kinds of equipment, other items are worth considering.

The REM pod

The *REM pod*, or *radiating electromagnetism pod*, is different from other ghost-hunting tools in that it radiates its own electromagnetic field. Traditional EMF meters are tuned to detect the fields produced by flowing currents of electricity or radio frequencies. Because the REM pod radiates its own EM field, it can detect much more, which, in theory, makes it easier for spirits to use the device to communicate. (See Figure 9-3.)

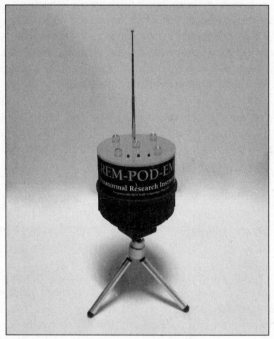

FIGURE 9-3:
A REM pod.

The REM pod can detect a difference in field strength whenever a conductive material enters into its EM field. The device's telescoping antenna allows for 360-degree coverage, which means that it should pick up anything that moves in and out of its field, including spirit energy. When the device is triggered, one of its five colored LED lights illuminates. An audible tone accompanies each of the lights — red, green, blue, yellow, and purple — to indicate the strength of the field disturbance.

It is an interesting device. Essentially, it is a capacitive circuit paired with an oscillator to generate an EM field. It is wrapped in a cylindrical-shaped case with the lights and antenna on the top. The technology it uses is not new. It is basically a modified Theremin, a musical device invented by Russian scientist Lev

Sergevich Termen in the 1920s. Unlike other musical instruments, the Theremin is played without making physical contact with it. Just like with the REM pod, the closer the musician moves their hand toward the instrument's antenna, the higher the note that it plays.

The device has five levels of sensitivity, set using a switch on the base, and this determines how close something, or its energy, needs to be to the device so that it is triggered. The REM pod also had automatic baseline adjustment. This means that if an object fell into the device's field, or something nearby was to switch on that produces a field, the REM pod would ignore it and readjust after a few seconds. It also has a useful function called *ambient temperature deviation detection*. The pod either makes a high- or a low-pitched noise to indicate a sudden change in air temperature. The noise is also accompanied by a visual signal in the form of a red or blue light.

The REM pod is a good alternative to paranormal researchers who have voiced their skepticism about the use of traditional EMF meters. These doubts are based on the fact that basic meters, like the popular K-II, cannot detect electromagnetic fields around the human body. This makes many question their usefulness — if they cannot detect a person, then how can they detect a spirit? The REM pod does not have this issue. It can be triggered by a person or an animal getting too close to it. This makes it easier to believe that a ghost may trigger the device.

When investigating, the REM pod should always be left in a stable location. It should not be carried around as a handheld device. Multiple devices can be used to track the movement of energy in the location.

When the REM pod is in position, consider calling out to the spirits that may be present and encourage them to interact with the device. Remember when doing this, though, that a ghost is unlikely to know what a "REM pod" is, so you should encourage them with phrases like "can you move toward the glowing box in the room."

Infrared motion detectors

Infrared motion detectors were included on the list of essentials for paranormal investigators because they serve several purposes. They can be used to secure an area from intrusion by the living, register the movement of energy fields, and even pick up temperature changes in the monitored area.

In the past, before the widespread availability of electronic equipment, researchers used string and tape to seal off rooms and doors that they were monitoring for ghostly activity. This insured that the locations remained uncontaminated and if the tape was broken on the door, the investigator had some idea that the room had been entered. Now, infrared motion detectors are available so that researchers can still seal off rooms and the meters serve the dual purpose of monitoring possible anomalous activity.

When searching for your own motion detector, look for a device that is not only triggered by motion but by temperature changes, too. A meter that monitors in the infrared range is able to pick up light changes, temperature changes, and of course, what cannot be seen by the human eye. By backing them up with a camera or video camera, motion detectors have become vital pieces of equipment when compiling evidence of a haunting.

When sealing off an area for investigation, simply place the meter outside of any door leading into the room that you want to remain closed. This can also work for larger areas by "closing" all the access points with motion detectors. This ensures that your paranormal experiments or monitoring is not interrupted and provides good evidence that any anomalous readings that are collected were not caused by human interference.

By spreading the motion sensors out through the area that is reportedly haunted, researchers should watch for them to be triggered by anomalous activity. If the alarms on the meters are set off, be sure to first look for a natural or artificial explanation for the alert. It possibly was set off by an animal, another researcher, or even an artificial surge in the electrical system of the site.

Temperature sensing devices

Paranormal researchers should almost make sure that temperature sensing devices are in their tool kit. Monitoring the ambient temperature of the site is critical. We are aware of the temperature of the surrounding air in our daily lives, based on what the weatherman tells us during the evening news. When a witness or researcher speaks of feeling a "cold spot" in a reportedly haunted place, it is within the ambient temperature of the location. This is where we need to focus our efforts when looking for temperature changes and abnormalities.

Many sensors that can quickly detect temperature changes are on the market. The first step is to make a record of the background, ambient temperature of the location. A basic thermometer works just fine for this. It does not have to be fast, merely accurate. This temperature device should be separate and independent from all other temperature-sensing devices, so the accuracy of any readings isn't contested later.

Then, we move on to our second unit. The best device to measure rapid changes in the ambient temperature is a device that can pick up temperature readings by the use of an external probe. Several are on the market, and some have metal probes that extend from the meter, whereas others have softer, flexible probes.

These devices are affordable and can be purchased from many electronic supply companies. Most of them have a measuring unit of fewer than three centimeters, which is capable of measuring the rapid changes to the temperature needed when looking for cold spots. A moving cold spot possibly can be tracked with such a tool because it can react so quickly.

When looking for a device like this, try to find one that is accurate, simple to use, and affordable. After you turn it on, most meters give you a new temperature reading every few seconds. Most meters also offer other options, like high and low limits, and sound an alarm when these limits are reached. An effective way of using them is to monitor an area with an array of these devices. By setting the alarms on the units to sound whenever a low temperature threshold is reached, we can easily focus on different parts of the location when needed. We can then have definitive temperature data from within the room, or at the exact location that we are monitoring.

Remember that because paranormal research is not an exact science, we have to check and double check and confirm and re-confirm any of the evidence that we collect in order for it to be seen as legitimate. Because many researchers report the presence of "cold spots," we need to find a way to measure them. Although we should never, ever discount the feelings and experiences of witnesses and investigators, we should also make every effort to legitimately verify such claims with the most reliable equipment that we have at our disposal.

Relative humidity gauge

This device is fairly inexpensive and can be used in conjunction with a thermometer to record the ambient conditions of an indoor or outdoor location. This enables you to record what the conditions were at the time of the investigation and may also help to rule out any natural effects that may appear in photos and video.

Because it has been theorized that residual hauntings may be caused by water embedded in the physical structures of some locations, a humidity gauge could become crucial when determining the humidity that is present.

Combination devices

One of the most convenient devices that can be used for investigation is a device that combinations several different pieces of equipment into one unit. MAG-TEMP meters offer simultaneous EMF and temperature readouts on one device, using an illuminated display. It has everything that you need to measure electromagnetic energy and temperature fluctuations and it fits in one hand.

Final Thought on Ghost-hunting Equipment

Choosing devices and gear for your paranormal research gives you much to consider. Technology improves all the time, and staying up-to-date on new devices, changes in the field, and the latest experiments is always wise. Electronic devices are an excellent way to collect valid evidence of the paranormal, but it is not the only way.

We must remember that ghost-hunting equipment is only as good as the ghost-hunter who uses it — and how they use it. Simple equipment can be just as effective in an investigation of ghostly phenomena as the most sophisticated apparatus, as long as it is in the right hands. The value of any report is only as good as the investigator who made it, and the best reports are never dependent only on the equipment being used.

Chapter **10**

The Dangers of Investigating

Research is the key to success when it comes to paranormal investigation. This not only includes the research into the history of the location that you plan to explore, but research into the various aspects of ghosts and hauntings, the best places to find ghosts, and the tools that you need with which to begin your investigations. All of this is very exciting, and you will soon be ready to begin your journey as a ghost-hunter. However, it would be negligent of me not to include some words of caution before you begin.

First, always be prepared. Before you begin your investigations, make sure you have all the necessary supplies. Dress appropriately for your excursion by wearing sturdy, comfortable shoes or bringing a jacket. Make sure that you have a cell phone for use in emergencies.

If you are investigating a property that is not your own, always ask permission. Having the property owner give written consent is often best to avoid any legal issues. If a property owner does not want you to investigate in a certain area, he probably has a good reason. To be on the safe side, always bring along your photo ID. Leave immediately and politely if the police or owners ask you to do so.

Safety during an investigation is always very important. If you are prepared by researching your location in advance, your exploration should be exciting and safe. In order to be cautious, though, you may want to bring along a first aid kit with bandages and antibiotic ointment for your team.

What Not to Do as a Ghost-Hunter

Many things can happen in the course of a paranormal investigation, and not all of them are good. The list that follows offers some ideas and guidelines of things that you should avoid:

>> **Never investigate alone:** Investigations are not only more exciting with a team; they are also much safer. Having other sets of hands allows you to have help during the investigation, allows you to have corroboration for anything strange that happens, and keeps you from walking into any problematic or volatile domestic situations at locations where you investigate.

The only time when I think this may be allowed is if the investigator has many years of experience and if their team is also present somewhere at the location. If a bad situation does arise, they can still contact someone for assistance.

>> **Never eat or chew gum during EVP sessions:** This seems like an obvious one, but you may be surprised. Eating or chewing gum while investigating is never a good idea, but it is even worse when trying to record credible EVP sessions.

>> **Never bring children to an investigation:** Team members for your investigation should always be made up of members over the age of 16. If a location is known for demonic activity, then look for members aged 18 and older who understand all the risks involved. This is legally smart in many ways and safer for everyone involved.

>> **Never go to a location without studying the layout and terrain:** Be sure you know what you are getting yourself into with your investigation in advance and in the daylight. Take notes, draw maps, identify parking, paths, and hazards, and anything else you need to do to verify the safety and accessibility of the site. Always keep a working flashlight with you, even during daytime ghost-hunts.

>> **Never assume the paranormal:** Never go into an investigation already assuming that the activity that has been reported has a paranormal source.

We must remain open-minded and cautious when starting a case. Percentages say that the activity may not be a ghost so unless we find evidence of our own, we cannot assume that a haunting is taking place.

» **Never review your evidence half-heartedly:** If you are going to record hours of tape during an investigation, then you must watch all of it, often frame-by-frame. The same goes for your hours of EVP. It all must be listened to and although it can be boring, it is a crucial part of the investigation.

» **Never be physically uncomfortable:** Dress for the weather and the location. Do not eat a heavy meal immediately before your investigation, but do not arrive hungry, either. Both can be distracting. If you take medication that could impair your judgment, talk to your doctor about being in rough terrain after dark and find out how risky it may be.

» **Never drink alcohol or use drugs during an investigation:** This is another guideline that would seem to be obvious, but too often, investigators have run into problems with team members who decided to have a few drinks before arriving at a location. This can be dangerous in many ways, not only physically, but mentally and spiritually, as well.

» **Never trespass on private property:** Always get clear and specific permission from the owners of private property before an investigation. If you will be on property that has been posted against entry after dark, contacting the authorities may be necessary. Getting permission in writing is always best. Bring along your own form to sign and make sure that it frees the owner from any liabilities caused by the investigation.

» **Never leave your cell phone in during an investigation:** Text messages, phone calls, and sounds from your smart phone can contaminate your investigations and can be very distracting. In addition, Bluetooth connections and incoming calls and messages — even when your phone is switched to silent — can disrupt equipment and audio recordings with interference feedback.

» **Never bring disruptive people to an investigation:** Never bring along anyone to an investigation who is not willing to take things seriously. Bringing someone who is loud, obnoxious, and disrespectful can ruin an investigation of even of the most actively haunted place. This is one of the worst situations that a dedicated researcher has to deal with.

» **Never be rude:** Not thanking the homeowner or manager of the location is always a bad thing to do and could impact your investigation and subsequent investigations. Always remember to thank everyone involved.

Health Hazards from Ghost-Hunting

Some experienced paranormal investigators in the field have pretty scary stories to tell. These stories are not about ghosts. They are about mold, mildew, health, and safety issues. One researcher even died from respiratory issues after spending the night at a haunted place.

Allergies

Allergies are often an issue for investigators, especially during the winter, when most investigations take place indoors. Energy-saving measures — such as storm windows and doors with weather stripping — means that air circulates less. This air may not be healthy, especially for those who have environmental sensitivities and indoor allergies.

Many investigators do not take allergy medications before an investigation, especially if that medication may affect their alertness. This can put them at greater risk for respiratory distress.

Location owners sometimes have blamed physical symptoms — like dizziness or depression in just one part of the location — on ghosts when the actual issue was something environmental, like allergies or fumes from a new carpet or an oil-based paint. This can affect the investigators who are also at the scene.

If anyone on your investigation team is allergic to pets, asking the site owner if he or she has animals in their home or business is a good idea. Many people isolate their pets before the investigation team arrives, so don't assume pets aren't in the house just because you haven't seen or heard them.

Dust and mold

However, allergies are just the beginning. Basements and attics often present all kinds of safety issues. Several otherwise healthy investigators ended up in the hospital with life-threatening respiratory issues after conducting research at sites that contained rodent droppings.

Attic floorboards can be old and may have never been intended to support much weight. Ask the location owner before you venture up there. Attics can also be filled with dust. This is not just bad for your photographs and video, it is also a serious allergen for a lot of people.

Basements are prime locations for mold and mildew. The problem may not be noticeable on stone or cement walls until someone starts wheezing and coughing. Cockroaches are another problem frequent found in basements. The insects aren't the issue, but their droppings are. They can cause terrible respiratory challenges for people with allergies.

Some people worry about visiting old tuberculosis sanitoriums because of concerns about air quality. Generally, tuberculosis can be spread only from person to person and only when the contagious person has an active case of the disease. Some believe that it can also be spread by breathing infected air during close contact. Even so, the infested air would no longer be present in an abandoned sanitorium. Wearing a mask during an investigation is a good idea, but not because of tuberculosis. Dust and disease-carrying animal and insect droppings are greater dangers.

Histoplasmosis

Bat droppings can also put you at risk. Bats (and sometimes birds) in attics and basements can cause serious respiratory disease and a significant threat in some areas. To be safe, avoid breathing dust in areas where animal droppings are found. Health officials recommend that people who enter such locations should wear a respirator that can guard against particles as small as two microns.

Every researcher should have, at the very least, a few simple, paper masks in his or her ghost-hunting tool kit. A basic paper mask can help protect your health, reduce your chances of an allergic reaction or asthma, or possibly save your life. Be sure to get a box for your team and carry masks with you, no matter where you are investigating.

Asbestos

For a casual investigator, exploring sites that may contain allergens, irritants, or dust, a basic mask should be adequate. Depending on your health concerns and the environment in which you are investigating, though, stronger protection may be needed, especially if biological hazards are a serious issue.

Asbestos was used for decades in buildings, as insulation, and as a fire retardant, before it was largely banned in the 1970s. It was especially prevalent in public buildings like hospitals, schools, and mental institutions — all favorite abandoned locations for paranormal investigators. Asbestos is inherently dangerous only when it is broken or crushed, when it releases microscopic fibers that can be deadly to inhale or ingest. Asbestos exposure is linked to the development of mesothelioma, a deadly cancer that affects the lining of the lungs or the abdomen. Mesothelioma has no known cure, and asbestos disease may take as many as 30 years or more after exposure to present symptoms.

If you suspect that asbestos is present in the building you are investigating, consider skipping the location, or at least invest in a high-quality respirator before the investigation. Always read the labels on masks and respirators and be sure that you have one that is qualified for the kind of particles that may be in the air.

Carbon monoxide

Another environmental hazard that many investigators forget about is carbon monoxide. It is an odorless gas that can pass right through all respirator masks and can be highly toxic at extremely low concentrations. If you are exposed to it, watch out for a headache or a "heavy" feeling. It can be mistaken for signs of spiritual oppression, but this is purely physical — and deadly.

3

Putting Your Paranormal Research into Action

Chapter **11**

Ghosts on Film: Using Your Camera to Capture Evidence of Ghosts

The birth of photography and the beginnings of paranormal research came within a few decades of one another. Photography, which began as little more than a few tentative experiments in the early 1800s, became commonplace by the middle part of the 19th century. It was about this same time when the so-called "spirit rappings" began at the Fox family home in Hydesville, New York and launched the Spiritualist movement and the scientific investigations of the movement that followed. By the early 1900s, with the introduction of the Brownie camera, photography had become wildly popular and so had the Spiritualist movement, with séances routinely held in family homes and mediums not only contacting the dead but also taking photographs of the departed. These days, with millions of photographic images being created annually with cameras and smartphones, photography has never been as important to the field of paranormal research as it is today.

With all these images come many mysteries, especially when we begin delving into the realm of the supernatural. We need to explore whether a strange photo shows merely a defect or a ghost and what we may be capturing when we photograph haunted locations. We take a look at how cameras are best used as tools in your investigations and also offer hints and tips on basic uses for cameras, using cameras in fieldwork, and even a guide to ruling out various types of flaws that may look like ghosts but are probably not.

When it comes to photographs, it is often necessary to spend more time discussing what is *not* a ghost, rather than what might be. Skeptics always maintain that "extraordinary claims require extraordinary proof." Although they use this statement to dismiss any type of phenomena that they personally do not believe in, it has some truth to it. A good investigator needs to have the tools to examine and analyze his or her photographs before putting them on display and claiming they are evidence of ghosts. We have all seen photos that claim to be ghosts and spirit energy that are not. With good information at your disposal, you can ensure none of those photos are yours.

There is a principle used in investigative work that maintains that the simplest explanation for something, which is the hypothesis with the fewest assumptions, is most likely to be correct. This does not mean that we should start dismissing any possibly genuine paranormal photos because it would be much simpler not to believe in ghosts but that we start analyzing them by looking for the non-paranormal explanations first. If a possible anomaly in a photograph looks like it could be caused by your camera flash on a reflective surface, then this is likely the case. By examining this idea first, and not assuming it must be a ghost because the location where the photo was taken is haunted, you may save yourself embarrassment in the future.

A Brief History of Photography

We begin with a history of photography, which is more relevant than you may think. In order to properly use a camera in paranormal research, the operator needs to know how that camera operates and how very different this device is from the human eye.

Capturing the light

Since the beginning of recorded time, man has created images of the things that surrounded him. In the earliest times, cave dwellers rendered likenesses of animals on the walls of their shelters. Ancient people crafted images on pottery and stone and the Middle Ages saw the birth of thousands of pieces of classic artwork. The 18th century saw a demand appear for pictures of people that were less expensive than the formal oil paintings that were commissioned by wealthier patrons.

Those of the middle class were able to obtain miniature paintings that were mostly silhouettes, created by a shadow cast from a lamp and then cut freehand by the artist from black paper. These shadow portraits were one-of-a-kind originals until 1786, when a device called a *physionotrace* made it possible to make multiple images. When the pointer of the device was traced over the lamp-created profile, a system of levers caused an engraving tool to reproduce the outline on a copper plate. Details, features, and clothing could also be added, and then the plate was inked and printed to make as many copies as needed. Soon artists and inventors began to speculate about creating an optical device that could produce the images directly.

An optical device like this, known as the *camera obscura*, was known in ancient times but there was no way to permanently record the images it obtained. Various portable models of the *camera obscura* were invented and in 1589, Giovanni Battista della Porta made note of using a lens rather than a hole to show the images. About 1665, Robert Boyle constructed a model that was the size of a small box and added a lens that could be extended or shortened like a telescope. This way, the image could be shown on a piece of paper placed across the back of the box and directly across from the lens. Scientists began using the *camera obscura* for solar observations and artists adapted it as an aid in drawing since they could easily trace the projected image.

Around 1800, the first experiments were conducted to try and enhance the *camera obscura* images. They were carried out in England by Thomas Wedgwood, who tried to copy paintings that were done on glass onto sheets of paper that were treated with silver nitrate. Unfortunately, the dark images were not permanent and because of their sensitivity to the light, could only be viewed by candlelight.

The first permanent images created by light were produced by a French inventor named Joseph Nicephore Niepce, who was also an amateur artist. He wanted to create a new printmaking technique of lithography but was not very skilled at drawing. He sought ways of transferring images directly onto the printing plate and even tried Wedgwood's methods but also found that the faint, disappearing images created a problem. Over time, Niepce discovered a varnish that was sensitive to light, remaining soft where protected from light and hardening wherever exposed. A plate coated with varnish and exposed by passing light through a drawing or print made on translucent paper could then be washed with a solvent that dissolved the soft areas and left a permanent image on the plate. These first *heliographs* came about in 1822, and Niepce continued working with them for five years before using a *camera obscura* to record an image on a coated pewter plate. This view was made from the window of his home and required an eight-hour exposure. It is regarded today as the "oldest surviving image produced by a camera."

Developing daguerreotypes

In 1835, William Henry Fox Talbot discovered the fundamental principle on which modern photography is based — the photographic negative from which many copies can be made. He also identified silver chloride as the silver compound that is most suitable for photographic prints. In 1840, he gave the name *calotype* to his improved process in which a latent image could be developed onto paper. Unfortunately, though, his work at that time was being overshadowed by a French process that produced a very different photographic image known as the *daguerreotype*.

This process was discovered in 1837 by an inventor named Louis Daguerre. The biggest drawback to this new form of photography was that to expose and process a daguerreotype plate, a lot of apparatus and work was required. First, the plate had to be placed in a hand vise and polished with a leather buff, using powdered pumice stone and olive oil. It was finished to a high polish and then placed in a box that had two compartments for iodine crystals and bromide water. The developer then had to watch the plate carefully and estimate when the desired degree of sensitivity had been reached. The prepared plate, loaded into a plate holder, was then placed in the camera, which consisted of two wooden boxes, one of which contained the lens and the other the focusing screen and holder for the plate. After the plate was exposed, which took about 30 seconds, it was removed and taken to the darkroom, where it was placed face down in the top of the developing box. In the bottom was a dish of mercury, heated by a lamp. As the mercury vapor developed the image, the process could be seen by candlelight through a yellow glass window in the box. When fully developed, the image was then fixed by a chemical treatment that removed the unused silver salts. The plate was then placed on a level stand so that it remained completely horizontal, then covered with a gold-bearing solution and heated. Finally, after it was washed and dried, the finished plate was covered with a decorated covering and a piece of protective glass and then sealed in a brass or foil frame. It had to be an airtight frame for the silver plate would tarnish rapidly if it was exposed to air.

Obviously, creating daguerreotypes was high maintenance work and very expensive and complicated. The work was so cumbersome that a photographer literally had to travel with a small laboratory that limited him to producing fragile, one-of-a-kind pictures that were *direct positives*, or mirror-imaged. In the portraits, the faces of the sitters were flattened in a way that made them look like they were in pain. Daguerreotypes were not only a burden to create but they were unflattering to those who paid to have them made.

Even with all the disadvantages, daguerreotypes captured the popular imagination. In March 1840, Alexander Wolcott and John Johnson, associates of Samuel Morse, opened the first portrait studio in the United States. The idea caught on and soon attendance at the daguerreotype portrait studio became essential in the social circles of the fashion conscious.

Working with wet plates: Ambrotypes and tintypes

By 1844, the daguerreotype process was virtually perfected, but even so, it was never meant to last. By the middle 1850s, a new photographic process, called the *collodion* or *wet plate* method, began to overshadow the daguerreotype and it lasted for several years in America.

The first wet plate method, the *ambrotype*, had a very short lifespan. This process, which used paper plates instead of silver ones, required much less work and was much cheaper to produce than the daguerreotype method. Despite its advantages, there were problems, too. Like the daguerreotype, each ambrotype was a one-of-a-kind image. If the subject desired an additional picture, he had to sit for another exposure or have his original copied. Because the image was quite fragile, the collodion positive had to be carefully packaged. It had to be fitted with a brass covering and then covered with glass, followed by a brass rim called a *preserver*. The package was then placed in a folding case that would protect it from damage.

The popularity of the ambrotype was sudden and far-reaching, lasting from the middle 1850s and into the early 1860s. Many Civil War soldiers chose this inexpensive process to immortalize themselves for their loved ones back home. But the process was not meant to last and was soon replaced by another type of collodion-positive method that gained its greatest fame during the Civil War.

The *tintype* came about in the latter part of the 1850s but did not become popular for several years. Like the ambrotype, the tintype used the same type of collodion, wet plate process but in this case, the process utilized a thin sheet of blackened iron. Thanks to this, it was nicknamed the "tintype," and the name stuck.

Although tintypes lasted well into the 20th century, when they were produced by the gelatin-silver bromide process, early tintypes were made by the collodion wet plate method. The thin iron plate that was used was coated with black varnish and then cut to size to be inserted into the camera. It was exposed in a camera that was often designed to permit all the chemical operations to be conducted inside of the camera itself. To prevent damage, the exposed plates were then given a protective coat of clear varnish.

Unlike the ambrotype, the tintype was developed as a positive image and so it did not have to be backed or even mounted in an elaborate matter that would allow the image to be clearly seen. The metal base was also less fragile, which is the reason that so many tintype images have survived into the modern era. Another advantage was that even though the tintype was also a one-of-a-kind photograph, multiple identical images could be created with a multiple lens camera. These cameras could expose four, six, or even more photographs simultaneously on a single plate. After processing, the duplicate pictures were then snipped apart with metal cutting shears.

Although the tintype photograph lacked the tonal range of the ambrotype, its relative inexpensiveness made it very popular, especially in America. The low cost also appealed to soldiers during the war, especially the lower paid Union enlisted men. Confederate tintypes became progressively less common, though, thanks to wartime shortages of sheet metal.

This practical and profitable method of photography continued to be used, despite the clamor for paper prints, until after World War II.

In the 1880s, Charles Bennett began work on a new dry plate process that allowed photographers to travel without a dark tent and wagon full of chemicals. This allowed them to make excursions with just a camera, tripod, and a few plate holders loaded with prepared dry plates. They could later be processed when they returned to the studio. Remaining popular until the 1920s, the gelatin dry plate glass negatives brought several important changes to photography, especially the means to measure the sensitivity of the plate.

Photographing movement

By 1886, improvements were also made that allowed for methods to calculate necessary lens apertures and exposure time. This led to radical advancements in photography. For the first time, photographs could be achieved that required exposures of fractions of seconds and the photography of moving subjects became practicable at last.

Because of the lengthy exposure times needed by the earlier photographic plates, any movement produced a blur. For this reason, not only were photos of moving people or objects out of the question, but even those who sat for portraits had to have their heads held by clamps that had to be fixed to the back of chairs. This is the reason why you never see any sort of photos from the Civil War era that are anything other than posed portraits or still landscapes.

Shuttered cameras first came into use about this same time. The shutters, consisting of flaps or sliding plates, created exposures as brief as one-fourth of a second. The instantaneous photo was characterized as a *snapshot* (a term applied to a hurriedly aimed shot) by Sir John Herschel. Such brief exposures permitted cameras to be freed from the tripod, which had been used by the photographer to prevent movement and then blurring of the picture. Now, with the addition of a viewfinder to aid in the framing of the photo, cameras could be handheld. The first small, box-type camera was invented by Thomas Bola. He called it a *detective* camera, and soon, diminutive models were hidden in bags, hats, and even in the handle of walking sticks. The glass plates remained a problem though, thanks to rather awkward mechanisms that held several dry plates at once. Such cameras came to be known as *magazine* cameras and became the forerunner to a revolutionary development in America that allowed successive snapshots to be made quickly.

Taking snapshots: The rise of Kodak

The dry photo process that had been devised by Charles Bennett gained the attention of an American named George Eastman. The Rochester, New York, bank clerk and amateur photographer was so impressed with the plates that he began manufacturing gelatin dry plates and selling them through a photographic supply house as early as 1880. He became the first person to do so in the United States.

Eastman soon sought additional ways to simplify photography, realizing that the complexity of it, along with the messy processes, was keeping it from being enjoyed by everyday people. Working with camera manufacturer William H. Walker, Eastman developed a holder for a lengthy roll of paper negative *film*. Although there had been earlier experiments with such things, the Eastman-Walker invention combined a roll-holding feature with very sensitive, lightweight material. It became an immediate success.

Soon after, Eastman designed a small, handheld camera that utilized the roll holder. Patented in 1886 with an employee named F.M. Cossitt, the small model was produced with a run of only 50 cameras. Too complicated and too expensive to do well, the entire lot was sold off to a dealer the following year. Two years later, in 1888, Eastman developed a new model that was made up of a small box that contained a roll of paper-based film that was enough for about 100 exposures. It was simple to operate but the photographer had to keep track of the pictures for there was no exposure counter. Eastman gave his camera the invented name of *Kodak*, which he felt gave it a firm, uncompromising moniker.

Although there had been earlier roll-film cameras, the Kodak was the first to be backed up by a service that processed the exposed pictures. Realizing that most people did not have the time, skill or inclination to develop their own film, Eastman adopted the slogan "You Press the Button, We Do the Rest." After completing the roll, the customer sent the camera to Eastman's factory in New York, where the film was unloaded, developed, and printed. After that, a reloaded camera was shipped back to the owner, along with the processed prints. After much success, Eastman introduced a new camera in 1889 with an improved shutter. He called this one the No. 2 Kodak.

At the end of that year, Eastman also introduced a new product that replaced the old paper-based film, which had been complicated to handle. The new product was a roll film on a celluloid base and with this clear, flexible material, the roll-film camera finally became practical.

The Kodak camera and the development of celluloid roll film launched the heyday of popular snapshot photography, although it took years to solve all the problems that remained. The need to expose 100 images, for example, was solved by shorter films and simpler methods of loading that did not involve sending the camera back to the factory. In fact, by 1891, cameras had been devised that even allowed the film to be loaded in daylight. Numbered markings were placed on the black backing paper that helped protect the celluloid film from light when it was wound on a spool. These numbers could be read through a window on the camera's back and they permitted the film to be wound a precise distance each time until a new number was centered in the window. Eastman incorporated the idea in his pocket Kodak of 1895 and the first of his folding Kodak cameras in 1897.

Despite all of this, Eastman still felt that photography was too expensive for the masses and he assigned his camera designer, Frank Brownell, to develop a simple camera that could be cheaply reproduced. The result was the Brownie Kodak, which was introduced in February 1900. (See Figure 11-1.) Even though most assumed that the name for the camera came from its creator, Frank Brownell, the designation was actually supposed to have been sparked by the popularity of the Brownies, the little fairies in Palmer Cox's children's stories. This was tied to Eastman's advertising strategy that stated that the Brownie camera had a "simple Kodak method that enables even a child to make successful and charming photographs."

FIGURE 11-1:
The Kodak
Brownie camera.

Shutterstock/Faraz Mujeeb

The Brownie captured the imagination of the public and photographic enthusiasm continued to spread. In 1893, the first practical motion pictures were made using Eastman's film and were shown on Thomas Edison's Kinetoscope viewing machine. The motion pictures were based on earlier experiments conducted by Edward Muybridge in 1878. He had arranged a series of cameras with shutters that were triggered by trip wires across the path of a galloping horse. This produced a picture sequence that showed the horse in motion. The 1893 images, shown at the Columbian Exposition in Chicago, were the first to show motion using a steady roll of film.

Improving over time: Further developments in photography

More significant steps in photography followed. One of the most important was the development of the camera flash. Although flash powder had been used for illumination of subjects almost from the beginning of snapshot photography, it was, not surprisingly, very dangerous. The flashbulb was invented in the 1920s and automatically triggered flashes came with professional cameras in the middle 1930s. The first simple flash camera, the Falcon Press Flash, came along in 1939.

Another development came in 1938 when the first fully automatic camera was developed. It used a photoelectric cell to move a meter needle, which was locked in place by the initial pressure on the shutter release. Then, a spring-loaded sensor linked to the aperture setting moved until it was stopped by a locked needle, automatically setting the exposure.

Among the most important developments in the field was the introduction of color photography. Prior to 1935, only black and white photos that had been hand-colored were available to the public. Kodachrome was produced at the suggestion of two musicians, Leopold Godowsky Jr. and Leopold Mannes. They proposed coating film with three different black and white emulsions, each sensitive to one of the primary colors of light. A single exposure, when processed, produced three superimposed images, each of which could be selectively dyed to yield a full-color picture. Kodachrome was initially introduced as a motion picture film but a version for still cameras was soon created.

About that same time, Agfa, in Germany, produced a film that used the same three layers, but the color-forming compounds were placed directly into the film's emulsion. The Agfa and Kodachrome systems are the basis for almost all color photography that is in use today.

More improvements in photography involved cameras that had "instant" features. The Polaroid Land Camera was marketed starting in 1948. Within a minute of being removed from the camera, the print yielded a sepia-toned image. It was a huge success and many improved cameras and film followed, including Polaroid color film in 1963.

The Kodak Pocket Instamatic later simplified the common problem of loading the film for the average person who wanted to dabble in photography. The Instamatic was introduced in 1963 and was similar to the Brownie but offered simple load-in cartridges that could be dropped in only one way.

Advancing to digital cameras

Today, most film cameras have been replaced by digital cameras, which save money on film and developing and offer instant results when a shot is taken. The origins of digital cameras can be linked back to the computer imaging that was being done by NASA back in the 1960s. During this time, NASA was preparing for the Apollo Lunar Exploration missions and in advance of men landing on the moon, they sent out a series of probes to map the surface. The probes relied on video cameras that were outfitted with transmitters that could broadcast analog signals back to mission control. The weak transmissions were often plagued by natural interference and television at that time could not transform them into images that were coherent.

NASA researchers soon began searching for ways to enhance the signals by processing them through computers. The signals were analyzed by the computer and then converted into digital information. The interference was removed, and the critical data could be enhanced to produce clear images of the moon. This was the first real digital imaging to be done but it would soon revolutionize photography as we know it. Digital technology was not only used by NASA to explore the solar system, but it also made possible a number of medical imaging devices, changed the world of entertainment, and made photography and video accessible to people who had never used it before.

The digital cameras of today capture images electronically and convert them into digital data that can be stored on a chip inside of the camera. The images can then be transferred and manipulated using a computer. Like conventional cameras, digital devices have a lens, a shutter, and an aperture but they do not use film. When light passes through the lens, it is directed to a light-sensitive chip called a *charged coupling device (CCD)*. The CCD converts the light into electrical impulses, feeds it into the processing chip, and then transforms that into digital information. Digital images offer many things that a standard camera cannot, freeing the photographer from film and optics and allowing the images captured to be transformed in ways that have never been available before.

All images that are seen by the human eye are formed from the energy given off by light. For the digital camera to store an optical image, it must be converted into digital information. A simple photograph is composed of a wide range of color and light variations and, like the spectrum of natural light that it represents, the tones of the photo are continuous and unbroken. However, a digital image consists of scores of points of light that have been sampled from the light spectrum. The range of tone is determined by the camera's capacity to store and sample different light values. The more expensive the camera, or at least the greater number of megapixels of light that it offers, the better image the photographer will obtain. When a photo is taken, the pixels in the image are assigned a place on the color scale that corresponds to its place and value in the optical image. The more pixels, the greater the range of tone for the image. After the camera has determined the proper colors and tone, the CCD calculates a sampling rate for the entire image.

Most digital images form within a fraction of a second and in that instant, an image made of light is transformed into a stream of numerical data that can be changed and altered to look just like anything that the creative photographer wants. Without question, digital cameras have permanently changed the world of photography — both the photography that captures the everyday world and the spiritual one.

Understanding Cameras

It has been written many times about how photographers and others "see the world through the camera lens," perhaps never realizing how radically different it is to physically see something rather than to capture it with a camera.

The human eye does work in some ways like the shutter of the camera. It opens and closes in a blink or can be closed at the speed of a long exposure. The lens of the human eye works to focus on what it is looking at in the same way that the focus ring on a camera can be used. The human eye does this by reflex, but the camera has to be manually focused, either by hand or by the camera's inner workings. The iris of the eye dilates to let in more or less light in the same way that the f-stop on a camera does. The retina of the eye receives an image and imprints it on the consciousness in the same way that images are captured on the camera's film. At that point, though, the comparison between the two comes to an end. The images that we see with our eyes are collected and analyzed by our brain and anything that we see is subject to adaptation and censorship by our personality. Images that are collected by the camera are captured just as they are and are not distorted by emotion or disbelief, freezing a moment of time and space in a way that our eyes cannot do. This may be why ghosts sometimes turn up in photographs even when they are not seen by the human eye.

A camera basically consists of two things: a box that is tight enough to keep out light and a lens. The lens collects the light from the object that is being photographed and focuses on the image. The box is sealed so that it does not take in any other light than what is coming in through the lens. Beyond that, cameras are also equipped with a shutter, a simple timing device that restricts the length of time that light is allowed to reach the film, and an aperture, which is a hole that is located just behind the lens. The aperture is opened wider or smaller to brighten the image. This is known as the f-stop and the larger the number, the smaller the aperture. A higher number allows more light than a smaller number f-stop. All these items can be adjusted with manual cameras, although today, most cameras are automatic, and these settings are handled by the mechanism of the camera itself.

These automatic cameras, known as *single reflex* cameras (or *SLR* cameras) were the most commonly used devices for professional photographers and paranormal investigators for many years. Members of both categories continue to use them today, although most have switched to a digital camera. With an SLR camera, a single lens handles the viewing and the taking of the picture, but this type of device also allows manual focusing and changes in f-stop settings, exposure settings, and more. They were a little complicated for amateurs but were worth the effort to learn to use. Many preferred simple point and shoot type cameras, which were very easy to use and handled all of the settings automatically.

Using a camera in an investigation

There have been long debates about what type of camera is best for an investigation. In reality, it all depended on preference, interest, and skill. Remarkable photos have been taken with everything from expensive SLR cameras to Polaroid instant cameras to even cheap, disposable cameras. The main thing to remember is that it's not the camera that's most important, but rather the person behind the lens. You need knowledge to be a great photographer and that knowledge should begin with how light is captured by the camera and how they actually work.

The light around us can be thought of as rays of energy that emanate from, or reflect off, every point of an object and travel from it in straight lines. These lines travel randomly, so the lens of the camera serves to control their progress. The curved lens collects and redirects the light, bending it as it does so. The thicker and more curved the lens is, the greater its ability to bend the light; and the more the light is bent, the shorter the focal length will be. When the lens is focused at infinity, it is one focal length away from the *focal plane*, where an image is actually formed. The operation of focusing the lens, whether done manually or automatically, brings the lens away from the focal plane and brings nearer objects into focus. When the lens is focused on a point a certain distance away, an area in front of and behind this point will appear very sharp on film. This is referred to as *depth of field.* Using the depth of field can be helpful to the photographer and not just for creating better-looking pictures. One way that it is useful is that it allows the photographer to focus the camera in advance of taking photos during times when there may not be time to manually focus an SLR camera.

The light captured by the camera is also connected to the camera's shutter. The shutter allows light to reach the camera by opening and closing at various speeds, from very fast to very slow. Using a fast shutter and a high-speed film, the photographer can literally freeze even fast-moving objects and also take pictures under very low light conditions.

If you decide to continue using a film camera, you have to make a decision about the best film to use for your investigations. Some of the most important questions involve the best kinds of film to use and what speed that film should be. We recommend that you use a well-known brand name film and make sure that it is not expired. If the film is outdated, it may not work properly, and the user will be very disappointed if it fails to develop correctly.

When it comes to the best speed of film to use, that answer largely depends on how, when and under what conditions you plan to use it. Whether the film is being used indoors, outdoors under lighted conditions, in low light, or even in total darkness all factor into what speed of film the photographer should be using. The smaller the number of film, like ASA 100, the slower the film speed is and the longer the shutter will have to be left open in order for it to gather sufficient light and gain the proper exposure. However, the benefit to a slower speed film is that it has a smaller grain and it makes the picture quality better and allows for better enlargements of the print. The drawback, though, especially to those who plan to use the film for paranormal research, is that slow speed films are difficult to use indoors and almost impossible to use in the dark.

If the user plans to shoot photos in the dark, or even inside of a building in dim or ambient light, we recommend using a faster film, such as ASA 400 or above. These higher speed films gather the available light much quicker and also allow the user to disable their automatic flash and to shorten the exposure time for their photos. However, the grain of such films is much larger, so enlargements will be limited, and the quality of the prints will be poorer than with lower speed films.

Most photographers today — from journalists to law enforcement — use digital cameras. More detailed information about using digital cameras in your investigations can be found later in this chapter, but, suffice it to say, you should always use a quality camera. The higher the number of megapixels available, the better your photographs are going to be. This seems simple, but there are a lot of things about digital cameras that you may not know.

Photographing the unseen: The history of spirit photography

Spirit photography is nearly as old as photography itself but when the first photographers found inexplicable images in their work, they assumed they were caused by unknown variables in the strange chemicals and new apparatus they were using. At the dawn of photography, it was nearly impossible to take pictures of people. With the exposure times of a half hour or more needed to impress an image on the paper films and coated plates of the day, it was impractical to expect anyone to sit still for so long. It was not until improvements came along in cameras, lenses, photographic chemicals, and processes that exposure times were reduced to a matter of seconds instead of dozens of minutes. By this time, people were flocking to the portrait studios to have their images immortalized in time.

Interest in the Spiritualist movement had been on the rise since the announcement of spirit rappings at the home of the Fox family of New York in 1848. Of course, no photographs were taken of the weird events at the Fox home because indoor photography was impossible for many years afterward, but the days of spirit photography were coming.

During that era, the photographer had to first prepare a plate by coating it with collodion, bathe it in silver nitrate, and then take the photo while the plate was still wet. Each new exposure was an exciting event but imagine how excited W. Campbell of Jersey City must have been when he achieved what is considered to be the first spirit photograph. At the American Photographic Society meeting of 1860, he displayed a test photograph that he had taken of an empty chair. There had been no one else in the studio at the time but when the plate was developed, it showed the image of a small boy seated in the chair. Campbell was never able to produce any other photographs of this sort and thanks to this, it would not be until the following year that the real history of spirit photography began.

Capturing ghosts: The strange case of William Mumler

On October 5, 1861, in a photographic studio at 258 Washington Street, a Boston engraver and amateur photographer named William Mumler developed some experimental self-portraits that he had taken and was startled to find that the image of a ghostly young woman appeared in one of the photos with him. He was said to have recognized the young woman as a cousin who had passed away 12 years before. He later recalled that while posing for the portrait, he had experienced a trembling sensation in his right arm that left him particularly exhausted. The photograph attracted great attention and it was examined by not only Spiritualists but by some of the leading photographers of the day. Mumler was soon overwhelmed by public demand for his photographs and he gave up his regular job to devote himself entirely to spirit photography. (See Figure 11-2.)

FIGURE 11-2:
A spirit photograph by William Mumler.

William Black, a leading Boston photographer who was known as the inventor of the acid nitrate bath for photographic plates, was one of the professionals who investigated Mumler and his methods. After sitting for Mumler in his studio, Black examined his camera, plate, and bath and kept his eye on the plate from the moment its preparations began until it was locked into the camera. After his portrait was taken, Black removed it from the camera and took it into the darkroom himself, where, as it developed, he was stunned to see the image of a man, leaning over his shoulder. Black was convinced that Mumler was the genuine article and could somehow entice the spirits to appear on film.

Others were not so sure. Mumler had never been interested in the spirits before he began taking photographs of them and his fee of $5 per photograph began to arouse the suspicions of many that he was just in it for the money. He became the object of great controversy and eventually moved to New York, where he then began charging $10 for photographs. His critics and the disbelievers howled once more. In spite of this, he still had many supporters. One of them was U.S. Court of Appeals Judge John Edmonds, who had originally come to Mumler's studio convinced the man was a con artist but left convinced that he could actually conjure up genuine psychic photos.

In 1863, a Dr. Child of Philadelphia reported that Mumler was willing to allow him to thoroughly investigate the matter of his spirit photos and, as he said, to try and find a rational explanation for the mystery. He permitted Child to watch all his operations in the darkroom, and out of it, and also allowed him to examine his apparatus. Dr. Child displayed the pictures made at the time, while he and several friends watched the entire process, from the plate cleaning to the fixing. He took the precaution to mark each plate with a diamond before it was used and yet on each one of them was a spirit image. Child had failed completely to discover any human agent that was responsible for the formation of the spirit pictures. Each of them differed considerably from one another and Child could not come up with a way to duplicate them.

However, the *extras*, as they came to be called, in Mumler's photographs did not amaze everyone. After much controversy, pressure from city officials led to him being arrested and charged with fraud. But the testimony of several leading New York residents, including famed Broadway producer Jeremiah Gurney who affirmed that as a professional photographer he had never seen anything like the images that Mumler produced, led to Mumler being exonerated and his case dismissed.

Exploiting spirit photography: Novelty photos and widespread fraud

Other photographers, both amateur and professional, soon began to appear, eager to capitalize on the success of William Mumler. In America and Great Britain, new studios began to open, and the photographers began to call themselves mediums, claiming the ability to make dead appear in photographs. Spirit photography soon became a popular pastime and tens of thousands of dollars were made from those who came to have their portraits taken.

Many of these photographs look blatantly phony today and many of the spirit photographers of the time were exposed as frauds. In typical spirit photographs, ghostly faces materialized, floating above and behind the living subjects. In others, fully formed spirits would appear, usually draped in white sheets. Unfortunately, the methods of producing such images were simple. The fraudulent photographers became adept at doctoring their work, superimposing images on plates with living sitters and adding ghostly apparitions and double exposures. The appearance of the fully formed apparition was even easier. Many cameras demanded that the subject of the photo remain absolutely still, sometimes for periods of up to one minute; all the while, the shutter of the camera remains open.

During this time, it was very simple for the photographer's assistant to quietly appear behind the sitter, dressed in appropriate "spirit attire." The assistant remained in place for a few moments and then ducked back out of the photo again. On the finished plate, it seemed that a transparent "figure" made an appearance.

This type of "trick photo" was first mentioned in photography journals in 1856. Ten years later, Sir David Brewster recalled the technique when he saw some of the early spirit photos that were produced. He remembered another photo that he had seen of a young boy who had been sitting on a step near a doorway and who had apparently gotten up and left about halfway through the exposure. As a result, the seated image was transparent in the finished photo. Brewster wrote: "The value and application of this fact did not at first present itself to me, but after I had contrived the lenticular stereoscope, I saw that such transparent pictures might be used for the various purposes of entertainment."

Ghost and spirit photographs and stereographs were sold commercially in America through the 1860s and 1870s but were nothing more than a parlor novelty and were not meant to be taken as genuine spirit photographs.

Other methods of obtaining fraudulent photographs were used, as well. Prepared plates and cut films were often switched and substituted by sleight of hand tricks, replacing those provided by the investigator. And although this may have fooled a credulous member of the general public, sleight of hand maneuvers and instances of assistants prancing through photos draped in sheets did not convince hardened and skeptical investigators that the work of the spirit photographers was credible or genuine. However, in case after case, investigators walked away stumped as to how the bizarre images managed to appear on film. For every fraud who was exposed, there was at least one other photographer who was never caught cheating. This is what has kept the curiosity of the public about the early spirit photographers after more than a century has gone by.

Gaining credibility

The 1870s saw the first general acceptance of something credible in some aspects of spirit photography. Several references to it appeared in issues of the *British Journal of Photography* and in other periodicals of the time. In the 1890s, J. Traille Taylor, the editor of the *Journal*, reviewed the history of spirit photography and detailed the methods by which fraudulent photos were sometimes produced. He approached the phenomenon as cautiously, not immediately disbelieving it, but studying it in a scientific manner. He used a stereoscopic camera and noted that the psychically produced images did not appear to be in three dimensions. He used his own camera, and he and his assistants did all the developing and photographing. Strangely, they were still able to produce mysterious results.

In 1891, the practice of spirit photography gained more credibility when Alfred Russell Wallace, the co-developer of the theory of evolution, spoke out with the belief that spirit photography should be studied scientifically. He later wrote about his own investigations into it and included a statement that he believed the possibility of it was real. He felt that just because some of the photos that had been documented were obviously fraudulent, that not all of them could be dismissed as hoaxes.

In 1911, spirit photography entered the mainstream with the publication of the book *Photographing the Invisible* by James Coates. It covered dozens of cases of spirit photographs in detail and was later revised and expanded in 1921. It remains one of the most comprehensive books on the subject during this period and it managed to bring spirit photography to the attention of those who were not Spiritualists.

Following the publication of the book, several noteworthy articles appeared on spirit photography, including one by James Hyslop, a Columbia University professor. He wrote an introduction to a series of experiments carried out by Charles Cook of two American spirit photographers, Edward Wyllie of Los Angeles and Alex Martin of Denver. Cook did extensive work with the two men in 1916 and provided them with his own plates and had them developed by a commercial studio. In this way, he eliminated any opportunity that the two men may have had to doctor the images. Cook concluded that the photographs submitted were genuine but, in these cases, thought the name *psychic photography* better matched the phenomenon. He believed that the two men actually produced the images through some psychical means, rather than actually photographing ghosts.

One of the most amazing spirit photographs in history was taken at Raynham Hall in England in 1936. The house was being photographed for an article in *Country Life* magazine when the image of the Brown Lady was accidentally captured on the stairs (see Figure 11-3). Photographic experts were unable to debunk it.

There remains debate today about the reality of spirit photographs of the past. The emergence of modern science in the first half of the 19th century had helped to dispel the superstitions of days gone by but scientists were unable to connect the mysterious evidence obtained by spirit photography to the progress they were making in other fields. Because of this, most of the investigation and research into the field was carried out by Spiritualists, who believed that far too many of the photographs were genuine, thus validating their often-unpopular beliefs. The debunkers of today simply point to the many blatantly fake images that were produced as proof that the entire field was corrupt. However, this is the sort of short-sighted thinking that has managed to stall the study of the paranormal and to prevent it from becoming an accepted field of science.

FIGURE 11-3:
The Brown Lady
of Raynham Hall.

Today, researchers in the paranormal have come to realize that the ability to photograph the unseen is no more improbable than the discovery of latent images in the early 1800s. Attitudes toward aspects of the supernatural continue to undergo radical changes and move slowly toward acceptance, even though these types of photos still involve an infringement on scientific assumptions and rules. Despite this, evidence of common ground between psychic phenomena and physical phenomena continues to grow and someday, perhaps the two will meet and explain just how spirit photographs are produced.

Photographing ghosts

Since the days when investigators were debunking mediums and ghost-hunters like Harry Price were prowling Borley Rectory, the camera has been an essential part of paranormal investigations.

Far removed from when the phrase *spirit photography* was coined during the Victorian era, this type of photography today involves many kinds of advanced techniques. Despite the gains in technology, it should still be subjected to the same kind of scrutiny now as it was then. It is imperative that a good researcher knows all that he can about his camera and how it works because the photographs he or she takes are one of the most important parts of an investigation. For this reason, it is vital that your entire team is aware of your protocols for using cameras in your investigations. Spirit photography involves many different techniques that can be used to try and capture ghosts and spirit energy on film.

To start with, it shouldn't matter what sort of technology you are using to try and obtain spirit photos if the photos themselves cannot stand up to the scrutiny of a practiced eye. In other words, just because someone claims that they have a photo of a ghost, does not necessarily mean that they do. Often, anyone with any experience with photography at all can spot the claims of those who want to *believe* they have a ghost photo. Many problems can occur even with the simplest cameras, including double exposures, tricks of light, camera straps, lens refractions, and even obvious hoaxes.

One big issue with all of this is that no one really knows how ghosts can show up in photographs when they usually cannot be seen with the human eye. Some believe that it has something to do with the camera's ability to freeze a moment of time and space in a way that the human eye cannot do. In addition, it has also been suggested that ghosts, or paranormal energy, may be at a different spectrum of light that is not usually visible to the human eye and yet the camera manages to sometimes pick it up.

This spectrum of light may have a lot to do with radiation that is caused by electromagnetic energy, which many researchers feel that ghosts may consist of. The range of electromagnetic radiation extends from the short-range energy expended by electrical appliances to the longest radio waves. Although we can only see the spectrum of visible light, camera lenses are more sensitive and, for this reason, we may be able to photograph further than we can see beyond the visible spectrum, including some portions of electromagnetic energy. This is one possible explanation for the extra images that appear in spirit photographs.

Of course, these are all theories. This may explain how ghosts appear in photos, or it may be a combination of every theory. Perhaps they are all correct, or perhaps none of them are. As with anything else to do with the paranormal, few researchers are ever in complete agreement as to how something works. Most ghosthunters simply find a method for producing ghost photographs and then adapt it to work in their own research. Most often though, ghosts are captured quite by accident, leaving no clues as to why a particular photo was successful.

Evaluating Anomalies in Photographs

When researchers begin to examine and analyze photographs they obtain during their investigations, they are, of course, looking for evidence of spirits. That evidence can come in a number of different variations and forms, including orbs and mists.

Understanding orbs

One of the most common images that investigators find are what are referred to as *orbs*. Orbs have provoked a lot of controversy within the paranormal field, and although many orbs can be explained, not all of them can.

So, let us look at the evidence. A typical orb photograph is usually one that is taken in an allegedly haunted place and somewhere within the photo is a hovering, round ball. Some of these orbs appear to be giving off light, whereas others appear to be transparent. It should be noted that orbs were pretty rare before digital cameras became common. In the middle 1990s, when digital cameras first began to appear at a price that consumers could afford, they were nothing like what we have today. The digital imaging chips, which allowed photos with a very low megapixel count, were then far inferior to traditional film photography. The chips they contained could create "noise" in low-light photographs that were mistaken for orbs. It seemed that when they were used in darkness, or near darkness, the resulting images were plagued with spots that appeared white, or light colored, and where the digital pixels had not all filled in. In this manner, the cameras were creating orbs, and they had no paranormal source at all.

But it was easy to believe they did. This was at a time when there was an upsurge in interest in the paranormal and the Internet was really getting started. A few websites started to say that those missing digital pixels were orbs and the idea spread.

Faulty digital cameras sparked the popularity of orbs in the early days of the Internet, but artificial orbs are created in other ways, too. The most common orb photos are merely refractions of light on the camera lens. This occurs when the camera flash bounces back from something reflective in the range of the camera. When this happens, it creates a perfectly round ball of light that appears to be within the parameters of the photo but is actually just an image on the lens itself. These kinds of orbs don't have to have a camera flash to be created. They can also be caused by bright lights in an area where the photo is being taken, by angles of light, and by many types of artificial lighting.

Artificial orbs are not only caused by lights and camera flashes. Other objects that end up in front of the camera lens and are mistaken for paranormal images include dust, moisture, pollen, insects, snow, rain, hair, ash, and scores of other semi-microscopic particles. In almost every case, camera flashes and any external lights reflect on the surface of these particles and they seem to "glow" as one may expect a ghostly image to do.

Unfortunately, dust is everywhere, even in the cleanest home, so imagine how much dust is in the old houses, abandoned prisons, and dilapidated hospitals where so much of our paranormal research is done. It doesn't take much more than a small, unnoticeable breeze to get those dust particles stirred up and blowing around. The majority of photographs taken under such conditions contain artificial orbs. Outside, conditions are even worse. Dust, pollen from the grass, and flying insects look especially spooky in photographs and in the greenish glare of a night-vision camera.

Although this all sounds very negative with respect to orbs, not all orb-like anomalies that appear in photographs and on video are artificially created photo flaws. I do believe that genuine anomalies like this do exist and remain unexplained. I have seen them, not only in photos, but in person and they do sometimes interact with investigators.

I believe that orb anomalies that are captured in photos and videos are partial manifestations of spirits. There is no way to explain incidents where, even in very dusty locations, only a single orb is captured. In my experience, these kinds of orbs almost always have corresponding activity — unexplained voices, readings on equipment, or even a physical touch. Many times, during my investigations and on *Ghost Adventures,* when someone is having an experience, or when we have heard a mysterious voice on the spirit box, someone will capture a visual anomaly or an orb. They have even been seen coming out of the spirit box, or even disappearing into the investigators themselves. During some of our investigations, we may roll as many as 50 hours of film footage and during that time capture only two or three orbs. In each instance, though, it was when other activity was also occurring.

The most important thing to do before accepting that you have captured evidence of such an anomaly is to always look for that corresponding activity. After that, do everything you can to rule out artificial and natural causes for them first. Look for lens refractions, light sources, and reflections that could cause a glare. Check the lighting conditions that may have caused an anomaly to look as though it's in motion. This can happen under low light conditions when the shutter of the camera stays open longer to allow in more light. If a dust particle or an insect was in front of the lens and moved, it can make it appear that it left a glowing trail of light behind out. After you have ruled out these potential photo flaws, it is very possible that you have documented some kind of paranormal energy.

Dealing with mists

Another type of unexplained anomaly that is often captured in photos is what some would call a "mist," "fog," or simply "energy." This type of phenomena is usually white in color and is often around people or somewhere around locations where investigations have occurred. It is almost never seen by the human eye but appears in photos with no explanation.

Such a photographic phenomenon is not new. It has been a staple of paranormal photographs for at least the last century or more. Most of the images seemingly had no natural origins and turned up in developed prints long after the image was taken. Whether or not these pictures actually show ghosts is yet to be firmly determined but they are strange and many of them — especially those of human-like figures — are incredibly unnerving. They do seem to show some sort of paranormal energy and are very difficult to dismiss as a flaw.

Even so, an open-minded investigator must be careful to rule out errors. We can do this meticulously examining all the photos of this type that we find. Often, the strange fogs seem to be very close to people in photos. Often this occurs when it's cold outside, and the fog is likely to be vapor from an investigator's breath or some other moisture exuded from the investigator's bodies or equipment. Or the lens of the camera may have fogged. This is usually noticeable by the way that everything in the photo is blurred or distorted.

Many people mistake cigarette smoke for ghostly anomalies. When photographed with a flash, it often gives off an eerie glow. Cigarette smoke is usually distinguishable by the fact that it is very thick and seems to give off a bluish color. An examination of the photo often even shows someone in the frame who is holding a cigarette, which is, needless to say, a tell-tale sign that it is smoke in the photograph. The reviewer can also examine the surroundings in which the photograph was taken. If it is a snapshot from a bar or tavern, more than likely it's smoke and not a ghost, even if the place is haunted. Unfortunately, whether you can see someone in the photo smoking or not, the location tends to negate the idea that it may be something paranormal in the photo. When it comes to paranormal claims, erring on the side of caution is always better.

When it comes to searching for a genuine photo of a paranormal "mist" or "fog," the best thing that you can do is to try and take one of your own. In this way, you can be sure of the conditions under which the photos were taken, making sure that no natural fog is present and that temperatures were well above normal at the time of the investigation. You will know that you were not smoking or fogging up your camera lens.

The most desirable type of anomaly to capture with your camera is an actual apparition. This is, without a doubt, the smallest section of paranormal photographs that exist. Such photos are rare, and proving whether these kinds of photos are double exposures or outright hoaxes is usually difficult. However, when they have been authenticated — usually by examinations from photo experts outside of the paranormal field, who can find no plausible explanations for how they were created — they cause a sensation.

In most cases of apparition photos, investigators have come to believe that the images are the result of residual hauntings. The apparitions are very much like photographs, or film loops, repeating their actions over and over again. In the same way that energy has imprinted itself on the location where the photograph was taken, it is possible that the camera has captured that energy as a photograph.

Photography in Paranormal Investigations

The idea of using a camera to investigate the supernatural has been around for more than a century and a half but the paranormal itself has been with us since the beginning of time. The Bible is filled with incidents of the supernatural. Auras, prophetic voices, and levitations have been recorded and attributed to saintly people like St. Francis of Assisi, St. Theresa, St. Joseph of Copertino, and others. Although these stories may have been written under the influence of emotion and fallible human memory, undoubtedly the accounts have at least some truth. One of the most believable is the story of St. Joseph of Copertino, who was beatified in 1753. It was recorded that his levitation was witnessed not only by the general public but also by members of his order and, on one occasion, by Pope Urban VIII himself. Just imagine how a photographic record of this event could affect our lives and religion today.

These days, we have a great advantage over our ancestors who witnessed paranormal events: Since the era of photography, we have been able to make a record of this type of event.

The scientific investigation of psychic phenomena began with scientists who gathered to discuss whether Spiritualist mediums could be studied scientifically. During the investigations that followed, many scientists reported and photographed their psychic abilities. Over time, the ability of these mediums to produce levitation and movements without physical contact was established but no real explanation of their talents was ever revealed.

Today, few paranormal researchers use their cameras to document the phenomena created by Spiritualist mediums. Most of us use the camera to document not only ghosts but the strange happenings that sometimes occur during our investigations of haunted locations. We are all hoping that our cameras will capture something truly incredible during an investigation. In some cases, they do.

Cameras are an excellent tool for providing legitimate evidence of the paranormal. When conducting investigations, it is essential that you remember that photographing ghosts is not an easy process. In fact, some experienced investigators spent their entire careers looking for ghost photographs and have yet to find any that they deem credible.

Many investigators only use a camera when they encounter anomalous readings with their equipment and others cover the location with their camera to document as much as they can. Do plan to take a lot of photographs when you are involved in paranormal research. It takes dozens (or even hundreds) of shots to come up with even one paranormal photo that you feel is genuine. With this being the case, try not to get discouraged if every investigation fails to turn up something paranormal. Just because you don't get any results with your camera, does not mean the location is not haunted. The camera is just like any other tool in your ghost-hunting kit. The results that you achieve with it do not stand alone, and it is always possible that you will not find anything with your camera, even though your research leads you to believe that something is truly there.

And when the camera does seem to work, you still must be careful. Turning to the camera for proof of ghosts does not ensure against mistakes and many ghost-hunters are fooled into believing that some erroneous photos are real. Be careful to do your research and know how to tell "accidental" photos from the real thing.

Here are some things to be aware of when experimenting with paranormal photography:

>> Be careful that you have nothing protruding in front of the camera lens. Believe it or not, this can be anything from a finger to clothing, items around you like trees, grass, solid objects, clothing, and even hair. People with long hair should make sure that it is pulled back tightly or tucked under a hat. Loose hair that ends up in front of the camera lens (which may be unseen by the photographer) and which gets illuminated by the flash can look very eerie.

>> Be sure that your lens is clean and covered when not in use. Even a small drop of rain, dirt, or moisture that ends up on the lens can show up in a photo. This would not be seen through the viewfinder, so you would never know that it was there.

>> Make sure the weather is cooperating with your photographs. Make sure that it is not raining or snowing. Glowing lights that are photographed during a rainstorm are not exactly overwhelming proof of the supernatural.

>> Make sure that conditions are not damp, promoting moisture or fogging, on your camera lens. This is where the recommended temperature and humidity gauges come in handy. Any fog-like images that later turn in your photos could have a natural explanation.

>> Be sure to point the camera away from reflective surfaces when using a flash. Avoid mirrors and windows and bright or polished surfaces. The light from the flash bouncing off this surface can refract back onto your camera lens and create artificial orbs or just simply ruin your photos.

>> Whenever you are attempting to photograph activity (not necessarily when simply documenting the location), always try and take a number of photos in

succession. Snap anywhere from four to five images in the same location, same direction, same posture, everything. If something shows up in just one frame, this can be very compelling and possible hard evidence of a paranormal image.

>> No matter where you are taking photographs, be sure to use a photographic log sheet to keep track of where the photos were taken, who took them, and whether they were taken randomly or because some strange activity was occurring at the time. This can be very important when it comes to analyzing the photos and looking for corresponding activity at the site.

Using 35mm cameras for investigations

Although fewer ghost-hunters are using standard 35mm cameras these days, photographic experts always tell you that nothing is better for authenticating photos than a standard film camera and a negative. Please keep that information in mind when doing investigations and when you are thinking of getting rid of that 35mm camera that you believe is obsolete.

Consider three basic types of film when photographing your investigations:

>> **Color film:** This is the simplest and most basic method of photography during both daytime and nighttime investigations. For interior locations, or daytime investigations, use a 200 ASA speed film. At night, a 400 ASA speed film, along with your camera flash, is recommended. You may want to experiment with your camera at night and make sure this is a high enough speed film for your particular model of camera.

>> **Black-and-white film:** If you prefer to try and experiment without the flash, thus cutting down the chance for false orbs and lens refractions, you will want to use a 400 ASA speed film. This film is ideal because it is more sensitive to ultraviolet light so you have a better chance of picking up something unseen by the human eye. In most cases, this film can be developed by just about any processor, but make sure that they know it is a black-and-white film so that it can be developed correctly.

>> **Infrared film:** One of the most reliable but difficult to use types of film for photography is infrared. Using it requires a lot of experimentation and money, but this type of film is sensitized both to light that we can see with the naked eye as well as to light of a different wavelength that is invisible to us. The film allows you to see, literally, what is beneath the surface, or what the human eye cannot see. Infrared does not detect heat, but rather sees and photographs radiation. It can *see* a level of radiation that is one spectrum below thermal radiation, and this is radiation caused by electromagnetic fields. Because we believe that paranormal energy also lurks in this same "dead zone," infrared film becomes a very helpful tool in ghost-hunting.

However, infrared film does require special filters to use, must always be kept refrigerated, requires special processing, and must always be loaded and unloaded into the camera under conditions of absolute darkness. Also, most automatic cameras cannot be used with infrared film. Most models have an infrared sensor inside to make sure that the film advances properly. This sensor will badly cloud your film.

Ghost-hunting with digital cameras

In the early days of commercially available digital cameras, they were completely unsuitable for paranormal research. They were immediately seen as beneficial by many investigators because they provided instant images and there was no wasted film and no development costs. They saved researchers a lot of money but the images they produced could not be authenticated.

Not only was there the issue with artificial orbs that were produced under low-light conditions, but there was no way to determine if a captured image was genuine or not. To be able to analyze a photo, two things had always been needed: a print of the photo and its negative. This was not something that a digital camera could provide, and because those early electronic images could be easily altered and manipulated, it was impossible to prove they were authentic.

Time and technology changed, though, and it is now possible to authenticate digital images. Over time, new cameras became available with greater numbers of megapixels, crisp, clean images, and a way to authenticate images that is as trustworthy as a negative. This information is called a *raw data file*. These files are uncompressed and unprocessed and an anomalous image that is examined using this option offers as much detail as a photographic negative. Digital cameras also offer access to the EXIF information about images that are photographed. EXIF is data that is embedded into the image when it is taken. It contains everything about the camera that took the image, including camera settings, date and time the image was taken, whether the flash was used, the ISO settings, and more. If anyone attempts to manipulate the image, the EXIF data contains this information, too. In this way, a person trying to analyze a digital image will be able to see whether it has been altered. If anyone attempts to change the EXIF data, it will destroy the image.

Even with this reputable technology, though, a camera cannot be the only tool used in an investigation. Reputable photographs should still be accompanied by good research and corresponding activity, whether the captured images can be authenticated or not.

Using full spectrum cameras

Full spectrum photography was something that paranormal investigators began using when the technology first became available on the market. It took several years before the prices of the cameras were affordable to the average researcher but, today, they are widely in use as both still and video cameras.

Standard cameras, in order to protect the image, and the camera, only capture a small range of light. Full spectrum cameras are designed to capture the entire light spectrum, including near ultraviolet (UV) and near infrared (IR) light. Because most researchers believe that spirits may be visible only in infrared and ultraviolet light, these cameras seem to have the best chance of capturing images and footage of spirits.

Most investigators likely already have a camera in their ghost-hunting kit that films in total darkness. These cameras (discussed in the next section) are incredibly useful but they are not the same as a full spectrum camera. What are commonly referred to as night vision cameras are showing you a composite recreation from the infrared light that is being reflected back to them. It shows nothing from the normal visible light, or from the ultraviolet range.

A full spectrum camera can accept and process all light, even beyond what the naked eye can see. This is what makes full spectrum cameras so important for paranormal investigating. A lot of things within that spectrum are hidden to us, shadows and anomalies that we could not see with our own eyes.

Using this kind of camera gives you several advantages beyond the obvious one of having a piece of technology that can do things that our eyes cannot:

>> No flash unit is ever needed for this kind of camera. The camera becomes your eyes to see in dark environments.

>> The full spectrum camera will not disrupt the location, which maintains the integrity of the investigation. With no bright lights and camera flashes, the investigator's eyes will not have to adjust to being constantly blinded. You can even work without a regular flashlight by carefully watching the camera's screen.

>> A full spectrum camera also eliminates false and artificial orbs that are caused by dust, pollen, and moisture. Because it does not have a camera flash, this is not an issue. If an orb or anomaly appears on camera emitting its own light source, then you very likely have captured a genuine paranormal image.

I believe that the use of full spectrum cameras represents the best opportunity that we have for capturing ghosts. While filming an episode of *Ghost Adventures* at St. Ignatius Hospital in Colfax, Washington, I was using a full spectrum camera and shooting down a hallway. I took about five photos in the exact same spot and in one of the photos, I captured a well-defined, misty, white figure, just standing there, staring at us. It was an absolutely incredible capture — so much so that I was actually jumping up and down in excitement!

Using Video in Your Investigations

Using video during investigations when you have a television show like *Ghost Adventures* is different than using it when you are investigating homes and buildings with your team. For my show, we have multiple cameras and a crew, which makes things easier in some ways and more complicated in others. For an investigator, video cameras have many uses in research, and they have become an important part of every investigation.

One of the main uses for a video camera in an investigation is to record your witness interviews. You may be surprised by what turns up on video that you could never have recorded in an ordinary audio file. Just the expression on someone's face or their mannerisms can often speak volumes about an event and bring to light facts that you may not have even considered. The only problem with this is that some witnesses are ill at ease in front of a camera. This can often make for a disjointed and nervous accounting of events. You should try the video camera first and, if that doesn't work, switch over to recording on audiotape instead.

Another advantage to the video camera is the ease with which you can document the location of the investigation. We always recommend that investigators draw up a map of the location and note the various areas where phenomena have been reported. This is much easier to do if you have covered the entire area with your video camera, too. Also, if you are writing the investigation up as a report, you can check your memory of the location by watching the video that you have recorded.

To most researchers, though, the main reason to carry a video camera into an investigation is for the chance to capture some sort of paranormal phenomena on film. In some cases, it may be anomalies that cannot be seen by the human eye or, in other cases, it may be something that occurred that we overlooked as we dealt with the many moving parts of an investigation.

Many anomalies have been captured on film under ordinary conditions while investigators checked out reportedly haunted locations. Some were filmed randomly, and others were captured while certain areas were under surveillance. This is another great use for video cameras during investigations. We recommend that you have several cameras available for every investigation. This allows you to monitor several sections of the site at the same time. You never know where activity may occur next. One of the cameras can be used to record the witness testimony, whereas the others can be used to thoroughly cover the entire location.

Reviewing footage

The grueling part of this is watching every single bit of footage you have recorded. You never know when something may turn up. Watch the recording frame by frame, if you have that capability. You may miss something during a general watch. Watching it frame by frame takes a lot of extra time but may be worth it. Many investigators have found that locations that they deemed "quiet" were actually very active when they slowed things down to see what they had missed the first time.

In the past, there were serious problems with video cameras during investigations that took place after dark. It was almost impossible to film after the sun went down without the use of extra light sources. This created issues with film, equipment, photographs, and more. In the early 2000s, manufacturers first introduced commercial video cameras that could record in total darkness. The filters in the cameras converted infrared light into a part of the spectrum that the human eye could see. A light emitted by the camera illuminated a dark location and converted it to an inverted white and green color. These cameras are readily available on the market today and are widely in use by paranormal investigators.

Being able to film under darkened conditions opened many possibilities for investigators. With several cameras at each location, we never miss anything that may occur, including moving objects, opening and closing doors, unexplained sounds, and much more.

Verifying anomalies

During investigations, researchers have also obtained footage of anomalous, moving images. Many of them seem to be lights that move independently of their surroundings and dart between people and objects. Few researchers can agree about the source and meaning of these anomalies. Most believe them to be orbs or at least some sort of paranormal energy.

If you happen to find something like this in your video, be careful to observe the object's movements and be sure that it is not some sort of dust particle or airborne pollen. Assurances can be reached in several ways, including the fact that dust has a distinctive way of moving on camera and usually drifts rather aimlessly back and forth as it settles. Heavier natural objects always fall straight down past the camera, following the laws of gravity. In most cases, actual anomalies have a movement pattern all their own and seem to have a purpose. They will not float side to side and drift slowly past. They move with purpose and may even interact with the investigators or the witnesses at the scene.

If you really want to be sure of what you are filming, you can do so. All that is required is to measure every object that can be seen on camera with a measuring tape, to use an inexpensive wind gauge, and to have a lot of patience.

When setting up a location to be monitored on video, you can first monitor the wind speed directly in front of any heating or air conditioning vents. After you have logged in the highest velocity speed from in front of the vent, you will be able to say with certainty that dust will not move faster than the air flow at the location unless someone walks in front of the video camera. After this data is collected, measure the distance of everything that can be seen in front of the camera, including the size of the room. Log this information in your notes next to the data from the wind gauge.

You can also adapt this to use in outdoor investigations. The summer months can be a hazard because of flying insects, which can look "spooky" on film but, with the right calculations, you can rule out natural explanations under these conditions, too. Simply follow the same steps of measuring items that are in the line of sight of the camera and then also place your wind gauge within view of the camera. That way, any changes in wind speed will be picked up in the video record and comparisons can be made next to any anomalies that are filmed.

For example, if your video moves at 30 frames per second, then an object that moves one inch between frames is moving at 30 inches per second. This is the reason why you need to know the distance of everything in a room in relation to a possible anomaly. When broken down, this would equate to about 1.7 miles-per-hour, which means that it could clearly be dust. However, if it was moving one foot between frames, it would be traveling at 20.4 miles-per-hour, which means that, it may be an insect, but it is not dust. In many cases, investigators have filmed anomalies moving much faster than this, sometimes as quickly as 60 (or more) miles per hour. Even the world's fastest flying insect (the Australian dragonfly, at 35 miles per hour) does not move that quickly. By having measurement and wind speed data from your investigation site, you can obtain some very reliable and authentic evidence of the unknown.

Remember that using a video camera is just like using any other device in the pursuit of the paranormal. It takes practice to be good at it and experimentation is essential. To be able to obtain credible evidence using video, you have to practice the same sort of caution that you use with anything else. Be sure that you carefully review any evidence you have before proclaiming it genuine.

Analyzing Your Photographs

Expect to take a lot of photographs during your investigations because most of the photos will contain nothing out of the ordinary at all. As an extension of that, plan to also look at a lot of photos that have nothing paranormal in them, too. Thousands of photos have been taken while attempting to photograph ghosts that are nothing more than bad pictures, containing images that can be mistaken for something paranormal or that are examples of outright fraud.

The first thing that you need whenever you are attempting to analyze your own photos, or someone else's, is a copy of the photograph and the negative or the digital data. You have to be sure that the image that appears in the photo is on the negative, decide whether it is a developing flaw or a case of someone who has gotten creative with their computer and wants you to believe that they have photographed a ghost. This tells you much of what you need to know, but other factors are also important.

Authenticating a photograph also means that you must know the conditions under which it was taken. We recommend that investigators keep a photo log, but the average person with an unusual photo must try and remember what was occurring when it was taken. Some of the most important factors are weather conditions, temperature, humidity, what was going on at the time, where the photo was taken, and more. It should also be noted what type of camera was being used. If it was a standard camera, the film speed should be noted. Also, it should be noted whether the flash was on and anything else that can be remembered. In addition, they need to know why it was taken, whether it was during an investigation, whether it was an attempt to capture a ghost, or whether it was simply because the place was known for being haunted and the image was caught by accident.

What to look for in paranormal photographs

Here are some things to look for when you are trying to determine whether the photos that you analyze have natural, or accidental, explanations.

>> **Out-of-focus photos:** Many photographs that people mistake for anomalous are often nothing more than blurred or out of focus pictures. Such pictures have many possible causes. Many pictures are blurred when the lens is set at the wrong distance, when the subject is too close to a fixed lens camera, or when the subject moves too quickly while the shutter is open. Moving subjects require fast shutter speeds and the faster the subject is moving, the higher the shutter speed required. Blurring can also happen when the photographer accidentally moves the camera, as well. This can be stopped by using a tripod or just by being much more careful about hand movement while using the camera.

>> **Dirty camera lens:** A dirty camera lens can cause all manner of problems, from blurred images to "mysterious" spots that appear in your pictures. The best way to avoid this is to always make sure that the camera lens is clean.

Never touch the lens with a finger. Always use a cloth or soft brush that is designed to be used on the sensitive glass. Spots that appear in your photos may be caused by dust particles or something else that ended up on the lens.

» **Scratched film:** If using a standard film camera, this can be an issue. Scratches can appear on photos in at least a couple of different ways, and often these scratches are mistaken for something unusual. They often show up as a sharp line or lines that cross the image on the film. The scratches can be caused by dirt inside of the camera back, by a rough rewinding of the film, or by mistakes during the development process. The best way to see whether the lines in the film are caused by scratches is to see if the marks are on both the negative and the print or on just the print alone. If the scratches are just on the print, then it means that it occurred during the processing. Reprinting can correct this problem if the image continues to be a concern. If the scratches appear on the negative, a check of the camera may reveal a rough spot in the film path.

» **Objects in the lens:** Make sure that nothing attached to you, whether fingers, hair, or clothing, can end up in front of the lens. An object that appears in front of the lens can be dark or black in color and usually has a hazy outline to it. These same objects, when illuminated by the camera flash, appear to be brightly lit and white in color.

» **Flash reflections and refractions:** Artificial orbs and false images can be mistaken for something paranormal. Camera flashes can cause these images to appear, along with lights, lamps, or even the sun when it reflects off something and then bounces off the lens.

» **Double exposures:** This can always be a problem with a film camera. Double-exposed photographs occur when the film in the camera is not fully advanced all the way or not advanced at all. Sometimes the last picture on the roll overlaps the second-to-last picture, which causes images from both photos to blend together into one. Usually this is obvious, but in some cases a subject from one photo will "mysteriously" appear in the other, looking like a transparent person — or a ghost.

» **Developing problems:** Unfortunately, many things can go wrong during the developing process that can cause otherwise ordinary photographs to appear paranormal. Uneven densities in the print can be caused by the uneven development of the negative. Stains and marks that appear on the print can be caused by inefficient rinsing and even weird colors in your photos can be caused by bad paper or improper developing. In most cases, developing problems are easy to spot and are rarely ever mistaken for anything paranormal.

Many things can go wrong when attempting spirit photography and it should be stressed again how rare authentic paranormal photographs actually are. Just remember that every photo that is alleged to be something paranormal should be intensely analyzed by the researcher before he or she is willing to state that it contains a ghost or anything unexplained.

If you are analyzing photos, be sure that you have a good working knowledge of cameras, films, and lens effects. You should know your camera, your shutter speeds, and what can happen with lens refractions, light reflections, and arcs. By doing this, you have spared yourself some embarrassment by finding flaws in some of your own photos. When you understand the natural effects that can occur, you will be confident about the photos you are taking.

When it's not a ghost

Most photographs that are mistakenly believed to be ghosts are the result of accidents, mistakes, and a lack of knowledge. It's rare that someone actually attempts to hoax a ghost photograph and pass it off to an investigator as the real thing. However, it does sometimes happen. Whoever said that pictures never lie obviously wasn't someone with photographic experience. Almost everyone knows that a photo can be easily faked. One way, which involves techniques using the camera tricks, Photoshop programs, smart phone apps, and other means, is by combining images.

In many cases, determining when a photo has been doctored and a ghost "created" is difficult, but it is certainly not impossible. In order to become adept at spotting trickery or mistakes in photographs that you are analyzing, you need to have a good working knowledge of how such photos are created.

>> **Combining images:** One of the oldest photographic tricks in existence is combining two or more images to make a composite. One of the simplest ways of doing this does not require either camera or darkroom fakery and dates to the days of studio photography in the late 1800s. Many portraits of the day were created by posing the subject in front of a pictorial backdrop that created the illusion that the people were part of the scene. There were wilderness scenes, lakeside scenes, drawing rooms, libraries filled with books, and even military and camp scenes. In their modern form, these composite scenes may be produced by front or rear projection.

Because most people use digital cameras now, these images can be much harder to analyze. You need to have a good working knowledge of Photoshop, which allows you to take images apart layer by layer and reveal whatever trickery may be involved.

>> **Multiple/double exposures:** Although double exposures can be produced by accident when used standard film cameras, they can also be created for deceptive reasons, too. In fact, most "ghost photos" created as a hoax were

done using this method. In the past, double exposures were easily created by simply not winding the film onto the next exposure. This could be done inadvertently, or on purpose, but these days, most modern cameras have features to prevent repeat exposures. However, even these cameras can be fooled into not advancing onto the next frame.

Digital cameras can also be used in this manner but most multiple exposures with digital technology are created after the fact. Using a digital photo program makes it possible to combine several images into one, creating a fraudulent ghost photo. An investigator also needs to be well-versed in the various smart phone apps that exist, which can literally place a "ghost" into an otherwise ordinary photo. Always try and stay up to date on what is new so that you will recognize the images that show up in the latest "ghost photo-graph" making the rounds online.

>> **Long exposure photos:** This is another method of creating "ghost photos" that has been around for a very long time. During the spirit photography craze of the late 19th century, some fraudulent photos were created by opening the shutter of the camera and allowing an assistant to enter the frame for a few moments and then stepping out. With a long shutter exposure, this created a semi-transparent figure that seemed to materialize within the solid setting of the studio. This is easily done today with just about any camera. Using a tripod, the camera is set up and the shutter opened. A person walks through the frame for a moment, creating an image that shows up on the finished print as a semi-transparent ghost.

Detecting trickery

It may not always be possible to detect trickery in a photograph. It could be a straightforward, untouched photo in which a scene was staged or faked in some way. It can also be very difficult to detect computer trickery in many cases. How-ever, many procedures and techniques for detecting photo hoaxes involve check-ing the source of the photo, the circumstances behind it, the negatives, and more. In some cases, the same techniques we use to detect accidental photos also apply because we can never be too careful when it comes to searching for authentic examples of the paranormal.

>> **Investigating the source:** When you are analyzing any photograph that you have questions about, always consider the source of the photo. If it seems too good to be true, it probably is, especially when the photo is coming to you from a person who cannot, or will not, tell you where it came from. It is not uncommon for photos to make the rounds on the Internet that seem to have no clear information about who took them, where they were taken, or when they were shot.

In other cases, even possibly authentic photos must be questioned because of their lack of a reliable source. This can be heartbreaking, especially when the photo may be real. A great example of those was a series of photos that went around a few years ago that seemed to show the ghostly image of a woman inside of a burning house. The photo showed no signs of manipulation but when research was done to try and find out the story behind it, several different sources and explanations emerged. One person explained that the photo had come from a minister in Tennessee. Another claimed that it was taken by a minister in Indiana. One said the house belonged to the minister's mother, his grandmother, and so on. Without an authentic source, there was no way to accept the photo as genuine, which was a shame.

» **Investigating the circumstances:** A good analyst needs to know everything he or she can learn about how and why a photo was taken. If the owner of the photo states that he snapped a photo of a ghost in a cemetery on a sunny day, but you check the weather report and see that it was raining, you should be cautious about what else he may be mistaken about. Find out if the photo was taken by accident or whether the photographer was purposely trying to obtain a photo of a ghost. Study the photo itself and look for problems, like when the "ghost" is perfectly framed in the center of the photo. If it looks too good to be true, it probably is.

» **Investigating the negatives/data files:** If you are analyzing a print photograph, always obtain the negative. This is a way to look for not only accidental problems that create a "ghost" but also a good way to detect trickery. The negatives may show actual retouching or yield evidence — like the edge of a photo within the negative's image area — that another photo was copied. If the photo owner refuses to give up the negative, or no negative exists, there is really no way to accept that the image may be genuine. Most people do not use print photographs any more, but if it is an older photo, this may be relevant.

This is also relevant when it comes to digital photographs. If the owner of a photo cannot or will not allow you access to the raw data files, something is likely amiss. Even if not, there is still no way that the photograph can be authenticated.

In a best-case scenario, an investigator should insist on all the raw data from images that were shot at the same time. Years ago, you would have insisted on the negatives from an entire roll of film. By studying the sequence of the photos, it may be possible to see if trickery has taken place. The data may possibly reveal practice shots that were done in advance of the hoax, or you may also find that the sequence of the photos does not match the photo owner's story.

Chapter **12**

Talking to Ghosts

Since the beginning of recorded time, man has had the desire to communicate with the spirit world. However, it was not until the heyday of the Spiritualist movement that conversing with ghosts became an everyday occurrence. The movement was founded by two young girls who established a method of communication, using a series of knocks and raps that eventually became a code assigned to letters of the alphabet.

It was the first step in improved communication that continues today. As Spiritualism grew in popularity, practitioners established what were called *home circles*, which consisted of groups of family members and friends gathered to attempt communication with the spirits. The knocking of the Fox sisters was soon abandoned by those who experimented with their own skills as mediums. These were not séances conducted by professional mediums but ordinary people who gathered to investigate the other side.

As time passed, those ordinary people began demanding new and improved methods of talking to ghosts, their demands were met by innovators and inventors who brought them planchettes and talking boards, radio devices and spirit boxes, and high-tech electronics that were designed to reach from this world to the next.

Paranormal investigators have been changing and adapting to the various devices that have been available to them for the last century and a half. We still have much to learn about the way that the voices of the spirits speak to us and the methods of finding a direct line to the spirit world.

Table Tipping

In the 1850s, it was not unusual to be invited to someone's house for tea and *table tipping,* one of the most popular home circle entertainments of the day. Those who participated in this type of séance were asked to place their hands on a small table and then wait until the table moved, turned, or tilted of its own volition. Not unlike spirit rapping, messages were tilted in code that corresponded to the alphabet. Séance participants would often communicate directly to the table by asking questions that it answered through turns and tips.

Although the process of table tipping dated back to the days on ancient Rome, it became enormously popular in America during the early days of Spiritualism. Spiritualists explained that table tipping worked as a result of a form of psychic energy that emitted from each and every object in the world. Mediums were supposed to be especially sensitive to this energy.

But table tipping was just as controversial as any other alleged psychic power. In churches, ministers railed against it as demonic and many physicians warned of the danger to one's sanity from participating in supernatural activities.

In 1853, famed British scientist Michael Faraday rejected Spiritualist explanations and announced his tests had produced the theory that table tipping had nothing to do with ghosts. The table moved thanks to the séance participants and their own "unconscious muscular action." Although many scientists agreed with Faraday, table tipping had its defenders who insisted that the movements were generated by spirit forces or some kind of psychic energy.

Automatic Writing

Another very popular phenomenon of the 19th century was *automatic writing.* As interest in Spiritualism grew and more people became involved in it, the tiresome and time-consuming method of knocking and rapping fell out of fashion and mediums began to produce messages through automatic writing. This was essentially writing that was done in an altered state of consciousness and was attributed to spirits of the dead. It was believed by some that the spirits literally manipulated the writing utensil in the hands of the medium to communicate, as the writer was often unaware of what was being written and would often scrawl out text in handwriting that was markedly different than his or her own. Others believed that perhaps the spirits communicated by forming messages in the mind of the medium, which were reproduced on the page.

Through automatic writing, mediums claimed to produce messages from famous persons of history, deceased authors, and even classical music composers. Other forms of automatic writing went beyond mere messages and included drawings, paintings, and even musical pieces that were allegedly inspired by the dead. In some cases, mediums or individuals with little or no artistic training would suddenly feel compelled to paint or draw in distinctive, professional styles. They felt taken over by a spirit, as if another hand was guiding their own.

Author and respected paranormal researcher Hereward Carrington described automatic writing as "non-conscious writing" and he believed that it was produced by spirit influences. Others believed that it was more likely that automatic writing consisted of material that was gathered in the unconscious mind of the medium and then put to paper as a message from the dead.

There remain many questions as to the authenticity of automatic writing, but there were many cases in which the messages were eerily precise. Just as with so many other facets of spirit communication, many mysteries remain unsolved.

Talking Boards

Automatic writing, like full-blown séances, was something largely embraced by professional mediums in the 19th century. Average people who were looking to satisfy their curiosity about the spirit world were looking for a more efficient way to reach the other side than by tipping tables.

In the winter of 1852–1853, about the time that the excitement of Spiritualism was reaching France, a séance participant proposed a better method of reaching the spirits than knocking on tables. He secured a pencil to a small upturned basket and allowed multiple sitters to write out messages received from the other side. The idea produced great results and, after some refinements to secure the pencil to a small, heart-shaped wooden disk, word of the invention spread across Europe. They called it a *planchette*, meaning "little plank." Planchettes came to America in 1858 when Spiritualist and social reformer Robert Dale Owen observed the device at a séance in Paris and returned to Boston with several of them. The invention caught on with mediums as a more elaborate form of automatic writing but never held much appeal for the general public.

A type of planchette would be part of a new invention that came along a short time later, though. It was a device that could be used by everyone and no psychic skills were needed. The *talking board* was born. It revolutionized the Spiritualist movement and made an impact that is still being felt today.

The history of the Ouija board

The origin of the first talking board — the Ouija — is shrouded in legend. The story goes that a cabinet and coffin maker from Maryland named E.C. Reiche devised this new method of communicating with the dead. He created a wooden lap tray with the letters of the alphabet arranged in two lines across the center of the board. Below these letters, he placed the numbers 1-10 and the words *YES* and *NO* in each lower corner of the board. He used a planchette with his board, after removing the pencil and placing wooden pegs on the bottom so that it could move freely around the board. One legend claims that Reiche named his board the Ouija because the name represented the French and German words for *yes* (*oui* and *ja*). Other versions of the story say that a spirit that spoke to him through the board told him that *ouija* was an ancient Egyptian word for *luck*. It is not, but the name was said to have stuck. (See Figure 12-1.)

The true story behind the invention of the talking board is not as mysterious, although it does have some unusual elements to it. It actually took seven men, from very different backgrounds, to create the first American talking boards. Those men were Charles Kennard, Harry Welles Rusk, Colonel Washington Bowie, Elijah J. Bond, William H. A. Maupin, William Fuld, and the elusive E.C. Reiche, a man about whom almost nothing is known and may have never existed at all. These men pooled their assets, cash, and resources to create the Kennard Novelty Co. of Baltimore, Maryland. All the men had two things in common. Each of them was a wealthy entrepreneur who was unopposed to taking risks, and all of them were Freemasons. Most likely they met through their association with this fraternal society, and they soon made a pact to start the company and to produce the first American talking boards.

FIGURE 12-1:
A Ouija board.

Shutterstock/Andrea Crisante

Colonel Bowie initially handled most of the matters involving the company. Rusk was named as president, as he had the most experience with patent law and was able to file all the necessary papers himself. Kennard had some land and buildings from a defunct fertilizer company, and he offered the property for use by the new firm. Because of this, his name was used on the masthead. Elijah Bond contributed little to the association, save for some ideas, and shortly after the patents were filed, he disappeared. William Maupin remains a mystery to this day. He was gone before the company even got started and the only proof that he even existed at all was his name on the patent filings. The most active investor in the company was a young varnisher named William Fuld. He played a major role in the daily operations of the company, including in production, and had many ideas of his own. Due to his age and finances, when compared to the other investors, he had to work much harder to achieve success. It took him nearly a year to begin his climb to the top.

Historically, William Fuld has been acknowledged as the inventor of the Ouija board, a fact that is confirmed by the remaining Fuld and Bowie families. At the time the company was created, Fuld had little money to invest, but the idea for the board became his contribution, which is what earned him a partnership and his name on the patent papers. He remains the name most connected to the boards today.

By 1891, the Ouija board was selling well, and on November 10 of that year, Charles Kennard filed a patent that would improve the performance of the board's plan-chette. This turned out to be his last act as a member of the Kennard Novelty Co. and one day later, he was removed from the board. Although the company bore his name and used his land, Kennard was said to have been a poor businessman and so he was voted out of the company. Years later, his descendants would claim that William Fuld drove Kennard out of business but most likely, it was Colonel Bowie. By 1892, Kennard was no longer listed in connection with the company, but Bowie was named as manager and Fuld as supervisor. The company moved from its original location and the name was changed to the Ouija Novelty Company.

A short time later, Kennard tried to sell another version of the talking board that he called the Volo. Bowie and Fuld hit back. They purchased the Espirito trade-mark from the well-known W.S. Reed Toy Company and they placed an exact copy of Kennard's Volo design on the back of their Ouija. Consumers loved getting two boards for the price of one and soon, Kennard's business was destroyed. He had no trademark for the Volo, so he tried to advertise the "Igili — the marvelous talking board" instead. This business also failed.

In 1894, the Ouija Novelty Co., which was turning out huge numbers of talking boards, moved to a larger location. Bowie remained in charge of the company with Fuld and Rusk at his side. A few years later, Bowie needed money for his other business interests, and he sold his share of the patents. Rusk left the company and production was turned over to Fuld.

Fuld now needed a partner. He was also a customs inspector and was unable to devote all his time to the Ouija business. In 1898, his brother, Isaac, became part of the business and they split the proceeds from the production of their talking boards and other games. By April 1901, though, the partnership was over. William and Isaac had a falling out and Isaac was immediately fired. The two of them never spoke to one another again, except in court. Their legal battles went on for years. They bickered about money, rights, and even about who had the authority to open mail addressed to the company.

Fuld soon changed the name of the company to the William Fuld Manufacturing Co. and endured a few years of declining sales, becoming so broke for a time that he operated the business from his home. But business would not stay slow for long.

Meanwhile, Isaac Fuld had started his own talking board business, breaking a court order that had been handed down by a judge during an earlier lawsuit. He began sending out samples of a talking board that he had created called the Oriole board. They were an exact duplicate of the Ouija with stencils cut out to replace the "Ouija" logo with "Oriole."

At this same time, William decided to expand his company and issued press releases that stated that he was preparing for "big business." He took a risk and moved his company to an enormous, three-story building and opened his doors again. The gamble paid off and Ouija board sales began to climb. Sales orders poured in and William enjoyed national acclaim.

He was, however, still dealing with his brother. In April 1919, William began mailing letters to stores who placed orders for Isaac's Oriole board. He warned them that the boards violated his patents and those who bought the boards were breaking the law. When Isaac found out about the letters, he filed suit against William. But William countered with the allegations that Isaac had violated the injunctions filed against him years before. Isaac's case was dismissed, and the judge ruled that he had copied and distributed the Oriole boards in violation of the injunction. A review of the trademark that he had filed revealed that it had nothing to do with talking boards — it was for billiards tables. Isaac was ordered to pay all of the court costs associated with the case and to never make another talking board.

With the court battles behind him, William continued to expand, offering cheaper forms of his board in an effort to combat knock-offs, a line of Ouija jewelry, and even Ouija oil for rheumatism. He also trademarked the Ouija board as the Egyptian Luck board, the Mystifying Oracle, and the Hindu Luck board.

William was realizing his greatest success when disaster struck on February 24, 1927. William always supervised any work that was done on the factory and when a flagpole needed to be affixed to the top of the three-story building, Fuld joined the workmen in the task. When an iron support that he was leaning on collapsed, he fell backward off the structure. He caught himself for a moment on one of the factory windows, but the force of the fall slammed the window shut and he plunged to the street below. Amazingly, Fuld survived the fall with only a concussion and some minor broken bones. On his way to the hospital in an ambulance, though, one of his broken ribs pierced his heart and he died.

William Fuld's children took over the company. Catherine and William A. Fuld ran the company until the youngest brother, Hubert, became president in 1942. Sales sagged for years but the talking board industry saw a renewed interest in the 1940s, around the same time that the Spiritualist movement enjoyed a brief revival. Many companies introduced their own talking board designs during this period, offering extravagant designs and colors, but eventually, disinterest and a declining market saw each of the companies fail. Soon, only Fuld remained.

The heirs maintained the company until 1966, when they sold out to Parker Brothers. Today, they own all the rights and trademarks to the Ouija board and they still produce it in large numbers. Now sold in toy stores, it remains a more cheaply made duplicate of the talking board that was sold in 1919.

Using a talking board safely

When it comes to paranormal research, the talking board is perhaps the most controversial method of spirit communication that exists. It can be used by anyone and requires no special powers to operate. It has been both condemned and praised in equal amounts as a method of communication with the spirits and, some say, a direct link to the dark side.

Using a talking board can be problematic for those not prepared to handle the consequences that may come from it. You may be talking to spirits, providing a channel to negative energy, or taking part in an interesting experiment in psychic phenomena. If you do decide to try it, a set of guidelines should always be followed:

>> The Ouija should be used by at least two persons at a time and can be placed on the laps of the sitters, or on a small table within easy reach of everyone. The sitters place their fingers lightly on the edges of the planchette, being careful not to push down too hard. If you should ever take part in a Ouija session, or witness one, where you can hear the sound of the planchette scraping on the board, or it seems to be unusually loud as it moves, something fishy is probably afoot. This means that someone is accidentally or willfully guiding the pointer, and the session should be stopped immediately. Any information received from the board is bound to be false.

>> When the session begins, we recommend that the sitters invite a spirit to come through and speak to them. The sitters are advised to add that they wish to communicate with a "willing" spirit. The reason for this is that some suggest that negative spirits try to come through and confuse the sitters. For this reason, it's best to state up-front what you are looking for from the session.

>> Questions should be asked and repeated in a slow and deliberate manner. Only one question should be asked at a time, and by a single person, to avoid confusion. The answers to the questions will be theoretically spelled out using the planchette.

>> To end the session, simply tell the spirits that you appreciated them answering your questions and being patient with you. Then, tell them you have no other questions and bid them goodbye. Some suggest that you move the planchette to the word *Goodbye* on the board so that no other entities come through.

This seems like a simple way of conversing with spirits but there may be a lot more to it than it appears on the surface. Many believe that the answers provided by the board are simply the unconscious movements made by the people touching the pointer. If this is true, then the Ouija is operated by nothing more than the power of suggestion. But if this is true, it makes it difficult to explain accounts of talking boards providing information that none of the sitters could have possibly known.

Others believe that the talking board is powered by the psychic portions of the human mind, spelling out answers to questions either by precognition, telepathy, or unknowing communication with spirits. By the latter, the board would be a mystical tool that is guided by the sitter's unconscious movements, which are in turn manipulated by the spirits. On the other side of the same coin, many researchers use talking boards to experiment with the effects of psychic phenomena, tracking the movement of the planchette as it is propelled by the human mind.

Some believe that it is not that complicated, however. They believe that the planchette is moved by the direct force of spirits, guiding the hands of the sitters. The Spiritualists believed this, as do many people today, feeling that the Ouija is an important tool in spirit contact, both good and bad.

Understanding the dangers of talking boards

This brings us to the bad reputation that talking boards have earned over the years. Malevolent forces, often masquerading as benevolent spirits, have been known to make contact through talking boards and cause emotional damage, pain, and even suicide. Even those who tend to disbelieve these overwrought and often unsubstantiated cases admit that people may become dependent on, or even obsessed with, talking boards. Their constant use can literally be hazardous to your health.

No matter what you may believe, the use of a talking board is not recommended for teenagers, overly emotional people, or anyone not equipped to handle what may occur as a result of the board's use. In many accounts of people using talking boards, their use is followed by strange happenings like voices, knocking, and moving objects in their home. Those who believe that talking boards achieve spirit contact say that the person used the board unprotected and thus attracted "lower entities" into their space. This can lead to a demonic haunting, which can be dangerous to everyone connected to the home and the board.

Talking boards may also work as a sort of lightning rod for activity. The forced concentration of the sitters incites a PK effect that possibly creates directed energy, or perhaps even opens a portal to the other side. The energy of the sitters, directed toward a common purpose, could cause lingering psychic activity in a location that may be mistaken for ghosts.

The best advice about talking boards is to avoid them altogether. They should never be considered a legitimate tool to be used during paranormal investigations. But if you decide that you want to experiment with them at home, be very careful. What started out as simple fun could turn into something for which you were not prepared.

EVP — The Voices of the Dead

A recording device is an essential piece of equipment in a paranormal investigation. It can be effectively used to keep notes for the researcher and as a way to record interviews with witnesses. There have also been many instances when paranormal phenomena have been captured on tape and this activity includes strange voices and bizarre sounds that cannot be explained. Most researchers believe that these strange anomalies, captured on ordinary tape, are communications from spirits.

The practice of attempting to record the voices of spirits is called *electronic voice phenomenon (EVP)*. The sounds that make up EVP are apparently sonic events of unknown origin, which can be heard, and sometimes captured in recordings, on various types of electronic apparatus, including tape recorders and even radio equipment.

The recorded voices come in diverse forms, sometimes seeming to speak in tongues, singing, or speaking in gibberish. The messages often make a sort of backward sense as though communication is difficult. They can also apparently call people by name and speak directly to researchers. They can be heard over telephones and as anomalous interference on tape recordings. Some of them seem to enjoy engaging in dialogue, answering questions, or supplying personal information about the researchers, possibly as a way of achieving credibility.

Of course, with all science, both conventional and paranormal, some investigators are so keen on finding evidence to support the validity of their field that they impose meaning on what may otherwise be random sounds or noise. This tendency seems especially prevalent when it comes to the recording and research of EVP.

But simple recorders are not the only instruments used to try and communicate with the spirit world. *Instrumental transcommunication (ITC)* is defined as using technical means to receive meaningful messages from the other side. The ITC method originated as a form of EVP but encompasses a myriad of techniques to make contact with the spirit world using television, radios, telephones, computers, and the popular "ghost boxes."

In this chapter, we take a closer look at the history of EVP, the story behind ITC, and the best methods and devices that investigators can use to capture and authenticate the voices of the dead.

The history of EVP

The invention of the phonograph by Thomas Edison paved the way for electronic voice phenomenon, the recording of unknown voices. In his early models, sound waves were recorded by a needle that etched into a wax cylinder. It was played back through a trumpet. To people in the late 19th century, the phonograph seemed beyond belief, just as some of our modern spirit communication devices seem today. Many of Edison's peers did not believe what they saw and heard. One scientist even stated that it was nothing more than a ventriloquism trick. It soon became apparent there was no trickery involved. Even more amazing was when evidence began to emerge that such devices could record the voices of the dead.

The first known recording of spirit voices occurred in 1901 when ethnologist Waldemar Bogoras went to Siberia to visit the shaman of a local tribe. Using a gramophone recorder during a spirit conjuring ritual, he recorded purported ghostly voices in English and Russian. This is considered the first spirit voices ever recorded by a modern instrument.

Although researchers were working with gramophones and wax cylinders, the first recording of a spirit voice on actual tape was achieved by Reverend Drayton Thomas who, during his investigations of the spirit medium Gladys Osborne Leonard in the 1940s, captured an audible, disembodied voice during a séance. He later came to believe that the voice was that of his dead father.

The psychic Attila von Szalay, who had been hearing disembodied voices in the air around him since 1938, started researching EVP with Raymond Bayless in the early 1950s. Their initial attempts with a 78-rpm record cutter and player were disappointing. Regardless, they continued their efforts using a device that Bayless invented. It consisted of a box with an interior microphone resting inside of an old-fashioned speaking trumpet. The microphone cord led out of the box and connected to a tape recorder. Almost immediately, the researchers began to hear whispers originating from inside of the box, which they managed to record. Von Szalay carried on taping for many years using an open microphone connected to a reel-to-reel recorder. (See Figure 12-2.)

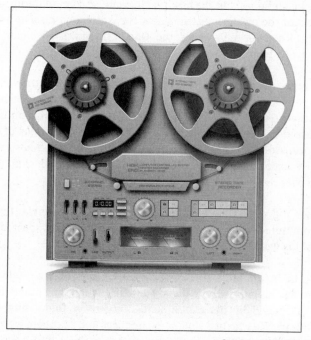

FIGURE 12-2:
A reel-to-reel
tape recorder.

Getty Images/Magnilion

Around 1959, Friederich Jurgenson, a retired Swedish opera singer, film producer, and bird watcher, was recording bird songs in the woods near his home. When he played back his tapes, he discovered that strange and garbled fragments of human speech had somehow made their way onto the recording. He had been completely alone in the woods at the time.

As he listened to the tapes, he found that the voices spoke in different languages. Also, he noted that longer phrases spoken by the mysterious voices often had improper structure and bad grammar and, in some cases, the syllables were stretched or compressed in a way that made it hard to understand what was being said. The strangest aspect of all was the eerie way that the voices seemed to reply to comments that Jurgenson inadvertently made. He began to hold conversations with the voices by recording questions and then later searching the tapes for answers.

Inspired to experiment further, he made other recordings and got more strange voices. He never heard them during the recordings, but they appeared during the playback. Even more in intriguing, the voices had personal information for him, plus they offered information about how to record more voices. He was once told by a voice that he was "being watched." Another time, he heard his mother, who had been dead for four years, speak to him using her nickname for him: "Friedel, my little Friedel, can you hear me?"

Then he began to hear the voices in real time as he listened to the radio while wearing headphones, but the best results were still heard during playback. A constant part of the mysterious transmissions was a loud hissing noise. Some of the speakers hissed out their words, too. One of them was a woman, who called herself Lena. She became his guide, assisting in his research.

By July 1960, the messages were coming in every day and the voices took over his life. Jurgenson listened to all of them, logged them into notebooks, and transcribed them. He gave up his professional career and devoted himself to the voices. He amassed thousands of recording and dozens of logbooks of notes. He heard from dozens of deceased family members and friends, whose voices he recognized. He experimented with a variety of techniques, including getting voices directly over the radio.

Jurgenson did more than simply record spirit voices. He was the first high-tech spirit communications researcher to undergo a profound spiritual awakening as a result of his work.

In 1963, he held a press conference to reveal his research, fully expecting to be ridiculed for his newfound beliefs. Some did laugh, but others took it very seriously, fascinated by his experiments. Jurgenson found himself contacted by numerous people who had similar experiences and by others who wanted to follow in his path. He published a book, *The Voices from Space*, which was accompanied by a recording of the voices.

By the time his books were published, Jurgenson felt completely changed by his work. He believed that because of his musical training, sensitive ear, and fluency in five languages, he had been chosen by some unknown force to be a pioneer of the metaphysical.

Jurgenson's research into electronic voice phenomenon inspired many other investigators, including Konstantin Raudive, a Latvian psychologist and philosopher. Raudive, who taught at Uppsala University in Sweden, was interested in psychic phenomena and survival after death. Intrigued by Jurgenson's experiments and convinced of his sincerity, he arranged to meet him in 1965. Jurgenson did demonstrations of Raudive that produced clear voices.

Raudive did his best to find natural explanations for the voices but he could not. He became convinced that the "voices of mysterious origin," as he called them, were genuine. He began his own intensive research, experimenting with microphone voices, which meant leaving a tape recorder running by itself; radio voices, obtained from within the white noise generated between stations; and diode voices, which were received with a crystal set that was not tuned to any station.

Results were not easy to obtain. Three months passed before Raudive heard his first voice — a man who responded, "That is right," to Raudive's observation that the dead had to deal with difficulty in communicating, too. As his work continued, he discovered that he developed an ear for hearing spirit voices as he continued to practice. When he listened again to some of his early tapes, he found that his recorder had captured many voices that he had not been able to originally hear.

Raudive found that radio produced the best spirit voices. He created his own prototype "ghost box" by manually and slowly moving his radio tuner dial up the broadcast band until he heard a voice that prompted him to start recording. Then, he turned on his tape recorder. When he played the tapes back, he heard voices that emerged from the radio static.

The spirit voices stood out from ordinary radio voices because of their paranormal features, such as peculiar rhythms and odd speech patterns. They spoke to him directly, used his name, offered personal information, and gave him advice on how to improve his recordings. Raudive made tens of thousands of recordings of electronic voices speaking in words and phrases in different languages. Some were clear and others sounded like poor telephone connections. Some of the words and phrases could be clearly understood, whereas others seemed to be speaking in code. Often, only one or two voices spoke but other recordings featured several voices speaking at once.

Raudive published a book in German in 1968 called *The Inaudible Made Audible*. In 1971, an English publisher, Colin Smythe, became interested in Raudive's work and asked psychologist and Cambridge scholar Peter Bander to translate it into English. Bander's initial reaction was one of disbelief. He thought the whole thing was too silly to be taken seriously.

But Smythe thought otherwise and decided to test Raudive's methods. Smythe recorded a woman's voice but her message was meaningless to him. He convinced Bander to listen to it and when he did, he received a shock. The voice was that of his mother, who had died three years earlier. Bander not only changed his mind about translating Raudive's book, but he also became one of the leading spokespeople for spirit voices. He went on to conduct his own research and write books on the subject.

It was Bander and Smythe who coined the term *electronic voice phenomenon*. Interest in EVP surged all over the world. Some researchers started as skeptics, trying to disprove the idea, but became converts themselves. One of those skeptics was Sarah Estep, who set up a reel-to-reel tape recorder in the basement of her Maryland home every night in 1976 to debunk the notion that the dead could speak to the living. In her belief, death was final — there was no afterlife.

In 1976, she read about EVP and the research of Jurgenson, Raudive, and others. She refused to believe that the phenomenon was anything other than wishful thinking and a trick of the mind. She decided that she would try the experiment herself, convinced she would receive no communications. Night after night, she set up the recorder, asked a series of questions, and left space for replies. Every morning, she reviewed her tapes. After a week of no answers, she decided that she would give it one more night. If nothing happened, she would end her EVP research and remain assured that there was no survival after death.

When she reviewed her tape the following morning, though, she received a shock. After her query, "Please tell me what your world is like," a clear female voice said, "Beauty." Sarah played the tape over and over. There was no mistaking it — she had made contact with the next world.

She continued her experiments but instead of more voices, she recorded silence again. Frustrated after a month of no results, she decided that the voice had been a mistake. She was on the brink of quitting again when a series of messages finally came through. All of them were encouraging, urging her not to give up. She continued to record, and although it took several months for her to accept the reality of EVP, she soon found that all her beliefs had been changed by the recordings.

In 1982, Estep founded the American Association of Electronic Voice Phenomena and became a worldwide leader in the study of EVP. Until around 2000, Sarah recorded daily on the reel-to-reel device that she had set up in her office. She received an average of three or four messages each day. She published several books about EVP and finally retired from the organization that she created in 2000. She turned its direction over to Tom and Lisa Butler, who broadened the scope of the association to include researchers from all over the world. The organization remains in operation today.

Classifying ghostly voices

While recording thousands of snippets of mysterious voices, Konstantin Raudive became the first researcher to classify EVP recordings. Sarah Estep also helped to develop the classification system that is still used by researchers:

>> **Class A:** The message is clear and easy to understand. It can be heard without headphones and people generally agree on which words were spoken.

>> **Class B:** This classification is less distinct but can be understood by a trained ear. Discerning message content on a recording usually requires careful listening through headphones, and not everyone always agrees about what words are spoken.

>> **Class C:** Faint and difficult to hear, these recorded voices require headphones to hear and amplification and filtering are often needed to understand them. Even then, the words may not still be completely discernable.

Experimenting with EVP

Following the research of Friederich Jurgenson, and the more recent experiments by Sarah Estep and others, EVP began to be accepted as a legitimate form of paranormal research. This has not, however, stopped it from being controversial.

Problems and questions arise because of the way that messages are normally recorded. They are rarely simple messages but often are fragments and sounds that require hours of listening to understand. Every researcher has listened to dozens (perhaps even hundreds) of recordings of what may be the voices of the dead. But we often ask ourselves what exactly we are hearing. We cannot be sure if they are the accidental recordings of other investigators, sounds that have no meaning, or authentic voices from the other side. In many cases, it is impossible to say.

Many researchers make the valid point that people have a natural inclination to project meaning onto otherwise innocent phenomena. Many tend to do this with EVP, to attempt to make the messages simpler or appear more mysterious than they really are. The human imagination tries to impose meaning on anything that appears to be intelligent sounds on the tapes. If no sense can be made of them, then an idea may be invented to support what we want to hear. The human mind tends to fill in the blanks, which can be a problem with EVP. Some suggest that if you listen to something enough times, you can hear anything that you want to hear. This problem is most apparent when someone with an EVP to share announces the contents of the EVP — or at least what he believes them to be — to listeners in advance. The power of suggestion easily takes over and destroys whatever credibility this experiment may have had.

Researchers with many years of experience have maintained that the authenticity of a recording is almost impossible to prove. No investigator can absolutely prove that the sounds were recorded naturally and are not the result of some interference or even an outright hoax. The only evidence a skeptic has is the word of the investigator, which, unfortunately, is never enough to prove anything. EVP has long been considered unverifiable evidence but only because many investigators are unwilling to take the time to verify their results with some simple safeguards to prove their recordings are authentic.

Although most investigators are very credible, much of their EVP research is not. Far too many investigators believe that simply leaving a tape recorder running and walking away from it is enough to prove that real ghosts have been recorded on their tapes. Unfortunately, this is not the case. This often opens the research up to criticism, but using by using detailed, restricted and well-monitored techniques to achieve EVP recordings, much of the room for error can be eliminated from your experiments.

>> Different theories exist about what kinds of recorders work best, but I always use a digital, handheld recorder for EVPs. The main thing to remember with these devices is that, if holding it, you need to make sure not to fidget, jostle, or move the recorder around too much. This can create sounds that can be mistaken for an EVP.

>> When using a digital recorder be sure to record at settings that do not compress the recording. Because we are not sure what part of the data contains paranormal artifacts, we must be careful not to destroy that material with compressions for a digital media player.

>> When recording, random locations are not recommended. Taking the recorder to a location you have good reason to feel is haunted is best. In addition, your EVP experiments should be conducted in the most active spot in the location. This obviously increases your chances for good results.

>> When you arrive, make handwritten notes of the weather and any natural or artificial sounds that can be heard where you plan to do your recording.

>> If you decide to record your audio in one location. You place the recorder in a secure spot, on the floor or on a table, and preferably on a rubber mat, which would reduce any sound traveling through the material to the recorder. I also like to place the recorder by itself on a tripod in some locations, eliminating any sound that may come from a table or floor.

And finally, the most important step to take when attempting to provide solid and incontrovertible evidence that anything that is recorded on your tape is genuine:

>> After setting up the recorder, set up three video cameras in the vicinity of the machine. One of the cameras should be aimed directly at the recorder.

The second should be aimed at the recorder and offer a wider view of the entire room or location. The third should be focused on the recorder, as well as on an EMF detector and a thermometer, which will show any atmospheric changes that occur during the recording.

» One of the most important aspects of the experiment is to stick to the question-answer format of attempting to record. Selected questions should be asked with at least a 20-second span between them to allow time for replies. Preparing the questions in such a way that they can be answered by a yes or no, or at least by words of one syllable, is best.

» After the session begins, the recorder should be monitored by at least two people and absolute silence must be maintained. It is imperative that verbal notes be made on the recording whenever any outside sounds are heard by those monitoring the tape. This is called *tagging*, which means that you "tag" the spot on the recording whenever an outside sound is made, like a car passing by, a dog barking, someone coughing, and so on.

» When reviewing the tape, if any sort of EVP is identified, go to the video record and see if the equipment detected anything. Checking the wide view of the room reveals whether any of the participants are responsible for the sounds.

» If you should capture something on your tape, have others listen to it to provide a confirmation of the sounds. Do not tell them what to listen for. They should discover anything strange on their own.

By following these guidelines — or your own version of them — you can not only be successful with your EVP experiments, but you can actually collect authentic evidence of the fact that the dead can communicate with the living.

Analyzing your EVPs

When you have a recording containing what you believe are anomalous sounds, then your analysis of it begins. You may have hours of recordings from an investigation and you must listen to all of it, carefully searching for any fragments of speech or sounds that do not ordinarily belong.

When attempting to analyze it, as well as playing it for other team members, you can cut out a section of your recording to feature the suspected paranormal sound for others but leave a few seconds before and after the event. This is important to establish the context of the suspected paranormal bit. If you just play the sound or voice to people by itself, they have no idea of the context.

High-quality audio editing software can be used to enhance voices and other paranormal sounds. This software can be crucial to your understanding of EVPs. In many cases, with recordings that I have obtained, spirits tend to speak faster or slower than what we can easily understand. By speeding up or slowing down the recording, the voices can be better heard and understood. You can raise the volume of the voices so that words become clearer.

Using audio software

These are worthwhile uses for audio software, but you must be careful with how much you use and with what enhancements you apply to the recordings. For instance, you can remove background noise from a recording, but the process is not perfect, and it inevitably alters the recording permanently, including the parts you are interested in. If a voice appears in a noisy recording, audio editing software may clarify it. If, on the other hand, the voice is just random noise that sounds like a voice, repeated use of noise removal and filtering could make the noise sound like a voice. You could end up listening to an artifact created by the overuse of audio enhancement rather than a real anomaly. Such audio enhancement processes are not "intelligent." They do not know when to stop; they just apply the same rules repeatedly. Each iteration gets further and further away from the original sound until it is completely lost.

Besides that, we want the background noise to remain in the recording. It provides an audio context and reassures the listener that the recording has not been manipulated. It can also provide clues to any possible natural explanations for what could be paranormal sounds. If the sound is louder than the background noise, then possibly it is a real sound that was not noted at the time and was forgotten. It could also be radio or electrical interference.

Far too many investigators manipulate their recordings with audio editing software. It may be done with the best of intentions, perhaps to point out the important snippet of sound, but this can also destroy evidence. Unfortunately, it is not always easy to tell if manipulation has occurred. Sound recordings have less information than photographs, making them easier to manipulate without people noticing. Try to avoid doing much with the software beyond raising the volume or changing the speed of the words in your recording.

Another benefit of using audio analysis software is being able to examine the waveform of your recordings. A waveform is an image that represents an audio signal or recording. It shows the changes in amplitude over a certain amount of time, giving you a visual view of what your recordings look like. When an EVP is discovered in your recording, it can have completely different characteristics than a human voice. By examining the waveform, you can see what your voice looks like in comparison to the EVP.

Assessing voice content

The most obvious way to analyze a sound recording is to listen to it, although this is also the most subjective method. Scientists have discovered that more of the process of hearing happens in the brain than in the ears. It is important to listen to large sections of your recording at one time so that you became used to the context of it, especially the ambient background level and other natural sounds. Listening to small sections can leave you with a false impression of the session and any anomalies found.

It is difficult to judge what caused a certain noise in a recording unless you return to the scene of your investigation and examine it carefully. You may be able to reproduce certain sounds by moving likely objects around but this does not necessarily mean that they were moved paranormally in your recording. This is the reason why using video cameras is so important for EVP sessions.

If you are working on an analysis with other members of your team, do not be surprised to find that people often disagree about the words that were recorded. EVP researchers often say that their messages made sense within the context of the recording, even if they do sometimes seem meaningless and cryptic when isolated. Of course, expectation and the verbal transformation effect are important in content. If you listen to the same words repeatedly, you will hear the words shift around to alternatives that sound similar. If, as often happens in EVP, you are told what words you are going to hear in advance, it is no surprise when you hear the expected message.

Although assessing content is always going to be a subjective process, some things can be done to overcome the more obvious biases. Perhaps the best way to sort this out is to find a small group of third-party judges, preferably those not interested in EVP, ask their opinion about the content, and then take a vote. You can include a few control voices in your sample, too. These controls can be ordinary voices saying known things. To make them sound more ambiguous, like an EVP, you can muffle the voice, perhaps by putting a cloth over the microphone of the recorder.

If you decide to try this method, be sure to remove all the recording before and after the EVP fragment that you want the group to judge. Interpretation can be affected by things said on the recording by people who were present during the investigation. For instance, if someone asked a question out loud and an EVP appears directly afterward on the recording, listeners may unconsciously interpret the EVP as an answer to the question. Do not tell anyone in the group what you believe the EVP says. Do not even tell them the context, because this may affect their expectations, too. If you tell them the recording came from a haunted house, they may be influenced to hear something about "ghosts" or other relevant words. Also, be sure to allow people the option of saying that they cannot hear any words at all, if that is the case.

Discerning paranormal voices from illusions

As you can see, it can be very difficult to discern a paranormal voice from an auditory illusion caused by the way the brain processes what it hears. However, some practical ways to find the differences exist.

One way is to try and break down any phrases captured in the recording into separate pieces. You can play them individually and see if they stand up as words on their own. You can also try and listen to the individual words and try repeating exactly what you hear, even if it sounds like a nonsense word. Reproduce your interpretation of the words as closely as you can and speak them into a recorder. Using audio software, you can then compare the frequency analysis of your real words with the same you have been examining.

During your analysis, look for natural causes that can be mistaken for anomalous sounds and voices in your recordings. While remaining silent during a recording session, investigators may not notice very faint sounds that seem amplified by a microphone. If anything does occur while recording, no matter how faint, speak aloud on the recording so that the quiet noise can be noted.

Also watch out for repeated or continuous background sounds, like electrical equipment like fans or pumps and the wind. All of these can seem quite loud and may come as a surprise when you play back your recordings. Be aware of electrical or radio interference, because this will only be noticed when the recording is played back. It would not have to be an obvious radio transmission. It could be just humming, buzzes, and whistles that your recorder "heard," even though you did not.

If, of course, you can eliminate all these natural causes and errors, you stand a very good chance of having a genuine paranormal EVP. Searching for these paranormal voices — or at least ruling out all the problems — is more difficult than it may seem at first. However, you can rest assured that if you do capture authentic voices, all the hard work that went into the process will be worth it.

Using Devices to Talk to the Dead

In the 1860s, it was a Scottish physicist named James Clerk Maxwell who predicted the existence of radio waves. More than three decades later, Italian inventor, Guglielmo Marconi proved that radio communication was possible by sending and receiving the first radio signal in Italy. In 1902, Marconi flashed the first successful transatlantic radio telegraph message from England to America and from that moment, the world was forever changed.

Suddenly, we had a way to communicate with someone thousands of miles away in real time. We could pass on news, information, and conversation in a way that had never been achieved before. As wondrous as this was, most people could not have imagined that radio waves would eventually support contact with beings much different from ourselves, from transcendent beings to the dead.

Instrumental transcommunication

In the decades that followed Marconi's grand experiment, inventors worked hard to duplicate and improve on his work. New devices appeared on a regular basis but some of the inventions were outside the norm. There were a number of researchers who were trying to create and adapt machines that could bridge the gap between the living and the dead.

In 1949, Italian Marcello Bacci attended a séance in London that changed the course of his entire life. He became fascinated with creating a way to directly communicate with the dead, while also removing the human factor of the séance medium. He soon began experimenting with what he called *direct radio voice method*, which meant tuning in spirit voices through his vacuum tube radio.

Bacci carried out his original experiments using the same methods as famous experimenters of the time like Friedrich Jurgenson and Konstantin Raudive. Frequently, the entities were able to refer to listeners by name, respond to questions directly, and give detailed information that only their relatives would understand. He carried out his sessions in his home, often in the presence of 70 or more people at a time. For those in attendance, there was no doubt that they were in direct communication with someone in the spirit world. Voices, they claimed, were often recognizable.

Bacci began his experiments by tuning into the white noise between stations on the band. By turning the radio knobs to just the right frequency, he could pick up spirit voices through the speakers, which passed on messages. The communications varied from as short as ten seconds to a maximum of four minutes. According to all reports, they were clear and differed from each other acoustically. When the communications ended, the normal static of the radio returned.

EVP can be difficult to understand. Often voices that are recorded are incredibly short, just one or two words, leaving them open to interpretation. Recording EVP is very different from what Bacci was doing. Skeptical researchers and scientists from around the world attempted to debunk Bacci's radio communications and all of them failed. There was no evidence whatsoever that it was a hoax.

Recently, voice recognition software, like that used by the FBI to conduct voice print analysis, was used to study Bacci's work. Like a fingerprint, voice analysis can be used with near certainty to confirm a speaker's identity. Voice recordings obtained from relatives from when they were alive were compared with the alleged spirit voices coming from the radio. Time and again, the spirit voices were proven to be an almost exact match. One voice even matched with an accuracy of 97 percent. Experts claimed that there was no way a voice that matched to that kind of accuracy could be anyone other than the person in question.

During scientific investigations, particular care was taken to see if any external form of transmission device was being used to create the voices. Scientists enclosed Bacci's radio on a special cabinet that blocked any form of external radio wave. This made no difference to the device. It still transmitted voices and messages.

Professor Mario Salvatore Festa, a Professor of Physics at Naples University, took things one step further. During one communication session, when the spirit voices were being received, Festa removed two of the valves from Bacci's radio. This should have effectively disabled the radio and yet the spirit voices continued to communicate. Baffled, he even removed the battery, but the messages did not stop, much to the amazement of everyone present. When Festa placed his ear against the speaker he was convinced that the voice was coming through the radio. It seemed impossible and yet, it happened.

It has been theorized that Bacci is a medium. Although he does not go into a trance, it has been suggested that he is the real communication device, transmitting the energy and personalities of those in the spirit world, through his contact with the radio. This could be the case, because some researchers asked Bacci to leave the room and their attempts to make contact through the radio were unsuccessful. It has since been concluded that for spirit contact to take place, Bacci must be present. To skeptics, this is a red flag, but even so, none of them have been able to debunk what happens with the radio.

Marcello Bacci became known as one of the world's foremost experts instrumental transcommunication (ITC) and wholeheartedly believes that he is in contact with the other side, offering messages of love and hope from the dead.

However, many of those who have experimented with ITC do not believe they are contacting humans who have departed. They believe their sessions are in touch with something else altogether.

It was in the 1980s that ITC developed into a new field all its own. Jules Harsch and Maggy Harsch-Fischbach of Luxemburg and Ernst Senkowski, a physicist and engineering professor from Germany, began attempting new spirit communication methods using records, radios, telephones, computers, and televisions. It was

Senkowski who christened the new field *instrumental transcommunication*. They envisioned using science to provide proof of the afterlife.

They began meeting once a week for recording sessions with radios and microphones. The voices that came through were typical of EVP. Some of them were loud and clear whereas others were faint and distorted. Soon, their device became more elaborate. It included two FM radios tuned near 87MHz, a black and white television set turned to a free channel, a sound generator, two ultraviolet lamps, and a loudspeaker with a filter. A fluorescent lamp and an incandescent blinking lamp with a one-second rate helped to establish rhythmic timing to produce speech. Maggy and Jules used a handheld microphone to record any words that came through.

The group sent out regular invitations for the late Konstantin Raudive to contact them but several months passed with no results. Then, in the spring of 1986, a clear voice came through that they were convinced was Raudive. After that, more communications emerged and the first voices came through the television set, but without any images. Most of the contacts lasted from between 10 to 15 minutes, mostly through the radios, but sometimes through the television, too.

Then, something changed. Another communicator, with a high-pitched, robotic voice, started making regular contact. This entity began lecturing the group on a wide range of technical and metaphysical subjects and started opening and closing every ITC session. When asked for a name, the group was told it had no earthly name. In fact, it had never been human. It claimed to be part of a group of seven ethereal beings — the "Rainbow People." They were a race of higher beings that were almost beyond the comprehension of humans. They existed in realms of timelessness and were assigned to help the Earth. They had to lower their vibration to get to the astral plane and communicate with the group.

The Seven described themselves as beings who provided assistance, guidance, and support to people on Earth. They had been particularly active with the Earth during critical periods of history. There had been six crisis points in the past and now the world was in a seventh critical period and they were trying to awaken humanity to a higher level of consciousness to be prepared for the end of times.

With the help of these beings, along with Raudive and other spirits, the home of Maggy and Jules became the world's first fully functioning ITC station in the world. As their work progressed, they received numerous telephone calls and radio messages from disembodied voices. Most of the calls came from Raudive, who delivered lengthy messages.

Their devices delivered mostly one-way communication, like traditional EVP, but by August 1986, Maggy and Jules patched together new gear that enabled two-way communication for a few minutes. This device, the *Gegensprechanlage*, or GA1, consisted of a radio with a built-in antenna, a shortwave radio placed in a separate room, two diode circuits with special antennas, a "frequency translator circuit" with a built-in microphone, and a small fluorescent lamp.

The first voice to come through the new device was Raudive, who praised their efforts. The GA1 produced better communications but the cosmic beings that Jules and Maggy had been speaking with warned them to only use it when instructed. Otherwise, they were told, they may wake up some morning in a parallel dimension. What this meant and how it would work was never explained.

According to Maggy and Jules, their ethereal contacts began overseeing all their communications. They enabled the energy in their links and helped them make contact with specific dead people whom the researchers requested.

Toward the end of 1986, they were given instructions about setting up a video experiment. In the months that followed, scenes and faces appeared on their television set. The images showed recognizable people and scenes from an astral plane that looked much like Earth.

Excited about these new results and convinced the public would be swayed by evidence of the afterlife, Maggy and Jules organized lectures and public demonstrations. They were ridiculed, criticized, and dismissed. Embarrassed, they withdrew from the public eye but not before getting the attention of those who shared their beliefs and wanted to be part of the experiment. Soon, these new researchers were making contact with their own spirit groups. The new communications were amazing. Their spirit beings left messages and images on computers, left messages on telephone answering machines, and appeared on television screens. The world of ITC had reached a new level of existence.

The research taking place in Europe came to the attention of an American who became a major figure in the ITC field. His name was Mark Macy and a battle with colon cancer in 1988 had caused him to reevaluate his life. He became a strict vegetarian and started alternative therapies for body, mind, and spirit. He also began to think more about survival after death and the afterlife. Unusual dreams troubled his sleep. In them, Macy found himself in laboratories where boxes on a table had tubes of light glowing inside of them. If he touched the table, his hand stuck to it like a magnet, while voices whispered to him about what he was seeing.

In 1991, he attended a conference about spirit communications and became interested in EVP. He quickly grew tired of short, cryptic messages and started on a quest to obtain long, clear, real-time messages and images. He began experimenting with radios tuned to different frequencies and eventually had some success. However, the messages told him that his mind was too much in turmoil. Macy interpreted the message to mean that he could only progress if he cleared his mind and focused his thoughts. He traveled to Europe and met with Jules Harsch and Maggy Harsch-Fischbach, as well as others. The trip gave him a clear vision and he decided to devote himself full-time to ITC.

Organizations formed across the globe, with Macy heading a branch of the Harsch-Fischbach association in the United States. The early years were filled with enthusiasm, cooperation, and excitement. The researchers were convinced that breakthroughs were coming that would get the attention of the entire world. But those days did not last. By the early 1990s, there were disagreements, legal issues, and money problems. Everyone had their own ideas about how to further the research. Some wanted to keep their work private whereas others wanted it to be open to the public. Serious rifts developed and skeptics attacked their work. The unified mind that had been stressed by the ethereal spirit beings never really materialized.

Mark Macy, along with most other ITC researchers, went on to pursue his own path. A variety of organizations are still devoted to ITC and spirit communications, though. For the most part, they work independently or in small groups, collaborating on occasion. Much of the current interest in ITC falls into two areas: those with an interest in ghost-hunting, and those who research survival after death.

ITC is a fascinating and wonderfully strange aspect of paranormal research that requires a lot of dedication and extensive protocols to achieve success. For those who pursue it, it can be a life-changing exposure to a world beyond our own.

Ghost boxes

Most investigators are familiar with what are commonly called *ghost boxes*, devices that usually consist of white noise generators, amplifiers, sound chambers, microphones, and a radio receiver. They are designed to make real-time connections with the spirits. They are different than EVP and unlike ITC, are not designed to remain stationary. Ghost boxes are portable devices that are designed to tune through radio stations across the dial, catching them for a few seconds, and with those words, and the static across the band, provide a method by which the spirits can speak.

These boxes became popular starting in the early 2000s and are still widely in use by investigators today. However, the first ghost box was actually designed several decades earlier when a Viennese electrical engineer named Franz Seidl got the idea to develop a device to talk to spirits.

The idea of the afterlife device was an afterthought. He had developed an instrument that allowed deaf people to hear, even some who had been deaf since birth. It sent a tone-modulated high frequency into the brain. Intrigued by the idea of EVP, Seidl combined tone-modulated high frequencies and a radio to create a device he called the Psychofon. Instead of turning a radio to the white noise between stations, the Psychofon rapidly scanned the radio bandwidth, looking for fragments of words.

In 1959, Seidl acquired a tape recorder and started taping animal and bird sounds as a hobby. But something strange happened during one of his recording sessions. When he played his tapes back, he heard a human voice that he was sure had not been audible when he started the recorder. A short time later, it happened again and this time, he unmistakably heard the voice of his dead mother calling his name. As he experimented further, he became convinced that the dead were communicating with him through the recorder.

With his recordings and the device that he constructed, Seidl believed that he had discovered a new form of "transcendental physics." He found that results were not entirely depending on the device but were heavily dependent on the cooperation of the spirits and the "mental readiness" of the experimenter. Psychic ability influenced results, as did preparing for a session by meditating first.

Seidl also tried photography during his sessions with the box and discovered that anomalous images appeared in many of his photographs. Before his death in 1982, Seidl often spoke of the many profound psychic and spiritual experiences that he achieved from his work. The schematics for Seidl's device are available on the Internet today and his methods have been widely followed. He led the way with the original ghost box but many followed in his footsteps.

The Koenig Generator

Another major influence on the development of ghost boxes and real-time EVP was Hans Otto Koenig, a German electronics engineer. Koenig entered the field as a skeptic in the early 1970s, trying to debunk EVPs with his own experiments. He changed his mind about the reality of the phenomenon after hearing the voice of his dead mother and several deceased friends.

Convinced that he had recorded the voices of the dead, he became obsessed with the idea of creating real-time, two-way communication. He experimented with background noises, such as running water and static. He realized that these noises contained ultrasonic sounds that were above the range of tape recorders. He thought that spirit communication may occur mostly in the ultrasonic range and spent the next eight years developing equipment that would reach far beyond what humans had the ability to hear.

He called the invention Koenig's Generator. It was a combination of four sound generators that mixed fixed ultrasonic frequencies, which in turn created an audible sound that resembled a police car siren, but with a constantly changing frequency. According to Koenig, when the spirit voices were mixed through the device, they were turned into audible sounds.

Koenig offered public presentations on his work and kept experimenting and building other setups that yielded longer sessions with less static. He conducted controlled experiments at different locations and researchers from around the world came to see his generators perform and went away convinced that Koenig had truly summoned the dead.

Spiricom

The first widely publicized ghost box device was called Spiricom. When news of its broke in the 1980s, it sent a ripple of excitement through the world of EVP research. But the excitement would not last and eventually, it cast a bad light over the entire field, which lingered for many years.

Spiricom was invented by George W. Meek, who received his bachelor's degree in engineering in 1932. He worked in product development but, in his spare time, was convinced that he could create technology that would provide real-time, two-way conversations with the dead. His interest in the paranormal remained throughout his career and he began saving money for early retirement. Finally, in 1970, he left his job and began investigating the paranormal full-time. For the next two decades, he worked on various projects before forming Metascience Associates, a partnership of several like-minded individuals.

Through mediums, they sought out advice and guidance from the dead about the best ways to build a communication device. With that assistance, Meek and his partners built a device called the Mark I, a bulky setup of a tape recorder, oscillators, amplifiers, transistors, timers, relays, and a 300MHz generator shielded from radio interference. With help from a medium, they began a series of high-tech séances. The partners sat around the medium, who attempted to communicate with the spirits, while the equipment stood ready to capture any direct communication.

The medium claimed to make contact but in session after session, nothing came directly through the equipment. The spirits explained that the situation was much more complicated than it appeared and involved more than just sound frequencies. More equipment was needed, as well as an "active application of energies" from those in the spirit world.

Spiricom became a series of devices, called the Mark I, Mark II, and so on. They would have the best luck with the Mark IV. The basic device was a modified ham radio that transmitted on the AM band. It had a tone generator that created 13 separate frequencies within the voice range of an adult man. The tones were combined into a regular audio carrier, which was broadcast via a 29MHz AM transmitter to a 29MHz AM receiver. The hope was that the spirits would use this frequency and the tones as vocal cords for creating words. If they did, the resulting sound would come out of a speaker. A cassette recorder for capturing the sessions was placed across the room from the receiver. The entire room served as a sort of Faraday cage, shielded from the interference of outside electromagnetic waves.

Meek became convinced that a medium may be the key to helping him succeed in his work. He had been interested in psychic abilities, especially healing, for many years. He believed that healers received assistance from the spirits to help people. If he could find a medium who already received help from the spirit world, it may put him closer to making his device a success. Meek eventually found a healer from Pennsylvania named William O'Neil and asked him to join his organization.

O'Neil seemed to have a natural gift of healing by laying on hands, and his professional background involved radio and electronics. He described himself as an artist, poet, and composer. He was also a ventriloquist; which critics would focus on years later. O'Neil seemed to be a perfect fit for the project but over time, it would become clear that most of the controversy that plagued Spiricom came about because of O'Neil, who died in 1992. He had many problems, including severe mood swings and constant financial troubles. He often complained about this work with Spiricom, insisting that it was an obstacle that kept him from the work he had been called to do. He repeatedly resigned, only to have Meek convince him to stay.

O'Neil may have had good reason to be hesitant about getting involved in Meek's experiments. A few months before he was first contacted about Spiricom, he had been doing his own research with radio frequency oscillators, trying to find the right frequencies to assist the hearing impaired. One night, he placed two oscillators on either side of an aquarium and had a frightening vision of human body parts forming inside of the tank. He was so shocked that he doubted his sanity and stopped all his experiments for two weeks. When he resumed them, he saw the same terrifying vision again. He stopped his research once more and even visited a doctor to make sure there was nothing wrong with him. He was given a clean bill of health.

Looking for answers, he had contacted the publisher of a psychic newsletter, who put him in touch with George Meek. When Meek asked him to get involved with Spiricom, he did not jump at the invitation. He had no desire to repeat the unnerving experiments. Then, two years later, in 1975, O'Neil had another strange experience. He was composing music on his guitar when an apparition materialized in front of him. The spirit, in a clearly audible voice, began to instruct him on how to improve his healing talents and how to build electronic devices that could be used for healing. Soon, he was having remarkable successes, including curing a woman of lymphosarcoma.

Meek finally persuaded O'Neil to work with him. O'Neil agreed reluctantly, still concerned about this mental stability. He insisted on remaining at his home near Pittsburgh. He worked on Spiricom there and communicated with Meek through letters. Progress faltered until July 1977, when O'Neil came face to face with the apparition of a man in a business suit. The spirit told him that he needed O'Neil's help to carry on his research and he, in turn, would help O'Neil sort through his failures and get back on track.

The mysterious figure said that his name was George Mueller and that, in life, he had been an electrical engineer and physicist and had once worked for the U.S. Signal Corps. When Meek heard about this, he investigated Mueller's claims. Almost everything checked out, including the dead man's Social Security number and death certificate. They even found a photograph of Mueller, as well as a book-let he wrote on electronics for the U.S. Army.

Despite these advancements, Meek still had to keep O'Neil from leaving the experiment. The medium complained of poor finances and said he needed to give up Spiricom research to earn money. His healing work was more important. Meek gave him money and again convinced him to stay.

O'Neil continued the experiments, eventually following his spirit assistant's advice and switching from the white noise preferred by most EVP researchers to audio frequencies. They served as an energy source for the spirits' "astral vocal cords." O'Neil made the switch but was still unable to capture the voices of his spirit guides on tape. He was discouraged by the setback and once considered leaving Spiricom. Things got worse in 1979 when an arsonist set fire to his home. Everything was lost, including all his research equipment. Instead of quitting, he vowed to rebuild his house and resume his spirit communication work.

On September 23, 1980, O'Neil had another breakthrough and recorded a 13-minute conversation with the spectral George Mueller. The voice of the dead man was monotone, with a continuous buzzing sound underneath it. For their first real-time conversation, it was surprisingly ordinary, but it was a start.

Over the next 18 months, Mueller periodically conversed with O'Neil on tape. The content of their conversations ranged from mundane to technical, with Mueller spending a lot of time focusing on perfecting the ability to communicate. Some-times the sessions ended abruptly without warning, as though the connection had been lost.

Meek's research associates tried their own experiments with Spiricom and other spirits besides Mueller came through. However, no one had the success with it that O'Neil had. But his success would not last. One day, Mueller warned him that he would not be able to stay forever. One month later, he vanished from the experiment without a farewell.

The end of the Mueller communications came as a blow to Meek, but he felt that he now had all the research he needed to break the news of Spiricom to the world. He organized a press conference in Washington, D.C. in August 1981 but the coverage of the event was spotty, at best. News coverage ranged from disinterested to disparaging. Undaunted, Meek gave dozens of radio interviews and kept playing clips of the O'Neil-Mueller recordings.

Meek's hopes of revealing proof of the afterlife to the world were soon dashed. The evidence failed to move the public. In order to silence the skeptics, he submitted the tapes for tests to prove that Mueller's voice was neither his nor O'Neil's voice. The tests upheld the recordings, but few seemed to care. Meek even sent out the schematics for Spiricom to hundreds of technicians, but no one could replicate his results. He now felt that he had wasted years on a project that had failed.

A short time later, though, Meek received a letter from a scientist who wished to remain anonymous. He told Meek that he and others had been pursuing similar work since 1946. Meek was on the right track, the scientist assured him.

Regardless, Spiricom was over. In the years that followed, Meek continued to fund research into spirit communications. Others received similar results, but no one could duplicate Spiricom.

After the project ended, William O'Neil deteriorated. Toward the end of his life, he was diagnosed with schizophrenia and was confined to the Torrance State Hospital in Derry Township, Pennsylvania. He died there in 1992.

Meek never wavered in his support for O'Neil but took the secret of the medium's schizophrenia with him to the grave. It was not revealed until both men had passed away. Meek died in 1999, leaving many unanswered questions in his wake.

Doubts had been raised about the authenticity of Spiricom as early as 1987. In the years after Meek's death, experimenters have examined the device and have tried to duplicate its success, but with no luck.

One of the first to raise questions about Spiricom was Alexander MacRae, a leading EVP researcher from Scotland. In 1982, he sent away for information about the device and received leaflets offering a Spiricom for $10,000, which he thought seemed expensive. Then Meek sent him a copy of the system and it seemed evident to MacRae that the price tag was to cover research and development costs. However, the system did not seem like any kind of mystical machine. The heart of it was a little radio that could be purchased from an electronic hobbyist's store for a few dollars. After some study, he concluded that there was no way that Spiricom could produce the results that had been claimed.

While in the United States, he attempted to make arrangements to see Spiricom for himself, but Meek gave him many reasons as to why it was not possible. MacRae never got to see Spiricom, but he did get to listen to the recordings that O'Neil made. He was unsettled by the many things that did not add up. Among them was the fact that no live demonstration had ever been offered of the device. In fact, there was no record of any communications with it after December 1981.

In 1983, Meek visited MacRae in Scotland. MacRae told him that he had doubts about Spiricom, but Meek said he believed the results to be true. He said that he had witnessed O'Neil working the device and had made a video of the session. Meek admitted that O'Neil insisted on being filmed with his back to the camera, which MacRae found odd. Meek said that he would let him see the video, but he never made a copy of it available.

Twenty years later, in 2003, MacRae finally saw the video. It reinforced an idea that he had about O'Neil doing the speaking for the alleged spirit, George Mueller. At no time did O'Neil and Mueller overlap each other's voice. MacRae also felt that O'Neil's body language him away, even with his back to the camera. He used the same dramatic upper-body movements while both he and Mueller were speaking. His final assessment of Spiricom was not favorable.

It was later learned that O'Neil was in possession of an electrolarynx at the time of his death. This is a medical device used to produce clearer speech by those people who have lost their voice box, usually due to cancer of the larynx. Some skeptics believe that O'Neil used this to alter his voice to speak as Mueller.

Other researchers, including Sarah Estep, had disappointing experiences with Spiricom and doubted its authenticity. Physicist Dr. Stephen Rorke undertook a comprehensive investigation of Spiricom evidence between 2003 and 2009 and concluded that the two-way conversations were not genuine. Although he was certain the evidence was hoaxed by ventriloquist O'Neil using an electrolarynx device, Rorke also thought the hoax was possibly a product of O'Neil's schizophrenia, combined with Meek's need to believe. In other words, both men may have genuinely believed that true results had been obtained.

But Rorke insisted that even if Spiricom was fake, it did not discredit EVP as a whole. There was too much data for it all to have been faked by everyone.

The evidence against Spiricom, as convincing as it may be to some, is still circum-stantial. With all the principals involved now gone, we will never know for sure what happened. Supporters of Spiricom contend that the device worked for O'Neil in a way that it did not for others because of his mediumistic abilities. Research-ers, including MacRae, have found that mediumistic abilities seem to be very important when it comes to spirit communications, even using an electronic device. Some researchers get results that others do not, even when using the same equipment and following the same procedures, which often makes validating the results extremely difficult.

This same problem would continue past Spiricom and continues today, with the assortment of new devices that have followed the research of the 1970s and 1980s.

Frank's Box and others

Frank Sumption was a licensed ham radio operator with a passion for the para-normal who created the first modern ghost boxes. His interest in a universal radio receiver that could contact the dead began in 1995 after reading a magazine article about EVP. Curious, he began trying to conduct EVP sessions but had little success at it. He put away the magazine and mostly forgot about it until he came across it again in 2000. He read the article again, decided to try again with EVP recording, and was shocked by his almost immediate success. He became fascinated with the idea of real-time communications and started his research to see how it may be possible.

During his studies, he came across a Danish researcher named Stein who was working with direct radio ITC. He would find an inter-frequency (a radio station without a signal) and search the white noise for voices. Stein conducted his direct radio experiments by sweeping the analog dial back and forth with his fingers, listening for mysterious voices.

Sumption also got a copy of EVP Maker, software created by German ITC researcher Steffan Bion. The software simply takes recorded audio and cuts it up into very small sound segments, which are then played back in random order. Listeners then listen for coherent messages within the sound bites. Sumption was impressed with the software but believed there may be something else that could work better for the process.

With ITC and EVP software on his mind, Sumption came up with the concept for the first Frank's Box in 2002. Using his skills as a ham operator, he began con-struction on the box from spare components that he had on hand. What he did not have, he salvaged from old discarded radios and television sets or purchased them from Radio Shack.

Frank's Box was nothing like the devices that had been used in the past, despite some similarities. It utilized the AM radio band and was much smaller than the bulky Spiricom devices. The box scanned the AM band, picking up bits and pieces of broadcasts and white noise. The end result was that users could ask direct questions of the box and receive a real-time reply. No playback was needed to hear the spirit voices — they were loud, often clear, and seemed to come from the other side.

Initially, Sumption thought that the best way to achieve communication was through random bits of audio. The first generation of Frank's Boxes supplied random audio generation to achieve communication. Until 2007, the boxes used a white noise generator, which fed a random voltage generation, which in turn was connected to a pre-built AM tuner from a car stereo system. As the random voltage fed through the system, the frequencies on the tuner would jump around. The rate at which these frequencies jumped was later controlled by a rate knob. This was just one of the many variations from the original box. As he continued to build Frank Box's, end users found that no two were exactly the same.

In 2007, a member of Sumption's web forum had the idea of making the ghost box utilize a linear sweep with a rate adjustment. This made it possible for the device to continuously sweep through the tuner frequencies. The results were amazing. Communications increased from single word replies into sentences that were built using multiple words. Sumption realized that the Frank's Boxes should not be limited to car stereo tuners and began using more elaborate, portable radios in the devices.

It was the linear sweep that launched a dozen or more similar designs. An ITC researcher named Bill Chappell thought that a regular radio should be able to accomplish the same linear sweep. He tinkered with a Radio Shack 12-469 in late 2007 and found a way to force the radio to constantly scan frequencies. After the radio was field-tested to positive results, more devices began to appear.

Frank Sumption's first and foremost interest was having his boxes be used for ITC research. To make this easier, he published the bulk of his schematics online for others to read and adapt. Ron Ricketts and a retired electronics engineer named Joe Cioppi used Sumption's schematics as a basis for the Minibox line and the Joe's Boxes. Many others have followed.

Sumption did not cease building and fine-tuning his boxes until his death in 2014. With each successive box, he tried something different. Some Frank's Boxes were linear only, some were only random, and a few boxes allowed for a device between random and linear frequency sweeping. He added filters, shortwave converters, and tone generators. To create better audio, he designed an internal echo chamber in some boxes and an external chamber for others. The echo chamber would take the audio generated by the frequency sweeping, send it through a tube to a microphone at the other end, and export it out through the speaker for listening. This added some reverberation to the voices that made them easier to understand.

Sumption built the boxes, used them at home, and then put them into the hands of ITC researchers who would make good use of them. He never put the devices up for sale. In his lifetime, he built 180 boxes. When he gave them away, he said that the voices from the box told him which researcher should have them.

Most of the Frank's Boxes that he built are still in use today. They have always been controversial — dismissed by some and cherished by others — but the Frank's Box has influenced the field of EVP research like before it has done, ushering in a whole new era of paranormal investigation.

Using the P-SB7 Spirit Box

The P-SB7 Spirit Box, created by Gary Galka, is one of the most frequently used devices on *Ghost Adventures*. (See Figure 12-3.) We have had a lot of success with it, starting back in 2009, when we did an investigation at the Trans-Allegheny Lunatic Asylum in West Virginia.

FIGURE 12-3: The P-SB7 Spirit Box during *Ghost Adventures*.

©Gary Galka, D.A.S. Distribution Inc..

The P-SB7 has provided groundbreaking evidence for us during our investigations. It seeks out paranormal voices on the EMF spectrum, and because we believe that spirits contain electromagnetic energy, it makes sense that we can hear them with this device.

It works by scanning the FM band, sweeping 119 different FM frequencies ranging from 75MHz to 87.9MHz, a full range of AM frequencies, and a unique high-frequency synthetic noise band, a.k.a. "white noise," where spirit voices seemingly can form words. The key is to focus hard and train the ear to distinguish messages formed in the white noise. The sweep speed has seven different speeds to choose from so you can experiment and choose the speed that is most comfortable for you and, of course, the speed at which you obtain the most EVPs. You can also sweep forward or backward.

To make room and allow power for the needed modifications, the internal speaker volume is low, so the external one provided (or any external speaker) must be used. A voice recorder or other recording device is important to use so you can review the EVP that is obtained.

The device was made specifically for paranormal investigators and has become so popular because it can be used by professionals and amateurs alike. It is small enough to be handheld, it can be connected to headphones and speakers, and it is backlit for use in dark locations.

When I have used it, it has been set very fast, so that each sweep stays on a station for only one-quarter second. The paranormal voices often can be heard on multiple sweeps. In many cases, we hear full sentences in the same voice. Hearing a full sentence over 14 sweeps, which is 14 different stations, cannot be explained by coincidence. You cannot go to all these stations and find someone speaking with the same voice.

Even stranger, we have used this device so without the FM and AM bands and have still captured voices. We have been underground, in remote locations, and with the P-SB7 inside of a Faraday Bag, which blocks out stations, and yet have still captured unexplained voices. Sometimes we leave this device on for 20 minutes without getting a single voice, and then I ask a question and get an immediate response that is relevant to my question.

I think one of the best-documented pieces of evidence that I received with the P-SB7 was when we were investigating the Perryville Battlefield in Kentucky. At the time, I had the curator of the museum with me when we were attempting a conversation in a former Civil War hospital. I asked several questions but there was nothing coming through. Then, a man's voice began to be heard. It was only this man's voice, every time that I asked a question. He answered a series of intelligent questions and when I asked him his name, he responded with "Daniel McIlwaine." The museum curator immediately went to his log and checked through the list of men killed during the battle at Perryville — Daniel McIlwaine was listed. He died on October 8, 1862.

I also used the P-SB7 at a house in Texas. The woman there was skeptical about the device and to test it, she told me that she and her mother, who had died in the house, had a secret word that they only shared with each other. I had no idea what this word was when we started our spirit box session. I tried asking questions for some time with no response but then I finally asked what the code word was that the deceased woman used with her daughter. The response was "Bossier." The woman with me grabbed my arm and began crying. "Bossier" was the correct word. It stood for "Bossier City" in Louisiana, where the two of them liked to go and gamble.

I tried an experiment with this box. I took two P-SB7 devices and put them side by side, within a few inches from each other. Then, I opened an audio program that allowed me to see waveforms. If there was any radio interference coming through, it would register from both devices. When I started the session, a voice came through but it only registered on one device, not the other. If it was radio interference, it would have come through both boxes because their antennas were literally only inches apart.

I cannot even count how many groundbreaking pieces of evidence that have been obtained using the P-SB7. It was created by Gary Galka after he lost his daughter in an automobile accident. I have been to his house and have communicated with his daughter, right in front of Gary and his wife. They validated her voice coming through.

So, I warn everyone who has never used a device like this, it really does work. Many people buy these devices with the idea that they are a toy. They are absolutely not. They have turned many skeptics into believers. Spending too much time with a spirit box of any kind can be dangerous. Getting too deep into communications can lead to attachments or even serious cases of possession if something dark decides to come through.

Using the Ovilus

Another device that we use constantly on *Ghost Adventures* is the Ovilus. (See Figure 12-4.) The device, designed by Bill Chappell at Digital Dowsing, was created to convert environmental readings into real words, offering direct responses to your questions. Theories suggest that spirits and other paranormal entities may be able to alter the electromagnetic frequencies and temperatures around us, so the Ovilus uses those frequencies to choose a response from a preset database of more than 2,000 words. The idea behind this is that an intelligent entity will be able to alter the environment in such a way that forces the Ovilus to "speak" an appropriate response. We do not know for sure how this works — but it does work.

FIGURE 12-4:
Ghost Adventures with an Ovilus device.

The device has been criticized for just offering random words when it is in "dictionary mode," but this is not the case. The "random" words are not random at all. The device uses readings from the environment to speak. It uses power points in walls, static electricity in the air, temperature changes — all these things are contributing to the readings. Spirits then use the atmosphere to manipulate the readings into words.

The spirits are also possibly picking a word in the dictionary that *sounds like* what they are trying to communicate. Quite often when the device speaks, it sounds like it is saying a word completely different than the one that appears on the lighted screen. The Ovilus is doing its best to choose the correct word but it may be slightly off. This usually changes during the course of the investigation as the spirit learns to manipulate the device in the way that it wants.

When using an Ovilus, it can be set up at a stable location inside the place you are investigating. The device can be monitored in the same way that you would monitor an EVP session, with equipment that includes cameras, temperature gauges, and EMF detectors. Ask questions and see what kind of replies you get from the Ovilus.

You can also take it with you and use it to get a reading from the entire location. When it is first turned on in the "dictionary mode," the device needs to calibrate to the environment, and you need to let it work itself through its initial readings. After that, the words that come through will seem less and less random and can be used for direct communications.

Just remember that, even though the Ovilus has more than proven itself as a worthy method of spirit communication, you must be cautious in some instances that you do not try and read too much into some of the responses. If they fit the situation, you may be making communication with a spirit. If not, do not try and force the circumstances to fit what the device is saying. It may still be trying to get used to the environment.

The Ovilus is another essential device for any investigator who wants to experiment with EVPs and direct voice communications. The warnings about spirit boxes also apply to the Ovilus. They can become dangerous if you get too deep into communications, so always experiment with them in moderation.

Chapter **13**

Putting It All into Practice: The Paranormal Investigation

This is a book about ghost-hunting. I have already discussed at great length the things you need to begin paranormal investigating, including the equipment to use, cameras and recording, and the methods to use when searching for spirits. This leads us to the investigation itself and the moment when you can put all the information that you have gathered into practice.

What to Do Before You Get There

One thing that paranormal investigator that is just starting out must do is to make it public knowledge that you are interested in hearing about strange events, haunted houses, and ghost stories in his area. After the word is out there, you are eventually going to get calls from people who want you to investigate their personal haunted houses.

One of the most important conversations that you have with the people who contact you is the first one. This conversation establishes the nature of the situation. To do this, consider some of these important points before getting involved with a serious investigation of a home or location:

>> Determine, if you can do so over the telephone, whether the person's report could have some sort of normal explanation. This may be hard to do in a telephone conversation, but try suggesting some non-paranormal reasons for the activity and see how the witness replies. Just be sure to explain to the person that you are not asking because you do not believe them. (They are already likely to start the conversation with "I know you'll think I'm crazy, but . . .") Simply explain that you need detailed information about the phenomenon they are describing. If one of your suggestions leads to an explanation about the events they witnessed, they may laugh a little with embarrassment, but they will be relieved that the problem was solved.

>> Find out why the person contacted you. Are they simply curious about a possible ghost? Do they expect you to make the activity stop?

>> Decide whether an on-site investigation is necessary. Find out how often the reported events occur, whether other witnesses are involved, and whether these witnesses are available for you to talk with, as well.

After talking to the witness, try and contact anyone else involved in the case who may be able to provide further information and then consider whether you plan to go to the location or not. Visiting the site is not always necessary. If the report of the "ghost" turns out to be an event that is explainable after a phone discussion, then it would not be necessary to investigate. This may also be the case when a report involves an isolated, one-time incident that did not occur again. In a situation like this, suggest that the witness keep a journal or a logbook of any activity. Then, leave it up to them to call you back and keep you updated about any new occurrences. Often, during that time period, the witness will realize the one-time event had a natural explanation or that it was an isolated incident that will apparently not be repeated. What had once seemed so frightening will no longer be, and you probably will not hear from them again. Although this may seem discouraging, it is not. The potential clients have been helped with little fuss, and there are always other cases for you to investigate.

On the other hand, if they do get back in touch with a list of additional activity, you will have an excellent timeline of events in the case and a written account of any incidents that took place before your hands-on involvement in the matter.

Always try to be an open-minded, but optimistically skeptical when dealing with witnesses. Depending on the person, they may be looking for reassurance that they are not crazy and that their experience has a logical explanation, even a strange one. You must start out by trying to prove that the situation may not involve a ghost. Don't listen to their story and jump to the conclusion that it is paranormal. People who are scared often misinterpret natural events as supernatural ones, and you have to be careful not to encourage the witness until you have actually investigated the location.

Another important thing to try and determine with this initial interview is whether the witness is mentally stable. This is not to make light of psychological issues. Nearly every experienced investigator has run into a situation of being contacted by someone who is not mentally competent. A little tact and diplomacy serves you well under these circumstances. The best thing to do in a situation like this is to bow out gracefully and suggest they contact someone with more experience in dealing with cases of that nature.

Tracking Down Leads

A good paranormal investigator is an ethical one. Our investigations must be conducted with sincerity, regard for the people and location involved, and by having the highest standards possible for the work that we do. It is never a good idea to go where you are not wanted, and you should never annoy or pester witnesses to paranormal events. But we are all looking for cases to investigate and haunted places to explore. Rather than harass people, a better way to start your career us to dig into public records or find books and articles about alleged haunted spots in your area. Many of these stories are purely folklore, but folklore can at least point you in the right direction to find authentic phenomena.

Many would-be investigators insist that this method is tapped out. Some say no haunted places exist in their area (hard to believe, but we can pretend it is possible), so they are not sure what to do next. One of the first things to do is to check the local newspapers, websites, and blogs each day. Reports about ghosts, and especially poltergeist activity, tend to make great back page and local mention stories, especially at Halloween. Also, make sure that your friends and family know of your interests and ask them to be on the lookout for any strange stories and articles that come along.

When you do find a story, though, it is unlikely that the address where something weird is happening will be printed, or that many details will appear. However, the names of the property owners and the main witnesses will usually be listed and those are great leads to start with. From there, you have a lot of options, both new and old. You can check local telephone directories online, but because most people no longer have landlines, this does not work as well as it used to. You can usually find the address of the location in a city directory, searching by the owner's name, or you can try tracking them down online or through social media.

From here, you have a few different ways to proceed. You can try finding someone who knows the owners of the house so that you can secure an invitation. This is the preferred method of access to the investigation, but it may not work.

The next suggestion is to try and contact someone at the local police station. The reason for this is that one of the first things that comes to mind for many families experiencing paranormal activity is that someone has broken into their house and may be causing the reported activity. For this reason, they usually contact the police first. Police officers can be very useful to you and even fill you in on small details in the case, but only if you handle it correctly. You must be able to convince them that you have a legitimate interest in the case and that you are not a lunatic. Play your cards right, and you may even get an introduction to the family.

Another course of action is to contact the family directly. The best way to do this is by a phone call or a letter because showing up on their doorstep with your ghost-hunter's kit is not recommended.

If the story about the possible haunting has been reported in the newspapers, it is likely that the witnesses will be receptive to your contact. However, the media can be very intrusive and unfair when they want to be. Their reports may have brought unwanted attention to the case or they may have reported the facts inaccurately. For this reason, approach the witnesses with caution and make sure they know your interest in the case is not only scientific but aimed at getting to the root of the problem, too.

Of course, private residences are not the only places to investigate. The business of ghosts has become very popular in recent years and it can often become a lucrative sideline for many unrelated businesses, like hotels and restaurants. Having a ghost can be great for revenue. Hotels sometimes charge higher rates for rooms that are renowned for spirit sightings. Likewise, some pubs, restaurants and public buildings can get away with charging steep prices for overnight ghost-hunts. These can be great places to investigate, especially when the stories have some legitimacy.

When you are new to investigating, start small. Try contacting a location that is unlikely to be inundated with requests from ghost-hunters. Be sure that you sound authoritative with your inquiries and be sure that you are prepared for the property owners to ask a lot of questions.

The more locations that you investigate, the easier that it will be for you to get into larger, more prestigious sites but this is something that takes a little preparation. The best advice is to initially submit your investigation requests in writing, by mail or even in person. You can always follow up your letter with a telephone call but in most circumstances, the first person who reads your letter is going to have to run the whole thing past whoever is in charge.

The following is an idea for a typical letter of introduction. Obviously, you'll want to fill in the blank lines with your name, your group name, and contact information. Just be sure to make the letter look as professional as possible. Here is an example:

Name of Contact Person

Name of Investigation Group

Address

Telephone

Email Address

Website Address (if applicable)

Name of Location

Name of Contact Person at Location (if known)

Dear _____ (or "To Whom it May Concern" if you don't have a contact)

Thank you for taking the time to read this letter. Permit me to introduce myself, I am _____ and I am the founder of a paranormal investigation group in the community called _____.

While conducting research into allegedly haunted places in the area, we came across information about your location and wondered about the possibility of researching the history of your place and possibly conducting a scientific investigation into any paranormal events that may have occurred there.

The investigation team will consist of _____ members (including myself) and we will be held accountable for any sort of damage that may occur to any property. We are also covered under our insurance for the sum of $_____. Although we have never had anything occur that would cause damage, we do hold ourselves responsible and are insured.

We would require access to your location for a period of three to five hours during the evening or night, in order to conduct a series of scientific tests that are designed to possibly collect evidence of the paranormal. We would also be very interested in speaking with any of your staff members who may be familiar with any folklore or history about the location, and also with anyone who may have encountered anything out of the ordinary in the past.

We will make every effort to conduct our investigations and interviews away from the view of the public, so we do not cause any disturbance to your operations. We will also inform the local police of our visit so that we do not arouse any form of suspicion.

If possible, we would like to visit the location in the daytime to have a walk around and familiarize ourselves with the place, meet with the staff and/or management and make notes of anything that may be of interest.

If you require any considerations to be met before the investigation takes place, please contact us and we'll be happy to meet with you and make our entire team aware of any concerns that you may have. In addition, we would welcome you to stay with us during the investigation, as your knowledge of the building will prove both interesting and insightful if we do encounter anything that may be regarded as paranormal.

Thank you again for your time and I hope to hear from you soon.

Sincerely,

_____

There is no guarantee a letter like this one will get you into public locations in your area, but it goes a long way toward establishing your credibility and serves as evidence of the fact that you take your investigations seriously and operate in a sincere, businesslike manner.

Guidelines for Your Investigation

If you decide to pursue the case and conduct an on-site investigation, there is much to know and consider before you get to the location. You should start off by doing your research. Look into the books and journals that you may have, and which may feature a case or two that includes incidents like the ones your witness is reporting. Do not assume that your case involves the paranormal before you investigate, though. Remember that what the witness is reporting may not be the only explanation for the activity.

Use this time to prepare for what to do when you arrive at the location. The following list of guidelines, ideas, hints, tips, and suggestions for investigating the paranormal offer you a lot of information. Not every guideline will fit your case, but many are valid for just about any situation. They are listed in no particular order:

» Try to make sure that all parties related to and who own the location have given their permission for the investigation, in writing if possible. You do not want anyone present to give you or the witnesses a hard time. This makes the investigation difficult, if not impossible.

» Keep your perceptions clear prior to the investigation. Never drink or smoke during or before an investigation. This will preserve your common sense, intuition, and sense of smell. Also refrain from wearing any heavy perfumes or colognes during the investigation, as it could be mistaken for something paranormal. Be sure to wear deodorant, however. You want to make a good impression on your clients and an investigator with bad body odor is not a way to do this.

» Arrive with an open mind. Always be aware that there may be a natural explanation for what is happening.

» Make sure that you bring along all the items that you need to properly conduct your investigation. Make sure that you know how to use your equipment properly and always try to find a natural source for your EMF readings before assuming that the detected energy is paranormal in origin.

» Avoid publicity and the media if possible when starting a case. You want to begin the case as unobtrusively as possible. Reporters, or people outside of your group, can add an unwanted dimension to the case. Media attention can also be disruptive with a witness who needs to be clear and coherent. Also, try to get the witnesses to refrain from inviting their friends over to watch. Carefully explain that you would like only people directed related to the case to be present.

» Avoid having any investigators from outside your group helping with the case, especially if you do not know them or have never worked with them before. They can bring unknown factors into the investigation, including trickery.

» Interview the witness in depth, repeating questions, if necessary. This allows you to tell how consistent the experience account is and whether any of the witnesses may be embellishing their version of the story.

» Look for a pattern in the accounts and try to see if the activity is related to only one person in the group.

» Become a part of the location. Try to blend into the background as much as possible and do not let the investigation turn into a spectacle. Also, make sure that your equipment is out of the way and not the focus of the entire household.

>> Make sure that the witnesses are comfortable with the investigation and understand what you are doing. You do not need to be technical with your explanations but make sure that they understand what the equipment is for and why you are taking so many photos, and so on. You will, at some point, run into a situation where the "haunting" has a natural explanation (like a banging water pipe or the wind), and you must be careful how you explain this to a witness. Some people will be relieved an alternate explanation besides a ghost exists, but if this is not handled right, some may feel that you think they were lying about the whole thing. Always explain the reasons why you think the activity has a natural cause, and if possible, demonstrate this for them.

On rare occasions, you will meet a witness who is actually lying, even if they imagine what they are telling you is the truth. This is also a situation to be handled delicately, and you should follow the same procedures you followed when you explained the activity's natural cause.

>> Remember that just because you want to study and research the activity (if it does prove to be genuine) the witnesses may not feel so inclined. In this case, the owner of the location must always take priority over the wishes of the investigator and help must be provided, if possible.

>> Try some field experiments to reconstruct the events. Let the witness walk you step-by-step through the encounter or experience and have them explain their feelings at the time.

>> Check with experts outside the paranormal field, like a plumber for an explanation of water pipes, an architect about the design of the house, an electrician about strange events with lights turning on and off, or any other kind of expertise that you need.

>> In the course of the investigation, remember to write down everything that occurs as soon as you can, no matter how small or insignificant it may seem at the time.

>> Be careful not to let your own beliefs influence the witness accounts in any way. They could be seeking the rational explanation that you are overlooking.

>> If you make public the information that you discover in your investigation, be sure that you have the permission of the people involved. Also, be careful of what you say and how you say it because the manner in which you present the information could influence the way that others perceive it.

>> If you do plan to make your information public, consider having releases printed so that they can be signed by the witness and the owner. That way, they are unable to come back later and say that you do not have permission to talk or write about the case.

>> Always carry some sort of identification. It is not uncommon for paranormal investigators to be questioned by the police or other local authorities during investigations. It is essential that you have express permission, if needed, to conduct your investigation, and you should keep any documentation you have pertaining to that in your possession at all times.

>> Always respect the location and whatever ghosts may be present. You should count yourself lucky when your team gains access to an investigation site and the location should always be treated with great respect. Always remember to clean up after yourselves, especially in a private location, because leaving a mess behind could guarantee that you are not invited back. It is also important to be respectful of the dead. It is the best way to be objective and conduct a professional investigation.

>> Always be polite. It does not cost you anything to have good manners. Whenever someone has invited you, or given permission to you, to do an investigation at their location, it is always good to follow that up with a thank-you letter, in addition to sending them a copy of your investigation report.

Keeping these guidelines in mind should assist you in pursuing an investigation. Obviously, these suggestions are not set in concrete, but they should help you in a manner that allows your investigations to be conducted in a professional manner.

Setting Up the Nerve Center

You have many things to do when you set up an investigation, but one of the most important is the creation of your *nerve center*. (Figure 13-1.) This is the audio-visual room for the investigation ahead. Here you can watch all the cameras you set up at the location and hear the investigators as they go about their tasks. This should always be the *least* active spot at the location. That way, the team members monitoring the cameras can move about freely and talk amongst themselves without contaminating the investigation. A perfect spot can be a detached garage or an isolated room, far enough away from the investigators to not be a distraction.

After your cameras have been set up throughout the house, you should go through the entire location with your team and make sure that all the camera views are visible on the monitor. Not only will the cameras capture all the action of the investigation, so to speak, they are also very important for capturing visual anomalies, apparitions, and poltergeist activity.

FIGURE 13-1:
The *Ghost Adventures* nerve center in action.

At least one of your team members should be on duty in the nerve center at all times. This allows that team member to monitor the entire location and to direct investigators to areas where activity may be occurring. It also facilitates communication between all the investigators, no matter where they are at the location. It is important for the team members in the nerve center to have all the research and history of the location. For example, when the investigators are participating in a spirit box session, the monitor can be checking out the authenticity of the information that is coming through the box.

The following steps provide a useful system for setting up the nerve center and the parts and moving pieces that go along with it:

1. **Find all the locations in the house that have been determined as *hot spots* either by the witnesses themselves or by your own investigation when you did a sweep of the house and picked up anomalous readings that could not be ruled out as artificial disruptions or electrical interference.**

2. **Use a number of cameras for the set-up. Run video cables to the monitoring system in the nerve centers.**

3. **Make sure you don't wash out an area with too much IR lighting. If you do this, you can make the area too bright to actually pick up any anomalies.**

   You want to find a good balance between the infrared lighting and the natural shadows. The ideal way to do this is to get a team member to stand in the middle of the location. If his or her skin tone is completely blown out white and you can barely see his or her eyes, you have too much light. Adjust that to get the perfect lighting.

4. **Set up a monitoring system.**

Several companies offer security and monitoring systems, most of which were designed for retail stores and companies. Many operate by Bluetooth or on a home Wi-Fi system. The systems often come with several cameras and professional monitors that offer multi-screen viewing on one unit. You can also hook up a recorder to these units so that you can go back and watch the tape later. Many of these units come with an extra-wide lens (because they are monitoring for intruders), which can be ideal for your investigation.

The only drawback of these systems may be the number of cameras for these units. Usually, each camera is surrounded by a ring of IR lights, which can pick up too much dust in a confined space.

5. **After getting your cameras placed, set up the rest of the equipment.**

We recommend you use EMF meters that can be used as stationary monitors. By aiming your camera and sound equipment in the direction of the meters, you will have a clear view of any disruptions in the location.

Consider also using a temperature and humidity gauge that can be monitored on camera, too. During an investigation, the researcher needs to make note of the temperature of the location and if possible, the humidity levels. Both readings may have an effect on the outcome of photos, video, and monitoring. As any sudden drops in temperature may signal the presence of something anomalous, this may be vital to the experiment's result.

Another great addition is a trigger object that can be monitored by the camera. For instance, a room at the location may be a nursery or bedroom where a child died and is alleged to linger behind. Placing some toys in the room, monitored by a camera, may achieve some great results.

Infrared motion detectors are also recommended. These units have more than one benefit. By monitoring the infrared spectrum of the location, it's possible that the units may pick up something that is unseen by the human eye. Investigators have often reported inexplicable alarms from these units, even when there was nothing to see. Later, they were surprised to find anomalies had been captured in their photos or on video. They also sometimes noted corresponding readings with their detection equipment. In addition, the units can be used to monitor the area for living persons, effectively sealing the area from entry.

By sealing off the area to everyone and monitoring it from a remote location, the investigator has effectively ruled out a source of activity that could be mistaken for paranormal. The human body does emit its share of electromagnetic energy and this could have an effect on the more sensitive meters. It also rules out temperature changes caused by the human body and eliminates the chance for minute dust particles in the air.

6. **Record the investigation.**

   You will have to go back later and watch all of the video, sometimes frame by frame, to see what may have occurred that did not immediately register with the monitors.

Starting and Conducting an Investigation

Investigations are best conducted with a team of three to six people (see Figure 13-2). This allows you to thoroughly investigate the entire location — without bumping into people from a large group — and to interview witnesses and record their statements without anyone feeling overwhelmed. A small group also allows you to avoid the distractions that arise and complicate investigations for researchers who work alone. Working alone is only recommended if you have many years of experience, and even then, it is best to have others present or nearby for safety and to corroborate any strange things that may occur. On the other hand, a large group is merely pointless, especially in someone's home, where things quickly become awkward and congested.

FIGURE 13-2:
Ghost Adventures team during an investigation.

©*Travel Channel.*

The following is a checklist guide for investigations. It is meant to be a list of helpful suggestions. Not every guideline works for every person, so use what you can from the list and adapt it to work for your own investigations.

1. **Make sure that the witness understands what you are going to be doing at their house or location. Make sure that they realize this can be an intrusive process. The more comfortable that the witness is, the better the investigation will go.**

2. **Divide up the separate functions of the investigation among the team members. Decide who will be handling each aspect: who will be photographing, who will be recording video, who will be using the available equipment, who will be in the nerve center, and so on.**

3. **Interview the witness in a secluded location with all the team members present.**

   Choose the team member who is the best interviewer to ask the questions. Be sure to ask what they know of the location's history and ask them to share their experiences there. Has anything affected them negatively there? Do they believe anything has followed them from the location? These are only general questions. More specific questions are suggested later in this chapter.

   Questions should be asked by one interviewer at a time, and the interview should be recorded on tape and if possible, video. One team member should take notes of everything that is said. Getting all the details of the case in this first interview is essential. The entire team should be aware of the history of the location. If an interaction with a spirit occurs, each team member can ask questions based on what they already know about the place. This helps the interaction to become more personal between the investigation and the conscious presence.

4. **After the interview, the team leader should take the group on a walk-through of the location.**

   The tech manager and the nerve center monitor should use this time to determine where all the cameras should go. Particular attention should be paid to those areas where the witness recalled an experience or sighting or where anomalies have been picked up using detection equipment.

5. **Another team member should make a photographic record of the location with his camera, documenting each of the locations, particularly the area where the witness reports seem to be most frequent. Using video, another team member should document the location in this manner also.**

6. **If the phenomenon occurs on a regular basis or has a set pattern, obtain permission from the witness to do surveillance of the area for an extended period. This is often referred to as a *ghost watch*, because it gets away from an active investigation and becomes more of a "watch and see" experience.**

   In these situations, researchers should come to the location, set up their monitoring equipment, and then wait to see what they can record. We have even been known to this as people sleep. Occasionally, witnesses tell us that the activity occurs only after they go to sleep, so we set up cameras to monitor them. During as episode of *Ghost Adventures* at Phelps-Dodge Hospital in Arizona, we interviewed a caretaker who told us that something touched him while he slept. We set up cameras, and he was right — we witnessed a presence touching his hand.

   This type of investigation should be done when you are relatively sure that you cannot explain away the reports of the witnesses, or after your own investigations have turned up something beyond the ordinary.

7. **If, when the investigation is over, you have turned up nothing, remember that this does not mean the location is not haunted. Even if you have tracked down all possible natural sources for the phenomena and ruled them out, the ghost could simply have been inactive while you were there. This is why follow-up calls and repeat visits are important.**

   You can't go to a location where witnesses have documented activity on their own, stay there for three hours, and then state that the place isn't haunted because nothing happened to you! Just because you showed up does not mean that the ghosts are ready to perform on command.

   If you have established a good relationship with the witness, they will not mind hearing from you again. Be sure to ask them to call you if anything else happens, and make sure that they keep a record of it. If anything occurs, go back and conduct another investigation, varying your technique to maximum effect.

Learning Ghost-Watch Skills

The ghost watch is usually the second step in the investigation, when the investigators have become relatively sure they cannot explain away the reports of the witnesses at the location. By now, the initial investigation had turned up something beyond the ordinary. It is no longer about just interviewing witnesses and ruling out natural events. With this type of experiment, the investigators set up monitoring equipment at the location to wait and see what occurs. It may be time-consuming, and even a little boring, but it often pays off.

Coming into a ghost watch, it helps if you have been able to establish a pattern for the reported activity. If witnesses say that activity happens at a certain time in the evening, this is the optimal time to set up. You will also want to center your watch in an active location where events have been previously reported.

You can conduct this experiment in several different ways. The first method is by using high-tech monitoring equipment, just like what you used in the nerve center for the operation. An investigator can place himself outside of the monitored area and watch any activity that occurs through cameras.

But in some cases, this type of ghost watch may not be practical. Not all ghost-hunters are as fully equipped as a nerve center requires them to be and not all homeowners are willing to allow large quantities of cables, wires, and equipment to be set up in their home. Some witnesses are happy to have you at the location, but not in such an invasive manner. As we are always required to honor the wishes of the location owner, we must adapt our investigations to suit their mood and desires.

Another method of the ghost watch can also be used, which is helpful for those on a limited budget. This method can be just as important to the overall investigation, and although you still should record as much of it as possible, usually one camera (or at the most, two) will do the trick. This method depends more on the alertness and common sense of the ghost-hunter than on high-tech equipment. Because it does not involve completely sealing off portions of the house, it is usually more palatable to the homeowner, too.

A ghost watch can also be used as a sort of remote investigation of locations that may be hazardous or dangerous because of the building conditions, air conditions, or even because of malevolent activity. The location is equipped in the same way — cameras, equipment, recorder, spirit box, and so on — but a two-way radio is also added. In this way, I can see and hear everything and can also communicate with any spirits present from the safety of the nerve center. Because the radios are connected along the electromagnetic spectrum, I have found this to be a method that has achieved some pretty incredible results.

One other method of the ghost watch will work if you do not have the time to sit and watch the cameras live through an entire night. In some situations, we have simply left the cameras and equipment at the home overnight, and set them up undisturbed to watch the homeowners sleep, for instance. Then, we return the next day, pick up the gear, and review the recordings at another time:

1. First, you need to secure the spot — a house, a single part of a house, or an abandoned building. Make sure that the perimeter is untouched and that no people or pets have access to it. If you are in a private home, be

sure to note how many people are present in the building. If one of them has a reputation for being a prankster, be sure that person — or perhaps his or her bedroom door — stays on camera. You want to make sure that you can rule out any artificial activity that may occur.

If you are investigating an abandoned site, you secure the perimeter so that no one can break in and contaminate the ghost watch.

2. **Seek out an area of the house/location that you want to monitor.**

The good news is that this does not have to be a single room, hallway, or staircase. Because the monitoring here is done more by man than machine, the investigation team can actually be scattered throughout the location. In this way, you can observe almost the entire house and perhaps even everyone who is in it. By stationing the group in different rooms, the team is in a good position to watch for both strange phenomena and fraud.

3. **If possible, equip each team member with a video camera to record anything (supernatural or otherwise) that occurs in their designated area.**

If this is not possible, have each team member keep track of everything that occurs and everyone who enters their portion of the house. These facts should be written in a notebook or voice-recorded. In this way, you will know the exact whereabouts of everyone should anything occur during the experiment.

4. **Carefully choose the investigators for the experiment.**

Waiting for something to happen can be boring, but team members must stay alert and be prepared for anything. Any member who is prone to fall asleep or become easily bored may not be your best choice to take part in this kind of experiment.

5. **Record and monitor video at all times.**

Those members who are monitoring their areas visually should remain on high alert and keep their still camera available. They should also keep a notebook and pen, a tape recorder, and any other ghost-hunting equipment close at hand. You never know when something remarkable may happen.

6. **Consider leaving an unmanned spirit box on camera during the ghost watch. It can be monitored from a distance for any communication that may come through.**

7. **Make sure team members have a good supply of energy drinks — coffee or their favorite soft drink — along with them.**

This type of experiment may last for hours, or it may last all night. Most likely nothing out of the ordinary will happen, but you have to be prepared if it does. It is bound to be a long night, and it could be an uneventful one.

8. **Have the team leader check in with the other investigators on a regular basis. This person can provide not only assistance when needed, but also perhaps extra batteries, refreshments, or even encouragement. This can keep the investigators on their toes and wide awake during a lengthy investigation.**

Some other things are worth thinking about, too, no matter what type of investigation that you are involved with. These are odds and ends and things that are worth keeping in mind:

>> If an investigation is worth doing once, then it is worth repeating. You should not be disappointed if nothing happens on the first investigation. Experts insist that you always do follow-up research at presumably haunted spots. Your vigilance and persistence will most likely pay off with something in the end. Even if it doesn't, though, you will have managed to establish a good pattern for future experiments. Or, at the very least, you have established what not to do the next time.

>> As part of the standard investigation, we recommend that team members prepare a diagram of the location on which they can mark questionable areas and spots where they picked up anomalies of any sort. These diagrams are important because a map of this type can be used to mark a designated area for team members as well as any odd happenings.

>> You need to decide what the investigators should be doing in their designated areas. The investigators literally interact with the location. There has been much debate as to what works better — silence or normal behavior. Opinions vary on this, and it really depends on the location itself. In a place where sounds carry in unusual ways (like an old theater), it is probably best that the investigators remain completely silent, or as silent as possible. On other occasions, they may be able to behave normally and quietly in whatever area has been designated to them.

   Keep in mind, though, your group members remain much more alert if they are allowed to move about to some extent and behave normally. Working under conditions of silence, and sitting still for hours at a time, can be exhausting. This can lead to errors in observation and leave the investigators stressed out and irritable, which are not the best conditions for an investigation. A compromise may be to alternate the periods of silence and restricted movement with periods of more normal behavior. Your investigation can continue much longer this way.

>> Another element to keep in mind during your investigation is the lighting of the location. When monitoring the entire location with cameras intended to film in total darkness, location lighting may be of benefit to you. It may increase the activity and also your chances of recording it. Many ghost-hunters prefer to

work this way, and it can be useful in situations where no one is walking or moving around in the monitored areas. This eliminates any concerns about people being injured in the dark, and your infrared cameras should be able to pick up any anomalous activity, as well as to check the readouts on the equipment under observation.

If total darkness is not practical, the lighting should be kept low. This allows investigators the ability to see without causing their vision — or any photographs taken — to be affected by the glare from too much lighting.

Low lighting is also of assistance in avoiding unwanted attention to your investigation. By having all the lights turned off at a location and having flashlights bouncing around and moving past the windows, the investigation could attract the attention of the neighbors or, in the worst case, the police. You can understand how this may look suspicious to someone passing by and this is yet another argument for the lights remain on but at a discreet level.

Chasing the Poltergeist

If an investigator remains in the field for a long time, he or she is eventually going to run into a case that has all the signs of a haunting, but it may not have the ghosts. A poltergeist outbreak can be a unique and baffling experience. Objects may violently move about during this kind of case, flying about the room, banging and crashing (early investigators dubbed these cases with the German phrase for "noisy ghost" for a reason), but some of these cases may have a human agent as the source of the activity, not a spirit.

If you get into this kind of situation, you first need to determine if the reported events are connected to actual ghosts or to one of the people residing in the house. To reach this point, a lot of interviewing and investigation must be done. If the case is an active one, it is very possible that sounds may occur, or physical items may be moved, while the investigators are present.

In these cases, your monitoring skills will be tested. It is essential that team members are stationed throughout the house and that cameras and recording devices are running constantly. In this way, you have the best chance of documenting the activity. Always check the items in the house that have been reported to move. Make sure such objects are solidly placed, not teetering on the edge of a table. Jump up and down and make sure that movement is not causing objects to move or fall. If your tests show that things are secure, make sure that your cameras are always focused on suspect items so that if anything does happen, you can capture it on video.

The most important thing to remember (whether you suspect the case is genuine or a hoax) is to keep the family members under constant observation. By keeping track of the movements of everyone present, you can authenticate the events that occur.

However, keeping the family under constant watch does present some problems. Because you do not want to seem like a kidnapper holding a group of hostages, you must be subtle about how you do this. If the homeowners feel that you do not trust them or that you think they are faking the whole thing, then they are likely to become offended and ask you to leave.

This is where your connection with the witnesses comes into play, and it's why every ghost-hunter must have some people skills. If they do not have them, they should never be dealing with the witnesses.

Rather than herd them into a group and stand over them, you should try and engage the family in conversation or explain to them that they should not move around too much with the idea that it may interfere with your testing equipment. Because people do not move around as much when you are talking or interacting with them, you should get them to talk about their interests, school, job, or whatever it takes to keep their attention. You may also consider allowing them to "help" with the investigation by keeping notes or making diagrams — essentially anything that will keep them busy.

If you think one family member is linked to the activity, keep them nearby. Just having that person close may trigger the activity to start. It may turn out that such a person is not the source of the activity. Maybe a spirit is connected to that person in some way, using their energy to manifest. That person may be able to provoke a response from the spirit simply by being present.

If, during the investigation, you suspect that a human prankster is at work, be sure to keep that person close to you and under surveillance. If the haunting turns out to be a hoax, this is your best chance of finding out. There have been many cases that start out with great promise and eventually are revealed to be the antics of an adolescent in the house whose playful pranks went just a bit too far. Although it may be the hardest thing that you have to do, revealing to the parents that you have a video clip of the prankster at work will certainly cure all the fears they had of their house being haunted. And if the phenomenon does turn out to be real, then your hours of investigation will have paid off.

Examining the House

Not every location that you investigate will be haunted. It is always best to approach each investigation with the idea that the reported events have a natural cause, rather than a supernatural one. Most investigators learn this by trial and error, discovering that many people who believe their houses are haunted are merely misinterpreting normal sounds for unnatural phenomena.

One of your main jobs is to check out the allegedly haunted house to see whether leaky or rattling pipes could be causing strange noises. Electrical problems, plumbing, weather conditions outside, and a variety of other natural problems can sometimes convince a property owner that they are being haunted. The investigator, however, can often quickly learn the truth.

For instance, if ghostly noises in the house seem to always occur at the same time each night, this usually means they have a natural cause. A flushing toilet at the same time each evening can lead to rattling walls and even "disembodied footsteps." Water pipes can play other tricks, as well. In fact, even water pressure in a kitchen faucet can seem like a ghost. The water pressure can build up to the point that the faucet begins to seep water, as though it was turned on by itself.

Faulty electrical work can also cause all sorts of seemingly bizarre manifestations, from tapping inside of the walls to light switches that turn on and off. When lights and appliances behave erratically, a check of the fuse box may reveal an outdated set of circuits. Besides being a fire hazard, it may also be the cause of what seemed to be supernatural events.

You may want to recommend that the family call in a good electrician rather than a ghost-hunter but be careful, though. Sometimes electrical and plumbing disturbances can actually be the first sign that a poltergeist outbreak is about to begin. There could be more going on what first meets the eye, so always remain open-minded about the location.

Examining the house should not stop at water pipes and electrical boxes. Other questions should be addressed. You may have to really dig deep, so to speak, to address all the concerns surrounding the strange events in the location. Has the house been checking for carbon monoxide or radon gas leaks? Has it been inspected for mold? These conditions can influence the minds of the occupants, causing illness and hallucinations. It is important to rule these things out.

What kind of soil was the house built on? Are there any underground rivers or water sources nearby? Could there be caves, tunnels, or even mine shafts beneath the house? This is part of the geological history of the property. They can show if the house may shift on its foundation, making noises occur or objects move about. Imagine that the homeowners tell you that the phenomenon normally occurs after a rainstorm. If so, you may check to see how much clay or chalk is present in the soil. As this kind of soil settles after a storm, it can put stress on the house, causing it to creak and shift.

These types of sounds and events could make even the most rational person wrongly believe that his or her house has been infested with ghosts. However, don't be too quick to judge. Just because a house has one leaky pipe or a faulty electrical outlet, this does not mean it is not haunted. Every incident, report, and happening must be considered to determine the authenticity of a haunting.

Investigating Outdoors

Conducting paranormal research in outdoor locations like forests, battlefields, and cemeteries should not be that different from conducting an investigation in a home or a building. Every investigation must be organized, have rules and guidelines, and a set of criteria to follow. Otherwise, we really cannot call it an investigation — it is simply an outing. Wandering around a location taking pictures may be enjoyable, but it is not research.

The first thing to do is to choose the site. It should not be done at random. Not every battlefield or cemetery is haunted. However, strange stories have been told, dark history has occurred, and people have encountered things they cannot explain in hundreds of outdoor sites.

After you find a location that seems promising, start looking into its history. This is where you decide if an investigation is warranted. You must decide if this will be legitimate research and you can make your decision based on the information learned by answering the following questions:

>> What is the history of this location?

>> What events have taken place here to lead you to believe that it may have become haunted?

>> What paranormal events have been reported in the past?

If the answers to these questions lead you to suspect that something ghostly may be taking place at the location, then you should consider organizing an investigation. Bear in mind that haunted history in some locations can be elusive.

Investigators provide historical evidence of a haunted house by gathering witness testimony and details about a ghost that may be present in a location. That information is then examined to try and match it to the alleged spirit when they were still alive. We can also collect testimony of events that occurred in the house to residents in the past and then match that evidence to current events that are now taking place. Having independent witnesses, of different time periods, with matching experiences makes for some very convincing evidence.

The problem with haunted outdoor sites is when we try and provide historical proof of the haunting. This is simpler with a battlefield than with a cemetery. It can be difficult to gather the data needed to explain why a cemetery is haunted, but it is certainly not impossible.

Tracking down battlefield haunts

When we think of hauntings, a haunted house usually first comes to mind. However, one of the best places to encounter the paranormal evidence that supports the intersection between the world we know and that of the spirit world is on a former battlefield.

Battlefields small and large dot our country from coast to coast. Some are mere roadside curiosities while others bewilder the visitor with their sheer expanse. Some battles were fought for freedom while others were open acts of aggression against an unsuspecting foe. Yet all were fought by brothers, sons, fathers, daughters, and mothers and all saw horrifying, unforgiving numbers of deaths.

At places like the Alamo, Shiloh, Antietam, Gettysburg, and the Little Bighorn, scared soldiers stood shoulder to shoulder and leveled their rifles at the enemy, firing as fast as they could reload. Cannons belched and the ground shook. The air was filled with smoke and the sickly sweet smell of blood. The screams of men in the throes of death were drowned out by the spine-chilling shrieks of injured and dying horses. The pall of death covered the land as far as the eye could see. Blood was spilled, limbs were torn apart, and bloated bodies rotted in the sun. Here, on these solemn fields, the seemingly inconsequential lives of thousands of young men were snuffed out in the proverbial blink of an eye.

Those mass casualties left a myriad of ghosts behind. Intelligent, interactive spirits, as well as residual hauntings, remain on the battlefields of the past. Many of these hauntings have been well documented, so finding out the history behind them or the locations on the battlefield where they are often seen is not difficult. Books have been written, documentaries filmed, and first-person accounts are readily available to the investigator.

Regardless, investigating a battlefield can be a difficult experience. We may know the history of why the location is haunted but proving it ourselves may be more difficult.

Tracking down graveyard history

Investigating a battlefield may be tough, but it is nothing compared to investigating a cemetery. History books provide us with details about what occurred on a battlefield, but a cemetery can be a complete mystery. These investigations must start from scratch.

The first thing you must do is to pick a site. You will not have home or building owners to help you out with their experiences. Your best bet is to keep your ears and your options open. You may be surprised at how many people have ghost stories to tell about local cemeteries, what may be around in the old folklore or what may be heard by everyday people who have encountered the unusual.

The most difficult part of the investigation is tracking down the cemetery's history, but this guide should help you to compile and complete and accurate picture of the cemetery that you are researching.

If you have heard about a cemetery that may be haunted, you will need to do two things: first, visit the cemetery for yourself; and second, research the history of the place so that you can get more knowledge about its background.

When you visit the location, be sure to go in the daytime. You need to study the layout and terrain, which may not be so easily seen after dark. If the cemetery has a caretaker's office, be sure to stop in and ask for maps and any available literature about the cemetery. In this first scouting mission, you are just trying to get an overall feel for the place. Be sure to take plenty of photos, stroll through the graves, and search out the older sections. Take your time in doing this and get a feel for the different kinds of markers that are on the grounds, the landscape, and anything else that may play a role in the history of the place.

After you have visited, you should start gathering historical information about the place. Make a checklist of events that may have occurred there to cause it to become haunted, including natural disasters, crimes, grave robbery, desecrations, and occult rituals.

Determining the type of cemetery

One of the first things to do is to determine what kind of cemetery it is. The following list describes several common types:

» **Church cemetery:** America's first cemeteries were the churchyards of New England the East Coast and here you can find the oldest burials. The tradition of church burials was started in Europe and carried on in America. When the churchyards became too crowded and the conditions unsanitary, town cemeteries were started. After that, land was usually set aside on the borders of towns where the cemeteries would be located. The early churchyards will not usually be laid out in neat rows like later cemeteries. The alignment of the graves tended to be haphazard and close. In many cities, and often in rural settings, churchyards are still in use today but those located away from the East Coast tend to be more organized and less crowded than the original sites.

» **Garden cemetery:** The garden cemetery movement began in Paris and later extended to America. The popularity of the movement came at a time when American attitudes toward death were changing from the grim reality of it, as typified by the skulls, wings, and frightening artwork, to finding beauty in death. This beauty was portrayed in the statuary and monuments and in the landscape architecture of the cemetery itself. Garden cemeteries are easily identified by the park-like setting of them, with pathways, ponds, trees, and benches for visitors. Before public parks were common, people came to the cemeteries on weekend afternoons to relax, walk, and have picnic lunches under the shade trees. Even the names of the cemeteries began to emphasize the beauty and back-to-nature settings with names like Greenwood, Laurel Hill, Spring Grove, Forest Lawn, Oak Ridge, and others. Garden cemeteries tend to be huge, sprawling places, so obtain a map if one is available.

» **Rural cemetery:** These types of cemeteries are a true piece of Americana and are easily found on the highways and back roads of the country. On many occasions, you'll find them well hidden along gravel roads and at the end of dirt tracks, abandoned and forgotten by the local populace. Other times, they will be on the edge of a small town, or a mile or two from town, and often on small hills to protect them from spring floods. Large monuments or mausoleums are rare because most of these cemeteries are small, which makes them simple to investigate but difficult to research. In these cases, check with the local genealogical society for information or talk with some of the old-timers in the area.

» **Memorial parks:** The first memorial park was established in Southern California in 1917 (Forest Lawn) and the movement has since spread all over the country. There is nothing inspiring about this type of cemetery, which is really the point. The flat, grassy lawns with their flush, stone tablets were designed to eliminate all suggestions of death. The cemetery has no monuments, and the grave markers are all situated against the ground so that lawnmowers pass right over them. The goal was to give the cemetery a more park-like landscape.

>> **Military cemetery:** The first large military cemetery in the country was established in Pennsylvania in 1863, shortly after the Battle of Gettysburg doomed the fate of the Confederacy. It was here that President Abraham Lincoln gave his famous Gettysburg Address and consecrated the place as hallowed ground. Currently, 119 national cemeteries exist in the United States, including Arlington Cemetery, and all of them are filled with rows of identical stone markers, marking the graves of men killed in battle and who were discharged from military service. The history of these cemeteries, especially those associated with the battlefields, can easily be obtained and offer a rich tale for the researcher. Many of them are as haunted as the battlefields located nearby.

>> **Potter's fields:** Potter's fields are graveyards where towns bury the poor, the unknown, the unclaimed, criminals, suicides, and illegitimate babies. Most often they are buried in mass graves or in individual graves with no marker. A potter's field is the greatest example of anonymity, a place where the names of the dead, if known, are usually placed only on the coffin itself. A pit is loaded with coffins until it is full and then the entire mass grave is given a single, numbered marker. No mourners are present when the earth is smoothed over this grave and no clergyman is there to offer a prayer for the dead. They can be stark, forbidding places.

Surveying the cemetery

As you are exploring the cemetery, try to get oriented with the general design of the site. One of the most common customs regarding cemetery layout is that most are on an east-west axis. The inscription on the monument may face east or west, but they can be anywhere, so check the back and all sides, too. Many ornate monuments, or those with lengthy stories to tell about the people buried beneath them, may have inscriptions on practically every surface. Some graves also have footstones, which makes it obvious which direction the body was placed, but most are laid with the head to the east and the feet to the west. This tradition follows the idea that the eastern sky will open on the Day of Judgment and the dead will rise from their graves to face the rising sun.

Gravestones and cemetery markers provide us with the greatest amount of information we can find about the history of the graveyard while at the site. For this reason, we should understand as much as we possibly can about them. Some basic information can be found on most tombstones:

>> Name of the deceased

>> Birth and death dates

>> Birthplace and place of death

>> Relationship or marriage information

>> Epitaph

Other information may appear as well, including service in the military, fraternal or service organizations, life accomplishments, and perhaps even a short biography of the deceased.

Also, just because a stone appears in the cemetery, this does not mean that the person is actually buried there. The marker could be simply a memorial that was placed there by loved ones. The body could have been lost in an accident or disaster and never recovered. Cemetery records, if they exist, should reveal that information.

Cemetery gravestones act as a road map to the past but unfortunately, vandals, pollution, and the weather can destroy these vital links. Weathering is a natural decaying process that affects porous objects that are left outside. When water gets into the cracks of a tombstone and freezes, it tends to expand, causing stress on the marker, especially older and more fragile ones. This makes the stone much more susceptible to accidents and damage from lawn mowers and rakes that are wielded by cemetery caretakers. Wind, rain, and sun can do damage also, and because the force of our weather patterns seems to move from west to east, many markers, especially marble ones, become eroded and are no longer legible. Be sure to note whatever information you can find on the markers in the section of the cemetery that you plan to investigate.

One of the best ways of finding out about the cemetery is through records, newspapers, local census records, and county histories but you can also get an equally good sense of time and place by surveying the cemetery itself. When you do this in conjunction with your research on paper, the cemetery will literally come alive for you. By surveying the site and reading though the tombstones (especially in smaller cemeteries) you should be able to find out a lot about the history of those buried there.

On some headstones, you will find information on where people buried in the cemetery migrated from, such as places of birth or inscriptions that tell of moving from one place to another. You can also use such information, including family names, to determine where their country of origin may have been.

A survey of gravesites can also give you an idea of how the people buried in the cemetery were affected by epidemics that swept through the region. If you find a number of graves that are dated 1918, it's possible that many of the deceased died during the Spanish Influenza epidemic of that year. Several graves that share the same date means that a check of the records could reveal a cholera, smallpox or any other common frontier epidemic killed people in the region.

Floods, hurricanes, tornadoes, fires, mine accidents, and other tragedies often claim the lives of a large number of people. On many occasions, the victim's tombstones will tell the story of the disaster, or at least that it occurred. If not, another check of records from a date that appears on many stones will likely provide the information that you need.

While you are in the cemetery, use your notebook to take a random sampling of about 40 gravestones that belong to adults that were at least 21 years of age when they died. Write down just the birth and death years and then sort them out by sex. Total the ages of the men and women and then divide that number by the number of individuals of each sex. The number that you come up with gives you an average age at death for men and women of the community. To be totally accurate, you have to go through the entire cemetery and do this, but this random sampling at least gives you an average.

Surveying and exploring the cemetery grounds is likely to give you pages and pages of information and believe it or not, most of it will be worthwhile, no matter how confusing it may seem at first. After you have finished your survey, research the names you compiled. The names may not mean much at first, but you are likely to have the names of city leaders, politicians, ministers, and more. Tracking down that history just may reveal the history behind the ghost stories you have heard about the cemetery. Linking that history to the real people buried there puts you one step closer to understanding the haunting.

Public records can provide information about the cemetery, as well as the local funeral homes, undertakers, and monument companies that used it. All these companies may have had records of the cemetery. If they are no longer in business, the local historical society may have access to their past records.

You can reveal the cemetery's history in other ways, too:

>> **Cemetery plat maps:** Although it may be hard to find plat maps (check the genealogical society) for old and defunct cemeteries, those graveyards still open for interments should have a map or register so that workers do not accidentally dig a grave where another is still in use. You can check for copies of such maps at the cemetery office or at a town or county office. Cemetery maps normally give the names of the person or person occupying the graves

and other details, such as the date of burial. This may be important if you survey of the cemetery pointed toward evidence of some unmarked graves in some areas.

>> **Cemetery deeds:** In the same way that purchasers receive a deed showing the ownership of a piece of property they have bought, those who purchase a cemetery plot also received a deed. A copy of it is usually recorded with the town or county where the cemetery is located, and the other copy is stored with the cemetery sexton. In the record, you will find the names of the buyer and seller, the amount paid for the plot, the lot number, and where it is located in the cemetery. This is the next likely step in research following the obtaining of a cemetery plat map.

>> **Cemetery transcriptions:** One of the best places to find more information about the cemetery is at the local genealogical society. Genealogists love cemeteries and are, in addition to records rooms and in front of their computers, the place where they spend the bulk of their time tracking down family histories. Over the years, many genealogists have taken the time to copy down cemetery inscriptions and have often had them privately printed into books that are stored in the local library or genealogical society so that others will have access to them.

>> **Cemetery records:** The superintendent's records typically give the name of the deceased, the date of the burial, and often, the exact location of the grave in the cemetery. In addition, the records sometimes list the original purchaser of the burial plot and who is responsible for the upkeep of it. When researching stories from a ghostly viewpoint, this just may be vital information if that person's relative is suspected of being the resident haunt. You can often find these records in the cemetery office itself or filed at the town or city hall.

Investigating your outdoor locations

After all the preliminary research of the site (whether it be a cemetery, battlefield, or some other outdoor location) is finished, you still have more to do before the actual investigation takes place. This includes returning to the location for some additional surveying and exploration, although this time it will be specifically in regards to the investigation that your team will be carrying out on the grounds.

Return to your location in the daytime and bring along a notebook and pen. A number of things need to be noted about the site before you can return at night:

>> Draw a map of the location, as close to scale as possible. Be sure to mark any landmarks or noticeable spots on the map so that other team members will be able to easily locate them. This may mean trees or monuments on a

battlefield or grave markers and mausoleums in a cemetery. These can all be used by your team to orient themselves between the cemetery and your map.

>> Take note of the location's surroundings. Be sure to notice what may be seen from the location during the investigation. If woods surround the area, check whether houses are visible on the other side of the trees. Even a small amount of light, or sound, from a nearby home or farm, could appear to be anomalous in any photos that may be taken or on any recordings that your group may make.

>> Take many photographs of the site in the daytime. That way, any nighttime photos can be checked for location and compared to areas that may be active.

After leaving the site, more preparation work needs to be done. One of the most important things can be accomplished by speaking with local authorities. If you are planning to conduct an investigation in a public location, you must find out what the state and local laws say about trespassing there after dark. In most cases, unless the site is otherwise posted, you will be asked to leave by law enforcement officials. If the site is posted, then you could be arrested or fined.

>> Try to get permission in writing from the owners of the location to conduct investigations at the site. This must be done through the authorities if it is a battlefield. They may have set times when it closes. Few cemeteries are privately owned and most belong to the local community or the township in rural areas. You can speak to the on-site superintendent about this. You may also contact the local police department and let them know that you will be at the site as a courtesy. This may be very important if you are unable to get written permission. If you can get permission, take the letter with you to the site.

>> After selecting the site and getting your clearances (if applicable), carefully put together a team of people to accompany you to the location. As with any other investigation, you should put together people who can take photographs, run the equipment, use the video camera, etc. Be sure not to tell them what to expect before the investigation. If they witness anything at the site that matches previous reports, this will strengthen your suspicions about the place being haunted.

>> After your team has been put together, prepare a variety of equipment that you want to take with you. Your team should be no larger than seven to nine people and no less than three. You will need the essential items from your ghost-hunter's kit, along with extra batteries, and these items, too.

- Flashlights (one for every team member)
- Clipboards and copies of location maps
- EMF detectors

- Cameras (one for every team member)
- Video cameras
- Infrared boosters to better illuminate the area
- Full spectrum camera
- Infrared motion detectors
- Thermometer to check weather conditions
- Game cameras, like those used by hunters, can be triggered by motion
- Thermal cameras, if available

Beyond this basic list, you should add whatever pieces of equipment that you feel would be useful in your particular location or investigation. Just be sure that you have a practice run with any new or unfamiliar equipment prior to the investigation. This is also suggested with new cameras and temperature gauges, as well. Most likely, you will be working in uncomfortable and dark conditions. The investigators should be familiar with the equipment before arriving at the location.

» Before you leave for the investigation, consider using the map that you have already made to decide where you would like to first set up the equipment. This may be based on previous reports from the location or insights by the team member who previously visited the site.

Going out in the Dark

Before the investigation begins, you may want to go over some ground rules with your team. You should keep many things in mind while getting the investigation organized:

» Never take on an investigation like this alone. A good team is required for legitimate research. Not only is safety important in an outdoor or an isolated location, but having more than one person to authenticate evidence and any incidents that may occur is essential.

» Do not drink or smoke prior to or during the investigation. The majority of evidence from the night comes in the form of photographs that have been obtained with corresponding evidence. If a team member is smoking, even if the smoke does not appear in any photos, it can destroy the credibility of any evidence that may be obtained.

» During the investigation, be sure to make a note of anything that occurs, no matter how small it seems. Before things start, be sure to also make a note of the following:

- Date and time of the investigation

- Name and location of the site

- Investigators/team members present

- Weather conditions (temperature and barometer readings and even the wind speed). Check the local weather service before leaving home

- Detailed list of the equipment being used

» Finally, leave the location exactly as it was when you found it. Be sure that you do not leave any trash behind and be sure that nothing is done to physically disturb the site. Even accidents can have a grave effect on the opportunity that you may have for future investigations at this site and others.

When you arrive at the location, find a place where you can set up your base of operations. At a point that is easily identifiable by the team members, you can leave your equipment cases and any non-essential items that do not need to be carried around the location. If possible, try to arrive at the site before dark so that all the team members can get a look at the place. Hopefully, the map that you made will have noted any hazards that may be encountered, but if not, this will give everyone a chance to see things for themselves.

When this is done, set up any stationary equipment you plan to use. Position the instruments in locations where they will not be moved, and have each team member make note of where everything is so that they will not stumble over it later. Make sure the equipment is in a position where it is most likely to encounter phenomena. If nothing occurs after a set period of time, then try moving it to another spot. After the equipment is in place, it is time to get started:

» Split the investigators into separate teams, with one person monitoring the cameras and stationary equipment and the rest checking out the location with various other types of equipment. You should be searching for all manner of activity and photographing any anomalies that may occur in order to provide corresponding evidence.

» Ideally, the investigation will last from 2–4 hours (depending on the amount of activity recorded) and this means that the location will have to be covered almost continuously during this time. Try to refrain from too many breaks and from leaving the equipment unwatched. Paranormal occurrences do not follow a pattern, so the investigator must be constantly aware.

>> If strange activity is found during the course of the night, the investigators should compare notes and try to pinpoint the most active areas of the location.

Even though the investigation ends for the night, it is far from over. All the data that you collected must be gone over, the recordings watched and listened to, and the photos studied. In an investigation such as this, you have a unique situation in that you rarely have any eyewitness testimony to collect. For this reason, the material that you have collected becomes even more important and essential to any theories that you may develop about the haunting.

If paranormal occurrences occurred, plan to do follow-up investigations. Plan to focus on the areas of the location that were the most active. You may see an increase in activity, or possibly even a decline. If this occurs, continue the same methods that you used in your initial investigation and see if the activity has moved to a different area.

Just remember that an investigation of this sort can quickly deteriorate into chaos if not handled properly. It is extremely important that the goals of the group remain focused and that the investigation is organized and well thought out. This is the best way for an outdoor, or cemetery, investigation can be considered successful.

Chapter **14**

Interviewing the Haunted

I nterviewing a witness may be the hardest thing that you have to do during an investigation. As any law enforcement officer will tell you, two witnesses rarely see the same incident in the exact same way. Paranormal investigators run into the same situation but in a different manner. In paranormal cases, a witness will see and hear something totally alien to them, something frightening, and something they don't understand. This makes our job even tougher.

People who are dealing with a haunting or a poltergeist outbreak are often highly agitated and stressed out. They may feel as if they are going crazy or that they will be labeled as unstable if they talk about what they have seen and heard. The paranormal may seem quite ordinary to an experienced researcher, but it is something completely bizarre to the average person.

An investigator needs to be able to assure the witness that their experiences are not unique. This must be done in a professional manner. You want your client to feel they are in good hands and that you respect both the client and their property. They must be comfortable with you, so establishing a good rapport with them is essential.

In the course of your investigation, you have already spoken with the witnesses over the telephone about the case, and you will then do a second, in-depth interview with them when you arrive at the location. Everyone in the affected household should be interviewed, although not necessarily at the same time. Collecting their accounts separately ensures less influence and cross-contamination. Everyone who is in any way a participant in the case — either a victim or a witness to the activity — should be interviewed. Many facts can come out during these sessions because clients are relieved to be able to talk about their experiences with sympathetic people who believe them.

Conducting a strong interview can be difficult for an investigator who is just starting out but developing the proper protocols for dealing with witnesses is essential to your future in the paranormal.

>> Check all the details of the account with the witness and make sure that all the outside facts, beyond their immediate experience, are in order. If they recall that it was snowing that night, check the weather conditions and see, because if it was not, that may not be the only problem with their memory.

>> Attempt to recreate the events if possible. Place each witness in the same position they were in when the encounter occurred. If they reported a strange noise, try to recreate that noise by natural means and make sure that normal possibilities are ruled out.

>> Try to get a full and complete report of everything that happened. This may be important later as the mind tends to forget slight details as time goes by.

At this point, let's suppose that you have followed all the rules of investigation and the case seems genuine. It appears that the witness statement holds up to scrutiny, but you must be certain. You must be objective when writing up your report. Do not let yourself be influenced by information you may have discovered while reading or something you experienced in other cases.

Your assessment of the witness testimony is very important to the case. You must decide if the witness is believable. If you have any doubts about what may have happened, you need to rule those out while you are at the location.

There are many problems that can occur when interviewing a witness and you need to be sure to eliminate all possibilities of fraud, deception, and mistakes during your interview.

>> A witness may be totally unaware of how some phenomena may occur. Check into the details. There may be something natural about the house that is causing the lights to go on and off or something like nearby train tracks that could be causing things to move about.

>> Eyewitness testimony is not always what happened — but what the witness believes to have happened. It is good to find out ahead of time if the witness is already convinced the house is haunted. This kind of thinking can easily color their testimony.

>> A witness can be influenced by information you give them. Be careful about what you say before the interview. Even joking about paranormal events can be bad.

>> The witness may be mentally unstable. This happens and it does so more frequently than we would care to admit. Paranormal investigators are not mental health workers so we can do little in this situation but try to extricate ourselves from the predicament as politely as possible.

>> The witness may deliberately fabricate events. This is a multi-level problem. Your client may have made the whole thing up, or your client may have had a real experience but cannot recall all the details, and filled in the blanks with false information. Either situation can destroy your entire case. If you believe that a client is lying and you continue on with the investigation, your credibility will be ruined. You must learn to do the best you can in determining when someone is lying to you. It will become identifiable by asking pointed and direct questions about the events.

Sample Questions for the Paranormal Witness

The following list certainly does not contain every question that you should ask a witness, but it should give you a good start. Add your own question or omit those that don't fit the particular investigation you are conducting. Add any questions that are pertinent to your case and customize your own questionnaire.

Before getting started with the list of questions, let the witness tell the entire story as they remember it. Then, start asking your questions, and you will notice that more details will start to emerge from the story. After that, try recreating the events in the locations where they occurred.

Also, before working your way through your list of questions, you may want to apologize in advance for the intrusive nature of your questions. You should explain that although many of them won't seem relevant, they must be asked. By having a complete picture of the person's experiences and beliefs, you will have a complete documentation of the case. Remember to stress that the answers they give you are completely confidential. This may help them to be more forthcoming with their information.

>> How was the phenomenon experienced? Were you alone at the time? Were others present? How many people saw the event?

>> If the phenomenon was visual — did it move or was it stationary?

>> How would you describe the visual phenomena? Was it a shadow? Was it light? Was it a recognizable form? Did it seem to have any form at all?

>> If it was sound phenomena — how would you describe it? Was it quiet or loud? Was it a sound that you recognized?

>> How would you describe the phenomena in general? Did you feel frightened by it? Disturbed? At ease?

>> Was there a smell involved with the phenomena? If so, how would you describe it? Strong or faint? Did you recognize the smell?

>> If there was a sensation of touch, how would you describe it? Was it slight or strong? Was it violent? What sort of feeling did it give you?

>> How would you describe the encounter as an experience? Did you sense that you were being watched? Did you sense a presence close by?

>> If any physical objects were moved — did you see it happen directly? Did you see movements of objects, or anything else, out of the corner of your eye?

>> Have you had any problems with electrical items? If so, describe them and where are they located? How are they located in conjunction with your encounter? Was there any disturbance of electrical items during your encounter?

>> What was your mood prior to the encounter? What was your state of mind? How were you feeling physically?

>> What activity were you involved in at the time of the encounter?

>> Did anyone die in the house recently? Do you know of anyone who died in the house during its history?

>> Was a séance held, or Ouija board used, in the house before the disturbance began?

>> Has anyone in the house reported frightening dreams or visions?

>> Do you have any pets in the household? If so, are there any areas that they avoid or growl at consistently?

>> Since the disturbances began, has anyone been physically harmed: scratched, bitten, or slapped?

The following questions are used to determine the background and the belief systems of the witness. They may shed additional light on their experiences and also provide answers about any information from the client that seems questionable.

» Do you believe that ghosts and other paranormal entities exist?

» Did you believe in them before your encounter?

» Do you ever visit allegedly haunted locations in groups or alone?

» Are you actively involved in a church or a religion?

» Do you agree with most of the teachings of your religion?

» How does your church feel about ghosts and the paranormal?

» Do you believe that angels have contact with people on earth?

» Does your family believe in the existence of ghosts?

» Do you have any knowledge about ghosts and the paranormal?

» Where does that knowledge come from (books, TV, etc.)?

» Did you believe this location was haunted before your experience?

» Has a member of your family, no matter where they may live, recently died?

» Are you currently taking any medication?

» Have you been treated recently for any serious illnesses?

» Were you drinking any alcohol near the time of your experience?

» Have you been treated for any mental illness?

» Do you believe that ghosts are real?

» Do you believe that people can influence mind over matter?

» Do you believe that people can affect their health through positive thought?

» Have you ever experienced déjà vu?

» Have you ever dreamed of events before they happened?

» Have you ever had a near death experience?

» Do you believe that other people's paranormal experiences are real?

» Do you believe in reincarnation?

» Have you ever experimented with witchcraft or black magic?

» What was the time and the exact location of your encounter?

> » What were the weather conditions at the time of the event?

> » Overall, how has this experience left you feeling? Scared? Confused? Interested in learning more?

After asking these questions, the investigator should make any related notes about the answers the witness gave and ask them if they can recall any other details about the experience. They probably would have given you those details while you were asking the questions, but it never hurts to ask.

It is imperative to record this entire interview and to have one of the investigators mark replies to the questions on a notebook separate to the one used by the main interviewer. This gives you several accounts that can be corroborated.

Interviewing Children

If interviewing a witness to a paranormal happening is the hardest thing you may do as an investigator, then interviewing a child is doubly difficult. Having children in a household that is undergoing a paranormal disturbance is frightening for everyone. Parents are worried about what is happening in their home and even more concerned about the effect that the haunting may have on their children.

Particular care has to be taken in these situations. Many believe that talking about the investigation in front of children or to explain to them what is going on is unwise. However, in far too many cases, the children in the house are important witnesses to the strange events. In fact, most children are far more sensitive to the paranormal than adults are and often make compelling witnesses to unexplained happenings.

Most importantly, though, never interview a child without the parent's express permission to do so. Not only can an unauthorized interview be detrimental to your investigation, but could land you in legal trouble, as well. In a later chapter, we discuss client release forms, but having one available specifically for anyone under the age of 18 is always a good idea.

Interviewing children is challenging for several reasons, including confusion and fear. Careful preparation before the interview will ensure that it proceeds smoothly and that you will obtain the information that you need for a successful investigation.

Be aware that many children are eager to win the approval of authority figures, or in this case, the investigator who they may see as having a job that they may have seen on television. This means that the child you are interviewing may try and figure out what you want (or do not want) to hear. Some children are emotionally susceptible to suggestion or manipulation. Be sure to tell the child that it is all right to say, "I don't know" or "I don't understand." Remember to give the child permission to pause the interview and correct you if any of your information is incorrect.

Use a comfortable setting for the interview and allow the child to choose where they would like to talk. Be sure to sit down when you do the interview so that you are at eye level with the child. Standing over anyone — especially a child — is intimidating. It is important to make sure that children feel secure during the interview. If they prefer to have a parent with them, be sure to encourage this.

Before you start your questions, tell the child what is going on and why you need the information. Use simple words and short sentences.

Make sure the child is questioned only once and by only one person unless a follow-up interview is needed. A detailed and well-documented report eliminates the need for multiple interviews that cover the same ground.

When you start the interview, begin by asking the child to recall anything they can remember about the reported events in the house. This allows the child to describe the experiences in their own words. Ask more focused questions later in the interview, depending on the age of the child and the child's willingness to talk. This approach reduces the risk of you accidentally influencing the child's account.

Before asking direct questions, you can set expectations that the child should provide accurate information by offering some instructions. The child's age may influence the number of instructions and, perhaps, the type of instructions that may be most helpful. For example, you may want to include instructions like:

>> "I was not there and don't know what happened. When I ask you a question, I don't know the answer to those questions."

>> "Only talk about things that really happened."

After the child's narrative account of the alleged incidents has been fully explored, you can then follow with more focused questions, asking for details, clarification, and other missing elements.

Sometimes, a child's recall of events is an important component in your investigation. If the child is interviewed skillfully, his or her account may be the crucial element in determining what kind of activity is taking place in the location. Just remember to make a solid plan before the interview, take your time, and never forget to have all your permissions in place before you start.

Chapter **15**

Authenticating the Ghosts

The past is never dead, in fact it's not even past.

WILLIAM FAULKNER

There is an often-used quotation that tells us that we should know our history because if we don't, we're condemned to repeat it. Although true, the above quote from William Faulkner is even more apt for ghost-hunters. Faulkner believed that the past lived on in the lives of the characters he created but for paranormal researchers, the past literally lives on in the hauntings that we write about, study, and investigate.

Hauntings are created by the events of the past, and, without history, we cannot truly understand them. If, after your investigations have been completed, you have come to believe that the location you are researching is truly haunted, your next step will be to find out why. What occurred to make this place become haunted? And who is it that haunts the place?

We have used cameras, technology, and various kinds of equipment to establish that paranormal events are occurring, but history offers us a different kind of proof. For example, a house may be considered haunted by its current occupants. When the past owners of the house are contacted, they tell the same stories, about the same events. This occurs even though the people have never met, do not know one another, and have not compared stories. It's difficult to dismiss such claims.

Ghost-hunting becomes like detective work when attempting to re-create the history of your haunted location. If you are researching a public building, your job may be easier. Many public buildings, including famous homes, are often mentioned in local history books. Even some of the strange events of the past, including the ghost stories, may be mentioned.

This is not always an easy job, but it is an important one. This chapter offers the best ways to track down the history of your location.

Reaching into the Past

All houses, just like people, have a past. You may find clues to what you are looking for right under your nose, like a child's growth chart that is hidden under layers of paint or even initials that are carved into a tree in the front yard. You don't even need an old house to make fascinating discoveries. Even new housing developments have a past. Think of the horror movies that we have all seen about houses that have been built on old cemeteries and then remember that these movies were inspired by actual events. Local legends, as well as land records, often help to uncover a compelling story.

All you need to get started is a little direction and a few tools: a sturdy notebook, a sharpened pencil, a magnifying glass for examining documents, a lot of curiosity, and plenty of energy. Searching through the past can be a tiring job but well worth the time and effort.

Start off easy and check out what the current occupants know about the house's history. Be prepared for some inaccurate information, though. There is a chance that the occupants, unnerved by the strange activity that is taking place, could shadow their information in a suggestive way.

You should also find out if any neighbors have been in the area for a long time. This is often a great source. The little old lady who has lived down the street for 50 years will remember many of the former occupants of the property. These nearby residents may also know whether any local folklore exists about the place. This type of information is usually only partially accurate, but don't discount it totally. Folklore can often point the researcher in the right direction, although sometimes by a meandering path.

The next step should be checking to see if anyone else has ever traced the history of the house in question. Each state has a state historic preservation officer who nominates structures that are "significant in American history, architecture, archaeology, engineering and culture" for listing on the National Register of Historic Places.

There are other places to look, too. The Historic American Buildings Survey and the Historic American Engineering Record have documented tens of thousands of historic structures and sites since 1993. Their reports contain measured drawings, photographs, and historical information, which is a treasure trove for any ghost researcher who is lucky enough to find the house he is checking out included in the survey. The data is available on microfilm and at the Library of Congress.

There are eight places to search for background information on your location.

Land deeds and directories

When you're researching an "ordinary" home that is not a historic location, you have to start from scratch. This means locating the land records in your area and digging in. Researching a house is much the same as doing genealogical research. You must start with the past and work backward. Land deeds record the transfer of ownership from a grantor (seller) to the grantee (buyer) and give you the grantor's name, marital status, and address (usually only the town and state). It also includes the grantee's name and address, the price of the property, and property description. Sometimes the deed also lists restrictions for the property, such as a ban on chicken or pig farms, sale of alcohol on the premises, and in older records, even a ban against property buyers of a certain race or religion.

Deeds can make for both invaluable resources and even fascinating reading. Keep in mind, though, that deeds record the ownership of the land, not of the houses. Most deeds don't even mention the buildings on the property, and you have to use the price of the property to guess whether the land was vacant at the time of the sale. Remember, though, just because someone's name does not appear on the deed does not mean that he or she did not live there. The house may have been rented out, and only by tracking down other listings will you be able to see who lived in the house.

In order to do this, try checking through what most towns call city directories. These are books that collect the names, addresses, and occupations of the people who lived in a city during a certain year. They usually also offer a "reverse" directory, which allows you to look up the address of the house and then find out the occupant of the house, instead of the other way around.

When you have a detailed timeline from the city directory, you'll have a listing of those who lived in the house and an idea of how long they resided there. At this point, you may consider sending a letter that requests information about any strange events that occurred in the house. The letter should be written as professionally as possible and should contain your contact information. Don't be surprised if you don't get a response. If they did not experience anything out of the ordinary, they are probably not going to feel the need to tell you that. However, if they also experienced the haunting that is reported by the current occupants, you may hear from them.

Newspapers

Even if you are unable to speak with the former residents, your timeline and list of occupants will continue to serve you well. You can use their names to start checking for stories and obituaries in local newspapers. There are a vast number of newspapers that are now available from online sources, but city libraries also have back issues of newspapers. They also usually have a directory for obituaries and of the dates in which they appeared in the newspaper. Genealogical and historical societies also keep copies of obituaries, or at least they may have a record of when they appeared in a newspaper. After you find the obituary, try and determine the cause of death. If the death was eventful in any way, there will also likely be a story in the general section of the newspaper for that day. As ghost-hunters are aware, murders, suicides, and traumatic deaths can certainly lead to a house becoming haunted.

If the death involved murder, suicide, or was under other questionable circumstances, then there was undoubtedly a police report filed about it. In this case, you are also in luck as police and coroner's reports are public record and can be obtained by anyone. In most cases, there may be a small fee involved and a short waiting period for the report.

Online resources

In addition to old newspapers, the Internet offers other help for investigators. One of the best is a website called DiedInHouse.com (https://diedinhouse.com), a unique database that provides users with death records associated with a specific address. The site was started by Ron Condrey in 2015 after research confirmed that someone had recently died in the house that he had just purchased. He assumed that would have been part of the disclosure process, but it was not. Knowing that other people probably found themselves in the same situation he was in, he decided to start the online database.

Currently, the site only offers data about the United States. It is also limited by technology because records only began to be digitized in the 1980s, so older homes are still going to take some sleuthing on your part. However, this is a great resource for those trying to find the identity for a restless spirit that is roaming a client's personal space.

Architectural drawings

A great source of information about the history of the house can be the builder's plans, although they can often be hard to come by. Some builders (especially with older homes) may have just kept the plans in their heads and modified them when needed. The best place to find them, though, is in the house itself. Home-owners often kept the plans in the attic, basement, or tucked away in a closet somewhere. If your research leads you to past occupants of the house, they may have accidentally taken the plans with them. Sometimes tracking down the heirs or descendants of the former occupants will help to find the drawings. You can also check with the state historical society and see if it has a drawing of the house or knows who to contact to get them. Many archives collect plans of architecturally significant buildings or those drawn by noteworthy architects. You may also consider looking in a book of house plans if all else fails. Many older homes were modeled from basic plans.

Maps

No house history research is complete without checking out the maps of the neighborhood. As you move backward through records and property changes, a map of the area will help to keep you oriented. Ask the Register of Deeds (or a related office) for maps that cover the neighborhood, such as surveys that were conducted when roads were widened or moved. In any older town, the roads were changed at least once to accommodate the coming of automobiles, as opposed to the horse and buggy. The house you are researching may appear as a small dot on the map or may be complete with details on a fire insurance map. It simply depends on what type of map you find.

A great resource is a plat map. When a piece of land is subdivided into streets, blocks, or lots, this information gets recorded on a plat map. Originally, these maps were hand-drawn and contained only a few details. Printed maps usually show streets, significant buildings, and houses, and rural maps show plots of land, cemeteries, and much more. Plat maps can be found at the office where deeds are filed or usually at the local library.

Many researchers also turn to birds-eye view maps, which are panoramic scenes of cities and towns that show buildings, trees, and homes from an overhead vantage point. Thousands of them were created for cities all over American between 1850 and 1900 but they show few details, and although they're striking and beautiful, they are only of assistance when dealing with well-known or highly visible locations.

Another type of map, which can be quite useful, is a Sanborn Map. Beginning in the 1860s, the Sanborn Fire Insurance Co. created maps to assess the fire hazard of buildings. The maps list construction details, such as windows and doors, and depict the size and shape of the insured structures. They also detail property boundaries and usage for about 12,000 cities and towns in the United States. Check with your local library to see if these types of maps are available in your area.

Biographical encyclopedias

If the people who lived in the house you are researching were notable in the community for anything, then they may be listed in the county or city biographical encyclopedia. These books were created for communities between 1870 to 1905 and list the accomplishments of local businessmen, bankers, and pioneers. Many of them also contain a portrait of the individual.

Building permits

Generally, before owners can make any major changes to their home, they need to obtain a permit from the town's building department, which may also be called the planning department or code enforcement division. These permits record the vital statistics of the home, including the number of bathrooms and bedrooms, porches, window locations, and more. Permits also include the names of the homeowners, when the work was done, and the contractors for the job. The information contained in a permit could play an important role in your research and provide clues to hidden aspects of the house, such as the location of former doors or windows, which may be useful when occupants report unexplained chills and drafts.

Photographs

A wonderful addition to your research would be a vintage photo of the house. You can often find photo files at local historical societies, libraries, and newspapers. Search under the name of a previous owner or the street address. You may also contact local real estate agencies to see if they have any photos of the house on file. When you visit a library or historical society, it's always a good idea to bring a current photo of the house with you. It may jog someone's memory and you can also use the photo for reference when looking through books of house styles.

All this information is of great use to you as you hunt for the history of the location. It gives you not only a record of who lived in the house but the things that may have happened there to cause it to become haunted.

Bringing the Dead to Life

The next step in your historical research is to connect the paranormal activity that has been reported in the location to a person who once lived there. Being able to do so creates powerful evidence of life after death.

In the previous section, city directories and obituaries were mentioned as ways to track the occupants of the location you are researching. Obituaries are like small biographies and are often written for the newspaper by funeral homes or by the relatives of the deceased. They often tell something about the deceased and his remaining family, as well as details about funeral services and where he was buried. The cause of death may or may not be listed in the obituary, but you can watch for clues within the notice as to what may have happened. Words like *died suddenly* may indicate an accidental death, a murder, or suicide or possibly just a heart attack or a stroke. The words *lingering* or *long illness* could suggest cancer, heart disease, or tuberculosis.

Here are some other ways to find information about the occupants of the location:

>> **Death certificates:** Death certificates are the official documents that record people's deaths and were first created to determine the frequency and distribution of fatal diseases. Many states did not have such a plan in place until the early 20th century, but modern death certificates are completed by several people. If a person dies in a hospital or other institution, then a nurse or staff member fills in the time and date of death. The doctor fills in the cause and then the funeral director, or one of their staff members, fills in the rest. The information is then retyped onto a new, blank form and then is returned to the doctor for their signature. After that, the funeral home then goes to the registrar for a burial permit. Usually, the funeral home will keep a copy of the certificate on file.

Death certificates, which are filled with vital information, can be confusing and hard to decipher but the more modern they are, the more they are likely to contain. Sometimes, information can be in error and often the cause of death can be obscured or covered up to protect a person's reputation or privacy. This is especially common with older certificates. For example, instead of *suicide*, you may find the cause of death was listed as *accidental*, or instead of *abortion*, you may find *uterine bleeding*. On older certificates, causes of death will often use archaic words for diseases so be sure to have some sort of glossary on hand while attempting to decipher them.

>> **Funeral home records:** Although this is a possible source for research, it's not a likely one. Many funeral homes will not have a problem accommodating you for research on people who have been dead for many decades, but they are unlikely to grant you access to anything recent. Funeral home records are private and so they are within their rights to restrict or deny access to records. Also, because they are private, the content in the records will vary from one location to another and from one time period to another, as well.

>> **Institutional records:** If your subject died in a hospital, asylum, tuberculosis sanatorium, poor house, or prison, then his death would have been recorded in that institution's records. These registers, which usually predate state ward registrations, may be kept in a separate death book or among the other entries in the main register book. Information is going to vary in them from one place to the next and certainly from one time period to another. In many cases, the institution (especially with asylums and tuberculosis hospitals) will have closed years ago and so finding the records may be tricky. To find out if the records still exist, contact the town, city, or county, or even the state historical society. They may have some idea to help you find them.

>> **Autopsy records:** Many death certificates can tell you if an autopsy was performed on your subject and if so, that record will then be filed with the hospital or with the coroner's reports. An autopsy is performed when a cause of death is uncertain, questionable, or suspicious. If the medical examiner suspects something unusual, then no consent is needed from the family for an autopsy. The details of these records are fascinating and just may provide many clues to the researcher in search of the strange.

>> **Coroner's records:** If you learn from your research that your subject died in an unusual way or under strange circumstances, you will want to check and see if a coroner looked into the case. Both medical examiners and coroners investigate suspicious deaths and the position of coroner predates that of medical examiners. The coroner, an elected position, was responsible for examining dead bodies for any sign of foul play. No special education was required, and it was not necessary to be a doctor. By the late 19th century, many states and cities began replacing the position of coroner with that of the medical examiner, who is required to be a physician. Some locations still use the elected coroner position or a combination of both.

If the coroner decided that the death appeared to be from criminal negligence or murder, then he held what was called an inquest and the records of these affairs hold huge amounts of information for both crime buffs and ghost researchers. Juries were appointed and witnesses were called to testify. The postmortem findings (autopsy records) were included, as well. Most coroners' reports are open to the public and should be followed up with newspaper research. There may be an obituary that was written, or, if the death was unusual, an entire report. If the death turned out to be murder or linked to a crime, there also be subsequent articles and possibly even court records if the case went to trial.

This information will assist you with what is perhaps the most important part of your research: connecting the ghost in the house to a person who once lived there. Acting like a detective, you have now linked the past to the present and have real evidence of life after death.

Chapter **16**

The Mundane Side of Ghost-Hunting

Ghost-hunting is not exciting all the time. As paranormal investigators, we know that a lot of our time during an investigation is going to be spent sitting around and waiting for something to happen. Although it's often a little boring, we always have the expectation that a weird happening is going to take place. This makes it worth all those hours that we spend waiting around for that excitement to happen.

But when the investigation is over, that does not mean the end to our responsibilities. There are hours of recordings to listen to and watch, photos to analyze, and a lot of paperwork that still must be done. We always have to keep track of the information, reports, and interviews that we collect during our investigations. We have a responsibility to both our client — and the rest of the paranormal community — to keep accurate records and to share information that leads to a greater understanding of the paranormal and how it works.

We have collected evidence, we have analyzed it, and we believe it to be genuine. Now, we need to present it to the public. It cannot be shown only to ghost enthusiasts and other paranormal researchers. Our hard work just may sway the mind of the non-believer. We must take a chance with the evidence we have and allow others to see it. If we are sure that our evidence is genuine, then we should have no problem presenting it to someone besides other ghost-hunters. Our belief system cannot be so fragile that we are afraid of being shown that we are wrong about something. We should have already attempted every possible natural explanation for the evidence that we believe to be real. If someone else suggests another one, then we have that much more ammunition for the next time that something possibly paranormal comes along.

This chapter examines what needs to be completed *after* the investigation. These tasks are not exciting and can even be a little dull, but they are very important if we want our investigations and our evidence to be taken seriously. This is probably best referred to as the "business side" of paranormal investigating but if you want to preserve the reputation and integrity of your work, it is essential.

Building Your Case Reports

You have completed your investigation and have done all that you can to address your client's fears with a rational approach and an objective eye. For the client, the investigation seems like the most important part of the process because it took place in their home, business or other location, but, in reality, it represents only a part of the work that must be invested in the case.

When it is over, the investigator must sit down and review all the material that was collected from the location so that a case report can be compiled. Evidence analysis and report writing can take weeks in some instances, depending on the complexity of the situation. There are many, many hours of audio and video evidence that has been gathered and an honest, thorough review can take quite a lot of time. Afterward, the team should gather for a discussion of the most compelling evidence, testimony, and personal experiences.

This is also the best time to continue to research all the facets of the case and suggest alternative interpretations of them. For example, if any of the occupants are taking a type of medication, you may look at its potential side effects, find out how it affects the body, and check to see if it could cause any perceptual anomalies that may be mistaken for paranormal experiences. Brain chemistry, physiology, and psychology are also complex factors. If a client is undergoing any physiological change, such as high stress, pregnancy, puberty or menopause, it must be considered as a potential influence. Household dynamics are also important. If the chemistry between family members or spouses and partners poses any significant challenge, then this also must be assessed as a possible influence on the case.

Be sure that when you are writing up your report, though, that you do not give the clients the impression that you are blaming them for their problems or that you think they are making things up. You are only looking for every explanation, including a paranormal one, as you study their case. Alternative theories and explanations should not be taken to mean that you are trivializing your client's concerns. You are simply trying to build a stronger case with an even-handed approach.

When the report is complete, it should reveal one of several conclusions:

>> **Explained:** Enough evidence was discovered to offer a rationale and ordinary explanation for the alleged paranormal experiences of the client. This can often be done at the site, at the conclusion of the investigation, but submitting to the client a report with a full explanation as to why you do not believe their home is haunted is always necessary.

When you can close a case as *explained*, it offers a happy ending for all involved. You have been able to put your client's fears to rest and you can also help them to correct the situation that was occurring.

>> **Inconclusive:** Evidence has been obtained that the events in the house may have a paranormal source but the analysis of it is inconclusive or disputed among the investigators. It is also possible that the facts in the case just do not add up or that no history can be found to explain the reported events. More simply, it may mean that nothing occurred while the investigation was taking place.

Labeling a case as *inconclusive* does not mean that the client has failed to convince you. Rather, it means that the evidence you collected did not convince you of a haunting. You may trust the client to be sincere in their reports of paranormal activity, and you can use the details of their testimony to help conduct the investigation, but your conclusions must rest in the strength of your own evidence because it was collected under controlled conditions and studied with a more objective eye than that used by the client.

If you find the client's accounts to be believable, then you should schedule a follow-up investigation. After that, it may be possible to change the category of the investigation from *inconclusive* to *haunted* or even *explained*.

>> **Haunted:** Although this designation may be the least often used, it is a valid one in many cases. Be sure that when you do support a conclusion of *haunted*, you do so reliably with a lot of evidence to back it up. Present all the data that you gathered and explain to the client why you came up with that conclusion. It must be up to them as to what the next course of action should be.

In most cases, you will likely want to continue your research, but that may not always be possible. Some families who have encountered frightening activity in their home simply want the spirit to leave. Unless you happen to be psychic, this is likely not something that you can assist them with. Your best bet is probably to refer them to an outside source that may be compatible with their principles and beliefs.

The first thing you can do, though, is to reassure the family that nothing will hurt them and assure them they can live peacefully with the haunting — at least in most cases. Continue your work, which can have some positive benefits. You can help the clients, through their own belief systems, to realize that they have nothing to fear. This helps to reduce their stress about the paranormal because they now understand it better.

If this does not work to their satisfaction, or they are involved in a haunting that is dangerous or possibly demonic, then it is time to take the next step. In this situation, you should turn to a member of the clergy or someone who has credible experience removing spirits.

If you or the clients know a minister personally, he or she may be your best solution. Ask this person to come into the house and pray for the soul of the deceased person. This is a psychological banishment that often works in convincing the spirit to leave.

This often has great benefit. It is also a great psychological relief for the residents because they have much more control over the spirit leaving then they first thought they did. In some cases, just the owners of the house asking the spirits to leave will do the trick. If the occupants are comfortable with this and can be convinced that it will work, have them give it a try.

If no minister is available, or if the family is not willing to try that approach, then your next step is to find someone who is an expert in getting rid of ghosts. The person you find doesn't have to be a professional medium; after all, many fellow investigators out there are sensitive to spirits and do this on a regular basis. If you do contact someone, make sure it is someone you are comfortable with or someone you have worked with before. If you have never done this before, ask for a referral from another investigator.

The difference between someone who is an investigator and a person who removes ghosts is that this person uses no equipment in what they do. They operate only with their senses and their minds. Remember, though, this is something that only works with intelligent hauntings. It is a spirit who did not move on after its death. The sensitive who comes into this situation must convince the spirit to move on through communication. They will talk to the spirits and help them to realize they are causing a problem by remaining behind. In most cases, the spirits do not even realize that they are dead and by developing a rapport with them, they can be convinced of this fact and assured that something better awaits them on the other side.

This can be effective, but not always. It almost always has a positive effect on the residents of the house, though, so this makes it worthwhile. The effectiveness often depends on the job that the investigator does as the mediator between the client and the medium. You will need to make sure the client understands what is going on, just as you did during your investigation.

With the report completed, it can be turned over to the client and a separate copy should be kept in your own files. The full report contains a synopsis of all your findings, along with some basic recommendations from practical fixes for high EMF sources to outside assistance for house blessings.

Unless your recommendation is a follow-up investigation to gather additional evidence so you can make a better determination about the case or to help assist in other steps, your involvement in the case officially ends after presenting your report. Just be sure to let the client know that if their conditions change or activity increases, you will still be available to help them.

Picking a Case Manager

Every paranormal investigation group is made up of a team. Usually, the team has a leader, someone who deals with all the equipment, and perhaps members who specialize in photography or recording EVP. There is also the often "unsung hero" of the group: the *case manager*.

The case manager not only handles the intake of new cases, but he or she manages all the date from ongoing investigations. They are also in charge of filing and organizing the old cases so that the data is accessible to the group and the client. It may be a somewhat thankless job, but most who do it love it because it gives them easy access to case files and the information they provide. But the job does not end there. Their biggest responsibility of keeping the investigations organized and running smoothly. They are on the front line when it comes to anything to do with the client. They manage witnesses and keep the team on track.

When choosing a case manager for your team, you want to find someone who is organized, can deal with client concerns, can keep an investigation on track, and can file the evidence when a case closes.

This is a list of just some of the things that a case manager does:

>> Screening calls and emails from potential clients

>> Contacting the client for the initial interview

>> Lining up witnesses to interview

>> Setting investigation dates and times

>> Securing access to the location

The case manager also deals with privacy forms, investigation consents, and disclosure statements. It is their job to make sure that nothing is released to the public without the client's consent.

In many cases, the lead investigator acts as a field coordinator for an investigation, working from the nerve center, and directing the team to target areas. However, if he or she is busy collecting evidence, then it often falls to the case manager to keep the investigation running smoothly.

When the investigation is over, the case manager usually stays in touch with the client to update them on the status of the report. They make sure that all the collected evidence is documented for the client. Then, the case manager meets with the client with the final report.

When it is over, the case manager stores all the evidence, answers any client follow-up questions, and closes the case. It is always a good idea for the case manager to also contact the clients just to check on them and inquire about any additional activity in their home.

Organizing Your Records and Files

Site assessment and investigation forms are essential for all your investigations. These forms allow investigators to record their experiences in an organized way. They become a part of your group's permanent record, and including the following is important:

>> Name of the investigator

>> Names of all investigators present

>> Date, time, and temperature

>> Location address

>> Equipment being used at the location

>> Any unusual events

An investigator's log and a photograph log can be separate forms or they can all be part of the same form, depending on how much information the investigator logs in the course of the investigation. In a personal log, the investigator can write down impressions and personal experiences, which may not always be the case in a standard investigation form.

Even the case manager organizes the files, all members of the paranormal group should be involved in the record-keeping. Each individual investigator logs all the facts and occurrences that may be relevant to the investigation. There may not be any obvious connections within one person's data and evidence, but when compiled with the rest of the team, it can fit together like a puzzle into one coherent picture.

After the investigation is completed, the case manager should gather all the other investigator's notes for review. The written record should be carefully examined so that anything significant can be noted.

If their review of the written material still leaves gaps in the understanding of the investigation, he or she must follow up with any team members whose reports seem incomplete. If one of your investigators consistently forgets to fill in information that is relevant to the investigation, the case manager needs to emphasize the importance of keeping detailed records.

The records, forms, and evidence for each investigation must be organized into a master system. A lot of evidence that is gathered is digital — audio, video, and photographs. It is recommended that as soon as a new case opens, the case manager assigns a name or number to it so that a file folder can be created. The individual investigators on the case can handle their stored media in several ways:

>> Investigators remove the digital media cards from their devices and place them in containers that are labeled by case, marked with their names, and gives them to the case manager.

>> Investigators keep the media cards but upload the files to their computer and send it to the case manager for analysis.

>> Investigators can also review files individually and add copies of what appears to contain paranormal activity to the file.

There are good and bad points to all three methods. Media storage can be lost and is not cheap to replace. It does, however, allow the case manager to control the data.

In the second method, the individual investigators are responsible for making sure that the evidence reaches the rest of the group. But all it takes is for one sloppy investigator to lose, accidentally delete, or forget about the evidence to harm your case.

The third method saves the case manager a lot of time, sparing them from many hours of reviewing evidence. It is risky when you have inexperienced investigators, however, who may miss something that a more seasoned investigator would spot. If you decide to go this route, do so only with researchers who have years of experience.

Whatever approach that you decide to use, the group should agree upon and follow a clear procedure. The files should be uploaded and put in a folder that is named according to the case. If more than one investigator did audio or EVP work, it may be necessary to create a subfolder within the audio subfolder with the case name and the name of the investigator.

Keeping your files organized is easy when everyone understands the system. The case manager may have to reorganize things occasionally, but everyone should attempt to keep the files consistent with names and recordkeeping.

Releases and Permission Forms

Every investigator should have forms that cover both you and the client in different types of situations. Some forms protect you or the client, whereas others spell out the procedures and clarify questions. A good form covers you legally and tends to reassure the clients that they are in good hands and dealing with professionals who are looking out for their best interests. Clients in historic sites, museums, and homes with expensive furnishings appreciate the reassurance that their location will be dealt with responsibly.

Investigators are almost always called into a location because clients feel anxious about what is going on around them. Your primary initial role is to calm and reassure the client. But one of his biggest fears may be the thought of being ridiculed in the community for believing that his house may be haunted. If this is the case, reassure him that a confidentiality agreement means that all his information will remain secret.

He may also worry that his home may be damaged by having a group of strangers searching for spirits in it. Part of any agreement between the investigators and the client should cover what behavior is expected from the team as they go about their investigation. If the client wants to add anything to the agreement about personal items that are not to be touched, rooms that are not to be entered, or anything else, the agreement should contain all these requests.

All groups should use a permission form to investigate a site. This form is perhaps the most commonly used method for gaining access to a location and protecting the group from any liability. There really is no way to legally conduct an investigation without it and those who do not bother are asking for trouble. Without this basic form, investigators can be arrested and charged with trespassing or even breaking and entering. Both situations would be terrible for your reputation.

To ensure that the form is legally binding, have an attorney create it for you or purchase one from a website that guarantees the form's viability. This is like a form of insurance. If the client later claims that the group did not have permission to enter the premises, or did damage to it, having a signed form can save you from a lawsuit, or worse. The form should be clearly written so that the rights and obligations of both parties are spelled out.

When a client contacts your paranormal group, seeking assistance, you evaluate the situation and decide if an investigation is needed. Likewise, the client must grant permission to the group to conduct the investigation, and he also must decide whether he wants the group to release any information that may be learned during the investigation. If a client is reluctant to fill out paperwork, go over it with him and make sure that he understands it. Answer any questions but make sure that he knows the investigation cannot proceed without the paperwork.

There is no single form for everyone to use. Most groups create the forms they need based on necessity and tailored to fit their individual needs. Most groups can get by with basic permission and release forms but at a minimum, you should always have an application to conduct an investigation form for the client to fill out and a form granting permission for a field investigation.

Release forms, like permission forms, come in several different variations. The release form serves to ensure the rights of the investigators and the client. Releases help both sides of the investigation feel comfortable with each other and make sure that no one is open to damage. The investigators must agree to keep the client's information confidential, and both sides may have to agree to not hold the other liable in the case of injury or damage that occurs during the investigation.

Make sure that you have all the necessary release forms:

>> **Permission to release confidential information:** This release gives the investigators permission to publish information that they gather about the case. If the client declines this form, then you must both sign an alternate form that promises to protect the client's confidentiality.

>> **Release from liability:** This form should protect both the client and the investigators.

In an earlier chapter, it was also advised that investigators get release and permission forms for the interviews that they are conducting with witnesses. Interviews often contain a lot of private information and although this is protected with the form that ensures confidentiality, most clients would feel better to have the additional coverage. This is especially important when it comes to interviewing children under the age of 18.

Even when it means more paperwork, we need to do all that we can to make our clients comfortable about the investigation. After concerns of a legal nature have been erased, both sides can continue without fear of reprisal. Of course, basic trust is needed to find such an arrangement and then is when an investigator finds that having an upstanding reputation is a great advantage.

Covering Your Assets

Paranormal investigation can sometimes be a risky business and even with consent and release forms, it does not hurt to have some insurance coverage. If you have a small group, having the individual members carry their own coverage is probably best. Members can insure their equipment, too. Full replacement cost insurance to cover equipment should be discussed with your insurance agent and you should make sure it is covered whether it is taken on an investigation, left in your car, or stored at home.

You can also obtain the kind of insurance that is used for events or for ghost tours. There are companies that provide this kind of insurance and although it can be somewhat expensive, it would be worth it if you plan to continue seriously investigating for a long period of time.

There are other kinds of "insurance," too. All groups agree that they should do everything in their power to make sure that no one gets hurt and that no accidents occur during an investigation. Remember the following things to ensure your investigations run smoothly and that everyone comes away from them unscathed:

>> Always have permission to investigate a site but leave immediately if a problem arises regarding your right to be there.

>> Follow proper investigative protocols.

>> Do not investigate alone. Always make sure other team members are somewhere at the site.

>> Bring along adequate equipment and supplies.

>> Bring a first-aid kit.

>> Examine the site for hazards in the daylight before the investigation.

>> Always stay in touch with other team members.

>> Make sure your transportation is reliable and maintain all vehicles used by the team.

» Never consume alcohol or drugs before or during an investigation.

» Have an agreed-upon signal to let members know if you need to leave the site in case of emergency.

Always remember that team members should never put each other in jeopardy or play pranks that may be dangerous. Everyone wants to have fun when they are pursuing this hobby, but not to the point that it becomes hazardous. The site is important to someone. It may be their home or their burial place, so try to act appropriately.

If one or more sensitives are in your group, pay close attention to them. They may be vulnerable to psychic or even physical attack because entities are drawn to them more than they are to other investigators. If they start behaving strangely or seem suddenly exhausted, they may need to be taken away from the location before they become ill.

Chapter **17**

When Things Go Wrong

Paranormal investigations do not always good as planned. As any experienced researcher can assure you, just about anything can, and does, happen in the course of an investigation, including accidents, mistakes, broken gear, power outages, unexpected storms, and worse. The best way to cope with such things is to try and have a good sense of humor about it. Usually, nothing can be done, especially when mishaps involve the weather.

In some cases, though, the things that go wrong do not have anything to do with nature or accidents. Some of them are much darker in origin, like physical and psychic attacks. Of course, some problems also occur that involve perhaps one of the worst elements of all — fraudulent investigators.

Afraid of Ghosts

Paranormal activity can range from slightly spooky phenomena, such as knocks and footsteps, to furniture being moved about and full-blown spectral appearances. Any of these things can happen during an investigation and under these circumstances, all that an investigator can do is react as professionally as possible.

When things do happen during an investigation, researchers must remain calm and try to be as objective as possible. Obviously, this may not be easy, but you should try to verify just what you are hearing or seeing and when possible, take notes. Even though a video camera or recorder will hopefully be operating, recording your own thoughts and feelings is important.

And here is the really hard part — try and keep the excitement to yourself.

In order to avoid any potential allegations of some group hallucination, it is important not to lead the other witnesses who are present with even a small description of the phenomena that is being encountered. One technique that has been suggested during an outbreak of activity is to simply state that you are "experiencing something." If anyone is else is also experiencing anything, they are told to write it down. Afterward, the written statements can be collected and compared with one another.

Of course, this is the ideal way of operating but rarely does anyone know just how they may react in the heat of an active investigation. This is where we begin to talk about what may happen when the witness (or the investigators) becomes frightened during the course of the investigation.

In many cases, the witnesses at the location do become frightened about the activity that may be occurring and have been known to occasionally call a halt to the proceedings. They may have called investigators to help decide whether the phenomena taking place at the location is genuine or not. As soon as they see that something strange is happening, and that others are seeing it too, they may want to end the investigation. This often happens because the location owner is afraid that by prolonging the investigation, they may make the ghosts angry or upset. It is quite common for them to change their view and decide that they want to leave it alone or that they want to get rid of the phenomena and refrain from making things worse. When this happens, the investigator has no other option but to do what the client wants.

In some cases, you may be able to reach a compromise with the owner. You may consider asking to continue your research on the condition that you help to find someone who may be able to get rid of the ghost. This is usually an ideal compromise, but it may not always be possible. No matter what you decide to do, the wishes of the location owner must be followed.

When working as part of a team, the fear threshold for the various members of the group is going to vary. Because all your team members became investigators because of their interest in the paranormal, they are likely not going to be afraid at the first sign of anything unusual. However, intense activity can have a remarkable effect on a person that you once thought of as a solid and fearless investigator. Many long-time investigators have had experience with fellow researchers who have dropped out of their team — and even stopped investigating altogether — because they were terrified during a case. Different people respond to things in different ways.

There have been cases where investigators have screamed, wept or have run in fear from a location because they are afraid. There is no way to know how a person may react in a specific situation. You may even find yourself the member of the team who becomes inexplicably unnerved by an experience that you thought would never bother you. It is easy for us to be rational and know that most ghosts do not hurt you in the light of day, but sometimes the energy of a location may affect us in a way that we could not have imagined.

If this does happen to you, try and remain calm. Fear can be a great instigator of activity at an actively haunted location. Just be sure that you do not start a panic. Your fear will quickly spread to other members of the team, and it may ruin the investigation. You may consider segregating yourself from the group — especially from the location owner if they are present — until your feelings of terror pass.

If another member of the team becomes frightened, take this person aside and get them away from the others present. Fear is contagious and anyone who asks to be removed from an investigation should step out immediately.

Equipment Failures

A type of mishap that every experienced investigator has dealt with on one or more occasions is the strange behavior of technology at haunted locations. Batteries drain and go dead. Audio recorders fail, cameras shut down, and equipment malfunctions. In a practical sense, this means that backup batteries and equipment are always needed so that you can sure that the phenomena that caused the equipment to fail can be recorded in some way.

If we accept the idea that paranormal activity causes some equipment to fail, then we must come up with a hypothesis about what is actually happening. There have been countless reports of appliances, televisions, radios and other objects being turned on by unseen hands, even sometimes when they are unplugged. There can be natural explanations for this, but such events are common at locations where paranormal happenings have been reported.

There is one theory that suggests that entities who are trying to manifest at a location will draw energy from the space around them, causing sudden temperature drops and the drained batteries that are often described by investigators. Occasionally, the investigators at these locations will be overcome by fatigue, as if the presence is draining energy from them, too.

Another theory is that increased electromagnetic energy and static electricity are present at most active paranormal locations. Most of today's digital devices use nickel-cadmium rechargeable batteries, which the manufacturers warn are susceptible to failure when they encounter both electromagnetic and static electric fields.

Either of these theories makes sense and reinforce the idea that extra batteries and equipment are always needed during investigations. You never know when something will go wrong.

Weather and the Paranormal

Almost every investigator can recall a time when he or she had to cancel an investigation because of weather issues. They were rained out, the power at the location failed, or perhaps they were unable to even make it to the location because of a snowstorm. Weather can wreak havoc on your research, but some interesting theories suggest certain types of weather may actually *enhance* paranormal activity.

The dictionary defines *weather* as "the state of the atmosphere at a given time and place, with respect to variables such as temperature, moisture, wind velocity, and barometric pressure."

Science tells us that energy cannot be created nor destroyed. It can, however, be transferred from place to place in one form or another. Weather is caused by a transfer or energy. Our planet is constantly keeping a balance between the solar radiation energy that comes from the sun and what is bouncing off the earth, back out into space. If paranormal entities use energy to manifest, then it seems reasonable to think that changes in weather conditions could potentially affect the amount of paranormal activity at a location.

For example, temperature and barometric pressure both change the energy of molecules in the air. Temperature is the measurement of the average speed of air molecules and as the kinetic energy of air molecules increases, temperature increases. Barometric pressure, or air pressure, is the result of molecules in the air colliding. When these molecules run into each other, electrons are exchanged, and electromagnetic energy is created. The more rapidly the molecules collide with each other and other objects, the higher the air pressure.

Theories exist to say that the energy involved with these two processes could influence the energy available to paranormal entities. By recording the temperature and the barometric pressure during your investigation, you may start to notice a pattern in activity in relation to the weather. However, be aware that changes in air pressure can affect some people physically. Many people get head-aches, migraines, and body aches from weather changes. These symptoms could be mistaken for signs of paranormal activity by clients or investigators.

The humidity at the location is also important during the investigation. Humidity is, of course, the measurement of the amount of water vapor in the air. Humidity helps regulate air temperature by absorbing thermal radiation from the earth and the sun. It is directly proportional to the latent energy that generates storms. Energy is absorbed during evaporation and released during condensation as rain. The process of water vapor condensing into rain releases energy. This may explain why investigators have noticed an increase in paranormal events during storms. But it may also offer a natural explanation for some potential activity. Rooms in which people feel uneasy should be checked for high humidity levels. This could indicate the presence of mold, which can cause headaches, dizziness, and nausea. If the mold is toxic, the symptoms can be much worse and include depression, memory problems, and breathing issues.

Besides contaminating your investigation with noise, the wind may influence paranormal events. Wind is created by a difference in pressure systems causing air to accelerate from areas of high pressure to areas of low pressure. Again, energy is being transferred from one place to another. Strong winds indicate a significant pressure difference between air masses, which is why heavy winds will usually accompany strong storms. If paranormal activity is related to energy, this move-ment of energy could create an increase in activity.

Thunderstorms are often listed as a cause for enhanced paranormal activity. Lightning is caused by a buildup of oppositely charged ions and when the buildup of ions is greater than the resistance of the air, lightning occurs. A lightning dis-charge generates electromagnetic fields, which are connected to paranormal activity. Thunder is basically a supersonic shock wave created when the energy in the returning stroke (temperature and pressure) is higher than the energy in the surrounding air. This makes it possible that this charge and subsequent discharge of the earth's natural electrical field could make it easier for paranormal entities to manifest. This means that a "dark and stormy night" for your investigation does not just make it spookier — it may have science to thank for the appearance of ghosts.

The paranormal remains a developing field, and you have no way to know for sure whether certain weather conditions enhance paranormal activity, but reports from investigators around the globe point to the possibility.

In the future, try not to think of bad weather as something that hampers your investigations. It may be just the thing that helps you to obtain the evidence you are looking for.

When Spirits Attack

Paranormal investigating can often be unnerving but imagine how much worse it may be if you find yourself under psychic or physical attack at a location. This has happened to myself and other members of the *Ghost Adventures* crew more times than I can count over the years. Our audience needs to understand that we have a very serious job and often put ourselves in dangerous situations to learn more about the afterlife. During our Halloween special in Ireland, Aaron had a very emotional and disturbing moment that we had to edit down. I feel there is a comfortable and acceptable level of what we choose to show the audience when things take a turn for the worse while we are trying to come into contact with evil spirits and demons.

I decided it was right to cut out a small portion of when Aaron was grabbed by a very dark force and had a breakdown after the event occurred. Many people will never understand that attacks are more than physical grabs and pushes. These entities can inject pure fear into your spine and let you feel this inside your body — something that you cannot feel yourselves watching on television.

The biggest thing I have learned is that seeing, and hearing, is not always believing. Everyone expects to go out and see a ghost or hear it talk. After years of investigating I have come to develop my sixth sense. This is the most important, but also the most dangerous, sense to use. After you develop this sense you will begin to feel these spirits, their emotions, their power. You open yourself up and let these spirits connect with you through energy.

When I do this and establish a strong spiritual connection, I have no way of knowing how long the spirit will stay in contact with me or what type of spirit it is — and that's the dangerous part. I've been on investigations where a spirit is channeling through me and I have extreme changes in my emotions — anger, sadness, confusion. Then I begin seeing visions that are not mine. They are theirs. There is no trace of time. My body goes stiff, numb, cold. Then when the spirit leaves, I can barely stand and speak. This is what I call a *lockdown hangover*, and depending on the severity of the interaction, I can be out of it for days afterward. I wonder what this does to my body. I do not think it is good for it.

More than just sensing the spirits, though, I have also been attacked by them. This is something that can happen to just about anyone when they put themselves into situations where angry, restless, or demonic spirits are present.

Here are some warning signs of a psychic attack:

>> **Tiredness and fatigue:** In this most common form of psychic attack, energy is drained from the investigator. He or she may even have a sense

of detachment, as if the things happening around them are unreal. Feeling drained and exhausted without good reason is an indication that something paranormal may be going on.

>> **Physical ailments:** Headaches, stomach issues, and unexplained pains may also be signs of a psychic attack. Negative physical reactions while investigating certain spots may be an indication of a paranormal event.

>> **Persistent or recurring bad dreams:** If you are not usually prone to nightmares and you suddenly start having recurring dreams about being hunted or oppressed, you may have picked up some sort of attachment while at a haunted site, which is now attacking you in your dreams.

Because psychics, sensitives, and paranormal investigators have existed in one way or another for the last couple of hundred years, practices employed to protect us from attack have varied according to cultures and time periods. Even some of today's most scientific investigators do not shy away from finding ways to protect themselves during ghost-hunts.

No matter what you may call different entities — ghosts, spirits, demons, elementals — far too many of them will attack and prey on people. However you decide to label them, the effect is the same. The paranormal universe is filled with all sorts of energies and entities. Investigating the supernatural can be like leaving the windows of your home open to intruders. Unless you take steps to lock the doors and windows you have opened, something unwanted can get inside.

You should always prepare and take precautions when dealing with the paranormal. If the wrong conduit is opened, it sometimes takes a very long time and a lot of effort to shut that down.

With time comes experience and investigators eventually learn what to look for and how to counteract the early signs of psychic trouble. Depression, despair, and anxiety are all red flags. An effective way of dealing with psychic oppression is to first ask what could have caused the feelings you are having. If no logical explanation exists, your depression could be paranormal in nature. The issue has to be sorted out before you decide to investigate again and put yourself into a situation that could be dangerous for you.

Situations can also be dangerous for witnesses and homeowners. Entities often became attached to people or places and launch terrifying attacks. The victims are usually disinterested in the paranormal before this happens, have done nothing to cause the events, and have no idea what is happening to them or why. This is the point at which paranormal investigators may be called in to help sort things out. They can attempt to restore normalcy in the home and assist the victims in dealing with the attacks. Although much of what is known is theory and speculation, having someone knowledgeable involved in the situation can be calming to the client.

There are dozens of accounts of entities who have attacked investigators and clients, causing injuries. Physical attacks have occurred with investigators being pushed, scratched, and even slammed into walls and knocked down flights of stairs. Most investigators come away with just bumps and bruises, but serious injuries can occur. Sometimes the attacks are not as violent and occur as dizziness, skin crawling sensations, and disorientation.

Violent attacks by human entities often occur because of a spirit that has become overly territorial and has decided that it does not want people living in its space. Entities of this kind do everything in their power to drive the residents away. Usually, they can be coaxed or forced into leaving or made to stop their activities by other means, such as rituals that put them to rest and offer protection for the clients who live at the site.

Just living with the stress and fear paranormal events can cause takes a physical toll after a while, especially if you have fears about the haunting being demonic. Even though most entities that we encounter are human spirits that have refused to cross over, demonic entities exist, and they can cause serious harm. The best way to protect yourself from a demonic spirit is to not draw its attention in the first place. If you must confront one, however, conduct a ritual or procedure to protect yourself before the exposure. This can take many forms, including meditation, white sage, prayers, or whatever is compatible with your belief system.

If a protection ritual fails, it may be time to call in outside help. Usually, when physical or psychic attacks get out of control, an experienced clergy member is called in to handle the situation. The idea that evil — in whatever form your beliefs perceive it — can inhabit people and places against their will — is a frightening concept. Unfortunately, you may be involved in a case for which no other explanation can be found. If it happens, find a person of faith, your faith or the client's, who can help.

Many investigators also seek assistance from warding and shielding, a former of energy barrier that is created by thought through visualization and prayer. This can help the investigator to hold off a physical or psychic attack.

It is also believed that this is useful in providing protection homes from negative energies. Some involve the protection of a divine white light, which they believe serves as a barrier between them and whatever forces they encounter during an investigation. The theory is that although entities and energies may not be inherently evil, confused and negative spirits can still cause problems. They may lash out and cause injury to innocent bystanders. After a house has been cleared of whatever entities haunted it, they also believe that a house blessing may act as a shield from further trouble.

Faking the Ghosts

The paranormal had been home to frauds, phonies, and hoaxers since the very beginning. Dating back to the days of Spiritualism, there have been those who have tried to trick people — usually, because money was involved — with fraudulent claims of "real" evidence of the paranormal. Unfortunately, such things continue to happen today and often for the same reasons — fame and fortune.

Just as it was in the 19th century, though, the majority of those involved in the paranormal field have good intentions. But the bad apples among us tend to give everyone a bad name. There are far too many examples out there of those who claim to be experienced investigators who are posting bad evidence, hoaxing activity, and trying to convince ghosts enthusiasts of things that are simply not true.

So, what is the best way to avoid getting caught up in a situation that involves fraud? For starters, you can make sure that you are always following the best guidelines on investigations and making sure that all your evidence is the best that it can be. Remember that corresponding evidence is the key to success and if you can show from multiple sources that paranormal activity is occurring, you can avoid claims of fraud.

There is no single right way to investigate claims of ghosts and the paranormal, except by using scientific methods and critical thinking. You can follow the step-by-step guides in this book, and they will start you in the right direction. What happens next is up to you, but the basic points here will never steer you wrong:

>> Never assume a ghost will be in a location before you have established that fact. One of the main things that questionable investigators do is to jump to the conclusion that a location is haunted before they have determined that to be the case. Only after that fact is established should you proceed to try and identify who that ghost may have been. Trying to communicate with a spirit that you do not know is there just makes you look unprofessional, or worse, it makes you look like a phony, playing things up for dramatic effect.

>> Avoid unfalsifiable claims and theories. For example, if something happens in response to your efforts during an investigation (i.e. some sound if heard), you cannot automatically assume this is a ghost. Similarly, if nothing happens, you cannot assume a ghost is there but decided not to make its presence known. This is not how science works. If you conduct an experiment, then you cannot interpret any or all contradictory results as proving your point. This is an unfalsifiable theory or claim (it can't be proven or disproven), so it's useless. An experiment in which any result — or no result at all — confirms

your assumptions is not an experiment at all. This sort of flawed methodology is the kind of thing that careless investigators use to justify their investigations, but so do fraudulent ones.

» Avoid those who peddle the "power of suggestion," and make sure that you do not do this yourself. This is a situation in which investigators manipulate their evidence to make it appear more ghostly. It is done in many different ways, but EVP recordings are often used by the worst offenders. In many cases, words are almost impossible to make out amid the static and buzzing and may be nothing more than background sounds. But that can change when ghost-hunters put words to those sounds. By suggesting words and phrases to the person listening to the recording, it becomes a flawed search for evidence.

The same thing can be done with the manipulation of electronic devices. Watches, cell phones, electric interference, and many other things can cause EMF detectors to light up like Christmas trees. This alone does not mean a ghost is nearby. This is the reason why corresponding activity has been stressed so many times within these pages.

» Be careful about who you work with. When you are putting together your investigation team, try and find reputable people, preferably ones you know personally and feel good about their legitimacy. It only takes one person to ruin the reputation of your group. Many investigators have been ruined by the actions of others on their team.

For example, many reputable sensitives and psychics are involved in the paranormal field, but thanks to the actions of a handful, many scientific-based investigators have reduced the role that they play in an investigation. For decades paranormal investigators have battled over the legitimate use of psychics in paranormal investigations. If it your group's credibility is in doubt, you must be cautious about your use of psychics.

During investigations, some psychics have been known to "personalize" alleged activity. The spirits will only talk to them and no one else. Some also claim to speak for the ghosts during an EVP session. There is no reason to bother to investigate a location if your psychic claims to be the exclusive spokesperson for the paranormal activity you were called in to investigate. Legitimate investigators would prefer that the spirits speak for themselves.

Most every investigator can agree that personal experiences do not prove or disprove a haunting. Only documented physical evidence can give your group creditability. Personal experiences are fascinating, but they cannot stand alone as the only proof.

Another problem is the inability to know if a psychic is acting or not when they sense a presence. They can become a distraction to the investigation and solid evidence that may have been collected in a case is missed because everyone is focused on what your psychic is doing.

Psychic ability itself remains under intense scrutiny. Those who do have a true gift are often overshadowed by frauds who claim to have psychic talents. They succeed in only driving more people to the conclusion that psychic abilities do not exist at all. And that is too bad. Research being done may one day prove that psychic abilities exist, but until then, you are likely to hear many grandiose claims of proof that are murky, at best. So, if you are trying to prove something that is unproven, it may be best to avoid something that is itself unproven as a tool.

It has been suggested that the best use of a psychic in an investigation is as a guide, giving investigators information that can help them collect solid evidence, such as where to place cameras and voice recorders. You may now want to risk your reputation with a "feeling."

Unfortunately, the worst-case scenario that we sometimes have to deal with is not someone who is "faking a ghost" for fame and fortune, but a person who is delusional because of alcoholism or mental illness. During an episode of *Ghost Adventures* that we filmed in Amarillo, Texas, we found ourselves in a situation where a woman was claiming that she and her children were being constantly scratched and attacked by a spirit. During our investigation, scratches did begin to appear on her back. I didn't see her scratch herself, but one of the other investigators did film some trickery with the video camera on his phone. In the clip, he saw her reach her arm very far around her back to scratch herself. I didn't see the footage until later but after I did, I had to keep in mind that she *could* have caused the injury herself.

Ultimately, we ended up bringing an exorcist to the house. While we were there, introducing her to the exorcist, her back got scratched again. When we examined the marks, we saw that they were on the lower part of her back, curving around toward the side, which is a common movement when someone scratches their own back. I asked the woman if it was possible for her to reach her arm back that far, which offended her. But when I explained that sometimes, under a demonic influence or attachment, it can make you subconsciously do things to yourself. When she attempted the movement, she couldn't do it. She explained that surgery on her shoulder prevented her from doing it. But, of course, we already had video footage of her reaching her arm all the way around her back.

I immediately realized that something else was going on with this family. I did some research on the mother and we uncovered some history of a criminal record.

Although I was convinced that we were dealing with a hoax, the worst possible thing that I could have done at that moment was to accuse her of fraud. An accusation can lead to immediate conflict, even violence. You do not want to get involved in that. You do not want to confront the family with accusations of faking the haunting.

You may wonder why I would give that advice, but I have a good reason: it truly is possible that a person can hurt themselves while under the manipulation of a harmful spirit. Your best bet may be to bring in a demonologist and suggest that they look for evidence of this kind of presence. They may be able to do things that you are not able to do.

Don't be too quick to judge a haunting. We never want to immediately assume that what is happening in a home is caused by a ghost, but we also don't want to prejudge it to be a hoax. Uncovering trickery can sometimes be as complicated as discovering the truth behind the haunting.

Chapter **18**

Going Beyond Just a Hobby

While paranormal investigation can be a serious business, it can also be exciting and a lot of fun. After trying their hand at a few investigations, a lot of researchers decide to try to take the hobby to the next level by starting a full-fledged group and offering investigation services to in their local community, region, and state.

This chapter discusses what you can do to successfully turn your hobby into a career.

Making Contact with Other Investigators

The best way to start your own group is to make contact with other investigators in your area. It is never a good idea to try to research cases by yourself. Consider finding some like-minded friends and individuals with a passion for the paranormal.

You can start looking for cases by going to the library or local newspaper and tracking down ghost stories, legends, and alleged haunted spots in your area. If they are public locations, then you are ready to begin experimenting with some of your newfound paranormal knowledge.

Building an Online Presence

TIP

The best way to get the word out that you are looking for cases and wanting to make contact with other investigators is through the Internet. You can meet and talk with ghost-hunters from all over the country who are often interested in sharing news and ideas about paranormal research and investigations.

Today, building a website is essential to attracting clients with active cases, getting the attention of fellow ghost enthusiasts who want to join your group, posting information and theories, and establishing yourself as a professional. A number of web services are available online and can help you build a thorough, interactive, and professional-looking website, even if you have no knowledge of HTML skills. Be sure to use one that will give you a credible website with good information.

It is true that you are offering a free service to the public, so a website might seem like an extravagance. Rest assured — it is an absolute necessity. Even if your site starts with only contact information and a small amount of text, it is better than nothing at all.

After your website is up and running, you and your team should get together and decide on the site's overall tone and message. After you map out the basics, start getting into the details of who will write the copy, who will maintain the site, who will monitor and reply to emails, who will gather new material, and more.

You'll also want to start building a presence on social media. Start a page for your group on Facebook, start sending out information on Twitter, and make sure that your group is easy to find. You will want to be an ongoing presence in your region, and you will want to maintain a consistent public profile.

Building a Presence in Your Local Community

Having an online presence is important (see preceding section), but you will also need to get established in your local area if you want to find new cases to work on. Most investigators work real jobs and do not always have the freedom to travel all over the country looking for cases. When getting started, it is best to focus on your state or part of the country.

To build a presence in your local community:

1. **Start by identifying some of the haunted places in your area and putting together a small packet with this information.**

   Include photos and any stories that you might have and collect it into something that looks as professional as you can manage. You don't have to be able to write to do this; just recount a few of the stories and your basic interest in the locations.

2. **Put together another packet of information about yourself and your new group.**

   It doesn't have to be a complete biography, just some items of interest about you and about your goals with the group. Everyone has access to simple computer programs for this, or you can visit your local copy shop for assistance.

3. **Go to your local newspaper and present the entire packet to a reporter who is assigned to the local area.**

   If possible, you may even want to talk to the highest-ranking editor who is available (call first for an appointment if necessary) because this person ultimately will decide how much, if any, coverage that you will get. It may also be worth it to get in touch with writers who do blogs about your local area. They often have tremendous reach and get a lot of attention.

TIP

Be sure to dress conservatively and make the best impression that you can. You do not want to come across as a nut with your packet and your presentation. As long as they know you are serious about the subject matter, you have a much better chance of success.

Needless to say, the best time to do this is in late September or early October. As far as the media is concerned, Halloween is the only time of year the general public is interested in ghosts. We all know this is not the case, but it seems to be one of the few times of year that the newspapers and local blogs pay much attention to what we do.

If everything works the way you want it to, you will do an interview. Hopefully, you will get the chance to present your thoughts and investigations in a positive light.

WARNING

When you are just starting out, you often must take whatever publicity that you can get, but always be cautious about what you say and how you word things when talking with any writer. You will often find that your quotes in the article or blog turn out to be off-handed remarks that you didn't think were being recorded. Try not to say anything that you do not want in print. There is a chance you will be disappointed with the finished article or post and if you do this long enough, you are doubtless going to appear in articles that either begin or end with the phrases, "Who Ya Gonna Call?" and "He Ain't Afraid of No Ghosts!"

It can be a disconcerting process but once your article appears, you will hopefully begin to see some attention and results from it.

Attending Lectures and Workshops

After a few years of investigations, you will have many stories to tell about your adventures, as well as knowledge to share about both paranormal investigating and haunted places. You may decide to share that knowledge with the public by offering presentations and classes.

Paranormal investigators may find themselves being invited to be guest speakers at regional events. If you are, this is often a good way to increase exposure for your organization. You can also do this on your own, in your own community. Local libraries and community colleges are often looking for people to present on various topics or to offer non-credit classes and workshops.

TIP

If your team had a particularly active case that can be shared with the public, put together a presentation of photos and EVPS, as well as any other evidence that you collected. People love to hear about local hauntings and to be exposed to the scientific approach to investigations.

Putting together paid classes or workshops can help defray the costs of new equipment or travel. A good class should always start with the fundamentals, from the first contact with clients to a description of an investigation and everything that follows. One or two members of your team can serve as instructors for the sessions, which might range from entry-level to advanced classes. You may even find a promising student who is asked to join the organization.

Starting a Ghost Tour

One of the great ways to meet the public and to generate publicity for your research is to offer a ghost tour of your local area. A ghost tour is a great form of entertainment that also manages to teach history and provide information about paranormal research. However, the average attendee of a ghost tour is not a researcher, but rather a person with a casual interest in ghosts.

Most tour attendees are looking for some scary fun. They usually do not want to hear about the science of an investigation, but you can still manage to slip that in. Mostly, they are interested in what happened in the past at a location, who it happened to, what is happening now, and, most importantly, will they have a chance for it to happen to them.

A successful ghost tour is all about interaction. It's about how the guest can interact with the location, the ghosts, and how the host interacts with them. You must be a people person to be able to host a tour. If you are shy, backward, and do not like public speaking, a ghost tour is not the right thing for you. If you do not have a good time, neither will your guests. Hosting a tour is just like performing on stage. The audience is only going to get out of it what you decide to put into it.

Another big issue is with hosts who do not know the material. If you are planning on hiring people to help you with your tours, be sure that they know every location on the tour backwards and forwards. Scripts are a bad idea, especially if your host sounds as though he or she is reading from it. Get rid of the notes and cue cards. If your host cannot offer a tour that seems spontaneous, you will lose business. Ghost tours must be both authentic and entertaining.

One of the greatest dilemmas about starting a ghost tour is deciding between a walking tour or a bus tour. Both tours can be great but when starting out, a walking tour is always the best idea.

There are a variety of reasons to not use a bus or vehicle, not the least of which is the overhead for the tour. As soon as you book a vehicle of any sort for a tour, you have automatically created an expense. Once you sell a ticket for the tour, you have committed to that expense and no matter how many people attend the tour, you still must pay the vehicle costs, no matter how many attendees actually show up.

In addition, if you are not careful, you can create a distance between yourself and the attendees on board the vehicle, especially if it is a large bus and some of the passengers are unable to see you. Everyone wants something to look at, they do not want to just hear your voice. If you do have to use a vehicle, though, there are ways to combat this. First, be sure to stand and speak where you can be seen by everyone aboard. Be sure that the passengers feel that they are a part of the tour by making sure that you speak "to" them, not just "at" them.

It is always best to have a bus tour with as much off the vehicle time as possible. This allows the passengers to feel as though they are visiting more of the locations first-hand and not just driving by and looking at them. They will also feel that they are more connected to the host, as well.

If you can offer a walking tour, do so. But if the haunted places in your area are so spread out that walking to them is not feasible, make the best of it by keeping your tour as interactive as possible.

Another question that often comes up is whether a tour creator needs to have written a book about the locations on the tour. It is not required but there are big advantages to doing so. Some of the most successful tours in the country have been based on books. Having a book that the tour is built upon gives a tour credibility and substance. In addition, it makes the tour more financially successful because people have something to purchase that they can take home as a souvenir. Also, reading the book often entices people to take the tour in the first place.

However, not everyone can write a book, nor the chance to publish one if they do write it. Just because your tour may not have a book that it is based on, does not mean that you cannot offer a great tour.

Starting a tour is as easy as finding the haunted places in your town or area. After that, though, there is still a lot of work to do. You must do all the necessary research about the history and hauntings of the sites. You will want to include as much history in the tour as possible. Not only does this give your tour credibility, but it also opens it up to people who might not necessarily be interested in ghosts.

In addition to the history, you also need to research all the haunts. Talk to the people at the location, find out as much as you can about the stories yourself. Never base your tour on the stories that you have heard around town unless there is absolutely no other source. Rumors and local gossip often turn out to be unreliable, other than as a starting place.

After talking to the people and researching the locations, you will need to begin on your tour route. This will need to be as smooth of a process for the attendees as possible. You need to have a starting location for the tour and then work the tour around so that you end up at the same location again. This will be important to your attendees, who will obviously need to return to where their cars are parked. You should then try and guess how long you will be visiting each location and then add up the times to determine the length of the tour. Remember to overestimate, especially with a walking tour, because the speed of the tour attendees will either make or break your schedule.

Once you have the locations that you want to visit, you should determine how many of these are public spots and how many are privately owned homes and businesses. With public places, you can always visit the spots, even during the evening hours, and should run into no problems if you have the proper clearances.

You may need to get permission from someone in authority for historic sites, parks, and especially cemeteries. With private spots, you have an entirely different set of issues.

Try not to use private residences on your tours. There are many reasons for this but the most important is that most homeowners do not want to deal with what comes after the tour — namely having people knocking on their door asking to see the ghosts. Most dealings with homeowners, even those who grant permission to have their house featured on a tour, will eventually come to an end. Most never realize what will happen when they give that permission and will eventually tire of the attention.

The only residences that work well on tours are those that have been advertised as being haunted or have appeared in books or articles about hauntings. They have become a matter of public record and it is fair game for any tour that wants to feature them. If this homeowner does not grant permission to have you on their property, though, be sure to feature the spot from no closer than the sidewalk.

Private businesses are a great asset for the tour operator. In many cases, if you do not wear out your welcome, you can often coax business owners into opening their shop, hotel, or restaurant exclusively for the tour. Not only is this great for you, but it is also great for the business owner. This brings in sales, especially for coffee shops and restaurants, which they would not have had otherwise. By bringing a group into their business, you have added something extra for the tour attendees and have also earned the goodwill of the business owner. Be sure to make time for this in your schedule but if possible, include a location (or several locations) like this on your tour. Everyone involved will thank you.

Once your tour has been set up the way that you want it, you have confirmed the locations with the owners or anyone who needs to grant permission, you need to attract the attendees. There are many ways to do this but start out by trying to work with your local tourism or visitor's bureau. More and more, cities are starting to realize the potential traffic from ghost tours and haunted places, so hopefully, you will get lucky in your area. Talk over your plans with a contact person there and you are likely to get them to help you spread the word. Make sure you have flyers, posters, and rack cards available for them to hand out or display at the visitor's center.

Make sure that the items are distributed to the shops and businesses in town who have expressed a willingness to work with you. If there are other shops in town that would be willing to hang up the flyers, make sure they have them, too. By bringing more people to town, it is a good thing for everyone. Your website and your social media sites are also a good place to advertise.

Once the tour is ready to start operating and you are ready to announce the dates when tours will be held, you will also need to figure out how admissions will be handled. There are many options for ticket sales. You can sell tickets through a local shop or business, through a visitor's bureau, by telephone, website, or ticketing company that deals with online sales. Established walking tours can also simply announce that a tour will leave at a certain time and place each night and just take along everyone who shows up. Your best option, however, is to sell tickets in advance.

At this point, your advertising can also go beyond posters and flyers to the local newspaper and television stations. Unless you have a lot of cash flow, though, this is not the best option with which to start. By planning the start of your tours in the fall, around the Halloween season, you may not need to pay for advertising at all. If you take the tour to newspapers and local blogs before the season, you might just guarantee your publicity for the tour. Almost every local news outlet is looking for local Halloween stories and a new ghost tour in town in just the thing. Once the story appears in the newspaper, you are sure to hear from the television stations, as well. Hopefully, you will soon be on your way to tour success.

4

The Part of Tens

Explore America's most haunted cities and towns

Find America's most haunted places

Identify signs of a haunted house

Chapter **19**

America's Ten Most Haunted Cities and Towns

We all know the song, dating back to grade school — America is a land of spacious skies and amber waves of grain, but it also happens to be a place filled with ghost stories. Ghost stories, just like the deeds and words of our Founding Fathers, are an essential part of American history. Eerie encounters with the unknown have been with us since the first settlers arrived on our shores. Even before that, the Native Americans had their own tales of mysterious lights, eerie apparitions, and sinister spirits. Tales of hauntings — and the haunted — have always been with us.

Nearly every community in the United States can claim at least one haunted house. Some have dozens, with the degree of how haunted each home might be varying by its history and, of course, by the person telling the story. Regardless of the truth behind every story, there is no denying the fascination of ghosts and the supernatural have to a large percentage of our population. Yes, there are still many who scoff at the existence of ghosts. However, many great people, even American presidents like Abraham Lincoln, Harry Truman and Franklin Delano Roosevelt, have harbored a belief in the spirit world.

Ghost stories are an integral part of America, and so I would like to take you along for a coast-to-coast (or perhaps we should say ghost-to-ghost) tour of the most haunted cities and towns in the country.

Virginia City, Nevada

Virginia City — where we filmed the first *Ghost Adventures* documentary — developed as a boomtown with the 1859 discovery of the Comstock Lode, the first major silver deposit discovery in the United States. Dozens of mines opened, drawing miners, suppliers, saloon owners, prostitutes, and outlaws, from all over the west. The population peaked in the mid-1870s, with an estimated 25,000 residents. In October 1875, what was called the Great Fire destroyed most of the city and left 2,000 people homeless. The city was rebuilt, but the output of the mines began to decline a few years later, ending Virginia City's glory days around 1880.

The town remains today as a time capsule of the 1870s. Many of the grand buildings remain but now serve as home to spirits. Haunted places in Virginia City include the Silver Queen Hotel, Piper's Opera House, Mackay Mansion, Gold Hill Hotel and Saloon, and, of course, the Old Washoe Club, which also makes the list as one of the most haunted spots in the country.

Gettysburg, Pennsylvania

The small town of Gettysburg in Pennsylvania is one of the most active paranormal hot spots in the country (see Figure 19-1). It was at this place where Union troops under command of General George Meade clashed with Confederate soldiers under General Robert E. Lee, resulting in the bloodiest battle of the Civil War. Over the days of July 1 to 3, 1863, more than 51,000 soldiers were killed, wounded, or went missing.

The carnage from the battle has left a permanent mark on the town, and there are literally dozens of haunted places in Gettysburg and on the surrounding battlefield, including the Jennie Wade House (once home to the only civilian killed during the battle), Devil's Den, Little Round Top, Iverson's Pits, National Soldier's Orphan Homestead, Gettysburg Engine House, and many others.

FIGURE 19-1:
The Gettysburg battlefield.

New Orleans, Louisiana

New Orleans is one of the most unique cities in America — and one of the most haunted (see Figure 19-2). Founded by the French in 1718, it was a colony into which France dumped its prisoners, criminals, and prostitutes. Built on the swamps of Louisiana, the city flew the flags of both France and Spain before becoming an American city in 1804. Destroyed once by fire, inhabited by pirates and voodoo priests, devastated by hurricanes and disease, the scene of a bloody battle during the War of 1812, and held by both Confederate and Union forces during the Civil War, the city has seen more than its share of history — and more than its share of ghosts.

Ghosts are found everywhere in New Orleans, from homes to hotels, churches, taverns, restaurants, and even alleyways. Some of the most famous haunted places include St. Louis Cemetery No. 1, Bottom of the Cup Tea Room, Beauregard-Keyes House, Gardette-LePrete Mansion, Andrew Jackson Hotel, Antoine's, Old Absinthe House, Lafitte's Blacksmith Shop, Bourbon Orleans Hotel, and, of course, the LaLaurie Mansion, which was known as The Haunted House in the city for decades.

Hollywood, California

Although it's officially been a part of Los Angeles for many years now, Hollywood is a world of its own. The "movie capital of the world" has drawn would-be actors, dreamers, and movie buffs since the first silent filmmakers came to California in the early 1900s. What began as a scheme for moviemaker Mack Sennett to make extra money with a low-cost housing development called Hollywoodland became a movie colony for artists, writers, and actors who came west to make it big. Today, Hollywood remains not so much a city, but a state of mind. It hasn't been incorporated since 1910, but it retains a strange allure for those with an interest in history, crime, and hauntings and for those who lived their life against the backdrop of the silver screen.

Dozens and dozens of hauntings are in Hollywood, most connected to the broken dreams faced by those who came to this place — and never left. There are haunted movie studios, haunted cemeteries, and haunted hotels like the Knickerbocker and the Hollywood Roosevelt. Some of the lingering spirits — as famous is death as they were in life — include Rudolph Valentino, Erol Flynn, James Dean, Jayne Mansfield, William Desmond Taylor, Thelma Todd, Sharon Tate, George Reeves, Bob Crane, and even Marilyn Monroe.

Salem, Massachusetts

Salem, located on the northeast coast of Massachusetts at the mouth of the Naumkeag River, was founded in 1626 by Roger Conant and a group of immigrants from Cape Ann. At first, the settlement was named Naumkeag, but the settlers preferred to call it Salem, derived from the Hebrew word for peace. The city grew into a thriving port and one of the largest cities in the state, outside of Boston. Of course, the events for which Salem is best remembered began in 1692. A local physician diagnosed several teenage girls as bewitched, which resulted in the hanging of 19 persons and one being crushed to death. When the hysteria had played itself out the following year, an edict was issued that released all people from prison who had been accused of witchcraft — but by then, the damage was done.

It should come as no surprise that an old city known for its rich witchcraft history and maritime trade is home to many legendary ghosts. Spine-tingling tales began as far back as the Salem Witch Trials of 1692, and today, the city is rife with spirited sites, ranging from Bunghole Liquors, a former Prohibition-era funeral parlor to Cinema Salem, an independent movie theater. Other spine-chilling locations include In a Pig's Eye, Murphy's, Hawthorne Hotel (named for Nathaniel Hawthorne, author of *The House of Seven Gables*, which is also in town), Old Burying Point Cemetery, and, of course, the Witch House, or the Corwin House, which was the home to Judge Jonathan Corwin, a lead figure in the Salem Witch Trials.

Savannah, Georgia

Established in 1733 when General James Oglethorpe and 120 colonists decided to build a city on a bluff along the Savannah River, Savannah became the first settlement in the last American colony of Georgia. A few decades later, it proved a strategic port city in the American Revolution and during the American Civil War. In 1778, the British took Savannah and held it until 1782. Eventually, a land-sea force of French and American troops reclaimed the city's independence. During the Civil War, Savannah suffered from sea blockades so fierce that its economy crumbled. Saved from the fires set by Union soldiers throughout the Southeast, the city was offered by Union General William Sherman as a Christmas present to President Abraham Lincoln. It's been said that Savannah was spared from fire because General Sherman was so impressed by its beauty that he couldn't destroy it.

Over the centuries, Savannah has suffered devastating fires, war, and yellow fever outbreaks that claimed the lives of thousands. But it survived and rebuilt itself, playing host to resilient citizens — and plenty of ghosts. Haunted places include the site of Gribble House, where notorious ax murders occurred, Marshall House, Factor's Walk, Madison Square, Moon River Brewing Company, and the infamous Pirate's House, one of the oldest structures in the city.

San Francisco, California

In 1835, an American, William Richardson, became the first permanent resident of a settlement then known as Yerba Buena. As more people came to the region, California achieved its independence and the town began to grow, but nothing like it would a few years later. On January 24, 1848, the first gold was found at Sutter's Fort, in the California foothills. Within months, San Francisco (renamed from Yerba Buena in 1847) became the central port and depot of the frenzied Gold Rush. Over the next year, arriving "forty-niners" increased the city's population from 1,000 to 25,000. The city was lawless and wild, with its Barbary Coast district full of prostitution and gambling. Construction of the Central Pacific Railroad drew thousands of laborers from China and San Francisco's Chinatown quickly became the largest Chinese settlement outside of Asia.

On April 18, 1906, a massive earthquake shook the city. The tremors broke water mains and triggered fires that raged for four days, killing 3,000 people, destroying 25,000 buildings, and leaving 250,000 homeless. The city rebuilt quickly with an improved city center and hosted the lavish Panama International Exposition just nine years later. San Francisco has continued to endure, drawing writers like Mark Twain and Jack London, becoming a center for the 1950s beat poets and for the Haight-Ashbury hippie counterculture that peaked with the 1967 "Summer of Love."

A city with such a long and storied history is undoubtedly a place to find a myriad of ghosts. Haunted places in San Francisco include some of the most legendary spots in the country, like Alcatraz, the infamous "escape-proof" prison located in the bay, and the Winchester House, which is in nearby San Jose. Other haunted places include Haskell House at Fort Mason, Neptune Society Columbarium, Curran Theater, San Francisco Art Institute, Queen Anne Hotel, and Sutro Baths, which was, in 1896, the world's largest indoor swimming pool establishment. It burned in 1966, but today accommodates more ethereal guests.

Alton, Illinois

This small Mississippi River town started out as a ferryboat landing in 1814 but soon grew into a thriving port. Author Mark Twain once referred to Alton a "dismal little river town," largely thanks to the dark history that the city experienced, which included death, disease, disaster, violence, murder, and even the scars of the Civil War. The town has endured over time, becoming home to the first state penitentiary in Illinois (later turned into a Confederate prison during the war) and to Robert Wadlow, the tallest man who ever lived.

Dozens of haunted places are in this small community, including the Mineral Springs Hotel, a 1914 building that attracted visitors from all over the Midwest to its mineral baths. The former hotel, shown in Figure 19-3, has more than its share of ghosts, including a man who drowned in the pool, and at least two documented suicides. One of the most active sites is the First Unitarian Church, haunted by a former pastor who hanged himself in the building. Other sites include the old penitentiary, Alton City Cemetery, Enos Apartments, a former tuberculosis sanatorium, and the McPike Mansion.

FIGURE 19-3:
The Mineral Springs Hotel.

Courtesy of American Hauntings.

Vicksburg, Mississippi

The land where Vicksburg is now located had a brutal history before the city was ever settled. The French built Fort-Saint-Pierre (1719) on the high bluffs overlooking the Mississippi River in 1719, but it was wiped out by Native Americans ten years later. In 1790, the Spanish tried again, and a sprawling community grew that was named for a Methodist minister named Newitt Vick. The settlement prospered as a shipping point. Because of its strategic location, Vicksburg was besieged by Union forces for 47 days during General Ulysses S. Grant's campaign for control of the river during the Civil War. Vicksburg surrendered on July 4, 1863. Since that time, the city has wrestled with racial unrest, has continued as a shipping port, and has become a tourist spot.

The town's long, and often bloody, history has left many ghosts and haunted places behind. Among them are the Vicksburg National Battlefield, McNutt House, the Genella Building, Kuhn Memorial State Hospital, and McRaven Mansion, which was used as a field hospital during the Vicksburg siege. At least 12 Confederate soldiers died here and were buried on the grounds.

Charleston, South Carolina

The new colony of Carolina got its start in April 1670 when travelers landed at Albemarle Point. They named the first community Charles Town in honor of their king, Charles II, but it did not have an auspicious beginning. They battled the French, Spanish, hostile natives, pirates, and rampant disease, but nevertheless, the community grew into a busy seaport. Ships carrying raw materials, deer skins, rice, indigo, and eventually cotton were exported to England and commerce was born. Ships returned heavy with staples and luxuries of Europe which lent a cosmopolitan air to the growing community. Even in its infancy, it had the reputation of being a "Little London" in the semi-tropic wilds of the New World. By 1740, Charles Town was becoming the most critical port in North America for exporting, and an economic boom surged across the colony.

The American Revolution brought an end to Charlestown's golden age. It would be divided by slavery, state's rights, and eventually, the Civil War. Battles occurred around the city, wreaking havoc on the plantations, homes, and citizens. Thousands died, and parts of the city burned. It would take years to recover, but by the early 1900s, Charleston was again a cultural center. The history of the city was preserved, and it remains one of the most beautiful cities in the South.

With a rich history that dates back more than 300 years, it is no wonder that it has so many ghosts and haunted places. Among the spooky sites are the Battery Carriage House Inn, For Moultrie, Dock Street Theatre, Old Exchange and Provost Dungeon, the Powder Magazine, Pink House, Poogan's Porch, Boone Hall Plantation, *USS Yorktown*, and the old Charleston Jail, which is haunted by the spirits of many inmates who died during their imprisonment, from murderers and pirates to prisoners of war and slaves.

Chapter **20**

Ten of America's Most Haunted Places

No matter where you live, it's likely you're not far from a historical site with a spooky history. On just about any day of the week, you can likely visit a haunted house in your area. But do you want to? Are you a believer in ghosts? You probably are since you are reading this book, but if not, it likely does not matter. Ghosts do exist. In fact, there are firm legal grounds for the belief in ghosts.

In 1991, a New York state court ruled that a seller must inform all potential buyers if a house is haunted or face the prospect of having to return the deposit. The ruling also declared that, for legal purposes, the house in dispute was haunted. The house was a lovely Victorian, located in Nyack, New York, which was purported to be haunted by spirits from the American Revolution. Wall Street bond trader Jeffrey Stambovsky had already placed a $33,000 deposit on the $650,000 house when he "decided that he didn't want to own a haunted house, and asked for the money back," Reuters reported. The owner, Helen Ackley, refused, saying in effect, "Let the buyer beware." But the court said there was no way Stambovsky could have known about the ghosts unless Ackley told him. They ordered that his deposit be refunded.

The courts are not alone in acknowledging the spirit world. A few years ago, Dr. Ian Stevenson, a clinical psychiatrist at the University of Virginia, got a lot of media attention when he stated that ghost sightings could no longer be dismissed as hoaxes or hallucinations. In an interview, he announced, "Evidence for these kinds of experiences are too frequent to be dismissed."

In other words, not everyone can be wrong.

Still skeptical? More people have seen ghosts than have walked on the moon. Most people have seen ghosts than have seen a dinosaur. Yet imagine how silly you would think someone was if they told you that they didn't believe in those things.

Ghosts are out there. That has been the point of *Ghost Adventures* all these years — to find that evidence, to experience that place, to come face-to-face with the spirit world and to tell our fans all about it. We have searched the country for haunted locations and found places that are rife with paranormal activity.

I have compiled a list of what I believe are some of the most haunted places that I have personally encountered. Read on — or better yet, visit them — if you dare.

Goldfield Hotel

In the almost ghost town of Goldfield, Nevada, is the historic and very haunted Goldfield Hotel. The town was born in 1902 when gold was discovered nearby. Within a few years, it was the largest town in the state. In addition to its numerous saloons, the city once boasted three newspapers, five banks, a mining stock exchange, and a population of nearly 35,000. By 1920, though, the gold was nearly gone, and the population was reduced to just 1,500 people. Three years later, a fire wiped out 27 blocks of homes and businesses. The town exists today with just a few hundred people and a number of restored buildings, including the Goldfield Hotel.

The hotel opened in 1908 to great fanfare. The four-story building of stone and brick cost more than $300,000 to build and included 154 rooms with telephones, electric lights, and heated steam. The lobby was paneled with mahogany and furnished in black leather upholstery, beneath gold-leaf ceilings and crystal chandeliers. Considered to be the most luxurious hotel between Chicago and San Francisco, the Goldfield Hotel appealed to society's upper crust, making it an immediate success.

Soon after the hotel opened, it was sold to George Wingfield, primary owner of the Goldfield Consolidated Mines Company, and hotel entrepreneur, Casey McDannell, who managed and operated the hotel. Wingfield was a multimillionaire by the age of 30 and became a political powerhouse in Nevada. After making his fortune in the gold fields, he went on to own a chain of banks, numerous ranches, and several Reno hotels, in addition to his interest in the Goldfield Hotel. He became a Nevada political fixer and one of the richest men in the state.

When Goldfield was in its heyday, the hotel entertained all manner of affluent guests. However, as the gold began to play out and Goldfield's population diminished, the Goldfield Hotel began a gradual decline. By the 1930s, it had become little more than a flop house for cowboys and undiscriminating travelers. During World War II, it housed Army Air Corp personnel assigned to the Tonopah Air Base 25 miles north of Goldfield. After the soldiers checked out of the hotel in 1945, the hotel closed its doors. Over the years, the Goldfield Hotel has changed hands numerous times, with each new owner promising to restore and reopen the old property.

Reportedly, several ghosts are at the old hotel, the most famous of which is a woman named Elizabeth. According to the legend, Elizabeth was a prostitute that George Wingfield visited frequently. When she turned up pregnant, she claimed the child was Wingfield's, who for a while paid her to stay away, fearful of how the scandal might affect his business affairs. However, when she could no longer hide the pregnancy, Wingfield was said to have lured her into room 109 of the hotel, where he chained her to a radiator. Supplied with food and water, she was left there until her child could be born. Some say that Elizabeth died in childbirth, but others contend that Wingfield murdered her after the child was born. Her baby was then thrown into an old mining shaft. Afterwards, rumors abounded that Elizabeth continued to visit Wingfield, and the sound of a crying child could sometimes be heard coming from the depths of the hotel.

The legends state that Elizabeth's apparition has been seen with long flowing hair, wearing a white gown, and looking terribly sad as she walks the hallways, calling out to her child. Others have reported her being sighted in room 109, which is often described as being intensely cold.

Elizabeth does not walk the hotel alone. Ghosts of two suicides haunt rooms on the third floor. Near the lobby staircase, the spirits of children are said to play pranks on visitors. And then there is the ghost of George Wingfield himself, who makes his presence known with cigar smoke.

Many believe that the Goldfield Hotel is a gateway to the next world. True or not, it has more than its share of strange phenomena, including footsteps, unexplained noises, and even poltergeist activity, as was seen during one of the *Ghost Adventures* investigations of the building.

Washoe Club

During the days when Nevada's Comstock Lode was turning miners into millionaires, the Washoe Club in Virginia City was created by mining magnates, artists, and writers as a place of luxury (see Figure 20-1). It soon gained a reputation throughout the West as a place to find extravagant accommodations, but it began as an idea.

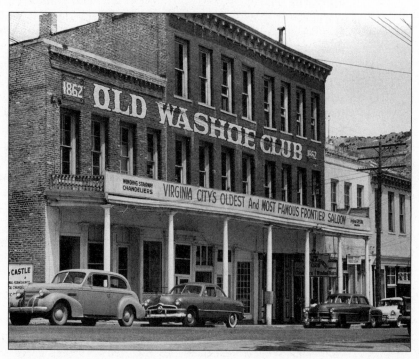

FIGURE 20-1:
The Washoe Club.

In February 1875, an organizational meeting was held among the notables who would soon put the Club's exclusive quarters to use. It housed one of the finest libraries east of San Francisco, an elegant billiard room, a parlor adorned with Italian marble and bronze statues, and a wine room that boasted an elaborately carved black walnut sideboard. The membership roster would include the greatest names from Comstock and West Coast history, and the guest register would bear signatures like General Ulysses S. Grant, actor-lecturer Artemus Ward, actor Edwin Booth, and railroad magnate Darius Ogden Mills, along with 50 other millionaires of international reputation.

The Washoe Club opened its quarters on June 1, 1875. According to reports in the press, applications for membership came in rapidly, but little did anyone realize that the Club was already in its glory days. Less than five months later, the palatial club rooms were consumed by a fire that destroyed much of Virginia City. Many of the members fell behind in paying the assessments on their membership, which made it difficult to find a new home.

But the Club persevered, and the new year, 1876, promised to be a prosperous one. The Club was organized again, and six months later, new Club rooms opened that were said to be "more elegant" than the originals. There was a new reading room with imported carpet, upholstered furniture, and steel chandeliers. There was another lavish billiard room, an elegant sideboard with the very best beverages and cigars, card room, wine room, and a hall for receptions.

By the time the Washoe Club was back to its renewed glory, the production of the mines had fallen drastically. A disastrous underground fire, in 1881, wreaked further havoc on the production of mines and on the ability of the Washoe Club members to continue to indulge in luxury. Membership continued to drop off and monthly dues were reduced, but that was not enough to keep the wealthy business owners in the failing city. A story in the *Territorial Enterprise* newspaper on September 9, 1897, simply stated, "The Washoe Club is no more."

The building that houses the Club, of course, survives and has since been renamed the Washoe Club as a reminder of the old days. A number of ghostly stories — and first-hand accounts — surround this place. The notoriety of the Club as an actively haunted place began back when the first *Ghost Adventures* documentary film aired on television. It included a scene at the Washoe Club where an apparition walked across the floor for a mind-boggling seven seconds.

Other stories are also told about the building. There are tales of a brothel that used to be on an upper floor. The story goes that a blonde prostitute was murdered on the third floor, and her killer took his own life in despair. There was also a young girl allegedly killed in the basement. Many have reported seeing the ghost of the prostitute on the spiral staircase that once led up the wealthy men's club upstairs. In fact, she has been seen so many times that patrons of the new club began calling her Lena. She has also been seen in front of the wall across from the bar.

Anyone who visits the Washoe Club will take something away with them — whether it is an appreciation of the history or a paranormal encounter. It is a place where I have never been disappointed.

Crescent Hotel

In the remote resort town of Eureka Springs, Arkansas, stands the gothic Crescent Hotel. Called by some the Grand Old Lady of the Ozarks, the hotel has served as many things over the years, and yet strangely, each incarnation has contributed to the legion of phantoms believed to walk the corridors of the building.

The Crescent Hotel was built on the ridge of West Mountain between 1884 and 1886. One of the main investors was the Frisco Railroad, which hoped to spur development in the region. It was an important time because of the national attention that had come to Eureka Springs for the "healing waters" that were bubbling from the earth nearby. During the late 1800s, people traveled from all over the country to take in the waters and to hopefully ease and cure their particular ailments. In addition, spring water was also bottled and shipped out, further enhancing the small town's reputation. The railroad made a fortune by offering excursion train trips to the town.

The hotel was massive and well-constructed. It is equipped with numerous towers, overhanging balconies, and granite walls that are more than 18 inches thick. Numerous renovations have altered the five-story interior, but the lobby is still fitted with a massive stone fireplace that dominates the room. At one time, more than 500 people could be seated in the dining room. Electric lights were included in the original construction, as were bathrooms and modern plumbing fixtures. The lawn outside was decorated with gazebos, winding boardwalks, and flower gardens, and guests were offered tennis courts, croquet, and other outdoor recreations.

The Crescent Hotel drew people from all over the country for the next decade, but as times changed, the wealthy began to have less interest in the "healing waters" and business for the entire town began to decline. In an effort to keep the hotel open, it was used as the Crescent College and Conservatory for Young Women, starting in 1908. The school became an exclusive academy for wealthy young ladies. During the summer, it still catered to the tourist crowd, but the money it made was not enough to keep the aging monolith in business. The school closed in 1924, and the hotel shut down five years later. There were a variety of owners and tenants after that, but no one could keep it operating on a regular basis.

On July 31, 1937, the hotel was sold to Dr. Norman Baker, a quack and flim-flam artist who claimed to have a cure for cancer. Baker, who made a fortune developing a calliope organ that played by air pressure instead of steam, was a born charlatan who was always just one step ahead of the law. He opened his first cancer hospital in Iowa but ran into legal problems over his "cure." He fled to Eureka Springs and bought the hotel. He spent a grand sum remodeling it into a hospital and then moved in with his medical staff and 144 patients.

He began advertising the hospital by saying that no surgeries or x-rays were used to save the lives of his patients. His "cures" mostly consisted of home remedies and drinking the local spring water. While scores of patients succumbed to their cancer, no reports exist to say that anyone was actually killed by Baker's treatments. Local rumor, however, had a different story to tell. The legends say that when remodeling was done at the hotel in later years, dozens of human skeletons were discovered hidden within the walls. These stories claimed that Baker was no harmless eccentric, but a dangerous and terrible man who experimented on both the dead and the living.

Truth or fiction, federal authorities caught up with Baker, and he was charged with using the mail to defraud the public about his false medical claims. He was convicted in 1940 and sentenced to four years in Leavenworth. The hospital closed, and Baker vanished into history.

The brooding old hotel stayed closed until 1946, when new investors took it over and began trying to restore the building. It wasn't long before the ghost stories began. Staff members began to receive frequent reports of strange happenings in the rooms and hallways. Guests have awakened in the night to find figures standing over them. Spirits have been seen sitting quietly in the lobby, vanishing when approached. A woman in a nurse's uniform has been seen pushing a gurney down a hallway later at night. An apparition near the staircase has been identified as Norman Baker himself, perhaps still trapped in the building where he harmed so many sick and dying people.

A few years ago, an antique switchboard from the days of the hospital was finally removed because of all the problems it caused. A staff member explained, "In the summer, we would get phone calls on the switchboard from the basement recreation room. There was no one on the other end because the room was unused and locked. We could check it out and find that the phone had been taken off the hook. There was only one way in or out of the place, and the key was kept at the front desk." The staff member checked the recreation room one night after a series of call and found the telephone in the locked room was off the hook. He fled back upstairs, and a few minutes later, the switchboard buzzer went off, coming from the same room. This time, he decided not to check it out.

Trans-Allegheny Lunatic Asylum

The story of the Trans-Allegheny Lunatic Asylum, formerly Weston State Hospital, is a familiar one in the long line of woeful tales from American asylums (see Figure 20-2). It was a designed to provide a safe place for the mentally ill, and like so many others, began with good intentions, only to become overcrowded and undesirable in the 20th century. But if one thing sets this place apart from others like it, even those with a reputation for being haunted, it is that the place once known as the Weston State Hospital is said to be infested with ghosts.

Library of Congress, Carol M. Highsmith Archive

FIGURE 20-2:
The Trans-
Allegheny
Lunatic Asylum.

The Weston State Hospital, known as the Trans-Allegheny Lunatic Asylum, was authorized by the Virginia General Assembly in the 1850s. Construction on the site, along the West Fork River opposite downtown Weston, began in late 1858. When the Civil War began in April 1861, the Weston State Hospital was still in the early stages of construction. At that time, the southernmost wing had been finished, along with the basement and foundation of the massive central structure. In June, Virginia's secession from the Union brought all work that was not related to the war effort to a halt. Following its secession from the United States, the government of Virginia demanded the return of the hospital's unused construction funds for its defense, but before this could occur, Weston was invaded by the Seventh Ohio Volunteer Infantry, who used portions of the completed hospital as a camp. Fighting occurred for the next several years, and control of the area changed hands several times.

During the war, the area where Weston was located became part of the newly organized West Virginia, which provided funds for work on the hospital after the war. The Trans-Allegheny Lunatic Asylum was finally completed in 1881. At that time, it was the largest hand-cut stone building in the United States, and second in the world next to the Kremlin in Russia. Its name was changed to Weston State Hospital in 1913 in an effort to remove the stigma caused by the words "lunatic" and "asylum."

Originally designed to house just 250 inmates in peaceful solitude, the hospital held 717 patients by 1880. The numbers continued to climb into the 1950s, when more than 2,600 patients were packed into filthy, overcrowded conditions. The asylum was overcrowded, which led to other problems, including violence. Several methods were employed to control the violent patients. These methods included straitjackets, solitary confinement, restraints, and the always popular *lobotomy*, which was widely used starting in the 1940s. After electroshock therapy was administered, the sharp tip of the orbitoclast was inserted at the corner of the eye until it reached the frontal lobes of the brain. With a few short sweeping motions, the frontal lobe had been disconnected — and the patient's life had been changed forever. With an overcrowded hospital and a staff that had little control over the horde of patients, the lobotomy gained popularity. Over the course of the hospital's history, more than 3,500 lobotomies were performed.

With hundreds and hundreds of the mentally ill living in a constant state of nightmarish insanity and with no help to be found, the inmates lived in a daze of anguish, pain, and utter hopelessness. It is no wonder that the imprint of their terror and madness has seeped into the walls and floors of the Weston State Hospital.

By the 1980s, the hospital's population was finally reduced due to changes in the treatment of mental illness. Those patients that could not be controlled, though, were often locked in cages. The hospital was finally closed in 1994 and sold at auction in 2007. New owners renovated the crumbling building and began offering historic tours. After the construction work began — and the tourists began to arrive — those who spent any amount of time in the asylum began to realize that the living were not alone in the old hospital. The dead were present, and they were making themselves known.

The Trans-Allegheny Lunatic Asylum was made up of different wards to facilitate the treatment of various kinds of patients. On the third floor, Wards C and F held the more physically violent men and women, with only a single locked door separating the two wards from each other. Many who have visited Ward F have reported being touched on the shoulder, pinched, or had their clothing pulled and hearing, whispers and, most eerily, the sound of the creaking wheels of gurneys being pushed down the empty corridors.

In Ward 2, located on the second floor, victims of a double suicide and a brutal stabbing have been said to wander the dark hallways, their dragging footsteps clearly being heard as they shuffle along the dark passageway. Witnesses claim to experience an icy grip of cold as the footsteps brush past, only dissipating when the sound is no longer heard.

One section of the hospital was long ago dubbed the Civil War Wing because it first admitted patients that had returned to their families from the war in such states of madness that no therapy of the time seemed able to reach them. The men suffered from shellshock, as it was known at the time. Visitors to this area of the asylum today have heard male laughter, coughing, and voices and have even been threatened by disembodied voices, warning them to leave the building. Over time, many of the staff members at the asylum simply refuse to enter this wing alone or at night. Many of them have reported being chased by the hurried footsteps of a man who cannot be seen. They also report the intense feeling of being watched, but searches of nearby rooms and hallways reveal that no one — no one visible anyway — is present.

If a single floor is more infamous than all others, it's the fourth floor, which was reportedly haunted even in the days when the Weston State Hospital was still in operation. The sounds of banging, footsteps, maniacal laughter, and haunting screams have been heard all over the floor. It is a place known to be so eerie that hospital workers refused to go up to the fourth floor without an escort.

Heavy footsteps trudged down the halls, accompanied by the sounds of distant crying, screaming, and moaning. Doors opened and closed on their own, banging sounds echoed off the pipes and door frames, and even the muted sound of conversation between two people have been heard — and recorded. No one was present at the time. Some have even reported seeing gurneys and wheelchairs slowly rolling down the corridors or across rooms by themselves.

One of the haunts of the fourth floor is said to be the spirit of a nurse. Legend has it that she was murdered decades ago by a patient who hid her body in an unused stairwell for nearly two months before her body was discovered.

Without a doubt, the most famous lingering spirit of Trans-Allegheny Lunatic Asylum is that of the young girl that has come to be called Lilly. She appears to be a child, perhaps three or four years of age. She wanders the hallways of the old hospital and seems particularly active when visitors ask her to play. No one knows who she was, although numerous legends surround this lost little soul. Some believe that she was an orphan, an abandoned child left in the care of the state and placed in the orphanage located on the site. The stories say that she lived for a few years and then died from pneumonia or tuberculosis, common killers of children in those days. Others claim that Lilly's mother was a patient at the hospital, a mad woman who gave birth to a child while she was locked away. If so, Lilly may have been left in the care of the orphanage since her mother would likely never be cured.

However she died, her spirit remains, wandering the halls of the abandoned asylum, perhaps seeking the mother who left her, or perhaps just looking for anyone who wants to entertain a lonely little girl. Some report the sounds of running and giggling whenever Lilly's spirit is around, while others have claimed to see the fleeting glimpse of a small girl in an old-fashioned dress as she hurries around a corner or vanishes up a staircase. Occasionally, she interacts directly with those from whom she seeks attention. A tour guide playfully rolled a ball down a hallway for her one night, only to have it abruptly change directions and return to them by some unseen force.

Queen Mary

The *Queen Mary*, shown in Figure 20-3, was commissioned in 1934 and for many years was the undisputed ruler of the oceans. She set sail on her maiden voyage in May 1936 and quickly became known as the ultimate form of international travel. During the 1930s, and in the years following World War II, her decks played host to the rich and famous and included guests like the Marx Brothers, Clark Gable, Charles Lindbergh, Amelia Earhart, Charlie Chaplin, Jean Harlow, Laurel and Hardy, and many others. The first-class passengers on the ship were treated to every imaginable luxury as the crew was trained to cater to the needs and whims of everyone on board.

FIGURE 20-3:
The *Queen Mary*.

©Travel Channel.

In 1939, though, the British government commandeered *Queen Mary* into military service. They gave her a coat of gray paint and started using her to transport troops. The majestic dining salons of the vessel became mess halls that served up 2,000 soldiers at a time. Her cocktail bars, cabins, and state rooms were filled with bunks, as was every available space below decks. Even the swimming pools were boarded over and crowded with cots for the men. The ship was so useful to the Allies that Hitler made her a marked ship and offered a $250,000 reward and hero status to the U-boat commander who could sink her. None of them did. But while *Queen Mary* was able to avoid the enemy torpedoes during the war, she was unable to avoid tragedy.

The horrific event occurred on October 2, 1942. The ship was sailing on a choppy ocean around the north of Ireland. She carried 10,000 American soldiers, bound for the Clyde River, where the men would disembark. Tragically, *Queen Mary* collided with a British warship, *HMS Curacoa*, killing 338 of the men on the other vessel. *Queen Mary* suffered only minor damage, and there were no injuries aboard the liner.

After that, she served unscathed for the remainder of the war. Following the surrender of Germany, *Queen Mary* carried American soldiers home from Europe and transported as many as 20,000 GI war brides to the United States. A year later, she was converted back to use as a luxury liner.

Her post-war service was largely uneventful. For several years, she and her sister ship, *Queen Elizabeth*, were the preferred method of transatlantic travel for the rich and the famous. As time passed, though, luxury ships began to fall into disfavor. It was faster, and cheaper, to simply catch a plane to wherever you wanted to go. The ocean liners were becoming a thing of the past.

In October 1967, *Queen Mary* steamed away from England for the last time. Her decks and state rooms were filled with curiosity seekers and wealthy patrons who wanted to be a part of the ship's final voyage. She ended her 39-day journey in Long Beach, California. The city had purchased the old liner, and she would be permanently docked as a floating hotel, convention center, museum, restaurant — and one of the most haunted places in America.

In addition to the wartime accident that caused *Queen Mary* to collide with another ship, other mishaps and bizarre deaths aboard claimed lives and left lingering spirits behind.

On July 10, 1966, John Pedder, a worker in the engine room, was crushed to death when the automatic door in Doorway 13 closed on him. The ship's first captain, Sir Edgar Britten, died only weeks after the liner's maiden voyage. During the war, when the ship was used as a troop transport, a brawl broke out in one of the ship's galleys and became so serious that the captain radioed a nearby cruiser to send a boarding party to break up the fighting. Before the escort ship's squad could arrive, a ship's cook was allegedly pushed into a hot oven, where he burned to death. There was also a report of a woman drowning in the ship's swimming pool and stories of passengers falling overboard, never to be seen again.

Another strange death on the ship was that of Senior Second Office W.E. Stark. His ghost has often been spotted in his former quarters and on deck. Stark died in 1949 after joking to some of his friends that he had taken a drink of a cleaning solution and lime juice, having mistaken it for gin. He made light of the situation, not realizing how serious it was to become. By the following day, he was sick in his bunk, and by the next, the doctor had advised his transfer to a hospital. The young officer grew even worse and soon lapsed into a coma and died on Thursday, September 22, 1949.

Another ghost believed to haunt *Queen Mary* is Leonard "Lobster" Horsborough, a former cook. He served aboard the ship for 15 years and then passed away on November 13, 1967, during the vessel's final voyage. He died from complications brought on by a heat stroke and eventual heart failure and was buried at sea. Since his death, tales have often been told of the kitchen area being haunted, and his presence is often seen, heard, and felt there.

In addition to these ghosts, there are also reported encounters with a man in white overalls who has been seen and heard many times below deck. He is dressed in the type of uniform worn by engineers and mechanics in the 1930s. There is also a spectral man in gray overalls who has also been seen below deck. He has dark hair and a long beard and is also believed to have once been a mechanic or a maintenance worker whose ghost stayed behind. A woman in white haunts Queen Mary, usually lurking around the main lounge in a white, backless evening gown. The stories say that she usually strolls over to the grand piano as if listening to music only she can hear or dances alone for a few moments before vanishing without a trace.

There are other spirits, too. Security guards, crew, staff members, and visitors have all been troubled by incidents that seem to have no explanation. Doors open and close on their own. They are locked one moment and then standing wide open the next, triggering alarms in the security office. This happens most often near the swimming pool and while the guards always look for the intruders, no one is ever found. Other reports of unexplained happenings include strange noises like footsteps when no one is there, banging and hammering like work being done on equipment, voices, cold spots, inexplicable winds that blow through areas that are closed off, lights that turn on and off, and more.

The strange events aboard *Queen Mary* continue, and it seems certain that events of the past have left an indelible impression on the decks, corridors, and cabins of the ship. They repeat themselves, over and over again, and create a haunting that is rivaled by few others in the annals of the supernatural.

Pennhurst State School

For decades, the primary treatment for people unable to fit into society was to place them in one of many sprawling mental hospitals, some of which held thousands of patients. Overcrowding and lack of funds led to inmates being deplorably treated by those in charge. It is almost impossible to imagine the horrors and brutality experienced by the mentally ill in the 19th and early 20th centuries.

Things began to change by the late 1950s, when the numerous abuses began to be reported. During the decade that followed, many asylums across the country were closed and left standing vacant — except for the many ghosts that still wandered their decaying halls.

Among these was the sprawling Pennhurst State School and Hospital (see Figure 20-4). It had opened in 1908 as the Eastern Pennsylvania Institution for the Feeble Minded and Epileptic. It was meant to be self-sufficient, a small community of its own with a power plant, farm, hospital, morgue, barber shop, and firehouse.

FIGURE 20-4:
Pennhurst State School and Hospital.

©*Travel Channel.*

When patients arrived, they were given a classification mentally, either as an "imbecile" or "insane" and physically as either "epileptic" or "healthy." Thousands of mentally disabled children, most of them abandoned by their parents, passed through the doors of the Pennhurst Asylum and entered a world that was more frightening than any they might have imagined.

Children and orphans were not the only inmates at Pennhurst, which was later dubbed as the "Shame of Pennsylvania." The asylum also housed immigrants that did not speak English, as well as petty criminals. What all the inmates shared were the appalling conditions and years of abuse and neglect.

It had been designed to house no more than 500 patients, but by 1912, the institution was severely overcrowded, and staff members were unable to give proper care to each patient. This led to terrible abuses. The asylum's staff would often tie the patients to their beds and leave them alone for hours and sometimes entire days. The inmates were left without food or water and without proper sanitation. Patients who showed aggressiveness were often drugged to calm them down. If a patient bit another inmate or staff member, their teeth were removed. This happened so often that, even years after the asylum closed, visitors would find teeth lying scattered in the tunnels beneath the buildings.

Things did not get better at Pennhurst in the 1950s. In fact, mistreatment and inhumane and dangerous conditions continued until 1968, when a new report about the hospital inspired a legal fight to correct the problems. The case went on for almost two decades before Pennhurst was finally closed.

When one considers the dark and harrowing past of the institution, it comes as no surprise that the "Shame of Pennsylvania" has a reputation of being one of the most haunted places in the country. Today, the old asylum is shrouded in ghost tales and reports of paranormal activity. Visitors have claimed to hear voices, shrieks, and murmurs of pain from former inmates of the facility. The hauntings are terrifying for multiple reasons. Aside from the typical fear of the paranormal, the ghosts of Pennhurst serve as a collective reminder of just how cruel society can be toward its own members.

Numerous investigations have taken place at Pennhurst — including those conducted by *Ghost Adventures* — and evidence of spirits has been obtained in the form of video, photographs, and eerie messages through EVP. Shadow figures and apparitions have been seen in various buildings. Objects have been hurled through the air, and many visitors claim to have been touched, pushed, and pinched by unseen hands. Some have also reported hearing the sounds of sinks being turned on and toilets flushing, even though no running water or bathroom fixtures are in the building.

Bobby Mackey's Music World

The building that stands today as Bobby Mackey's Music World (see Figure 20-5) has a long and bloody history in the northern Kentucky and Cincinnati area. It started out as a slaughterhouse in the 1850s and was one of the largest packing houses in the region for many years. Only a well that was dug in the basement, where blood and refuse from the animals was drained, remains from the original building. The slaughterhouse closed in the early 1890s, but it gained lasting notoriety a few years later after the decapitated body of a young woman named Pearl Bryan was found nearby. The murder trials that followed were some of the most spectacular in the state and led to the hanging of the two killers.

FIGURE 20-5: Bobby Mackey's Music World.

The murderers refused to say what had happened to Pearl's head.

One of the most persistent rumors in the area claimed that it had been thrown into the well at the old slaughterhouse, a short distance from the murder site. The slaughterhouse had been empty for years, but legend had it that it was used by occultists for magic rituals. The well was used for the remains of animals that were killed during sacrifices. This occult group was allegedly made up of society people from Cincinnati and the surrounding area, including county officials, judges, attorneys, and members of law enforcement. They made sure that the location of her head remained a mystery. Whether this theory had any truth to it, the fact remains that the head was never found — and many believe it vanished into the well at the slaughterhouse.

After the murder, the building was silent and empty for many years. It was eventually torn down, and a roadhouse was constructed on the site. During the 1920s, it was a speakeasy and popular gambling joint. Local lore has it that during this period, several murders occurred in the building. None of them were ever solved because the bodies were normally dumped elsewhere to keep attention away from the illegal gambling and liquor operation.

After Prohibition ended in 1933, the building was purchased by E.A. Brady, better known to friends and enemies alike as Buck. Brady turned the building into a thriving tavern and casino called the Primrose. He enjoyed success for years but eventually the operation got the attention of syndicate mobsters in Cincinnati. They came to Brady, looking for a piece of the action. Brady refused offers for new "partners" and ignored demands to buy him out of the Primrose. Soon, the tavern was being vandalized, and customers were being threatened and beaten up in the parking lot. The violence escalated until Brady became involved in a shooting in August 1946. He was charged, and then released, in the attempted murder of small-time hood named Albert "Red" Masterson. This was the last straw for Buck, and he sold out to the gangsters. Brady committed suicide in September 1965.

After Brady sold out, the building re-opened as a nightclub called the Latin Quarter. It was during this period that the legends about the building gained another vengeful ghost. According to the stories, the daughter of the club's owner, a young woman named Johanna, fell in love with one of the singers who was performing there and became pregnant. Her father was furious. Thanks to his criminal connections, he had the singer killed. Johanna became so distraught that she attempted to poison her father. She failed but did succeed in taking her own life. Her body was later discovered in the basement of the club. According to the autopsy report, she was five months pregnant at the time.

Business did not fare well after this. During the early 1950s, new owners of the bar were arrested several times on gambling charges. In 1955, Campbell County deputies broke into the building with sledgehammers and confiscated slot machines and gambling tables.

Bad luck continued to plague the owners of the tavern. In the 1970s, it became known as the Hard Rock Café, but authorities closed it down in early 1978 because of some fatal shootings on the premises.

In 1978, Bobby and Janet Mackey purchased the bar. Bobby Mackey was a well-known as a singer in northern Kentucky and had recorded several albums. He scrapped his plans to record in Nashville in order to renovate the old tavern. Once the bar was opened, it immediately began to attract a crowd — a crowd that soon realized that strange things were happening in the bar.

Carl Lawson was the first employee hired by Bobby Mackey. He was a loner who worked as a caretaker and handyman at the tavern. He lived alone in an apartment in the upstairs and spent a lot of time in the sprawling building after hours. When he began reporting that he was seeing and hearing bizarre things in the club, people around town first assumed that he was simply crazy. Later on, though, when others started to see and hear the same things, Lawson didn't seem so strange after all.

Lights turned on and off, the jukebox turned on by itself, even when unplugged, and doors unlocked on their own. Soon, things went from weird to frightening. The first ghost that Lawson spotted in the place was that of a dark, very angry man behind the bar. A short time later, Lawson began to experience visions of a spirit who called herself "Johanna." She would often speak to Lawson, and he was able to answer her and carry on conversations. The rumors quickly started that Lawson was "talking to himself." Lawson claimed that Johanna was a tangible presence, though, often leaving the scent of roses in her wake.

Odd sounds and noises often accompanied the sightings, and Lawson soon realized that the spirits seemed to be the strongest in the basement, near an old-sealed up well that had been left from the days when there was a slaughterhouse at the location. The lore of the area, Carl knew, stated that the well had once been used for occult rituals. Some of the local folks referred to it as "Hell's Gate." Although he wasn't a particularly religious man, Lawson decided to sprinkle some holy water on the old well one night, thinking that it might bring some relief from the spirits. Instead, it seemed to provoke them, and the activity in the building began to escalate.

Soon, other employees and patrons of the place began to have their own weird experiences. Bobby Mackey was not happy about the ghostly rumors that were starting to spread around town. He didn't believe in ghosts and didn't want his customers thinking that his staff was crazy. He was sure there was nothing more to the stories than wild imaginations, but then when his wife, Janet, revealed that she had also encountered the club's resident spirits, Mackey was no longer sure what to think. Janet told him that she had seen the ghosts, had felt the overwhelming presences, and had even smelled Johanna's signature rose scent.

Once Janet admitted that she had seen the ghosts in the building, other people began to come forward. Stories from staff members and customers attracted the attention of writers and ghost enthusiasts, who came to regard the bar as a place they had to visit, at least once. Many came and were too frightened to return.

Strange activity continues to occur at Bobby Mackey's Music World, despite several attempted exorcisms of the site. It's as though the dark and bloody history of this place refuses to let go of the hold that it maintains on the present. And that bloody past will likely continue reaching out from the grave for many years to come.

Winchester Mystery House

Legend has it that the story of the Winchester Mansion, shown in Figure 20-6, began after the death of the husband and daughter of Sarah Pardee Winchester, a young woman from a wealthy New Haven, Connecticut, family. Her husband, William, was the heir to the Winchester rifle fortune and left his widowed bride very well off. After the death of William and their daughter, Annie, Sarah became a recluse, teetering on madness. She grieved deeply, and like many others at the time, she visited a spiritualist medium, hoping for comfort. However, the medium had a dire warning for her — there was a curse on the family, caused by the thousands of deaths attributed to the repeating rifle that the Winchester company had invented. Sarah was told that she needed to start a new life and build a home for the spirits that had fallen because of the terrible weapon. If she continued to build the house, she would live. If she stopped, she would die.

FIGURE 20-6:
Winchester
Mansion.

©Travel Channel.

Shortly after the séance, Sarah sold her home in New Haven and, with a vast fortune at her disposal, moved west to California. She believed that she was guided by the hand of her dead husband, and she did not stop traveling until she reached the Santa Clara Valley in 1884. There, she found a six-room home under construction and convinced the owner to sell it to her, along with the many acres of land that it rested on. She tossed away any previous plans for the house and started building. She had her pick of local workers and craftsmen. For the next 36 years, they built and rebuilt, altered and changed, and constructed and demolished one section of the house after another. She kept 22 carpenters at work, year around, each day. The sounds of hammers and saws sounded throughout the day and night.

As the house grew to include 26 rooms, railroad cars were switched onto a nearby line to bring building materials and imported furnishings to the house. The house was rapidly growing and expanding, and while Sarah claimed to have no master plan for the structure, she met each morning with her foreman, and they would go over her hand-sketched plans for the day's work. The plans were often chaotic but showed a real flair for building. Sometimes, though, they would not work out the right way, but Sarah always had a quick solution. If this happened, they would just build another room around an existing one. The foreman could never figure out where his employer got her ideas, but to Sarah, they came quite easily.

One of the first rooms that had been added to the house had been a séance room. It was located on the second floor in the center of the house. It had been designed with no windows and with a single entrance. No one ever entered it but Sarah. She would go into this room and attempt to "commune with the spirits," sitting quietly in meditation until the spirits placed their structural ideas for the house into her head. She would then ponder these ideas and place them on paper.

As the days, weeks, and months passed, the house continued to grow. Rooms were added to rooms and then turned into entire wings, doors were joined to windows, levels turned into towers, and peaks and the place eventually grew to a height of seven stories. Inside of the house, three elevators were installed, as were 47 fireplaces. Countless staircases led nowhere, a blind chimney stopped short of the ceiling, closets opened to blank walls, trap doors, double-back hallways, skylights were located one above another, doors opened to steep drops to the lawn below, and dozens of other oddities existed.

Sarah was intrigued by the number 13. Nearly all the windows contained 13 panes of glass, the walls had 13 panels, the greenhouse had 13 cupolas, many of the wooden floors contained 13 sections, some of the rooms had 13 windows, and every staircase but one had 13 steps. This exception is unique in other ways. It was a winding staircase with 42 steps, which would normally be enough to take a climber up three stories. In this case, however, the steps only rose nine feet because each step was only two inches high.

While all of this seems like madness to us, it all made sense to Sarah. In this way, she could control the spirits who came to the house for evil purposes, or who were outlaws or vengeful people in their past life. These bad men, killed by Winchester rifles, could wreak havoc on Sarah. The house had been designed into a maze to confuse and discourage the bad spirits.

Each night, at midnight, Sarah and her spirit guides met in the séance room. She traveled down the hallways in a strange course that would be sure to confuse any ghost who was following her.

Sarah remained a recluse in San Jose. In all the years that she lived in the city; she was only seen outside her walls one time. She refused to meet with any callers, no matter who they were, except for one — President Theodore Roosevelt. Roosevelt managed to get into the house, but no record remains as to whether he actually spoke with Sarah or not. Some visitors were not even that lucky. Prominent religious leader Mary Baker Eddy was turned away at the gate.

The house continued to grow, and by 1906, it had reached a towering seven stories tall. Sarah continued her occupancy, and expansion, of the house, living in melancholy solitude with no one other than her servants, the workmen, and, of course, the spirits. In April of that year, the house was badly damaged by the San Francisco earthquake. It took workmen hours to rescue Sarah from the room in which she had been sleeping.

Workers spent months repairing the damage, and then the expansion of the house began once more. The number of bedrooms increased from 15 to 20 and then to 25. Chimneys were installed all over the place, although strangely, they served no purpose. Some believe that perhaps they were added because the old stories say that ghosts like to appear and disappear through them. On a related note, it has also been documented that only two mirrors were installed in the house. Sarah believed that ghosts were afraid of their own reflection.

On September 4, 1922, after a conference session with the spirits in the séance room, Sarah went to her bedroom for the night. At some point in the early morning hours, she died in her sleep at the age of 83. She left all her possessions to her niece, France Marriott, who had been handling most of Sarah's business affairs for some time. In her will, Sarah had a couple of unusual requests. She asked that her casket be carried out of the house through the back door. Sarah had never used the front entrance. She also requested that all subsequent owners of the house allow the ghosts to still be welcome there and that they keep the property in good repair and tell all visitors about Sarah's project.

In time, the house was sold as a tourist attraction. It was initially advertised as having 148 rooms, but the floor plan was so confusing that that every time a room count was taken, a different total came up. The place was so puzzling that it was said that the workmen took more than six weeks just to get the furniture out of it. The rooms of the house were counted over and over again, and in 1933, it was estimated that 160 existed, although no one is really sure if even that is correct. Today, the house has been declared a California Historical Landmark and is registered with the National Park Service as "a large, odd dwelling with an unknown number of rooms."

Most would assume that the house must harbor at least some of the spirits who came there at the behest of Sarah Winchester. Others dispute this, saying that no ghosts ever walked it halls. The mansion is nothing more than too much money in the hands of an eccentric woman. However, based on the haunting activity that is still reported there, the Winchester Mystery House seems to have more than its share of ghosts.

Some of the first paranormal reports occurred back in the 1970s, when visitors and staff members began reporting strange sounds, footsteps, and voices that could not be explained. Two writers who spent the night in the house in 1979 reported the sound of a piano playing in the darkness. They were in the house alone. In addition, they had no idea that Sarah often played the piano late at night when she could not sleep and that, like the piano they heard that night, two of the keys were badly out of tune.

Staff members have the most compelling tales of spirits in the house. Many of them have claimed to see the ghost of Sarah herself among the maze of rooms. One day, several employees were buffing the floors on the second level of the house when they heard footsteps on the floor above them. They were the only ones in the building at the time. On another night, a staff member was locking up the house for the night, and as he walked the entire route of the tour, he shut down the lights as he went. He then locked the doors and walked out to the parking lot to get into his car. When he turned and looked back at the house, all the lights on the third floor had been turned on again.

A security guard for the house once admitted that they often have a lot of false alarms at the house, with the security system being tripped, even though no one is ever found inside. Strangely, when they go to investigate, the alarms are usually found to have been triggered from the inside, even though the exterior alarms have not been bothered. Security guards have also reported banging doors, mysterious voices, cold spots, and doorknobs that turn by themselves.

There is no question that this is one of the most unusual homes in the entire country, and, if all the stories are to be believed, it is one of the most haunted ones, too.

Waverly Hills Sanitorium

During the 1800s and early 1900s, America was ravaged by a deadly disease known to many as the *white death*: tuberculosis. This terrifying and very contagious plague, for which no cure existed before antibiotics were discovered, claimed entire families and occasionally entire towns. Many tuberculosis patients were advised to seek out drier climates in the west, which brought relief for many.

Isolating the infected and giving them the opportunity to rest became the preferred way of dealing with the disease, for which there was no cure. The idea of seeking "healthy air" gave rise to the expansion of sanatoriums. They were not just for the wealthy. The contagious poor were also encouraged or even pressured into entering one of the state or charity-run sanatoriums. The movement became the most popular in the early 20th century. Rest, sun, fresh air, rich food, and moderate exercise were part of the patients' daily routine.

But a cure was still decades away, and no matter how well-intentioned the methods of the scores of tuberculosis sanatoriums across the country, little could be done to save the lives of those afflicted by the disease. As a result, hundreds of thousands of people perished within the walls of the hundreds of hospitals, which could be found in almost every town, county, and state across America.

There are many such hospitals where the ghosts of the past are said to linger behind, but none as famous as the former sanatorium that overlooks the city of Louisville, Kentucky.

In 1900, Louisville, Kentucky, had one of the highest tuberculosis death rates in America. On low swampland, the area was the perfect breeding ground for disease. To try to contain the disease, plans were made for a two-story wooden sanatorium on a windswept hill in southern Jefferson County. The land where the hospital was built had been purchased by Major Thomas H. Hays in 1883, and he constructed his family home on the hilltop. He called it Waverly Hill.

An initial wooden hospital, with open air pavilions and tents for the patients, opened in 1910. It eventually proved inadequate. More construction was completed, but it was not until 1924 that work began on the Waverly Hills Sanatorium that still stands today. It opened two years later.

Built in the collegiate gothic style, it was considered the most advanced tuberculosis sanatorium in the country. Even so, many of the patients succumbed to the disease. No medicine was available at that time to treat the infection, and so patients were offered rest, fresh air, and large amounts of healthy food. Patients were placed in front of wide, open windows on the upper floors, on sun porches, and on the roof, no matter what the season.

Sadly, though, the main use for the hospital was to isolate those who had come down with the disease and to keep them away from those who were still healthy. Families were tragically divided with parents, and even children, forced into the sanatorium with little contact with their loved ones.

Treatments for tuberculosis were sometimes as bad as the disease itself. Some of the experiments that were conducted in search of a cure seem barbaric by today's standards. Patient's lungs were exposed to ultraviolet light to try to stop the spread of bacteria. Other treatments were less pleasant — and much bloodier. Balloons would be surgically implanted in the lungs and then filled with air to expand them. Another operation removed muscle and ribs from a patient's chest to allow the lungs to expand further and let in more oxygen. This blood-soaked procedure was a "last resort," and many patients did not survive it.

While the patients who survived both the disease and the treatments left Waverly Hills through the front door, many others left through what came to be known as the "body chute." This tunnel was constructed at the same time as the main building, and it traveled 500 feet to the railroad tracks at the bottom of the hill. One side of the tunnel had steps that allowed workers to enter and exit the hospital without having to walk the steep hill. The other side had a set of rails and a cart powered by a motorized cable system so that supplies could be easily transported from the railroad stop to the hospital on top of the hill. Air ducts leading from the roof of the tunnel to above ground level were incorporated every hundred feet to let in light and fresh air.

In time, the tunnel was used to not only bring up supplies, but to send out the dead as well. It was believed that the sight of the dead being taken away was not good for patient morale. With that in mind, staff members began using the motorized cart to discreetly lower the bodies to the bottom of the hill and into waiting hearses or onto a passing train.

There are many inaccurate reports as to how many people died during Waverly Hills' decades of operation. Some claim that tens of thousands died there, but records show that approximately 6,000 people died at Waverly Hills between 1911 and 1961. It may not be as many as some legends claim, but it is still a tremendous number of deaths to have occurred in a single structure.

By the 1930s and 1940s, medicines had started to be developed to prevent tuberculosis. New treatments were devised, and the sick began to survive the illness. New cases of tuberculosis in Louisville dwindled over the next decade. It reached a point that it was no longer cost-effective to operate a hospital the size of Waverly Hills. It closed in 1961.

A year later, the hospital reopened as Woodhaven Geriatrics Sanitarium. The reputation of the place suffered after allegations of abuse and patient mistreatment. Budget cuts led to horrible conditions, and in 1982, the facility was closed by the state of Kentucky.

The buildings and land were auctioned off and changed hands many times over the course of the next two decades. In 1983, a developer purchased the property with plans to turn it into a minimum-security prison for the state of Kentucky. Plans were dropped after neighbors protested, and a new idea to turn the former hospital into apartments was devised. A lack of financing caused this plan to be abandoned. It was finally sold to the current owners in 2001.

By that time, the once stately building had been nearly destroyed by time, the elements, and vandals who came looking for a thrill. It was a magnet for the homeless looking for shelter and teenagers, who broke in looking for ghosts. The former hospital soon gained a reputation for being haunted, and stories began to circulate of resident ghosts, like the little girl who was seen running up and down the third floor solarium, the little boy who was spotted with a leather ball, the hearse that appeared in the back of the building dropping off coffins, the woman with the bleeding wrists who cried for help, and others. Visitors told of slamming doors, lights in the windows when no power was in the building, strange sounds, and eerie footsteps in empty rooms.

Other legends told of a man in a white coat who was seen walking in the kitchen and the smell of cooking food that sometimes wafted through the room. The kitchen was a disaster, a ruin of broken windows, fallen plaster, broken tables and chairs, and puddles of water and debris that resulted from a leaking roof. The cafeteria had not fared much better. Even so, many people reported hearing footsteps in the room, seeing a door swinging shut under its own power, and the smell of fresh baked bread in the air.

Perhaps the greatest — and most controversial — legend of Waverly Hills was connected to the fifth floor of the building. This area of the old hospital consisted of two nurses' stations, a pantry, a linen room, a medicine room, and two medium-sized dormitories on both sides of the two nurses' stations. One of these, room 502, is the subject of many rumors and legends and just about every curiosity seeker that had broken into Waverly Hills over the years wanted to see it. This is where, according to the stories, people had seen shapes moving in the windows and had heard disembodied voices.

According to the stories, a nurse was found dead in room 502 in 1928. She had committed suicide by hanging herself from the light fixture. She was unmarried and pregnant. It is unknown how long she may have been hanging in this room before her body was discovered. And this would not be the only tragedy said to be connected to room 502. In 1932, another nurse who worked in the same room jumped from the roof to her death. There are no records to say these stories are true, but based on the numerous experiences that have been reported in this area over the years, it seems likely that something out of the unusual happened. Like the rest of the former hospital, many ghostly encounters have taken place here.

Literally hundreds of paranormal investigations have been conducted at Waverly Hills, including those with the *Ghost Adventures* crew. Visitors, volunteers, and investigators have experienced ghostly sounds, heard slamming doors, saw lights appear in the building when there should have been none, had objects thrown at them, have been struck by unseen hands, have seen apparitions in doorways and corridors, and much more.

This place can turn just about anyone into a believer in ghosts.

The Haunted Museum

I don't think that I could have picked a better location for The Haunted Museum, shown in Figure 20-7. The 1938 mansion, owned by prominent Las Vegas businessman Cyril S. Wengert, already had a history of ghosts when I bought it. I had been looking for a haunted, historic house in the city to offer tours. I found some and tried to buy some, but it seemed that, at the last minute, something would happen, and the deal would fall through. Frustrated, I was driving around one day, and, while at a stop sign, I spotted the mansard roof of the house, which seemed really out of place in Vegas. So, I circled around and saw that it was for sale and bought it.

Soon after, I heard from the State Bar of Nevada — the attorneys who owned the place — that the house was very haunted. I knew right then that my prayers of finding a historic building had been answered. I got inside and realized the first time I walked through it that I could feel spirits. And then I learned that all the employees would line their offices with salt at the door because many of them had been personally affected by attachments that followed them home. I have since discovered that the house was abandoned in the '70s and it became known as the "witch house" because of the dark rituals that took place in the basement.

I soon realized that it was not a simple coincidence that I got this house — the house chose me! When I first walked through the door, not only did I feel the spirits, but I could actually see what each room was going to be used for. Soon, these haunted and cursed objects from all over the world began coming to me, almost dropping into my lap. It's very hard to find authentic, genuine, haunted objects, but as soon as I bought the building, so many of them began coming at me. There's no other way to put it. Stranger still, these items just fit perfectly in each of the rooms in the house. I felt that I was being guided by different energies and spirits to open up the museum.

FIGURE 20-7: At the Haunted Museum.

My interest in a museum dates back to my initial interest in the paranormal as a child. When I was a very young boy, I was already scouring local garage sales with my mom in search of odd and spooky collectibles. My fascination with the unusual has turned into a life-long pursuit into the afterlife and communicating with the dead. For 15 years before opening The Haunted Museum, I traveled the world investigating the paranormal. I investigated buildings with horrific histories, I dealt with people possessed by demons, and I offered help to people in some of the most serious situations you can imagine. I don't play a paranormal investigator on Ghost Adventures — it's my life. It intrigues me that there are forces that are dark and positive, that are not of flesh and bone, that wander the earth with us.

I have always been fascinated with objects that contain very powerful energies, from curses to human spirits. I have Wyatt Earp's bible. I have artifacts that are very dark, including a chalice that came from the estate of Anton LaVey, founder of the Church of Satan. There is light and dark. I find that all religions are interesting. We all have different gods and beliefs. We're all different, so the artifacts in the museum are different and unique.

The museum was designed to reflect that. Every room in the house has its own energy. I built it like a puzzle, where each piece fits perfectly. Every room has a different environment. I've tried to own many pieces of historical mystery and to tell the story of them. Throughout this book, I mention haunted objects that now reside in the museum, but there are hundreds here — true, cursed, haunted objects.

I have Jack Kevorkian's death van, the cursed Ed Gein cauldron, Bela Lugosi's haunted mirror, Peggy the Doll, the mummified head of a man who was accused of witchcraft, and the Dybbuk box, which is one of the most haunted objects in the world. Whenever I buy this stuff, I must know its provenance. I have to buy it from the family of where it came from or I have to look into it. As a collector, those are the only type of objects that I want — I don't want to have to wonder, "Is this real?" I have met the people who have been affected by them.

The objects are placed in the museum in a way that hopefully doesn't put people at risk, but I can't guarantee that. That's why everyone who comes in must sign a waiver. Since the museum has been open, hundreds — probably thousands — of people have been affected by the objects inside. But people are aware of the risk when they enter the rooms. The Haunted Museum is a collection of dark and light, and it's a place of curiosity for people to come and maybe have an experience.

The Haunted Museum is like a giant experiment, where I took all these cursed and haunted objects and put them into one place together. It's like a chemist putting these chemicals together in one concoction to see whether an explosion occurs. One of the items here is the Demon House Staircase. I ended up bulldozing that house. I could have kept it open and opened it for tours, but after what I saw it did to me and others, I bulldozed it to the ground. I did take the staircase, though. The staircase was what all the police departments from different jurisdictions said was where the portal to Hell was. Underneath that staircase was the dirt where the police found all the objects that were used in a necromantic ritual.

I took the staircase, the dirt, and the objects. Once construction workers started installing it at the museum, two of them lost their personalities. They just went numb — like something felt like it was taking the life out of them. A little doll mysteriously appeared on the staircase one day when we had it in the other room. No one moved it and put it there. A black stain appeared on the outside of the door, too, without explanation. After the staircase was installed, the construction workers ran out of the building. They walked off the job and refused to come back. I later heard that they were involved in a serious traffic accident a short time later. It was so serious that some of them had to be airlifted to Los Angeles. That is one of the reasons why visitors are required to sign a waiver stating that they understand the risks associated with the place before they can go inside.

Over time, as the museum has grown and I have obtained more objects, it has become one of the most haunted places in the country. The Haunted Mansion is unique became I have placed this collection of artifacts under one roof on top of a building that already has a haunted history to it — it's like a nuclear reactor of paranormal activity.

So many people who have visited The Haunted Museum had had experiences. These experiences are not just of sight or sound or sense of touch; they're a sixth sense experience that stays with you forever. That kind of thing can leave a lot of people shaken up.

Rapper Vanilla Ice also had a frightening experience at the Haunted Museum when he visited a room full of REAL Oddfellows skeletons. As he was sitting in a chair he felt something touch him on his neck causing him to jump out of his seat and refuse to go back into that room.

I wrote about the Dybbuk Box and its effect on the many people involved with it, including musician Post Malone. He was a complete skeptic but had one of the most intense paranormal encounters ever with the Box. He is now a believer. I also included the Devil's Rocking Chair, which was involved in a controversial murder case and demonic possession. But those are not the only artifacts in the museum that affect visitors.

I bought quite a few items from the boat connected to the mysterious death of Hollywood legend Natalie Wood, including candlesticks, life vests, a table from the galley, and the radio that Natalie's husband, Robert Wagner, used to call hotels asking about his missing wife. It is the radio from which people seem to sense very negative energy. (See Figure 20-8.)

My collection also includes the false teeth of murderer Charles Manson, bone fragments, the hospital gown that he died in, and a painting of Manson with Manson's ashes in the eyes. This is a common medium for the painting's artist, Ryan Almighty, who uses human blood and remains to create his artwork. When I got it, it took its place alongside other Manson items like a bloody handprint, paintings made with Manson's urine, and jewelry made from his hair and under-wear. The painting is especially unsettling, though. It's a little more charged with energy and a little more creepy than the other objects.

Another odd artifact has ties to the Titanic. I acquired a haunted mirror that once belonged to Titanic's captain, Edward John Smith, which came with a letter of authenticity written in 1922. The letter claims that Smith's housekeeper saw him in the mirror after he died in the Titanic disaster. She continued to see his spirit in the mirror every year on the anniversary of his death. After investigating relics from Titanic during an episode of Ghost Adventures, the mirror was just some-thing that I had to have.

FIGURE 20-8:
Artifacts from Natalie Wood's yacht. Posing with Captain Dennis Davern of the Splendour yacht who was onboard the night Natalie lost her life.

©Courtesy of Zak Bagans, The Haunted Museum.

The Haunted Museum experiment will continue for many years to come. The darkness of many of the objects causes things to manifest at the museum. To witness those manifestations as an investigator is incredible. But this is my life. I don't just do it for a TV show. Yes, it's dangerous, but it's both interesting and scary. I was driven to creating one of the most haunted places in the country, and I can't wait to see what happens next.

Chapter **21**

Ten Signs Your House Is Haunted — and What to Do Next

When strange things begin to happen in the average person's home, they start looking for an explanation, wondering whether their house might be haunted. The first thing to do is to try to see whether the strange noises and other occurrences that you believe are taking place have a natural explanation. Do you have window leaks that might cause cold drafts? Could the footsteps in the attic be caused by mice?

Try not to let your imagination run away with you. This is easy to say and much harder to do. People are frightened by the unknown and by things that they don't understand. Try to relax and keep your eyes and ears open for anything on the list that follows.

Unexplained Temperature Drops

One of the easiest ways to tell whether spirits are present in your home is by paying attention to the temperature. If you experience unpredictable shifts in temperature, this could mean that you are indeed in the presence of an other-worldly entity. The reason for this is pretty straightforward. Ghosts require energy, and when they are present, they pull energy from the environment. Accordingly, their presence is directly associated with sudden drops of temperature.

Electrical Glitches

Electrical glitches can include anything from ringing phones with no one on the other end of the line to flicking lights, televisions that turn on an off, and more. Problems with electricity is a classic clue that reveals a ghostly presence is nearby. Ghosts exist within another dimension and need conduits to make contact, which is why audio and video recording devices have become so well-known as methods of communicating with the spirits.

Unusual Smells

One of the most common ways to identify the presence of a ghost is through scent. Ghostly smells will usually be somewhat familiar, like perfume, flowers, or the distinctive aroma of pipe tobacco. Sometimes, the scents can be less pleasant, like that of sulfur, which has been connecting to negative hauntings. The smells can manifest and then disappear with no explanation.

Movement of Objects

If you start seeing doors open and close or notice that things seem to disappear from one part of the house only to show up in another, unrelated spot, you may have a ghost. It is not often that ghosts build enough energy to interact with physical objects, but it does happen.

Unidentifiable Sounds

The clomping sounds of boots on the staircase, footsteps going up and down hall-ways, and disembodied voices in the night are all signs that your house is likely haunted. While strange sounds are often more closely connected to residual hauntings, it is also possible that you have a spirit on your hands who wants your attention.

Odd Behavior from Your Pets

If your pet begins spending an inordinate amount of time in a certain area of your home or having a reaction to something that is unseen by you, then it is very possible they are making contact with a paranormal entity. Animals can pick up on sounds, smells, and sights that are not detectable to humans. In addition, dogs are also known to foresee imminent earthquakes, tornadoes, and other natural phenomena. So, it is no surprise that your pet can also feel the presence of a ghost.

Feelings of a Nearby Presence

Many people who find themselves living in a haunted house will speak of feeling a presence in the house that they cannot explain. This may manifest as feeling someone standing over your shoulder, close behind you, or even in the room with you when you can see no one is there. It is also possible to feel as though you are being watched, wherever you go in the house. It is possible that a spirit is trying to make contact with you but is unable to get your attention in any other way.

Sensation of Being Touched

Ghosts also try to get your attention through touch, perhaps a tug on your hair, a touch on your shoulder, or, in more negative situations, a push on a staircase, scratches, bruises, or worse. If this is something that you start experiencing in your home, then it is very possible that you have an unwanted presence there.

Seeing Shadows and Movement

If you suddenly start seeing the apparition of a person standing in a corner, who vanishes when approached, it has become very obvious that you have a ghost situation. Most sightings will be much more subtle, though. You may start to see flickers of movement out of the corner of your eye, but when you look straight at the spot, nothing is there. You might also see shadows that do not belong, moving in the opposite direction of the light. If this becomes a common occurrence, you may have spirits in the house.

Feelings of Depression and Sadness

When you have feelings of overwhelming sadness and depression in your home, it may not just be because of your mental state. There may be an outside influence, especially when the feelings tend to go away once you leave the house. In many cases of negative and oppressive hauntings, homeowners are plagued by heavy feelings and depression, which cannot be easily explained. This may be a clear sign that something is wrong with your property.

Actions You Can Take

If you are experiencing any, or most, of the items on this list, then it is possible that your house may be haunted. If you can, try to determine whether your possible ghostly activity has a natural cause.

Keep a log or journal

The next thing to do is to keep a log or journal of any activity that occurs in the house. This is a great way to not only recall the events when they are fresh in your mind but also to see whether a pattern of activity exists.

In your log or journal, record the following details:

>> The exact time and date when the activity occurred

>> Everyone who was present and what they experienced

>> The weather conditions at the time

Discovering a pattern to the events can help find a cause for them later on, or it may reveal a natural cause of the activity, such as the furnace kicking on at a certain time or a nearby freight train passing by. If the activity is determined to be genuine, it will make it easier to decide on the best time or day for a paranormal investigation.

Decide what you want to do

That brings us to the next decision you will need to make. You can either learn to live with the novelty of a ghost in your house, or you can get in touch with a legitimate paranormal researcher to help you understand it better. You may be unwilling to share your house with a ghost and want to get rid of it. If that is the case, an investigation team can help you determine the veracity and extent of the haunting first.

Contact a qualified paranormal investigator

It is now time to get in touch with a qualified paranormal investigator who can come into your home and determine what sort of activity is taking place. This is not as easy as it sounds. Hundreds of websites on the Internet claim to be affiliated with paranormal research, and it would seem that you have scores of ghost-hunters to choose from. Unfortunately, this is not the case. But the following is a bit of helpful information that can help that may help you choose an investigation team for your home.

>> Make sure that they have a telephone number to make contact with. Also, make sure that the contact information on their website lists a first and last name of the persons who are actually doing the investigations.

>> Try to determine from the website whether the investigators are someone that you would like to have in your home. Remember, the website is the method of advertising that they chose to offer their services through, and if the site is questionable, the ghost-hunters might be, too. Anyone can put up a website, but the quality of the material on it will speak volumes about who is behind it.

>> Legitimate investigators will not charge for their services. If you are asked to pay for an investigation, then you should look for someone else. Only services that produce concrete and tangible results are worthy of payment, and paranormal research is too unpredictable for that. In most cases, very little may occur in an investigation, and no one should be expected to pay for that.

>> Once you believe you have found an investigator that you are comfortable with, you need to check his qualifications for an investigation. Ask how long he has been involved in paranormal research and about investigations in the past, especially those involving private residences.

Once you have a ghost-hunter to work with, they will need to determine whether an on-site investigation of your home is needed. They will do this by asking a lot of questions and will need to know that you have already tried to rule out natural explanations for the phenomena and perhaps even that you have compiled dates and times for the reported events.

Preparing for an on-site investigation

WARNING

Should the researcher then decide that an investigation of the house is warranted, then prepare for an "invasion." Even though most research groups will consist of no more than five to six individuals, a good team can seem like many more. An investigation can be very invasive, and photographs and video will be taken of the house. The investigators will ask you to describe the events that occurred (perhaps several times), and your statement will be recorded. They will ask you dozens of questions, and many of them will seem unconnected and perhaps even embarrassing. Bear with them, however, because the questions do have a purpose, and the investigators will be working to try to not only legitimize your story but also to determine whether the reported activity is real.

Here are some things that you should be aware of when it comes to paranormal investigations:

>> The investigators should not be drinking or smoking at any time.

>> The investigators should arrive at your home with open minds. No one is trying to debunk your reports but must keep an open mind to all possibilities. Good investigators must remain noncommittal until they have had a chance to gather their evidence.

>> Make sure that the investigators seem to know how to use all their equipment. If there is anything that you do not understand, be sure to ask them to explain what it is used for. If they cannot, you may have a problem.

>> Unless the investigation was set up through you with a local television station or newspaper, the investigators should not be accompanied to your home with a reporter or media person. This should never occur without your permission. The investigators are duty-bound to keep all aspects of your case confidential unless they have your permission to disclose anything.

>> You can help by making sure that everyone who experienced anything unusual is present on the night of the investigation and that you keep away friends and relatives who want to come over to watch the proceedings. This can be very distracting to you and to the investigators and can interfere with an accurate investigation.

>> If you become uncomfortable with what is going on at any point in the investigation, you have the absolute right to call a halt to everything. The investigators are present at your request and are guests in your home. They should be given the respect that such a title signifies, but they also must respect your feelings and fears as.

As the investigation continues in your home, the team members will divide up their duties and while you are being thoroughly interviewed, other investigators will be filming and mapping the house, taking photos, and looking for any anomalies with their equipment. They will likely ask you to show them where any odd happenings took place and may ask you to recreate what you were doing when they occurred.

Following up

If activity occurs during the investigation, this will be exciting for everyone involved. If it does not, and yet the investigator believes there is a strong possibility of genuine phenomena, he may request a follow-up investigation. A good investigator researcher will always follow up on a case. If you do not hear from him and the phenomenon persists, then call him yourself. Do not be afraid to get in touch with him and ask him to come back.

It is possible that an investigator will tell you that they believe your house is haunted. You may be comfortable with that, or you may want to try and get the haunting to stop. However, unless your investigator is psychic, they will not be equipped to get rid of the ghosts that may be haunting your house. Most ghost-hunters are merely investigators. They do not talk to ghosts and do not see them around every corner. This normally means they will contact an outside source.

If you have a family minister, the ghost-hunter will likely suggest that you get in touch with this person and ask them to come to the house and to pray for the soul of the spirit that is present. This is not an "exorcism" but simply an attempt to get the ghost to leave in peace. It can be of great benefit to you and your family, as well.

If a willing minister is not available, then the investigator should be able to suggest or find an expert in getting rid of ghosts. They may not be a professional medium or psychic but someone who is sensitive to spirits and who has a good reputation. It should be someone the ghost-hunter has either worked with before or someone who was referred through a legitimate source.

Paranormal research has several goals. Not only is the investigator seeking evidence of ghosts, but he or she is also there to help the person who called them in to investigate the case. It is the investigator's main responsibility to alleviate the fears of the witness and to help them deal with the activity they are experiencing. The homeowner should ever be shut out of the investigation but should be treated with the utmost respect. We all know that we fear the things that we understand the least.

Index

About the Author

Zak Bagans is currently the host, lead investigator and executive producer on Travel Channel's *Ghost Adventures*.

After graduating from film school in Michigan, Bagans moved to Nevada to pursue a career in documentary filmmaking. There, he met fellow "Ghost Adventures" investigator Aaron Goodwin. In 2004, they began filming what became an award-winning documentary about paranormal investigations in Nevada. The concept was turned into a series for the Travel Channel, and it continues to be the highest-rated series on the network today. Bagans also hosts and serves as an executive producer for other Travel Channel programs like *Ghost Adventures: Flashbacks at Zak's, Aftershocks, Deadly Possessions, Paranormal Paparazzi, Paranormal Challenge,* and *Netherworld.* In 2018, Zak directed and starred in the documentary feature film, *Demon House,* which chronicled his investigation into what is widely known as the country's most authenticated case of demon possession.

Bagans is also the owner/curator of the famed Zak Bagans' The Haunted Museum in Las Vegas. His museum twice won Best Museum in Las Vegas (*Las Vegas Review Journal*), Best Attraction in Las Vegas (*Las Vegas Weekly*), and the coveted City of Las Vegas Mayor's award for historic preservation and design.

He has also penned two books with Kelly Crigger: *I am Haunted: Living Life Through the Dead* (Victory Belt, 2015) and *the New York Times bestseller Dark World: Into the Shadows with the Lead Investigator of the Ghost Adventures Crew* (Victory Belt, 2011).

Bagans currently resides in Las Vegas, Nevada.

Dedication

For all my incredible fans and those eager to explore the mysteries within the paranormal field.

Publisher's Acknowledgments

Senior Acquisitions Editor: Tracy Boggier

Project Editor: Kelly Ewing

Editorial Assistant: Matthew Lowe

Production Editor: Mohammed Zafar Ali

Cover Images: Author Photo © TravelChannel; Basement © spxChrome/Getty Images

Dummies is the global leader in the reference category and one of the most trusted and highly regarded brands in the world. No longer just focused on books, customers now have access to the dummies content they need in the format they want. Together we'll craft a solution that engages your customers, stands out from the competition, and helps you meet your goals.

Advertising & Sponsorships

Connect with an engaged audience on a powerful multimedia site, and position your message alongside expert how-to content. Dummies.com is a one-stop shop for free, online information and know-how curated by a team of experts.

- Targeted ads
- Video
- Email Marketing
- Microsites
- Sweepstakes sponsorship

20 MILLION
PAGE VIEWS
EVERY SINGLE MONTH

15 MILLION UNIQUE
VISITORS PER MONTH

43%
OF ALL VISITORS
ACCESS THE SITE
VIA THEIR MOBILE DEVICES

700,000 NEWSLETTER SUBSCRIPTIONS
TO THE INBOXES OF
300,000 UNIQUE INDIVIDUALS EVERY WEEK